History of Universities

VOLUME XXXIII/2

2020

History of Universities is published bi-annually

Editor:

Mordechai Feingold (California Institute of Technology)

Managing Editor:

Jane Finucane (Trinity College, University of Glamorgan)

Editorial Board:

R. D. Anderson (University of Edinburgh)
L. J. Dorsman (Utrecht University)
Thierry Kouamé (Université Paris 1 Panthéon-Sorbonne)
Mauro Moretti (Università per Stranieri di Siena)
H. de Ridder-Symoens (Ghent)
S. Rothblatt (University of California, Berkeley)
N. G. Siraisi (Hunter College, New York)

A leaflet 'Notes to OUP Authors' is available on request from the editor.

To set up a standing order for History of Universities contact Standing Orders, Oxford University Press, North Kettering Business Park, Hipwell Road, Kettering, Northamptonshire, NN14 1UA Email: StandingOrders.uk@oup.com Tel: 01536 452640

History of Universities

VOLUME XXXIII/2

2020

Special issue

Reshaping Natural Philosophy: Tradition and Innovation in the Early Modern Academic Milieu

GUEST EDITOR
ANDREA SANGIACOMO

OXFORD
UNIVERSITY PRESS

OXFORD

UNIVERSITY PRESS

Great Clarendon Street, Oxford, OX2 6DP,
United Kingdom

Oxford University Press is a department of the University of Oxford.
It furthers the University's objective of excellence in research, scholarship,
and education by publishing worldwide. Oxford is a registered trade mark of
Oxford University Press in the UK and in certain other countries

© Oxford University Press 2020

The moral rights of the author have been asserted

First Edition published in 2020
Impression: 1

Published in the United States of America by Oxford University Press
198 Madison Avenue, New York, NY 10016, United States of America

British Library Cataloguing in Publication Data
Data available

Library of Congress Control Number: 2020941841

ISBN 978–0–19–289383–3

Printed and bound by
CPI Group (UK) Ltd, Croydon, CR0 4YY

Contents

Introduction: Natural Philosophy in the Early Modern Academic Milieu

Andrea Sangiacomo

0. The playground

Was there continuity or discontinuity between early modern natural philosophy and the previously dominant Aristotelian tradition? Did the emergence of a 'new' natural philosophy during the seventeenth century mark a radical break from previous traditions? Or did early modern natural philosophy simply emerge out of the background of late Aristotelian and Renaissance debates? Did *novatores* aim to make a 'revolution' in natural philosophy or a 'reformation'?[1] Did they operate from within universities or outside them and against them?

Over the last few decades, intellectual historians, and especially historians of early modern philosophy and science, have debated these and related questions intensely. Natural philosophy underwent dramatic transformations during the early modern period, so it is not without reason that the 'new' science has been popularized as a key feature of early European modernity and canonized as the 'Scientific Revolution'.[2]

---

[1] The model of 'reformation' is defended by Daniel Garber, 'Galileo, Newton and all that: if it wasn't a scientific revolution, what was it? (a manifesto)', *Circumscribere. International Journal for the History of Science* 7 (2009), 9–18.

[2] For classical accounts of the Scientific Revolution see Herbert Butterfield, *The Origins of Modern Science* (London, 1957); Alexandre Koyré, *From the Closed World to the Infinite Universe* (Baltimore, 1957); Alfred Rupert Hall, *The Scientific Revolution, 1500–1800: The Formation of the Modern Scientific Attitude* (Boston, 1966). This narrative has also been reworked and developed by more recent historians, see Stephen Gaukroger, *The Emergence of a Scientific Culture: Science and the Shaping of Modernity, 1210–1685* (New York, 2006); Id., *The Collapse of Mechanism and the Rise of Sensibility. Science and the Shaping of Modernity. 1680–1760* (New York, 2010); Id., *The Natural and the Human. Science and the Shaping of Modernity, 1739–1841* (New York, 2016); Floris Cohen, *How Modern Science Came Into the World. Four Civilizations, One 17th Century Breakthrough* (Amsterdam, 2010); John Henry, 'Essay Review. The Scientific Revolution: Five Books about It', *Isis*, 107 (2016), 809–817.

Independently of how one understands this revolution, it is crucial to appreciate that the early modern reshaping of natural philosophy was not restricted to the laboratory or the observatory where a few heroes of the new natural philosophy made their discoveries. The revolution also took place in classrooms and universities throughout Europe, in newly-founded scientific academies and in private circles; in intellectual exchanges and sometimes in harsh controversies, spreading within and beyond the universities. Undoubtedly, early modern natural philosophy witnessed a reshaping of the canons and authorities used to establish and convey the contents of the discipline. Canons and authorities are socio-historical constructions, deeply rooted in political, religious, philosophical, and scientific debates. To change the canon in a field of study is to subvert hierarchies of powers and recognition. Struggles between conflicting powers ensue and often redefine authorities. The early modern academic milieu was the playground where these struggles became strikingly apparent.

This monographic issue of *History of Universities* presents new materials and case studies in order to deepen our understanding of the role of the academic milieu in the early modern reshaping of natural philosophy. The expression 'academic milieu' captures the idea that authors working both within and outside of early modern universities (and sometimes *both*) are members of a shared environment, which thrives on the continued exchanges and interactions across boundaries and borders. In this way, the expression encompasses something broader than the strict definition of university understood as a socially, politically and geographically determined institution of higher education, but stops short of becoming an umbrella term for any heterogeneous intellectual context.[3] Focusing on the academic milieu will provide us with a better understanding of two groups of authors: (i) those who operated within universities and who, from within this institutional context, were active in defending or reshaping established traditions, and (ii) those who did not belong to any formal institution but did try to establish new institutions, authorities and traditions by competing with those already in place.

The methodological intuition at the core of this approach, which is developed in various ways throughout this collection, involves looking at the *interactions* between these two groups of authors and at the internal. From this perspective, the focus on the academic milieu is a methodological

---

[3] Willem Frijhoff, 'Patterns' in *A History of the University in Europe*, vol. 2: *Universities in Early Modern Europe (1500–1800)*, ed. Hilde De Ridder-Symoens (Cambridge, 1996), 43–113, discusses the difficulties of adopting an overly rigid definition of 'university'. Frijhoff stresses the need to understand the role and practices of academic institutions in a more dynamic way, by emphasizing the way in which academic institutions were embedded in their political, social, historical and cultural environments.

and heuristic device aimed at fostering a relational and dynamic approach to the history of universities and their role in the reshaping early modern natural philosophy. By focusing on this academic milieu as a space for intellectual conflict and scientific struggle, the contributions included in this volume aim to reconstruct aspects and features of the early modern scientific landscape and uncover the diverse ways that early modern natural philosophy was re-conceptualized.

The advantages of this approach can be better appreciated by recalling the issues that accompany the still widespread narrative of the Scientific Revolution. In general, one of the major problems with that narrative is that it explains the evolution of natural philosophy by reference to a group of 'innovative' authors (mostly operating outside the universities) who struggled against a group of more 'traditionalist' Aristotelian authors (who dominated the academic milieu) in order to establish and disseminate new practices in natural philosophy. However, neither of these groups was in fact homogeneous and their evolution and interactions were much more complex than this contraposition might suggest.

Concerning the camp of the alleged 'innovators', it is increasingly clear that no coherent agenda or conceptual framework can capture all the different orientations endorsed by historical actors.[4] Consider, for instance, the implementation of mechanical explanations (i.e., those based on the notions of matter and motion only) in natural philosophy. Different supporters of 'mechanical' philosophy were in fact drawing from a range of often heterogeneous sources.[5] Furthermore, mechanization is often taken to entail a rejection of final causes in physics.[6] However, recent scholarship suggests that this was not always the case. In fact, several early modern authors were ready to rework different notions of final causation in their mechanical philosophy.[7] Moreover, not only did mechanization have a very limited impact in domains such as biology and medicine,[8] but it seems

---

[4] Daniel Garber, 'Why the Scientific Revolution Wasn't a Scientific Revolution, and Why It Matters', in *Kuhn's Structure of Scientific Revolutions at Fifty: Reflections on a Science Classic*, eds. Robert J. Richards and Lorraine Daston (Oxford, 2016), 133–148.

[5] Walter R. Laird and Sophie Roux eds., *Mechanics and Natural Philosophy before the Scientific Revolution* (Dordrecht, 2008); Daniel Garber, 'Remarks on the Pre-History of the Mechanical Philosophy', in *The Mechanization of Natural Philosophy*, eds. Daniel Garber and Sophie Roux (Dordrecht, 2013), 3–26.

[6] Steven Shapin, *The Scientific Revolution* (Chicago, 1996), 30–46.

[7] Margaret Osler, 'From Immanent Natures to Nature as Artifice: The Reinterpretation of Final Causes in Seventeenth-Century Natural Philosophy', *The Monist* 79 (1996), 388–407; Laurence Carlin, 'Boyle's teleological mechanism and the myth of immanent teleology', *Studies in History and Philosophy of Science*, 43 (2012), 54–63; Andrea Sangiacomo, 'Aristotle, Heereboord and the polemical target of Spinoza's critique of final causes', *Journal of the History of Philosophy* 54 (2016), 395–420.

[8] François Duchesneau, *Les modèles du vivant de Descartes à Leibniz* (Paris, 1998).

also chronologically confined to mid-seventeenth-century approaches.[9] However, scholars disagree on whether it is possible to clearly oppose seventeenth-century mechanist physics with eighteenth-century 'vitalism'.[10] The case of 'experimentalism' (i.e., the 'new' experimental way of investigating the natural world), is no less controversial.[11] While it is true that disparate authors such as Cartesian philosophers, members of the Royal Society of London, and Dutch professors all appealed to experimental practices, they integrated them into rather different conceptual frameworks.[12] Hence, 'experimental' philosophy looks like little more than an umbrella term for a variety of different approaches.

A growing trend in recent scholarship emphasizes that, far from being avatars of ossified traditions, universities were in fact laboratories for the constant adjustment and transformation of concepts and practices.[13] It is problematic to take the 'Aristotelians' as a unified polemical target for the proponents of 'new' approaches. In fact, given the different orientations within the Aristotelian group, controversies and polemical arguments were, in many cases, only relevant to *certain* specific Aristotelian authors or doctrines.[14] What's more, it is increasingly clear that ongoing transformations in the academic milieu created a more fertile background for the spreading of new approaches in natural philosophy.[15] A number of

[9] See e.g. Gaukroger, *The Emergence of a Scientific Culture*.

[10] Charles Wolfe, 'Review-Interview with Stephen Gaukroger', *Journal of Interdisciplinary History of Ideas*, 5 (2016), 1–13.

[11] Peter Anstey, 'Experimental Versus Speculative Natural Philosophy', in *The Science of Nature in the Seventeenth Century*, ed. Peter Anstey and John Schuster (Dordrecht, 2005), 215–242.

[12] Mihnea Dobre and Tammy Nyden eds., *Cartesian Empiricisms* (Dordrecht, 2013).

[13] Charles Schmitt, *Aristotle and the Renaissance* (Cambridge Mass., 1983); Cees Leijenhorst, Christoph Lüthy, Johannes Thijssen, 'The Tradition of Aristotelian Natural Philosophy. Two Theses and Seventeen Answers.' In *The Dynamics of Aristotelian Natural Philosophy from Antiquity to the Seventeenth Century*, eds. Cees Leijenhorst, Christoph Lüthy, Johannes Thijssen (Leiden, 2002), 1–30.

[14] Paul Grendler, *The Universities of the Italian Renaissance* (Baltimore and London, 2002), 267–313, discusses the case of Italian universities during the Renaissance and the seventeenth century. Grendler shows how Aristotelian natural philosophy was steadily maintained in the curricula of Italian universities but 'the quality of university Aristotelian natural philosophy in the late sixteenth and early seventeenth centuries varied from university to university and scholar to scholar' (ibid. 310). According to Grendler, the situation changed dramatically in the second half of the seventeenth century, which witnessed a collapse of Aristotelianism and the affirmation of experimental natural philosophy.

[15] Charles Schmitt, 'Science in the Italian Universities in the Sixteenth and Early Seventeenth Centuries', in *The Aristotelian Tradition and Renaissance Universities*, ed. Charles Schmitt (London, 1984), 35–56; Mordechai Feingold, *The Mathematicians' Apprenticeship: Science, Universities, and Society in England, 1560–1640* (Cambridge, 1984); Id. ed., *Jesuit Science and the Republic of Letters* (Cambridge Mass., 2003); Laurence Brockliss, *French Higher Education in the Seventeenth and Eighteenth Centuries: A Cultural History* (Oxford, 1987); John Gascoigne, *Cambridge in the Age of the Enlightenment. Science,*

Aristotelian authors were open to new developments and to accommodating them in the established frameworks taught at universities.[16] Reciprocally, the progressive integration of the 'new' natural philosophy into the university milieu was crucial for the acceptance and dissemination of these 'new' approaches. For instance, Cartesian philosophy was not only remarkably resonant, but also received crucial developments thanks to the efforts of various academics who sought to transform it into a systematic framework capable of competing with the scholastics.[17] The circulation of Newton's physics and the reshaping of its mathematical and theoretical apparatus was crucially affected by generations of eighteenth-century professors who taught, refined and adjusted the views originally presented in Newton's works.[18]

This body of scholarship suggests that trying to identify well-defined groups or factions in terms of their 'innovative' or 'traditionalist' agenda is not only extremely difficult but may easily lead to a misinterpretation of the complexity of early modern debates. Instead, this complexity is better tackled by focusing on the exchanges through which authors belonging and operating in the same academic milieu collectively contributed to reshaping the way in which natural philosophy was conceptualized, practiced and taught between the seventeenth and eighteenth centuries. The notion of an academic milieu shifts the research focus from the qualitative contraposition between 'traditionalist' and 'innovative' groups of authors to the topographical contrast between groups and individuals operating within or outside universities. This latter focus does not assume that university professors, for instance, were necessarily 'traditionalist' or that outsiders were necessarily 'innovative'. Rather, it takes the academic milieu itself as the background against which it is appropriate to assess the interplay between tradition and innovation across the boundaries of established institutions and throughout the space of early modern intellectual life.

Religion and Politics from Restoration to the French Revolution (Cambridge, 1989); Marco Sgarbi, *The Aristotelian Tradition and the Rise of British Empiricism. Logic and Epistemology in the British Isle (1570–1689)* (Dordrecht, 2013).

[16] Laurence Brockliss, 'Curricula', in *A History of the University in Europe*, vol 2: *Universities in Early Modern Europe (1500–1800)* ed. Hilde De Ridder-Symoens (Cambridge, 1996), 563– 620; Roy Porter, 'The Scientific Revolution and Universities', in *A History of the University in Europe*, vol. 2: *Universities in Early Modern Europe (1500–1800)*, ed. Hilde De Ridder-Symoens (Cambridge, 1996), pp. 531–562; Mordechai Feingold, 'The Mathematical Sciences and New Philosophies', in *The History of the University of Oxford*, vol. 4: *Seventeenth-Century Oxford*, ed. Nicholas Tyacke (Oxford, 1997), 319–448.

[17] Roger Ariew, *Descartes and the First Cartesians* (New York, 2014); Tad Schmaltz *Early Modern Cartesianisms: Dutch and French Constructions* (New York, 2016)

[18] Eric Jorink, Ad Maas eds., *Newton and the Netherlands: How Isaac Newton Was Fashioned in the Dutch Republic* (Leiden, 2012); Elizabethanne Boran and Mordechai Feingold eds., *Reading Newton in Early Modern Europe* (Leiden, 2017).

The contributions included in this volume aim to develop this approach along two main axes of research: (1) the reconstruction and exploration of the dialectics between tradition and innovation in the reshaping of natural philosophy; (2) the attempt to constitute and consolidate new traditions in natural philosophy. The first axis of research concerns the seventeenth century in particular and the interplay between the still-dominant late scholastic framework and the spread of new approaches. The second axis of research, meanwhile, concerns the eighteenth century, in which the space opened up by the demolishing of the scholastic tradition is progressively filled and replaced by the construction and consolidation of a new academic tradition. The first five contributions in this volume are more connected with the first axis of research, while the next four contributions are more concerned with the second.

The geographical focus of this volume is, for the most part, Northern Europe (Germany and the Low Countries in particular), although it also encompasses figures and groups working in France, Britain and Italy. The interplay between different geographical regions is an important factor in the early modern development of natural philosophy.[19] It is well established that the Dutch Republic was a crucial laboratory for the reception, circulation and transformation of new ideas.[20] France was also a pivotal hub for both the creation of a 'Cartesianian Scholasticism'[21] and for the reception of British natural philosophy; Baconian at first and, later, Newtonian.[22] The British context itself was deeply influenced by developments of natural philosophy on the continent.[23]

This volume offers new materials that bring to light the intense exchanges that animated intellectual, academic and scientific life across early modern Europe. In doing so, the volume does not consider the reception of ideas as a one-sided process in which ideas flow from a centre to the periphery of a certain intellectual environment. Instead, this volume supports a more dynamic model in which ideas are constantly transformed

[19] Roy Porter and Teich Mikulás, eds., *The Scientific Revolution in National Context* (Cambridge, 2012) offers a systematic analysis of how 'The Scientific Revolution' unfolded in and affected different European countries. Notice, however, that the notion of 'Scientific Revolution' is a somewhat problematic historiographical construction. The present collection avoids using this term, focusing instead on 'natural philosophy' as a discipline and denomination which was commonly accepted by historical actors themselves.

[20] Wiep van Bunge ed., *The Early Enlightenment in The Dutch Republic 1650–1750* (Leiden-Boston, 2003)

[21] Ariew, *Descartes and the First Cartesians*; Schmaltz, *Early Modern Cartesianisms*.

[22] Élodie Cassan ed., *Bacon et Descartes. Genèse de la modernité philosophique* (Lyon, 2014); John Shank, *The Newton Wars and the Beginning of the French Enlightenment* (Chicago, 2008).

[23] Giovanni Gellera, 'The Scottish Faculties of Arts and Cartesianism', *History of Universities*, 29 (2016), 166–187.

as they travel among authors, traditions, institutions, languages and places. Rather than offering purely internalist explorations, the contributions show, in different ways, the unfolding of dialogues and debates between figures and authorities coming from different regions, periods and backgrounds. The underlying methodological intuition is that it is only by investigating how ideas were actually debated, reshaped and explored among different authors and scenarios that historians can gain a deeper grasp of the meaning and implications that those ideas had in the historical context in which they emerged and were circulated.[24]

1. Exploring the dialectics between tradition and innovation

The dialectics between tradition and innovation does not necessarily involve opposed camps but emerges *within* the Aristotelian tradition itself. Roger Ariew's contribution to this volume emphasises this point. The main focus of Ariew's contribution is to show how Aristotelian authors used Aristotelian principles that they deemed more fundamental to deny other Aristotelian tenets they regarded as secondary. Ariew illustrates this general point by taking as a case study the early seventeenth-century debate on comets. In particular, Ariew focuses on the role played in this debate by the Flemish academic Libertus Fromondus (1587–1653), professor of philosophy and theology at Leuven, who was actively engaged in debating the 'new' science with many natural philosophers around Europe, including Descartes and Galileo.

Questions about the nature and location of comets had not been definitively decided by 1618, a year marked by a succession of three comets visible to the naked eye, culminating in the great comet of 1618. These events resulted in the publication of multiple treatises about comets by numerous observers, including those of Libertus Fromondus and Galileo Galilei. Fromondus criticises the Aristotelian account of comets but rejects Galileo's explanation as well. In his *Treatise on the Comet of 1618*, Fromondus argues that the comet he observed is not a fiery exhalation because of: (i) the height of such exhalations, (ii) the nature of fire, (iii) its lack of scintillation, (iv) its motion, and (v) its tail. These five arguments are alike in that they are all basically Aristotelian arguments employed to attack an Aristotelian conclusion. Fromondus uses some entrenched Aristotelian principles against the conclusion, which is also Aristotelian, that comets are terrestrial exhalations. For Fromondus, as it was for Tycho Brahe,

---

[24] A full-blown defence of this method is offered by Mogens Laerke, *Les Lumières de Leibniz: controverses avec Huet, Bayle, Regis et More* (Paris, 2015), 11–46.

superlunary comets would count against the solid spheres and for fluid planetary heavens. However, not everyone took the route followed by Fromondus. One might even count Galileo among the traditionalists, or at least among Tycho's opponents, when it comes to comets. Horatio Grassi, a Jesuit astronomer, argued against Aristotle by referring to the lack of an observable parallax for the comet of 1618. Galileo disputed his findings, contending that one cannot use the parallax of a comet to calculate its location. In his *Meteorology* (1627), Book III, *De Cometis*, Fromondus rejected Galileo's account and argued for the anti-Aristotelian view that some comets are supra-lunar. The take-away point here is that Fromondus made significant modifications to his Aristotelianism to accommodate astronomical novelties such as supra-lunar comets. While he could be thought of as a traditionalist, spending his whole career as an academic, he made changes that went well beyond what could be described as the articulation of the Aristotelian tradition.

It is also noteworthy that other prominent academics were willing to embrace and appropriate the new doctrines defended by the *novatores* and integrate them in the academic curriculum. The contributions by Stefan Heßbrüggen-Walter and Nabeel Hamid in what follows focus on the case of Johann Clauberg (1622–1665) first rector of the new University of Duisburg. Heßbrüggen-Walter reconstructs the controversy between Gerard de Neufville (1590–1648) and Johann Clauberg about the comparative merits of Bacon and Descartes in the university classroom. This controversy had a crucial pragmatic dimension, which involved evaluating the question of how Baconian and Cartesian philosophical projects could meet the pedagogical needs of the university as an educational institution. The exchange between de Neufville and Clauberg shows that textbooks of natural philosophy contain important discussions of pedagogical practice. De Neufville taught philosophy and medicine in Bremen, where Clauberg was his student between 1639 and 1644. De Neufville criticises Bacon's contention that the natural philosopher must entirely abandon the tradition of his discipline and fears that a revolution of natural philosophy along Baconian lines may well take centuries. In the meantime, he argues, professors still need something to teach to students. Therefore, he envisions a Baconian *philosophia nov-antiqua* that reintroduces certain aspects of Aristotelian science into a broadly Baconian empirical investigation of nature. Clauberg's criticism of his teacher focuses on two perceived weaknesses. First, Baconian doubt renders natural philosophy unteachable; while Cartesian doubt does not, because it can be dissolved comparatively quickly. Second, de Neufville's evolutionary approach may inadvertently convey false doctrines to students, thereby preventing their epistemic progress. The only defence against unexamined opinions is the suspension of judgment. Besides that, he argues, de Neufville's pragmatic worries are unfounded: Cartesians are successful professionals in theology, medicine, and in the university itself.

Clauberg's positive attitude towards Cartesianism and his reasons for embracing it are further explored in Hamid's contribution, which focuses specifically on how Clauberg adjusted the scholastic tradition to accommodate Descartes' philosophy, thereby making the latter suitable for teaching in universities. Hamid highlights two related motivations behind Clauberg's synthesis of Cartesianism with tradition: a pedagogical interest in Descartes as offering a simpler method, and a systematic concern with disentangling philosophy from theological disputes. These motivations are brought into view by situating Clauberg in the closely linked contexts of Protestant educational reforms in the seventeenth century (associated with figures such as Jan Amos Comenius), and debates concerning the proper relation between philosophy and theology (notably litigated in the so-called *Hofmannstreit* around 1600). Hamid argues that Clauberg retains an Aristotelian conception of ontology for purely philosophical reasons; specifically, to give objective foundations to Descartes's metaphysics of substance. Hamid concludes that Clauberg should not be assimilated either to Aristotelianism or to Cartesianism or, indeed, to syncretic labels such as 'Cartesian Scholastic'. Instead, he should be read as transforming both schools by drawing on a variety of elements in order to address issues local to the Protestant academic milieu of his time.

The next contribution, by Helen Hattab, explores the same dialectics between traditional and new natural philosophy. This time, however, the focus shifts away from the courtyard of universities and towards the *novatores* and their own appropriation and reworking of traditional methodological and pedagogic approaches. Hattab's contribution shows how the established tradition worked not only as a polemical target but also as a crucial resource that nourished the growth of alternatives to academic and Aristotelian approaches. Hattab develops this point by discussing in detail the problem of method in Spinoza and connecting it with its scholastic background. Early proponents of new sciences, like Bacon, Galilei and Descartes were aware that in advancing new philosophies of nature they were also introducing new methods of *investigating* nature. Hence, they eschewed communicating their discoveries by the standard Scholastic Aristotelian teaching methods of textual commentary and syllogistic disputation of questions. Instead they attempted to instruct their readers by means of aphorisms, dialogues, autobiographies and even fables. By the mid-seventeenth century proponents of controversial philosophies appropriated more familiar didactic genres to convey their radical doctrines. For instance, the first book of Thomas Hobbes' *De Corpore* follows the familiar order of standard Scholastic Aristotelian logic textbooks, and Baruch Spinoza's *Ethics* emulates Euclid's *Elements*, by presenting astounding conclusions about nature and extension *more geometrico*. There is a long-standing debate regarding whether Spinoza's geometrical method is a method of discovery or merely a method of presentation. Hattab's contribution examines Spinoza's reflections on method in the *Treatise on the Emendation of the Intellect* in the context of contemporaneous conceptions of analysis and synthesis found in the works of Zabarella, Burgersdijk, Descartes and Hobbes to identify the most plausible readings of his method in the *Ethics*.

2. Exploring the establishment of new traditions

The second axis of research in this volume moves to the late seventeenth century and the eighteenth century. While the idea of a tradition may suggest something long-established and immutable, it is important to realize that traditions have origins, developments and sometimes collapse. Moreover, while some traditions are successful in establishing themselves, others are abortive or simply do not manage to propagate their tenets. Appreciating this element of contingency in the fate of different traditions is important when it comes to understanding why *some* traditions are more successful than others in emerging as the new dominant framework.

Jaworzyn's contribution focuses on an apparently obscure and seemingly abortive tradition, namely, the Parisian 'sect' that Caspar Langenhert (1661–1730?) attempted to found, which Jaworzyn sees as developing in Langenhert's engagement with the work of Arnold Geulincx (1624–1669). Geulincx was professor of philosophy in Leiden and combined his sympathy for Cartesian metaphysics and natural philosophy with a thoroughly Calvinist agenda in theology and ethics. Due to his premature death in the plague of 1669, Geulincx's legacy remains difficult to assess. Jaworzyn explores the 'egoism' supposedly advocated by Langenhert in the *Novus Philosophus* (1701–2) and at a controversial school he opened in Paris in 1701. Jaworzyn argues that the unusual doctrines of *Novus Philosophus* most likely developed in response to ambiguities Langenhert saw in Geulincx's physics, for which he provided a commentary in the 1688 *Compendium Physicae*. Geulincx's supporters agreed that his physics was broadly Cartesian, but they also emphasized the crucial addition of a kind of occasionalism based on an epistemic condition on causation. Nevertheless, where Swartenhengst, Bontekoe, and Flenderus differed in regard to their reading of the extent of Geulincx's occasionalism, Langenhert held that Geulincx did not develop his occasionalism consistently. Langenhert claimed that neither Descartes nor 'occasionalists' could prove that the external world exists and that the existence of bodies outside of us is merely a hypothesis, and ultimately dispensed with accounts of causation in metaphysics. On this basis, Jaworzyn argues that Langenhert developed an occasionalism 'without occasions in the external world' and shows that this view is a product of philosophical debates that animated the academic discussions at Leiden. By showing that Langenhert developed these views in his critical encounter with Geulincx, Jaworzyn demonstrates that Geulincx's influence, understood as the extension of his ideas as much as their adoption, was more varied and geographically wide-ranging than often thought. Equally, by exploring some of its more unusual manifestations in *Compendium Physicae* and *Novus Philosophus*, Jaworzyn goes some way to uncovering the breadth of the teaching of (broadly) Cartesian physics.

Moving from a seemingly abortive new tradition to a very successful one, the next contribution, from Pieter Present, focuses on Dutch Newtonianism. Newtonian natural philosophy emerged during the eighteenth century as the new dominant approach and is one of the most successful 'new' traditions. This is not the result of Newton's work alone but rather depended on the joint effort of a number of academics who sought to introduce Newton's philosophy in their university teaching. Interestingly, this effort led to significant reworkings and important adaptations of Newton's own view. In his contribution, Present offers a case study of one of the most important Dutch Newtonians, Petrus van Musschenbroek (1692–1761) and the implementation of 'Newtonian Philosophy' in Dutch universities. The Dutch Republic played an important role in the dissemination of Newton's philosophy where it found its earliest proponents, who were instrumental in the spread of Newton's ideas on the continent. Van Musschenbroek was one such figure who, during his life, took up professorships at the universities of Utrecht and Leiden. In a letter to Newton written at the beginning of his academic career, van Musschenbroek explicitly stated that it was his aim to spread the 'Newtonian philosophy' in the university and, from there, to the rest of Dutch society. Present analyses van Musschenbroek's defence of the 'Newtonian philosophy' in his academic orations and examines the rhetoric used to present Newton's philosophy in the textbooks van Musschenbroek wrote for his teaching activities. Present shows how van Musschenbroek uses a specific account of the institution of the university and its tasks as a leverage in his defence of the 'Newtonian philosophy' and his attack of the existing tradition of Cartesian philosophy in the university.

Universities represented the main infrastructure for higher education in early modern Europe. Nonetheless, the seventeenth and the eighteenth century witnessed the development of a number of scientific societies that were not university-affiliated. These societies often played a prominent role in the spreading of new views and operated as autonomous (and sometimes competing) centres of knowledge and authority in the shaping of the early modern debates about natural philosophy. In his contribution, Christian Leduc focuses on the way in which the relationship between the fields of philosophy and science was the object of intense debate at the Berlin Academy. Originally founded by Leibniz in 1700, the Berlin Academy was reformed in the 1740s under Frederick II. The reform aimed at multiple reorientations, but one of its most important components was the creation of a class of speculative philosophy. While other important institutions, such as the London and Paris academies, mainly focused on sciences, Frederick II wished for his academy to propagate research in metaphysics, psychology, and morals. Members were thus recruited on the basis of not only their scientific achievements but their philosophical contributions as well. Leduc draws attention to two points related to the Berlin Academy during the second half of the eighteenth century. Firstly, the existence of a class of speculative philosophy was not only exceptional, but also represented a unique environment to discuss the relationship between philosophy and sciences. Indeed, there were a number of papers devoted to these questions, in which the authors reflected on the way research should be made in the context of an academy. They were obviously aware that speculative philosophy has to explain how science and philosophy are done in the Academy. Secondly, Leduc analyses some key papers in which members of the Academy try to determine what they call the 'academic spirit'. An important source is Maupertuis' paper entitled 'On the duties of academicians' of 1752, in which he explains his views, as president, about the division of classes and the advantages of carrying out research in an academy. But there are other important contributions; particularly that of Formey who, as secretary, wrote several papers on these questions, but also of Dieudonné Thiebault, Jakob Wegelin, and Christian Garve. These discussions took place at distinct periods and express different ways of conceiving of the production of academic scholarship. Most importantly, their representation of speculative philosophy changed, to the extent that some believed that this field should no longer be discussed in the context of the academy. Christian Garve maintains this view in his paper of 1788, which expresses a major change in the history of the institution. This position is also accompanied by a gradual disappearance of speculative reflections.

Is it possible to derive a new narrative about the transformation of early modern natural philosophy from the way in which natural philosophy was systematized in academic textbooks and publications? This question is at the centre of Andrea Sangiacomo's contribution. Sangiacomo introduces the notion of 'normalisation' as a way of studying and explaining conceptual changes during relatively long periods of time. Normalisation concerns the mutual adaptation of certain ideas and existing traditions. Sangiacomo argues that the academic milieu is the best scenario to study normalisation, since it is in the academic milieu that the constant exchange between (and clash of) tradition and innovation becomes more apparent. Sangiacomo provides the methodological underpinnings of his account of normalisation and offers a preliminary implementation of it by focusing on the role of 'occasional causality' in natural philosophy (i.e. the account of causality that understands causes as *sine quibus non* conditions devoid of any intrinsic efficacious causal power to bring their effect about). To do so, Sangiacomo considers four authors: Pierre Sylvain Régis (1632–1707), Johan Christoph Sturm (1635–1703), Petrus van Musschenbroek (1692–1761), and Immanuel Kant (1724–1804). These authors were all university professors, except for Régis, whose work was nonetheless intended to provide a Cartesian textbook comparable to those used in university courses. Except for Kant, these authors are all (as yet) relatively obscure figures, who do not routinely feature in early modern discussions of causation. Sangiacomo argues that these four authors progressively normalise an account of 'occasional causality'. According to Sangiacomo, the reason why occasional causality is normalised is because it is most conducive, in the early modern scenario, to preserving (under a different guise) a fundamental ontological commitment to the coarse-grained nature of reality (i.e. the ontological view according to which reality is made up by ontologically discrete and reciprocally independent entities), which all four authors are extremely recalcitrant to abandon. According to Sangiacomo, this preliminary conclusion shows that studying normalisation may open up a new way of understanding the evolution of early modern natural philosophy. However, he stresses that a proper study of normalisation requires the introduction of quantitative methods in the study of the history of universities, philosophy and science.

3. Looking at the background

The contributions in this volume intervene in the ongoing debate concerning the complex role played by the academic milieu in the early modern reshaping of natural philosophy. They draw attention to different facets of a scenario in which intellectual, philosophical, social and scientific issues are deeply entrenched. They also call for renewed methodological attention to the way in which particular authors or conceptual changes are understood and studied by today's scholars. In particular, these contributions draw attention to the dynamic nature of conceptual exchanges across different places and backgrounds and between innovation and tradition, and consider the academic milieu the focal point from which to observe these exchanges.

One of the aims of these contributions is to show the complexity of the dialectic between 'tradition' and 'innovation' that took place across the early modern debate on natural philosophy. This, in turns, calls for a renewed effort to map the geographical interplay of different regions and academic institutions. Only by embedding philosophical and scientific debates in the concrete historical and geographic scenario in which they took place is it possible to fully appreciate their contribution to the European discussion.

Crucial areas of Europe are not yet well integrated in the international scholarly debate on the role that the academic milieu played in the reshaping of early modern natural philosophy. For instance, one macroscopic absence (in Anglophone scholarship at least) is that of Spain and Portugal, which were two world-empires and first-order political players in the early modern landscape. The Iberian Peninsula hosted one of the most solid and resilient scholastic traditions, which continued to be active throughout the early modern period. Perhaps due to the emphasis on the role of *novatores* in the master narrative of the Scientific Revolution, these areas have not received sufficient scholarly attention, since they did not seem to witness the emergence of analogous anti-traditional figures or were not receptive to the 'new natural philosophy' in the same way in which other areas of Europe were.[25]

The interplay between scholastic and non-scholastic approaches was a vital element in the evolution of early modern natural philosophy. Early modern scholasticism witnessed its own internal evolution and tried to develop new ways of addressing enduring problems or incorporating new approaches in the existing frameworks. Once one abandons the narrative

---

[25] See David Goodman, 'The Scientific Revolution in Spain and Portugal' in *The Scientific Revolution in Natural Context*, eds. Roy Porter and and Teich Mikulás (Cambridge, 2012), 158–177 at 171: 'Iberian scientific and technological activity, once so conspicuous, collapsed towards the end of the sixteenth century and remained unimportant for most of the seventeenth century when elsewhere in Europe there was a cluster of scientific talent and discovery. So complete was the collapse that it is difficult to find a single Iberian contributor to the European Scientific Revolution of the seventeenth century. The pattern is the same for both Portugal and Spain: sixteenth-century activity, seventeenth-century stagnation followed by a campaign to rescue the countries from the darkness of scientific backwardness. What was the cause of this intellectual deterioration? Iberian historians have continued to give the explanation favoured by the philosophers of the Enlightenment: the cause was religious fanaticism. This can be supported but the issues are complicated.'

of the 'Scientific Revolution' and rather focuses on the continuous evolution of the academic milieu, it should be possible to reconsider how contexts in which no 'Scientific Revolution' seemingly occurred nonetheless reacted, resisted and adapted to the evolution of natural philosophy unfolding around them. The contributions presented in this volume offer a number of suggestions and examples about how this line of research could be further developed and applied to different cases.[26]

Faculty of Philosophy
University of Groningen
a.sangiacomo@rug.nl

[26] This volume emerged from a conference (originally entitled 'Teaching the new science: the role of universities during the Scientific Revolution') organized by Andrea Sangiacomo at the University of Groningen (15–17 June 2017), as part of the activities of his NWO-veni research grant 'Occasionalism and the secularization of early modern science: understanding the dismissal of divine action during the Scientific Revolution.' A profound thank you goes to all those who attended the conference and contributed to the discussions that nourished the collective effort that underpins this collection. In particular, I am very grateful to Laura Georgescu, Martin Lenz and Doina-Cristina Rusu for the inspiring methodological conversations on different approaches to the history of philosophy and science.

Fromondus versus Galileo on Comets

Roger Ariew

Introduction

Libertus Fromondus (or Libert Froidmond, 1587–1653) was associated with colleges and universities the whole of his life. He was educated in the humanities by the Jesuits in Liège (near his birthplace, Haccourt sur Meuse, Belgium) and studied philosophy in Louvain at the collège du Faucon, 1604–1606. There he befriended a Dutch student, Cornelius Jansen of Acquoy, the future Jansenius, Bishop of Ypres. Fromondus did not pursue his studies but instead went to teach rhetoric, first at the abbey Saint-Michel in Anvers, 1606–1609, and then back in Louvain, 1609–1614. He taught philosophy in Louvain starting in 1614, until he received a doctorate in theology in 1628, when he joined the faculty of theology. After Jansenius was appointed bishop in 1636, Fromondus assumed his chair as professor of Sacred Scripture. During his final illness in 1638, Jansenius entrusted the manuscript of his *Augustinus* to Fromondus, who arranged for its publication in 1640 (as he had previously for other theological commentaries by Jansenius). Fromondus's early works (which I will be discussing below) were composed during the period he was teaching philosophy at Louvain, and concerned natural philosophy: *Saturnalitiae Coenae, Variatiae Somnio sive Peregrinatione Caelestis* (1616); *Dissertatio de cometa anni 1618* (1619); and *Meteorologicum libri VI* (1627, with a second edition in 1642). While he wrote a number of theological commentaries (published posthumously in 1653 and thereafter), he also continued publishing natural philosophical and mathematical works after 1628, including *Labyrinthus sive de compositione continui* (1631); *Commentarii in libros Quaestionum naturalium Senecae* (1632); and *Ant-Aristarchus sive orbis terrae immobilis adversus Philippum Lansbergium* (1631).[1] Fromondus's book

[1] The work is a critique of the Dutch Copernican Philip van Lansbergen. Jacob Lansbergen replied with a defense of his father's work, *Apologia, pro commentationibus Philippi Lansbergii in motum terrae diurnum & annuum: adversus Libertum Fromondum*

Roger Ariew, *Fromondus versus Galileo on Comets* In: *History of Universities*. Edited by: Mordechai Feingold, Oxford University Press (2021). © Oxford University Press.
DOI: 10.1093/oso/9780192893833.003.0001

on the labyrinth of the continuum, sometimes described as a 'reactionary scholastic diatribe against atomism,' may have been Fromondus's most influential work, because of the interest given to it by G. W. Leibniz.[2] Apart from his published and edited works, Fromondus is perhaps best known for the letter he wrote to René Descartes, which he sent to Descartes through the intermediary of his faculty of medicine Louvain colleague (and former philosophy student), Vopiscus Fortunatus Plemp. The letter was in response to Descartes's sending Fromondus and Plemp copies of his *Discourse on Method*. Descartes likely had met Plemp and possibly Fromondus before 1637, but the main reason he sent the *Discourse* to Fromondus was because the *Meteors* was one of its appended essays and Fromondus, of course, had published a *Meteorology*.[3] The correspondence between Descartes and Plemp continued with Fromondus as a silent partner.[4]

Fromondus's letter to Descartes shows him to be a reactionary anti-atomist scholastic as well. As part of his response, Fromondus sent Descartes his *Labyrinthus sive de compositione continui*, that is, his tract against Epicureans and atomists, and argued against what he saw as Descartes's over-reliance on atomistic and mechanical principles. Concerning Descartes's account of body in the *Meteors*, Fromondus commented: 'the composition of bodies from parts of diverse shapes... which cohere with one another as if with hooks, seems too crass and mechanical.'[5] He appeared astonished that

theologum Lovaniensem, in 1633, and Fromondus replied as well with *Vesta, sive Ant-Aristarchi vindex* in 1634. For more on this debate, see Rienk Vermij, *The Calvinist Copernicans. The reception of the new astronomy in the Dutch Republic, 1575–1750* (Amsterdam, 2002), esp. 1, chap. 5.

[2] The comment is by R. T. W. Arthur in G. W. Leibniz, *The Labyrinth of the Continuum: Writings on the Continuum Problem, 1672–1686*, trans. R. T. W. Arthur (New Haven, 2001), 388, n. 12; for a more positive view of the relations between Fromondus and Leibniz, see Carla Rita Palmerino, '*Geschichte des Kontinuumproblems* or Notes on Fromondus's *Labyrinthus*? On the True Nature of LH XXXVII, IV, 57 r°-58v°,' *The Leibniz Review* 26 (2016), 63–98 and 'Libertus Fromondus' Escape from the Labyrinth of the Continuum (1631)', *Lias, Journal of Early Modern Intellectual Culture and its Sources* 42 (2015), 3–36.

[3] 'I received several [sets of objections] recently from Mr Fromondus of Louvain, to whom I sent one of the books because he wrote on Meteors. I replied to him the day after I received them. In fact I rejoice when I see the strongest objections made against me are not as worthy as the weakest I make against myself before establishing what I wrote'. René Descartes, *Oeuvres de Descartes*, ed. Charles Adam and Paul Tannery, 2nd. ed. (Paris, 1964–1974), I: 449. Henceforth AT volume, page.

[4] Plemp wrote at least five letters to Descartes: the first one on 15 September 1637 to acknowledge reception of the copies of the *Discours* and to send Fromondus's reaction to it (AT, I, 399–401); at the end of November or the beginning of December 1638 (lost but see Descartes to Plemp, 20 December 1637, AT, I, 475); in January 1638 (AT, I, 497–504); March 1638 (AT, II, 52–54; and 20 April 1638 (?) (lost; see Descartes to Plemp, August 1638, II, 343–345).

[5] AT I, 406; Also AT I, 402: 'he unknowingly, I suppose, adopts Epicurus' physics, something crude and somewhat crass, not sufficiently polished, as most people believe, instead of the precise truth'.

Descartes would want to eliminate forms and qualities and sensitive and vegetative souls; as he said,

> He [Descartes] appears to say that heat, something of the same nature as what warms up hay, should be able to accomplish in a human body all the operations of an animal, with the exception of the actions proper to the rational soul. Therefore, without any other soul, such as the sensitive soul, the heat of hay is able to see, to hear, and so on. Such noble actions as vision and the like do not appear able to be produced by so ignoble and brute a cause as heat.[6]

At the end of his letter Fromondus summarized his objections with the following: 'Descartes hopes to explain too many things with location in space or local movement; and they cannot be explained without real qualities, or I understand nothing.'[7]

Despite these exchanges, we should be wary of treating Fromondus as a rigid dogmatist. Constantijn Huygens found his remarks insulting,[8] but Descartes did not take them in this way. Twice, Descartes used the analogy with a game of chess to describe the exchanges he had with Fromondus, that is, he thought both he and Fromondus were playing a game, acting out respective roles. In his reply to Plemp about Fromondus, Descartes said:

> I am very surprised it made him believe that his writing caused me to be annoyed or irritated, because I was not so in any way. I do not think I even uttered the slightest word against him without his having said similar or harder things against me first, so that, thinking he liked this style of writing, I somewhat forced my nature, which is normally disinclined to disagreement with others. I thought that, in this case, if I answered his strong attack too softly and gently, my game would have pleased him less. Those who play chess or checkers against each other do not for that reason stop being friends, and indeed among them some skill in the game is in itself a bond of friendship, so I crafted my reply to gain his goodwill.[9]

[6] AT I, 403. Also AT I, 406: 'He does not seem to recognize any sensation but that which takes place in the brain. But when an animal is burned on some part of its body, is there not some operation of touch at the location that makes the animal perceive a dolorific quality there? This at least is what we see and experience rather than trying to imagine it in the head'.

[7] AT I, 408.

[8] See AT II, 653–54: 'I do not know whether Mr Fromondus's blind philosophy will have led him to the edge of a reply, *such that he asks to be punished again*, but regardless, I beg you that the communication not be denied to me with respect to what you hold me to be competent and capable to judge. I am delighted to see what affronts I would deserve if I freed myself to give you such a rude and ill-founded question, and how you would feel about it with your incomparable patience.... after Fromondus there is no significant offense. Read me always after him, please'.

[9] AT I, 475. In his reply Descartes rejected the assertion that he was an Epicurean or atomist, exaulted in his 'crass mechanical philosophy', and discussed phantom limb pain to counter Fromondus's 'dolorific quality'. See AT I, 413–30.

And in response to Huygens's pique, he repeated: 'As for Mr Fromondus, the small disagreement between us was not worth you knowing about.... Moreover, this dispute happened between us like a game of chess—we remained good friends after it was finished, and we only send compliments to each other.'[10]

Thus, I propose to investigate the limits of Fromondus's scholasticism and to use the evidence of his earlier writings in the service of that investigation, specifically concerning what Fromondus wrote about comets and whether he treats Aristotle and previous scholastic views about comets with deference in those works.

The Setting for Thinking about Comets: Astronomical Novelties, 1610–1618

In March 1610 Galileo published the *Sidereus Nuncius*. The work contained an account of the astronomical discoveries he made, using a spyglass he fashioned for himself based on a Flemish toy;[11] it described mountains on the moon, plus more stars than ever seen before, and the motion of four moons around Jupiter. But Galileo was not done making discoveries with his spyglass. In August of the same year, he wrote a letter describing the odd shape of Saturn, which appeared to have two lateral stars accompanying it,[12] and, by the end of December, responding to a query from his follower Benedetto Castelli, he recounted the changes in Venus from a small round object to a larger one, and then to a waning and waxing crescent. Castelli had asked, at the beginning of the month, whether Galileo had looked at Venus through the spyglass because, as he put it, given Copernicus's system, 'in which they both believed,'[13] Venus must be revolving around the sun, and, therefore, it ought to exhibit phases like those shown by the moon. Thus, to be added to the novelties of the *Sidereus Nuncius* were the 'handles' of Saturn, the phases of Venus (and Mercury), and, ultimately, the newly observed sunspots. All of these phenomena were to be made public by Galileo in his 1613 *Letters on Sunspots*, in which he also argued that they are evidence for the theories of Copernicus and the Pythagoreans—something he had not done directly in the *Sidereus Nuncius*.

---

[10] AT II, 47–52.
[11] For more on the Galileo's telescope, see Massimo Bucciantini, *Galileo's Telescope*, trans. Catherine Bolton (Cambridge, 2015).
[12] Galileo Galilei, *Opere*, ed. A. Favaro (Florence, 1890–1901), 5: 410.
[13] Galileo, *Opere*, 5: 481.

Galileo also set about to hold exhibitions of the newly discovered phenomena, but not all of these turned out perfectly well. At times, the guests at the displays were not able to see the novelties—or anything at all, for that matter—with their spyglasses. Such accounts have led commentators to see resistance and irrationality in the reception of Galileo's observations;[14] others have attempted to turn the matter on its head, contending that the resistance was warranted.[15] But irrational or seemingly irrational reactions were simply not the rule. In fact, as early as November 1610, the Jesuit mathematicians at the Collegio Romano had constructed their own spyglass and were making independent observations.[16] Initially skeptical, they were in a position to answer some wide-ranging queries about Galileo's observations by the head of the Collegio, Cardinal Roberto Bellarmine, within a week of his request. On 19 April 1611, Bellarmine wrote to the Jesuit mathematicians asking whether they could validate Galileo's observations, saying that he himself had seen some very wonderful things concerning the Moon and Venus through a spyglass. Bellarmine asked whether they could confirm 'the multitude of fixed stars invisible with the naked eye,... that Saturn is not a simple star but three stars joined together,... that the star of Venus changes its shape, waxing and waning like the Moon,... that the Moon has a rough and uneven surface,' and 'that four movable stars go around the planet of Jupiter.'[17] So, in the first half of 1611, Bellarmine could ask the Collegio Romano mathematicians about Galileo's observations, both about those published in the 1610 *Siderius nuncius* and those later disseminated in correspondence, in this case, the 'handles' of Saturn and the phases of Venus.

---

[14] For example, Stillman Drake asserts: 'The arguments brought forth against [Galileo's] new discoveries were so silly that it is hard for the modern mind to take them seriously.... One after another, all attempts to cleanse the heavens of new celestial bodies came to grief. Philosophers had come up against a set of facts which their theories were unable to explain. The more persistent and determined adversaries of Galileo had to give up arguing and to resort to threats.' Stillman Drake, *Discoveries and Opinions of Galileo* (New York, 1957), 73–74.

[15] Paul Feyerabend notoriously argued that '[Galileo] offers no theoretical reasons why the telescope should be expected to give a true picture of the sky....Nor does the initial experience with the telescope provide such reasons. The first telescopic observations of the sky are indistinct, indeterminate, contradictory and in conflict with what everyone can see with his unaided eyes. And the only theory that could have helped to separate telescopic illusions from veridical phenomena was refuted by simple tests'. Paul Feyerabend, *Against Method* (London, 1978), 99, 121.

[16] See Henrique Leitão, 'Jesuit mathematical Practices in Portugal, 1540–1759', Michel John Gorman, 'Mathematics and Modesty in the Society of Jesus: The Problems of Chistoph Grienberger', and Mordechai Feingold, 'The Grounds for Conflict: Grienberger, Grassi, Galileo, and Posterity', *The New Science and Jesuit Science: Seventeenth-Century Perspectives*, ed. Mordechai Feingold (Dordrecht, 2003), respectively 229–248, 1–120, and 121–158.

[17] Galileo, *Opere*, 11: 87–88.

The mathematicians Christopher Clavius, Christopher Grienberger, Odo Malcote, and Giovanni Paolo Lembo responded in the affirmative on April 24, agreeing that, using the spyglass, more stars can be seen than ever before, there are 'handles' to Saturn, phases of Venus, and moons around Jupiter. However, they did not think that mountains on the moon could be observed. They granted the great inequality of the moon's surface, but added: 'Father Clavius thinks it more probable that the surface is not uneven, but rather that the lunar body is not of uniform density and has rarer and denser parts.'[18] Clavius, the author of an important and extremely popular scholastic textbook in astronomy, *Sphaera*, was even moved to include a brief account of the Galilean novelties in the ultimate edition of his work, published that year:

> I do not want to hide from the reader that not long ago a certain instrument was brought from Belgium.... This instrument shows many more stars in the firmament than can be seen in any way without it... and when the moon is a crescent or half full, it appears so remarkably fractured and rough that I cannot marvel enough that there is such unevenness in the lunar body. Consult the reliable little book by Galileo Galilei, printed in Venice in 1610 and called *Sidereus Nuncius*, which describes various observations of the stars first made by him.

He didn't stop there, discussing also Galileo's unpublished observations concerning Venus and Saturn:

> Far from the least important of the things seen with this instrument is that Venus receives its light from the sun as does the moon, so that sometimes it appears to be more like a crescent, sometimes less, according to its distance from the sun. At Rome I have observed this in the presence of others more than once. Saturn has joined to it two smaller stars, one on the east, the other on the west. Finally, Jupiter has four roving stars, which vary their places in a remarkable way both among themselves and with respect to Jupiter—as Galileo Galilei carefully and accurately describes.[19]

Clavius finished his discussion with a programmatic stance, saying that the new astronomical observations should be accounted for within the received astronomical theory: 'Since things are thus, astronomers ought to consider how the celestial orbs may be arranged in order to save these phenomena'.[20] Unfortunately, Clavius died that year, so the task of reconciling Aristotelian astronomy and the celestial novelties was left to others.

[18] Galileo, *Opere*, 11: 92–93.

[19] Christopher Clavius, (Mainz, 1611), 3: 75; trans. James M. Lattis, *Christoph Clavius and the Collapse of Ptolemaic Cosmology* (Chicago, 1994), 198.

[20] 'Quae cum ita sint, videant Astronomi quo pacto orbes coelestes constituendi sint, ut haec phaenomena possint salvari'. Clavius, *Opera mathematica* 3: 75: trans. Lattis, *Between Copernicus and Galileo*, 198.

The Galilean novelties traveled far,[21] making their way to Louvain by 1615. At the time, Libertus Fromondus was a young professor of philosophy; he was asked to preside over some quodlibetal exercises that year. Fromondus published his contribution to the discussions in 1616 and inserted an astronomical fantasy, *Peregrinatio Caelestis,* in the publication.[22] As he said in the preface to the work, he wanted to give his students a taste of the wonders that he and others had seen through the telescope; Fromondus regretted that he did not have as good an instrument as Galileo's, which allowed him to distinguish the triple system of Saturn, and with which Fromondus speculates he might have discovered more and more curious things. In his fantasy, a guardian spirit (*Genius*) riding the winged horse Pegasus took a dreaming Fromondus up to the heavens. There, Fromondus observed the rough surface of the moon, the sunspots, the phases of Venus, and the moons of Jupiter. He then noticed Saturn's triple system and referred to Galileo as having first made the discovery (citing at length from a letter of Galileo of November 1610) and he mentioned the Milky Way with its many stars—more stars than ever seen before—first seen through the telescope. In the process, Fromondus disputed the Aristotelian theory of elements and the existence of the sphere of fire. He allowed that the moon might be covered with water. And because of the existence of superlunary comets, he rejected the mechanism of solid spheres, epicycles and eccentrics, in favor of a fluid ethereal substance. In his fantasy, Fromondus made a number of statements

---

[21] On 4 June 1611, the College of La Flèche held the first memorial celebration of the death of Henry IV. Henry le Grand, the patron of La Flèche, had his heart buried at La Flèche, with all appropriate pomp. The students, including even the young René Descartes, composed and performed verses in French and Latin for the memorial. These compositions were published for posterity as *Lacrymae collegii Flexiensis.* One of the French poems from the collection had the unlikely title, 'Concerning the death of King Henry the Great and on the Discovery of Some New Planets or Wandering Stars Around Jupiter, Made the Previous Year by Galileo, Famous Mathematician of the Grand Duke of Florence'. In the poem the sun revolved around the earth; but, taking pity on the sorrow of the French people for the loss of their King, it offered them a new torch: the new stars around Jupiter. The students of La Flèche, and by inference, their Jesuit teachers, appear to have had no objection to the telescope. They even praised its use and Galileo's results. *Sur la mort du roy Henry le Grand et sur la descouverte de quelques nouvelles planettes ou estoilles errantes autour de Jupiter, faicte l'année d'icelle par Galilée, célèbre mathématicien du grand duc de Florence,* in Camille de Rochemonteix, *Un collège des Jésuites au XVIIe et XVIIIe siècle: le collège Henri IV de la Flèche,* (Le Mans, 1889), 1: 147–148. Moreover, in Paris, during 1614, Théophraste Bouju published *Corps de toute la philosophie,* a basic philosophy textbook advertised in its subtitle as 'all of it by demonstration and the authority of Aristotle'; in it one finds Bouju asserting that the moon 'appears with this variety and deformity in it which is not in the other stars, as the Dutch lenses clearly show. And the cause of this defect might be that the moon is close to the lower bodies, in which obscurity and deformity dominate'. Théophraste Bouju, *Corps de toute la philosophie* (Paris, 1614). 1: 388–89 (chap. XLII: De la lune).

[22] Libertus Fromondus, *Saturnalitiae Coenae, Variatae Somnio, sive Peregrinatione Caelestis* (Leuven, 1616).

approving of the Copernican system and the hypothesis of a plurality of inhabited worlds, which he thought consistent with Copernicanism.[23] Still, though only flirting with the Copernican hypothesis, Fromondus showed himself to be very well acquainted with the Galilean celestial novelties.

Despite its popularity, not everything went well for Galileo and his astronomical discoveries in 1616. On February 24, the Holy Office prepared an assessment of two propositions attributed to Copernicus: (i) The sun is at the center of the world and completely devoid of local motion; (ii) The earth is not at the center of the world, nor motionless, but moves as a whole and also with diurnal motion. The Church asserted, of the first proposition, that it is 'foolish and absurd in philosophy, and formally heretical since it explicitly contradicts in many places the sense of the Holy Scripture, according to the literal meaning of the words and according to the common interpretation and understanding of the Holy Fathers and the doctors of theology,' and with respect to the second, that it 'receives the same judgment in philosophy and that in regard to theological truth it is at least erroneous in faith.'[24] The examination of the two propositions were conducted specifically with Galileo in mind, since the very next day Cardinal Bellarmine 'was ordered to call Galileo before himself and warn him to abandon these opinions; and...should he not acquiesce, he is to be imprisoned.' The record shows that Bellarmine warned Galileo on February 26 and Galileo 'acquiesced to the injunction and promised to obey.' The order was given for the edict to be published on March 3 and, on March 5, Copernicus's work was placed on the *Index of Prohibited Books*: 'the Congregation has decided that the books by Nicolaus Copernicus (*On the Revolutions of Spheres*)...be suspended until corrected.'[25]

The news of these events took a while to travel to Louvain. If Fromondus is to be believed, he became aware of the condemnation of Copernicus only at the end of 1618, having been informed of it by his medical school colleague Thomas Feyens (or Fienus); Fromondus complains about his lack of precise knowledge of the condemnation. He writes: 'But what did I recently hear from you about the Copernicans, most honorable person [Feyens]? That one or two years ago the most holy Paul V had them condemned? Until now I had not yet heard about this, nor I imagine, had any of those very learned and Catholic men in Germany and Italy, who, like

---

[23] Georges Monchamp, *Galilée et la Belgique: essai historique sur les vicissitudes du système de Copernic en Belgique (XVIIe et XVIIIe siècles)* (Paris, 1892). 34–43; Tabitta Van Nouhuys, *The Age of Two-Faced Janus: the Comets of 1577 and 1618 and the Decline of the Aristotelian World View in the Netherlands* (Leiden, 1998), 240–245.

[24] Maurice Finocchiaro, *The Galileo Affair: A Documentary History* (Berkeley, 1989), 146.

[25] Finocchiaro, *The Galileo Affair*, 147–49.

Copernicus, are supposing the earth to rotate.'[26] The Church's condemnation of Copernicus would need to be taken into account by the Catholic, Jesuit-educated Fromondus. As we have said, Fromondus, in his fantasy, disputed the Aristotelian theory of elements and the existence of the sphere of fire and, because of the existence of superlunary comets, he also rejected the mechanism of solid spheres, epicycles, and eccentrics, in favor of a fluid ethereal substance (similar but not identical to a Stoic *pneuma*). Thus, in 1615, Fromondus accepted a cosmology like the one adopted by Tycho Brahe.[27]

Comets seem to provide a powerful argument against the heterogeneity of the sublunary and superlunary regions of the world. The standard view is that the new star of 1572, and Tycho Brahe's measurement of the parallax of the comet of 1577 concluding that the comet was in the heavens, and thus to be incompatible with the existence of the 'crystal' spheres, epicycles, and eccentrics of the Aristotelians, had dealt a heavy blow to the traditional view of the immutability and perfection of the heavens.[28] But Tycho Brahe's parallax measurement was neither universally accepted nor without conceptual difficulties. As the textbook author Scipion Dupleix explained in 1607,

> Because they look like true stars, because of their flame, several ancient philosophers, and even Seneca and the common people ignorant of this matter still, take comets to be true stars. But this ignorance is too crass, given

[26] Libertus Fromondus, *De Cometa anni 1618. Dissertationes* (London, 1670 [1619]), 50. See also Monchamp, *Galilée et la Belgique*, 46–47; Van Nouhuys, *The Age of Two-Faced Janus*, 294–95.

[27] See Peter Barker and Bernard Goldstein, 'The Role of Comets in the Copernican Revolution', *Studies in History and Philosophy of and Philosophy of Science* 19 (1988): 299–319. I should specify that Fromondus accepts a fluid ethereal substance in the heavens, but he is clear in his rejection of Stoic or Tychonic *pneuma*, which he thinks is the result of mixing up corruptible and incorruptible substances. See Fromondus, *De Cometa anni 1618*, 4, and Christoph Meinel, 'Les Météores de Froidmont et les Météores de Descartes', in Anne-Catherine Bernès, ed., *Libert Froidmont et les résistances aux révolutions scientifiques*. Actes du Colloque Château d'Oupeye, 26 et 27 septembre 1987 (Haccourt, 1988), 106–29. For more on the issue of celestial motion through the ether, see Edward Grant, *Planets, Stars, and Orbs: The Medieval Cosmos, 1200–1687* (Cambridge, 1994), esp. chap. 18. See also see Miguel A. Granada, "A quo moventur planetae? Kepler et la question de l'agent du mouvement planétaire après la disparition des orbes solides', *Galilaeana* 7 (2010): 111–141.

[28] See, for example, Stephen Gaukroger, *The Emergence of a Scientific Culture: Science and the Shaping of Modernity, 1210–1685* (Oxford, 2006), 99, 171. The 'crystal' spheres are a rhetorical move by Tycho. Aristotelians did not use crystal spheres for their planetary heavens, though some accepted solid spheres for their epicycles and eccentrics. A crystal sphere was traditionally postulated as the ninth sphere, above the firmament of fixed stars, representing the Biblical water above the firmament. Tycho could have no argument that places his comet above the firmament, crashing through the crystal sphere; rather his argument would be that the lack of measurable parallax of the comet would place it above the sphere of the moon, whose parallax is measurable. See also Grant *Planets, Stars, and Orbs*, chap. 14.

that stars are all in the heavens and comets are in the region of air below the moon, as is demonstrated by astronomical instruments [note in the margin: Regiomontanus, *de Cometis*].[29]

Dupleix's reference to Regiomontanus, a marginal note on his comment about astronomical instruments, indicates that, some decades after Tycho's measurements, some scholars still preferred Regiomontanus's earlier parallactic measurements concluding that comets are sublunary.[30] As Dupleix implies as well, the question of the composition of the heavens and the nature and location of comets was a standard dispute between the Stoics, such as Seneca, and the Aristotelians. But, as with most everything Stoic, fluid heavens could also be incorporated into Aristotelianism. Théophraste Bouju argued as an Aristotelian in 1614 that there is no sphere of fire and no absolute division between the sublunary and superlunary world, but Bouju upheld the de facto incorruptibility of heaven;[31] he posited some kind of ethereal substance in the heavens, and even accepted, in principle, the possibility of substantial change in the heavens, with the Stoics, but he maintained a standard Aristotelian account of comets:

> [comets] move from east to west in accordance with the motion of heaven, although they do not do so with regularity. The height of their motion is less than that of the planets and other stars; it demonstrates that they remain in the middle region of the air, in the same way as do those lights in the form of stars which seem to fall from heaven, which are only meteors, of the nature of comets, and not true stars, being generated and corrupted almost in the same instant.[32]

However, Bouju accommodated other novel astronomical phenomena, such as novas; he stated:

> We have seen in our time, during 1572, a new star appearing in Calliope and lasting two years. In the beginning this star seemed to surpass Venus in size and clarity and two months later it decreased in these respects, such that it no longer seemed to exceed a star of the third magnitude; it kept this quantity for the duration of two years, when it disappeared. It cannot be said that this star was in the air where comets usually happen, because it appeared in

---

[29] Scipion Dupleix, *La physique*, ed. R. Ariew (Paris, 1990), 423–24.

[30] For more on Regiomontanus' measurements, see Jane L. Jervis, *Cometary Theory in Fifteenth-Century Europe* (Wrocław, 1985).

[31] Bouju (1614), 380–81 (chap. XXXI: Comment le ciel peut estre et n'estre pas incorruptible): 'Since it does not appear to us…that the sun is of another matter than the other lower bodies, its incorruptibility must arise from its more excellent form than theirs or because contrary agents which can corrupt and alter it do not rise up to it, although it is corruptible with respect to its nature, in the manner of air and other elements'.

[32] Théophraste Bouju, *Corps de toute la philosophie* (Paris, 1614), 600–01 (1. Phys. 11, chap. 12: Des Comettes).

the same way to all who saw it, in whatever region it was, and it always moved from east to west like the other stars; this could not happen if it were located only in the middle region of air, the place of comets.[33]

Bouju showed himself to be open to the possibility of comets moving well above the region of air, something he accepted for the nova of 1572, but he did not think he had enough evidence in 1614 to claim that any comet resided there.

Questions such as the nature and location of comets had not been definitively decided by 1618, a year marked by a succession of three comets visible to the naked eye, culminating in the great comet of 1618. These events resulted in the publication of multiple treatises about comets by numerous observers, not the least being those of Libertus Fromondus, of the Jesuit Horatio Grassi, and of Galileo, responding to Grassi, in defense of his own position, as elucidated by his disciple, Mario Guiducci.[34]

Fromondus and the Comet of 1618

Fromondus wrote his treatise on the great comet of 1618 as a response to a dissertation on that comet which he requested from his colleague Thomas Feyens; he then proceeded to publish the two treatises together. Feyens's treatise used his observations of the comet to dispute the Aristotelian theory of comets as burning terrestrial vapors and reworked arguments from Seneca to support the view that comets belonged to the genus of heavenly bodies, thus placing comets above the sphere of the moon. Ultimately, Feyens used the observations of Tycho Brahe and of Galileo to argue against both the existence of solid planetary spheres and the incorruptibility of the heavens. Consistently with the Church Fathers and Scriptures, Feyens adopted the view that there are three heavens: the fluid planetary heaven delimited by the solid firmament of the fixed stars, above which is located the Empyrean, that is, the resting place of the blessed.[35]

---

[33] Bouju, *Corps de toute la philosophie,* 381.

[34] There were very many treatises published on the Comet of 1618. See Stillman Drake and C.D. O'Malley, *The Controversy on the Comets of 1618* (Philadelphia, 1960); Monchamp, *Galilée et la Belgique* 44–5; and Victor Navarro-Brotons, 'Astronomy and Cosmology in Spain in the Seventeenth Century: the New Practice of Astronomy and the End of the Aristotelian-Scholastic Cosmos', *Cronos* 10 (2007): 15–39. For more on the general general issue on the ways in which heaven and earth were unified in the early modern period, see Grant, *Planets, Stars, and Orbs,* and the chapters in the edited collection of essays by Miguel A. Granada, Patrick J. Boner, and Dario Tessicini, eds., *Unifying Heaven and Earth: Essays in the History of Early Modern Cosmology* (Barcelona, 2016).

[35] Monchamp, *Galilée et la Belgique,* 54–56; Van Nouhuys, *The Age of Two-Faced Janus.* 253–276. For the three-heaven theory, see Roger Ariew, 'Theory of Comets in Paris during

Fromondus received Feyens's treatise very favorably, even claiming (ironically) that as a result, one can see that the comet foretold the death of a Prince, namely, Aristotle, whose theory of comets as meteorological phenomena the Peripatetics needed to bury.[36] And Fromondus's treatise, like that of Feyens, systematically argued against the Aristotelian theory. Fromondus's work is composed of eight chapters: a descriptive first chapter about the great comet of 1618, regarding its appearance and motion, and five subsequent chapters consisting of arguments about various aspects of that comet. In these chapters, Fromondus argues that the comet of 1618 is not a fiery exhalation: because of (i) the height of such exhalations, (ii) the nature of fire, (iii) its lack of scintillation, (iv) its motion, and (v) its tail. The treatise ends with a chapter about the distance and magnitude of the comet, and another, extremely short chapter, about whether comets presage other events on earth.

The interesting thing is that the five arguments are alike in that they are all basically Aristotelian arguments employed to attack an Aristotelian conclusion: Fromondus uses some entrenched Aristotelian principles against the Aristotelian conclusion that comets are terrestrial exhalations. In the argument about the height of terrestrial exhalations, Fromondus argues that such exhalations would have to rise beyond the maximum height for terrestrial exhalations, to where comets are usually observed, and in the process would become extremely subtle and rare. But then, according to Peripatetic theory, they would have also become incapable of being observed on earth.[37] Moreover, if comets were fiery exhalations, they could not last as long as they did, because of the 'volatile and dissoluble nature of fire.'[38] And if comets consisted of fire, they would scintillate. Fromondus thus places comets in the genus of planets, which shine with 'calm and quiet luster,' as opposed to the fixed stars, which 'scintillate and vibrate as fires.'[39] This leads him to an interesting discussion of the hypothesis that the stars and some planets rotate around their axes, causing some of the scintillation, with such phenomena as sunspots, the phases of Venus, and moons around Jupiter and Saturn brought into play for or against the hypothesis—which, in the end, he leaves undecided.

Fromondus's more conclusive arguments against the Aristotelian cometary theory come in the next two chapters. He agrees with Feyens that the comet of 1618 followed a circular path, but also gives it its own proper

---

the Seventeenth Century', *Journal of the History of Ideas* 53 (1992), 355–372 and *Descartes among the Scholastics* (Leiden, 2011), chap. 6.

36 Fromondus, *De Cometa anni 1618,* 31.
37 Fromondus, *De Cometa anni 1618,* 39.
38 Fromondus, *De Cometa anni 1618,* 41.
39 Fromondus, *De Cometa anni 1618,* 42, 44.

motion. A circular path, or a segment of a great circle, instead of an up and down motion, would indicate that the comet's motion was like that of the heavens, not like that of a 'fluctuating fire in the changeable, unstable airy regions.'[40] Finally, for Fromondus, the comet's tail cannot have consisted of fiery exhalations more subtle than those forming the head of the comet, because, as he observed, the comet's tail is always pointing away from the sun. According to Peripatetic principles, as wielded by Fromondus, an exhalation or fire should either be seen pointing toward the sun, because that is the side that would be rarified by the heat of the sun, or upward, because of the tail's rarity, as compared with that of the comet's head.[41] Anti-solarity, or the dependence of the comet's tail on the sun, indicates to Fromondus that the comet is a kind of lens refracting the solar rays in different directions away from the sun, depending upon the density of the comet's head.[42]

Having demolished from his own perspective Aristotle's account of comets based on the Aristotelian theory of elements and their motions, Fromondus proceeded to construct a new account of comets. For Fromondus, superlunary comets counted against the solid spheres and for Feyens's (and Tycho's) fluid planetary heavens. Fromondus rehearsed a possible Copernican plurality of worlds explanation of comets as planetary exhalations arising from planets viewed as systems of elements, on analogy with the elements around our earth,[43] but rejected the hypothesis for a simpler one, in which comets originate out of ethereal matter. Comets, then, are formed through condensation or rarefaction of celestial ether, coagulated for various lengths of time; they are like planets wandering above the sphere of the moon, describing a circular motion.[44]

Fromondus's account of comets fit reasonably well that of Tycho, though the reasons he gave for his account were different: Fromondus understood that he was not able to make sufficiently accurate measurements of the comet's parallax, or lack thereof; however, he also thought that if the comet was sublunary, he should have been able to discern some measure of parallax.[45] One can see as well, in the course of his treatise, that he accepted fully all of Galileo's novel observations, but, even though he might have been tempted by the Copernican hypothesis, in the end he did not think that those observations, or his own observations of the comet of 1618, were evidence for it.

[40] Fromondus, *De Cometa anni 1618*, 45.
[41] Fromondus, *De Cometa anni 1618*, 47.
[42] Fromondus, *De Cometa anni 1618*, 48.
[43] Fromondus, *De Cometa anni 1618*, 54.
[44] Fromondus, *De Cometa anni 1618*, 56.
[45] Fromondus, *De Cometa anni 1618*, 50.

Not all scholastics took the route followed by Fromondus and Feyens; that is, not all the scholastics who accepted the novel astronomical observations adopted some kind of Tychonic or Stoic system, as it is often asserted. For example, the Parisian professor Jacques du Chevreul accepted the new astronomical observations, but rejected the Copernican system. He also rejected Tycho's solutions, maintaining a more traditional Aristotelianism. In his treatise, Du Chevreul discussed the method of parallax in general, and the issue of the parallax of comets,[46] but did not decide the question fully.[47] Du Chevreul adopted a probabilistic language on questions about the matter of the heavens and its incorruptibility. He inserted a disputation with the 'neoterics', who claimed that the heavens are corruptible, on the basis of such astronomical phenomena as new stars (that is, novas) and comets. In his replies, again couched in probabilistic language, he denied the conclusiveness of the moderns' observations and of their parallactic measurements. He then followed tradition in dividing the stars into fixed and wandering stars. Du Chevreul tells us that Plato, Aristotle, and all others to the present generation observed seven wandering stars or planets: Saturn, Jupiter, Mars, the Sun, Venus, Mercury, and the Moon. But he also asserts that Galileo, that preeminent mathematician, discovered four planets circling around Jupiter and two new planets concentric to Saturn. Thus, Du Chevreul counts thirteen planets agreed by all, that is, six new ones on top of the seven classically known ones. He further multiplies the count by noting that others add another thirty new planets circling about the Sun, namely the sunspots that Jean Tarde calls the Bourbon stars.[48]

The discoveries acknowledged by Du Chevreul entail modifications in the doctrine of the number of the heavens. According to Aristotle and the Aristotelians, the number of heavens, distinguished by their different motions,[49] is at least eight; instead, Du Chevreul counts only five planetary heavens: those of Saturn, Jupiter, Mars, the Sun, and the Moon.[50] Missing in this count are the heavens for the new planets and those of Venus and Mercury. Du Chevreul asserts that, as shown by the optical tube, Mercury and Venus circle around the Sun, that is, they can be found above, below, and next to the Sun. Thus, the center of their orbs must be the Sun; any other arrangement would require the interpenetration of orbs, causing a vacuum—and this is impossible in nature. According to Du Chevreul, only the astronomers of his generation, using an optical instrument that can detect more stars in the Milky Way and other parts of the firmament,

[46] Jacques du Chevreul, *Sphaera* (Paris, 1622), 47–51.
[47] See Du Chevreul, *Sphaera*, 83–85.   [48] Du Chevreul, *Sphaera*, 80–85.
[49] Du Chevreul, *Sphaera*, 136.   [50] Du Chevreul, *Sphaera*, 152.

can see that Venus and Mercury are located next to the Sun, above, and below it. Venus and Mercury thus orbit the Sun as the Moon orbits the Earth, within the Sun's heaven.[51] The situation is similar to that of Galileo's stars around Jupiter and the two 'planets' circling Saturn. The same is true for the thirty Bourbon planets or 'shadows' around the Sun.

It is not difficult to see that Du Chevreul is the legitimate heir to Clavius: he has managed to accept the observations made by Galileo in 1610–1613 with the assistance of the telescope, but does not regard these phenomena as evidence for either the Copernican or the Tychonic system. He accepts Galileo's observations from more or less within the framework of Aristotelian cosmology, as received before 1610. This is made quite clear in his chapter on eccentric and epicyclic orbs. There, he argues for the necessity of eccentrics and epicycles and formally rejects Tycho's view of the universe. He asserts that Mars cannot be below the Sun, as Tycho would have it, because that would make the heavens permeable and go against the appearances.[52] Further, in his section on the matter of the world, he denies the kind of language the followers of Tycho used, that the stars wander in the heavens like fish swimming in water.[53] Tycho's measurement of the parallax of the comet of 1577 did not settle the matter for Du Chevreul; it did not require him to think of the planetary heavens as liquid and permeable. In his lectures on Aristotle's *Meteorology*, he continued to claim that comets are sublunary flames.[54]

But scholastics were not the only ones to have rejected Tycho's parallactic measurements and his fluid heavens. One might even count Galileo and his disciple Guiducci among Tycho's opponents. The Jesuit astronomer Horatio Grassi argued against Aristotle's cometary theory based on the lack of observable parallax for the comet of 1618. But Galileo and Guiducci disputed his findings, contending that one cannot use the parallax of a comet to calculate its location: 'Whoever wishes the argument from parallax to bear upon comets must first prove that comets are real things.'[55] For Galileo and his disciple, parallax is a valid method only

---

[51] Du Chevreul, *Sphaera*, 153–154. Thus Du Chevreul's five heavens are, in order: (1) That of the Moon; (2) of the Sun, consisting of the Sun itself in the middle of its heaven, surrounded by the Bourbon stars, Mercury and Venus; (3) of Mars; (4) of Jupiter surrounded by the four Medicean stars; and (5) of Saturn, in the middle of which Saturn sits, with two concentric orbs or satellites.

[52] Du Chevreul, *Sphaera*, 153–154.   [53] Du Chevreul, *Sphaera*, 72.

[54] Jacques du Chevreul, *Commentarius in libros Meteorologicos*, ms. Cherbourg, Bibliothèque municipale Jacques Prévert (1635), fols. 514–590, at fol. 547.

[55] Galileo, in Drake and O'Malley, *The Controversy on the Comets of 1618*, 186–87. Galileo is quoting from a debate between his student Mario Guidicci and Grassi, supporting Guiducci against Grassi.

when one has a real and permanent object; for example, one cannot use the parallax of a rainbow to calculate its location. Thus, the parallax of a comet (or its lack of parallax) cannot give us its superlunary location and is not evidence for concluding that the Aristotelians are wrong (or for concluding further that there is an imperfect terrestrial object in the heavens) unless, of course, we had previously accepted comets as objects whose nature is terrestrial, and not meteorological phenomena or mere appearances. Though Galileo does not need to think that the heavens are heterogeneous, in 1623 he proposed that comets are luminous reflections of atmospheric exhalations, an account similar to the one he had proposed in 1606 and similar to the Aristotelian account; quoting Galileo: 'The substance of the comet... may be believed to dissolve in a few days, and its shape, which is not circularly bounded but confused and indistinct, gives us an indication that its material is more tenuous than fog or smoke.'[56]

Fromondus and Comets, 1627–1650.

Fromondus understood Galileo's opinions about comets, but in Book III, *De Cometis,* of his 1627 *Meteorology,* he rejected them, arguing instead for the anti-Aristotelian view that some comets are supra-lunar. In *De cometis,* Fromondus repeated the arguments from his shorter 1618 tract, with a few interesting changes. Fromondus's discussion is divided into four parts: chapter 1, on the place in which comets are generated, with arguments about parallax and whether comets are celestial or sublunary; chapter 2, on the matter of comets, whether they are drawn from celestial or from terrestrial and aqueous matter; chapter 3, on the formal, efficient, and final cause of comets, with a single article about whether comets presage events on earth; and chapter 4, on the properties of comets, including arguments about the tails of comets, their light, their motion, magnitude, and duration. Given that Fromondus is talking about comets generally, he argues that some comets are celestial but also allows that some are sublunary. Thus there are two kinds of comets: those generated in the heavens, that share the motion and matter of the stars, and others that are sublunary and drawn from terrestrial elements.[57]

Still, in his chapter on the location of comets, Fromondus is clear that many comets have a smaller degree of parallax than that of the moon; thus

---

[56] Drake and O'Malley, *The Controversy on the Comets of 1618,* 229.
[57] Fromondus (1670 [1642]), chap. 1, art. 6: 'Cometa aliquos esse sublunares', 115.

comets move among the stars.[58] This leads to Fromondus's critique of the parallactic views of Scaliger, Rothmann, Claramontius, and Galileo. In fact, Fromondus describes in detail the argument by Galileo and his disciple Guiducci against the use of parallax for measuring the distance of comets. As he explains it, positional visual phenomena such as parhelia, halos, and rainbows are to be located below the heavens next to us but evince no measurable degree of parallax. Comets, then, could have no measurable parallax and still be some kind of terrestrial exhalations in the sublunary region. Fromondus understands that this is the conclusion of Guiducci and Galileo, but rejects it. He notes that comets are not visual phenomena but lucid bodies like stars, and that they frequently move from place to place, from South to North *and vice versa*—that which a mere positional appearance could not do.[59] Fromondus revisits the opinion of Guiducci and Galileo that comets are terrestrial exhalations in his second chapter, on the matter of comets. Against their view, he repeats his analysis from 1618 that such exhalations climbing so high would become so rarified that they would become invisible.[60] Moreover, in his fourth chapter, on the motion of comets, Fromondus argues that terrestrial exhalations do not have the lengthy motions exhibited by comets; if Galileo and Guiducci were right, the proper motion of comets above the moon would measure only one or two degrees of arc for the whole of their duration.[61]

Fromondus argues against Galileo and Guiducci on three separate occasions. On one of these occasion he singles out an argument as belonging to Guiducci alone, that the curvature of the comet's tail is caused by refraction. Fromondus dismisses this explanation, arguing that if this were so, the comet's tail would be more curved at the horizon, where greater and more vapors are in abundance. He asserts that such a phenomenon was not observed for the comet of 1618 or for earlier comets. Fromondus had obviously considered seriously Galileo's views and those of Guiducci— well enough to reject them—and well enough to be able to differentiate between them.

While Fromondus was more confident in 1627 that their lack of parallax indicated that comets were celestial, indecision about the parallactic argument and Tycho's measurement of the parallax of the 1577 comet

---

[58] Fromondus (1670 [1642]), chap. 1, art 1: Cometa quidam caelestes sunt, ex minima quorundam parallaxi, 100.

[59] Libertus Fromondus, *Meteorologicorum libri sex* (London, 1670 [1642]), chap.1, art 2: Argumentum Parallaxeos frustra eludunt Scaliger, Claramontius, Galilaeus, 103–104.

[60] Fromondus, *Meteorologicorum,* chap. 2, art 4: Non omnium caelestium Cometarum materiam, esse terrestres halitus, 126–129.

[61] Fromondus, *Meteorologicorum,* chap. 4, art 4: De Motu Cometarum, 155–156.

continued. For example, François le Rées, in his 1642 *Cursus philosophicus*, had a long discussion of comets and parallax, pro and con Aristotle, including Tycho's observations, finally concluding for Aristotle—just barely. Instead of resolving the question of their parallax, he merely discussed various options he seemed to think were all ultimately consistent with Aristotelian principles, if not Aristotle's actual doctrine about comets being fiery exhalations. In order of preference, the possibilities were: comets could lack parallax and be above the moon, not in the upper region of air; they could be old stars; or their parallax could be observed, consistently with Aristotle's opinion that they are sublunary fiery exhalations.[62] Similarly, René de Ceriziers in 1643 discussed various opinions concerning comets, including the possibility that comets are engendered in the heavens but are corruptible, that they are exhalations attracted by the sun, and that they are wandering stars having different motions above and below the heavens than the planets (requiring the hypothesis of fluid heavens, which he rejected). De Ceriziers asked: 'But why would we not see comets ordinarily, if they were stars? Why would they not have the shape of other stars?', and concluded: 'Let us believe with the Philosopher that comets are exhalations that are ignited in the upper region of air'.[63] In Louis de Lesclache's 1651 philosophy textbook, under the topic of 'fires that form mainly in the higher region of air, like comets, and that happen only infrequently', Lesclache wrote: 'The difficulties that philosophers have in discovering the place of comets must not occupy the minds of those who seek knowledge of natural things in order to acquire knowledge of God'.[64]

But the denial of superlunary comets seems to have been waning by mid-seventeenth century. For example, one can read in the textbook of the Protestant, Pierre du Moulin, in 1644: 'Aristotle holds that comets are fiery exhalations; but the astronomers of this time have observed that a comet was above the moon. If that comet was a fiery exhalation, it would have always kept its tail behind it, in the manner of a torch, which when carried always keeps its flame behind it. And the fact that it was seen by so many in so many countries demonstrates its great height.'[65] Du Moulin, like Fromondus, invoked anti-solarity to argue that some comets are not fiery

---

[62] François le Rées, *Cursus philosophicus* (Paris, 1642), 2.2, 14–26. Le Rées' possibilities were previously discussed in Jean Crassot, *Physica* (Paris, 1618), 475–76.

[63] René de Ceriziers, *Le philosophe françois* (Paris, 1643), 363–64.

[64] Louis de Lesclache, *La philosophie en tables, divisée en cinq parties* (Paris, 1651), 68, table xi of the physics.

[65] Pierre Du Moulin, *La philosophie, mise en francois, et divisée en trois parties, sçavoir, elemens de la logique, la physique ou science naturelle, l'ethyque ou science morale* (Paris, 1644), 5, chap. 3, 103–104.

exhalations.[66] He also constructed an argument about the distance of comets based on their being visible at many places at the same time; this is obviously a common-sense way of getting the parallax arguments across.

Du Moulin, like Fromondus, concluded that there are two kinds of comets, sublunary fiery exhalations à la Aristotle, and celestial objects: 'I believe that both opinions are true and that there are two kinds of comets. The comets of the first kind are miraculous and celestial and above the moon; and consequently they are more meaningful.'[67] By the second half of the seventeenth century, one can find a number of Aristotelians accepting comets as celestial objects: 'Both the form and matter of comets are celestial; thus a comet is a star, not a fire'; 'Comets are celestial; in truth they are planets.'[68] One can even find the successor to the two comets theory, in which both kinds of comets are non-miraculous, in the fashion of Fromondus:

> It must be said that there seem to be two kinds of comets: some are permanent bodies placed in heaven, appearing and disappearing with respect to us; others are only meteors produced by terrestrial exhalations, appearing in the highest regions of air and being ignited there. Proof of the first part. Most of the comets recently observed are certainly higher up than the moon. Now, there cannot be any new production in this part of heaven, as needed for the second opinion. Therefore, these are permanent bodies.[69]

There turned out to have been no difficulty with comets being stars, except that if they were stars, they could not have become sublunary. As far as I can tell, no one ever suggested (nor could they have lived to suggest) that a comet crossed the division between the sublunary and superlunary world. On the other hand, if a comet, seen as a star, had a path that carried

---

[66] Du Moulin, unlike Fromondus, however, expected the moving fiery exhalations to point away from their direction of motion and not away from the sun.

[67] Du Moulin *La philosophie*, 4, chap. 3, p. 104. Brockliss argues that dismissal of anomalous physical phenomena as miraculous was a standard move at the time. See L. W. B. Brockliss, *French Higher Education in the Seventeenth and Eighteenth Centuries: A Cultural History* (Oxford, 1987). 375. See also Renaudot's conférence on comets, in which three out of four speakers are concerned with the signification of comets, their portending the death of a great personage. There is a discussion of some of the conférences (including the one on comets) in chap. 2 of Geoffrey V. Sutton, *Science for a Polite Society: Gender, culture, and the demonstration of enlightenment* (Boulder, 1995).

[68] Petrus Iaubert Bonaviolensis, Student thesis, In Collegio Cadurcensi Societatis Jesu. Bibliothèque Nationale, Cabinet d'Estampes AA6 (1657). One can find a similar theory in de la Vigne's thesis: 'II. Coeli tres numero et specie distincti; figura rotuindi sunt; natura corruptibiles, si Empyreum excipiamus: liquidum praeterea Firmamentum. Eorum materia est eadem sublunariu'. Guillelmus de la Vigne, Student thesis, Jesuit collège du Mont, Caen ms. 468 (1666).

[69] Antoine Goudin, *Philosophia juxta inconcussa tutissimaque Divi Thomae dogmata* (Paris, 1726 [first ed., 1668]), 3: 197.

it across the celestial spheres, then a revision of the solid eccentric-epicycle model would be called for. One might be led to adopt a Tychonic or semi-Tychonic system on account of comets, a path taken by many Jesuits.[70] Ultimately, the Tychonic system was also taken up as a modification of a general Aristotelian point of view.

Fromondus, du Chevreul, Bouju, *et al.* were all forward-going scholastics, accepting Galileo's novel observations, but in various respects not accepting the Copernican or Tychonic systems. Fromondus flirted with Copernicanism, but clearly, he had to take into account the fact that the Catholic Church had decided against it; and he had fundamental Aristotelian commitments motivating him to reject it as well. All of these thinkers made significant modifications to their Aristotelianism to accommodate the astronomical novelties. Du Chevreul accepted Venus, Mercury, and sunspots as moons of the sun, together with moons of Jupiter and Saturn, all within a modified Aristotelian system of eccentrics and epicycles; Bouju rejected the Aristotelian theory of elements and the sphere of fire on Aristotelian grounds and Fromondus corrected Aristotle's account of comets based Aristotelian principles, making room for superlunary comets. The changes Fromondus, du Chevreul, Bouju, *et al.* made were different from one another, but all of them could be said to have used Aristotelian principles they deemed more fundamental to deny Aristotelian tenets they regarded as secondary.[71]

Department of Philosophy
University of South Florida
rariew@usf.edu

---

[70] As late as 1651 one can find Paris writers denying the Tychonic system and defending what they called a semi-Copernican system (the earth rotating on its own axis, but not revolving around the sun—in other words, a return to the speculation of Nicole Oresme). For similar kinds of arguments, using observations to conclude for fluid heavens, see C. J. Schofield, *Tychonic and Semi-Tychonic World Systems* (New York, 1981).

[71] While all of them could be thought as normal scientists—in this case, Aristotelians—they all made changes that went well beyond what could be described as the articulation of the Aristotelian paradigm (or exemplar) or as part of the sequence of theories in the Aristotelian 'research programme'. Using Lakatosian language, they all could be said to have fundamentally altered their paradigm or changed part of the core of their research programme.

Institutioni Scholasticae Minime Accommodata: De Neufville and Clauberg on not Teaching Bacon

Stefan Heßbrüggen-Walter

Introduction

The university as an institution serves a dual purpose: it is committed to the search of truth, but at the same time it must train professionals for the needs of society at large. The construction of a curriculum must take both functions into account. Students should not concern themselves with obvious falsehoods. But at the same time, the material they encounter in the classroom must, in the end, enable them to be responsive to the requirements of the profession they take up after finishing their studies. Within the early modern university, the same held for the study of philosophy: the task of the teacher was to convey truths. But at the same time practitioners had to keep in mind that students would advance to the higher faculties, training as pastors, lawyers, or physicians. So when reflecting on 'teaching the new science', teachers of philosophy had to grapple with two problems. They had to consider to which extent the material they presented was true, or at least truth-conducive. And they had to ask themselves to which extent the new paradigm was teachable, i. e., to which extent it was compatible with the institutional constraints imposed by the vocational function of the university. So when the Bremen Baconian Gerard de Neufville and his Cartesian student Johann Clauberg disagreed on whether to teach a modified version of Bacon's project or Cartesian methodology, this was not only a disagreement about the one correct way to investigate nature. Their views also had a pragmatic dimension: evaluating the question how both philosophical projects could meet the pedagogical needs of the university as an educational institution. Moreover,

Stefan Heßbrüggen-Walter, *Institutioni Scholasticae Minime Accommodata: De Neufville and Clauberg on not Teaching Bacon* In: *History of Universities*. Edited by: Mordechai Feingold, Oxford University Press (2021). © Oxford University Press.
DOI: 10.1093/oso/9780192893833.003.0002

their exchange shows that textbooks did contain discussions of pedagogical practice. Authors were not content just to 'compress and express the elements of *Fachwissenschaft* for students'.[1] Such a transmission of pedagogical know-how might have been of less concern for students, but it certainly was relevant for colleagues and administrators. They as well as students may have been part of the target audience of such texts.

De Neufville was born in 1590 in the small German town of Wesel as the grandson of the well-known cartographer Gerhard Mercator.[2] He studied first in Steinfurt, presumably with Timpler, then in Leiden where he received the *magister* degree in 1609. In 1610, he obtained a position as *professor extraordinarius* of mathematics in Heidelberg. One year later, in 1611, he moved on to the Reformed *gymnasium* in Bremen, teaching there with minor interruptions until 1644.[3] In 1616 he received an additional degree as medical doctor in Basle, advanced to the professorship in medicine in Bremen in 1624, and became the first city physician in 1638. He died in 1648. The work under consideration here, his textbook on general natural philosophy, was published in 1645.[4]

There is not much agreement on de Neufville's philosophical stance in the existing scholarly literature. Francesco Trevisani believed incorrectly that de Neufville's *Physiologia* had been lost.[5] He comes to the conclusion that de Neufville was a Melanchthonian.[6] Simone de Angelis classifies de Neufville correctly as 'an early example of the reception of Bacon in Germany'.[7] But de Neufville articulated substantive criticism of Bacon's views as well. I will argue that his views are best understood as an attempt to create a synthesis of natural history and Aristotelian logic, a Baconian *philosophia nov-antiqua*.[8]

---

[1] Anthony T. Grafton, 'Textbooks and the disciplines' in *Scholarly Knowledge: Textbooks in early modern Europe*, eds. Emidio Campi, Simone De Angelis, Anja-Silvia Goeing, Anthony Grafton, (Geneva, 2008), 11–36, 12.

[2] The following is a summary of the biographical information in C. A. E. Lorent, 'Gerh. de Neufville' in *Biographische Skizzen verstorbener Bremischer Aerzte und Naturforscher*, Aerztlicher Verein zu Bremen (ed.), (Bremen, 1844), 71–80.

[3] Some background on the Bremen *gymnasium* can be found in Wilhelm Schmidt-Biggemann, 'Die Schulphilosophie in den reformierten Territorien' in *Ueberweg Grundriss der Geschichte der Philosophie. Die Philosophie des 17. Jahrhunderts*, eds. Helmut Holzhey, Wilhelm Schmidt-Biggemann, Vilem Mudroch, 8 vols. (Basle, 1988–2002), 4/2: 392–474, 423–24.

[4] Gerard de Neufville, *Physiologia seu Physica Generalis* (Bremen, 1645). In the following cited as *Physiologia*.

[5] Cf. Francesco Trevisani, *Descartes in Deutschland: Die Rezeption des Cartesianismus in den Hochschulen Nordwestdeutschlands* (Münster, 2011), 95.

[6] Cf. Trevisani, loc. cit., 65.

[7] Simone de Angelis, *Antrophologien: Genese und Konfiguration einer 'Wissenschaft vom Menschen' in der Frühen Neuzeit* (Berlin/New York, 2010), 269.

[8] De Angelis concedes that de Neufville does not believe that there are obvious contradictions between the basic tenets of Aristotelian logic and Baconian method. Cf. de

Clauberg was born in Solingen in 1622, and he studied in Bremen between 1639 and 1644. In this period, Johannes Combach taught philosophy; in theology we find the irenic professors Crocius and Bergius. De Neufville's interest in Comenian philosophy may have been an important factor in Clauberg's intellectual development. We can guess that Clauberg's move to Groningen in 1644 was, at least, in part motivated by his wish to be close to his friend Tobias Andrae, a member of Comenius's circle.[9] Clauberg then took up teaching positions in Herborn and later in Duisburg, where he died in 1665 at the age of 42.

Verbeek emphasises the relevance of de Neufville for Clauberg's intellectual development in general terms, but without any specific references to the philosophical views of Clauberg's teacher.[10] Savini claims that Clauberg's views on the possibility of 'metaphysical induction' are tied to studies of Bacon with de Neufville.[11] Both Trevisani and Savini assume that the root of the central Claubergian notion of premature judgments lies in de Neufville rather than Descartes.[12] And Savoni notes that Bacon is quoted in Clauberg's *Oratio inauguralis* (1650).[13]

Ulrich Leinsle has shown to which extent Clauberg's *Ontosophia* is influenced by Comenius. These influences may have been mediated by de Neufville.[14] When Comenius spent a few days in Bremen, he apparently met with de Neufville several times and both men discussed a possible employment of Comenius in Bremen.[15] De Neufville and Comenius agreed both in their general admiration for the Baconian project and its assessment as ultimately utopian. But their search for an alternative that would be applicable in the 'real world' led them in different directions. Comenius believed in the project of Mosaic physics, the possibility to ground natural philosophy in Scripture.[16] De Neufville held that it was

Angelis, loc. cit., 272. But he misses the fact that de Neufville aimed to unify both in a coherent theory.

[9] Cf. Theo Verbeek, 'Johannes Clauberg: a Bio-Bibliographical Sketch' in: *Johannes Clauberg (1622–1665) and Cartesian Philosophy in the Seventeenth Century*, Theo Verbeek (ed.), (Dordrecht, 1999), 181–199, 182.

[10] Cf. ibid.

[11] Cf. Massimiliano Savini, *Methodus cartesiana et ontologie* (Paris, 2011), 48.

[12] Cf. Savini, loc. cit., 124, quoting Trevisani.

[13] Cf. Savini, loc. cit., 180–81, quoting Johann Clauberg, *Opera omnia philosophica* (Amsterdam, 1691), 693.

[14] Cf. Ulrich Leinsle, 'Comenius in der Metaphysik des jungen Clauberg' in: *Johannes Clauberg (1622–1665) and Cartesian Philosophy in the Seventeenth Century*, Theo Verbeek (ed.), (Dordrecht, 1999), 1–12, 2–4.

[15] Cf. Leo van Santen, *Bremen als Brennpunkt reformierter Irenik: Eine sozialgeschichtliche Darstellung anhand der Biografie des Theologen Ludwig Crocius (1586–1655)* (Leiden/Boston, 2014), 270.

[16] Cf. Ann Blair, 'Mosaic Physics and the Search for a Pious Natural Philosophy in the Late Renaissance', *Isis* 91 (2000), 32–58, 41.

the complete abandonment of Aristotle and the philosophical tradition that was ultimately responsible for the failure of Bacon's project.

I will first discuss de Neufville's analysis of the state of the art in contemporaneous philosophy of nature: there are irreconcilable differences between Aristotelians, dogmatic, and empiric philosophers. The only resolution is to adopt the Baconian method that combines experiments and induction. But de Neufville's agreement with Bacon is qualified. Philosophy of nature must investigate not only definitions, but also causes. Bacon's polemics against Aristotelian logic are misguided: a reformed natural philosophy still needs syllogisms, because only syllogistic proof can show us how experiential facts hang together and form a coherent theory. And scientific knowledge of nature must presuppose that we can be aware of some universals without needing inductive proof.

While these arguments concern the 'internal' problem of how the teaching of natural philosophy can lead us to truths, we must also address what could be called the 'external' question of how Bacon's theory would fare within the university as an institution that is, at least in part, tasked with a vocational mission. In this context, we must note that it is possible to read Bacon's philosophy as claiming that we need to stop teaching natural philosophy altogether. If we have to give up all that we believed to know about nature, if we must abandon all the findings of natural philosophy accumulated over centuries, natural philosophy could no longer function as an academic subject within the university. We would have to start from a clean slate and wait for successful experiments and inductions furnishing us with fresh insights into nature, before these insights could be conveyed to eventual students. This is why de Neufville proposes to continue teaching those parts of established doctrine taken to be probable (*verisimilis*) by those who have the competence to judge them.

Clauberg, on the contrary, agrees with Bacon that a profound revolution in philosophy is needed and that the evolutionary approach promoted by de Neufville must fail. But he also accepts de Neufville's diagnosis that a revolution along Baconian lines is not feasible. For Clauberg, the way out of this dilemma is to follow Descartes rather than Bacon. We should subscribe to Cartesian 'metaphysical' doubt as a methodological premise rather than to Baconian 'physical' doubt. Since the refutation of 'metaphysical' doubt requires proof rather than experimentation and induction, it can be dissolved much easier. And it involves no merely probable opinions. Clauberg takes such opinions to be a risky proposition, because they would weaken the resolve of the Cartesian student to give assent only to those facts that can be known clearly and distinctly. This strategy can be justified not only in the abstract: Clauberg claims that it is also superior in the pragmatic dimension of vocational training.

De Neufville on why natural philosophy needs Bacon

De Neufville makes the case for Bacon's method in natural philosophy by way of exclusion: since all other approaches to natural philosophy are fallacious, Bacon's path is the only one that remains open: skepticism about knowledge of nature, scholastic approaches to natural philosophy, and 'dogmatic' and 'empiric' reformers of natural philosophy have nothing viable to offer.[17]

De Neufville's anti-skeptic arguments are not very sophisticated. All men by nature desire to know. God has created us as spectators of the universe. If the skeptic was right, we would have been created as beings that are incapable of filling the role set for us by our creator.[18] But in spite of our capability to know the natural world, the project of natural philosophy has not yet been a success. If we measure its progress against the achievements in pure mathematics and the mechanical arts, i. e. mixed mathematics, we must acknowledge that '... [sc. the subject matter of natural philosophy] is to a large extent uncertain and rests on shaky foundations: dissenting opinions and controversies in all matters pertaining to nature are satisfactory proof of that, because they demonstrate [sc. only] a wavering [sc. adherence to] truth'.[19]

Scholastics are not named explicitly, but it is easy to identify them as targets of de Neufville's objections. Scholastics disregard sense perception and experience as a precondition of knowledge. They cannot explain how to get from sense perception to full knowledge of nature, and they take no interest in having principles that are certain. Instead, they are preoccupied with preconceived opinions and empty reasoning. The number of arguments brought forward is more decisive than the weight they may have.[20] These misguided investigatory practices are complemented by faulty

---

[17] Cf. Francis Bacon, *The New Organon*, eds. Lisa Jardine and Michael Silverthorne, (Cambridge, 2000), book 1, Aph. 95, 79. In the following quoted as *New Organon*.

[18] Cf. de Neufville, *Physiologia*, praef., [2]: 'At vero, hujusmodi verae ac certae cognitionis et scientiae rerum naturalium hominem capacem esse, quod negant Sceptici, satum ostendit innatum omnibus scientiae desiderium: quod frustra eisdem naturaliter insitum esse, dici nulla ratione potest. Nec consentaneum est, Deum hominem, quem sapientiae suae spectatorem, in hoc universitatis theatro, constituit, fini huic perfecte quantum fieri potest, obtinendo inhabilem fecisse.'

[19] De Neufville, *Physiologia*, praef., [3]: 'ipsa, uti quidem communiter tradi solet, magna ex parte incerta sit ac fragilibus admodum fundamentis nitatur: id quod dissentientes ubique de rebus physicis Philosophorum opiniones et controversiae, quae vacillantis ubique veritatis certissimum testimonium perhibent, satis superque comprobant.'

[20] Cf. de Neufville *Physiologia*, praef., [3]: 'radix et fons malorum est, quod homines, qui veritati in hac scientia inquirenda operam navant, non satis adhaereant sensui atque experientiae, mediaque ab istis initiis rite scientiam excitandi non recte adhibeant; sed, vel auctoritatibus aut praeconceptis opinionibus praeoccupentur, vel, loco certorum principiorum,

methods of teaching: truths about nature cannot be taught in disputations *ad utramque partem* or by merely following authority. Disputations introduce a lot of vacuous and artificial problems into the debate that can thus easily end up as a mere fight over words (*logomachia*).[21]

So natural philosophy is in dire need of reform. Again following Bacon, de Neufville divides advocates of such reforms into two camps: *empirici* and *dogmatici*.[22] *Empirici* trust the power of the senses, *dogmatici* emphasise the role of reason. De Neufville argues for a middle way between both extremes: we must allow for reason to supplement the testimony of the senses and to correct its errors. But still cognition can only be about objects insofar as it is based on the senses; only the senses allow the mind to attain true and certain knowledge through observation and experience.[23]

De Neufville counts both 'mosaic' natural philosophers and Cartesians as *dogmatici*. 'Mosaic' philosophers like Lambert Daneau, Otto Casmann, or Conradus Aslacus claim that natural philosophy should be built on scriptural truth, not unaided reason.[24] These principles are unassailable, because they rest on scriptural authority. Natural philosophy then consists in the deduction of truths from these incontrovertible first principles which are based on the authority of revelation. De Neufville objects against the 'mosaic' view that Scripture does not contain much that would help us

vanas atque invalidas ratiunculas secentur, quae ut plurimum numero, non pondere aestimantur.'

[21] Cf. de Neufville, *Physiologia*, praef., [4f]: 'Ex quibus haud difficulter [sic!] perspicitur, veritatis in rebus naturalibus inquisitionem frustra tentari per disputationes, quibus quaestio qualibet in utramque partem ventilatur, adductis variis rationibus atque auctoritatibus: quo in genere inquisitionis scholae omnes hucusque tanto conatu laborarunt. Quod enim hac ratione, in inquirenda veritate, nihil proficiatur, sed contra rerum cognitio pluribus et majoribus difficultatibus implicetur et involvatur, atque a rebus solidis ad umbras, h. e. vanas merasque de iis opiniones et fere logomachias, ut et digladiationes de horum vel illorum illustrium Auctorum sententia, traducatur, superiorum temporum experientia atque historia hactenus luculenter testatam fecit.' On Bacon on disputation cf. Stephen Gaukroger, *Francis Bacon and the transformation of early-modern philosophy* (Cambridge/New York, 2001), 10f.

[22] Cf. Bacon, *New Organon*, book 1, Aph. 95, 79.

[23] Cf. de Neufville, *Physiologia*, praef., 3f: 'Qui vero reformationem aliquam tentarunt, non omnes eadem via progressi sunt. Quidam nimium sensus, ut Empirici, aliis nimium rationi ut Dogmatici plerique tribuunt: quum tamen vera et legitima veritatem certam inquirendi methodus rationem cum sensu et experientia legitimo modo copulare et sociare debeat, ita videl.[icet] ut, in ea cognitione, quae naturae lumine perficitur, ratio quidem sensuum defectus suppleat et errores corrigat, omnem tamen cognitionis suae certitudinem a sensibus atque experientia mutuetur et hauriat. Et hoc quidem ideo, quia rerum cognitio petenda est a rebus ipsis, quibus ut vera sit et dicatur, conformari debet: unde, ad veram et certam rerum cognitionem acquirendam, mentis cum rebus ipsis commercio opus est; quod non aliter, quam sensuum opera, per observationem atque experientiam, institui atque obtineri potest.'

[24] Cf. Blair, loc. cit., 37, on the background of de Neufville's selection, its context, and alternative proposals who to count as a member of this group.

to develop a comprehensive philosophy of nature. Nor can all of its insights be validated through experience. Finally, Scripture is intended to teach us how to obtain salvation through Christ rather than to contribute to our knowledge of the natural world.[25]

The second group of *dogmatici* is suggestively similar to Descartes and his followers, although de Neufville does not name them explicitly. Still, the parallels are fairly obvious:

> Others search in natural philosophy some general or universal principles, from which they would be able to deduce and derive everything else infallibly and with a certain and evident reason, using demonstrations that are structured as a continuous series. We see this happening in mathematics, too, for example in Euclid's work: here, so many different things are gradually collected and proven through necessary and evident demonstrations, and from a few definitions and common notions that are known and manifest to the senses.[26]

So these *dogmatici*—we could call them neutrally 'mathematical natural philosophers' – want to base their work on 'general and universal principles', or, in the terminology of Descartes's *Discours*, 'the simplest and most easily known objects',[27] i. e., those objects that are most simple and most accessible to our cognitive efforts. These starting points allow the deduction of everything through a series of demonstrations.[28] These deductions are in turn taken to be certain, evident, and infallible. The paradigmatic example for the application of this method is Euclidean geometry.

[25] Cf. de Neufville, *Physiologia*, praef., [5f]: 'Hanc ob causam nonnulli, scripturae s. nobis divinitus revelatae auctoritate potissimum, de rebus naturalibus certi aliquid definiendum esse, contendunt: inter quos praecipue est Lambertus Danaeus, qui Physicam Christianam, ex sola fere scriptura s. collectam et deductam, concinnavit. Idem statuunt Otto Casmannus in Prolegomenis Cosmopoeiae et Uranographiae Christianae praemissis, Conradus Aslacus lib. I. physicae Mosaicae cap. 1 et alii. Quanquam vero non diffiteor, Christianum philosophum omnino decere, ut nihil statuat, quod veritati divinitus revelatae repugnet; negari item non potest, etiam de rebus naturalibus hinc inde sparas in S. literis quaedam inveniri, quae ad naturalem philosophiam illustrandam magisque confirmandam facere possunt, et inter haec nonnulla quoque de quibus ratio per sensum et experientiam sufficientem informationem habere nequit: certum tamen est, ejusmodi pauca admodum esse, neque eo modo tradita, uti eadem a naturali philosopho scientia certa atque evidenti comprehendi debent; et constat, scripturam s. nobis longe alio fine a Deo esse traditam, videl. [icet] ut nos, de voluntate Divina nostraque salute per Christum obtinenda, erudiat.'

[26] De Neufville, *Physiologia*, praef., [6f]: 'Alii in physicis generalia quaedam seu universalia principia quaerunt, ex quibus deinde reliqua omnia per demonstrationes, continua serie ordinatas et depositas, certa atque evidenti ratione et infallibiliter deduci atque inferri queant; ut in mathematicis fieri videmus, exemplo operis Euclidei: in quo, ex paucis quibusdam definitionibus et communibus notionibus, sensu notis ac manifestis, tam multa et varia, per demonstrationes necessarias atque evidentes, paulatim inferuntur et colliguntur.'

[27] René Descartes, 'Discourse on Method', in René Descartes, *Philosophical Writings*, trans. J Cottingham et al., 3 vols. (Cambridge/New York, 1985), 1: 111–51, 120.

[28] Cf. Descartes, loc. cit., 120.

Geometry starts from a few definitions and shared notions (*notiones communes*). Then a series of necessary and evident demonstrations is used to derive new and and non-obvious insights—a method that can also be applied outside mathematics:

> They believe that there can be similar first principles for any natural science which can be known directly and are unchangeably true and which are general and universal. These principles contain general reasons that are abstracted from the things themselves through induction and serve as standards for knowing them. And from these principles all other highest, middle and particular [sc. propositions] can be derived, chained together through a series of demonstrations. They enjoy the same obviousness used in proofs of mathematical propositions, since there it is necessary to adhere to the first [sc. premisses] and last propositions [sc. conclusions] with the same degree of belief, because of the continuous and uninterrupted demonstration of truth.[29]

In other words, we need only to find a few self-evident principles that contain general notions (*communi rerum rationes*) by way of abstraction from things themselves. As soon as we have such principles, we can then derive from them all kinds of insights of varying generality. Both principles and deductions will be as obvious as geometrical proof and demand the same unqualified assent, because each deductive step will be as evident as a single inference in a proof.

De Neufville's objection is fundamental: there are important differences between mathematics and natural philosophy. Ignorance of these differences leads to a false conception of principles and their role in natural philosophy. De Neufville focuses on the differences in what constitutes a proof in both disciplines. In mathematics, proofs from premises or through a *reductio ad absurdum* are a matter of reason. But the ultimate starting point of a mathematical proof, definitions and 'shared notions', must rely on the senses.[30] Diagrams must be used to make obvious the connections

[29] De Neufville, *Physiologia*, praef., [7]: 'Ad eundem modum existimant, in naturali aliquaque scientia, prima quaedam principia per se nota et immotae veritatis, et quidem generalia seu universalia, quae communes rerum rationes, ab ipsis rebus per inductionem quandam abstractas, tanquam earundem cognoscendarum normas, complectantur, dari posse, e quibus deinde reliqua omnia summa, media, infima, concatenata a quaedam demonstrationum serie deriventur, et quidem ea evidentia, qua propositiones mathematicorum solent demonstrari, ut tam postremis, quam primis, necesse sit adhiberi fidem, propter continuatam et nusquam interruptam veritatis demonstrationem.' See also Descartes, loc. cit., 120.

[30] Cf. de Neufville, *Physiologia*, praef., [7f]: 'Etenim media demonstrationum mathematicarum ut plurium sunt rationes quaedam priores, jam ante demonstratae, aut absurda quaedam, quae, e contradictoria positae propositionis, contra ea, quae jam demonstrata sunt, inferuntur, prima etiam principia, in quae mathematicae demonstrationes tandem

that underlay a proof.[31] But, more importantly, the essence of a mathematical concept can be understood without any deeper investigation. This is not true for natural philosophy. Here, we must rely on our comprehension of the essence or nature of the thing to be examined. This essence is expressed in a definition that can then be used to deduce further properties of the thing in question. But such definitions are not to be determined beforehand by simple evidence of the senses, as in mathematics.[32] They are the end result of a prolonged investigation a posteriori, relying on induction and the results of multiple observations and experiments.[33] Conversely, any conclusions a priori must have been based on non-universal, i. e., experiential principles with a limited domain of applicability. Thus, all proofs constituting natural philosophy must ultimately rely on propositions that are based on experience.[34] But 'mathematical natural philosophy' discards the testimony of the senses, when it holds that all properties of natural bodies can be reduced to size, figure, and movement. This reductionism conflicts with empirical evidence, because experience demonstrates clearly the indispensability of qualities, substantial forms, and active potencies in natural bodies. Reductionists—de Neufville names ancient atomists, Sebastian Basso, and Descartes—thus cannot explain all of nature.[35]

resolvuntur, sunt, vel definitiones, vel communes notiones, quae solo sensu, absque laboriosa aliqua inquisitione, statim comprobantur.'

[31] Cf. de Neufville *Physiologia*, praef., [8]: '[...] unde, in mathematicis, omnia et definiuntur et demonstrantur ad sensum, h. e. ita, ut tam definitiones, quam demonstrationes, per diagrammata quaedam oculis et sensui velut subjiciantur, adeoque sensu ipso immediate quasi firmentur et stabiliantur.'

[32] Cf. de Neufville, *Physiologia*, praef., [8]: 'In physicis vero demonstrationibus, longe aliter se res habet. In illis enim medium demonstrationis est, vel natura seu essentia subjecti, quae definitione ejusdem explicatur, ... vel subiecti quaedam causa. ... At, tam definitiones rerum naturalium, quam causae earundem, ut et affectionum illis inhaerentium, non possunt ex generalibus quibusdam principiis cognosci, sed, longa et difficili admodum inquisitione, ex variis et multiplicibus experimentis, per analysin et divisione investigari, et inductione examinari ac probari debent'.

[33] Cf. de Neufville, *Physiologia*, praef., [8f]: 'unde fit, ut in omnibus et singulis demonstrationibus physicis, et quidem non in generali tantum, sed et specialibus philosophiae naturalis partibus, major propositio semper, minor ut plurimum, sit ... talis quae a priori demonstrari non possit, sed solum a posteriori colligi, et quidem per inductionem ex observationibus atque experimentis, aut insuper quoque per demonstrationem a posteriori seu ab effectu'.

[34] Cf. de Neufville, *Physiologia*, praef., [9]: 'Ex quibus tandem liquido constat, omnes et singulas conclusiones physicas, quae per veras et proprie dictas demonstrationes a priori inferuntur, tam in speciali, quam generali, physica, cognosci ex principiis, non communibus et universalibus, e quibus continuata demonstrationum serie deriventur, ut fit in mathematicis, sed propriis et determinatis ac vernaculis, sibique quodammodo adaequatis, quae a posteriori solum ex observationibus atque experimentis, uti diximus, colliguntur; ac proinde totam rerum naturalium scientiam observationibus atque experientiae, tanquam basi et fonti omnis certitudinis atque evidentiae, potissimum inniti.'

[35] Cf. de Neufville, *Physiologia*, praef., [11f]: 'Contra inveniuntur alii, mathematicis praecipue speculationibus assueti, qui omnes corporum naturalium differentias, proprietates,

But de Neufville disagrees with the *empirici* as well.[36] They believe that experiments about a certain class of natural objects would be applicable to completely different domains, too.[37] Alchemists assume that a complete account of nature can be given using the results only of chymical experiments.[38] Gilbert in his experiments with magnets, or Fludd, Campanella, and Telesio in their philosophy of nature based on heat and cold limit their investigations to one aspect or factor that then forms the basis of an explanation of nature as a whole. But no *empiricus* takes in nature in its totality.[39]

So none of the competing factions in natural philosophy, neither scholastics nor reformers, can propose a truly satisfactory way to conduct inquiry in this discipline. The only way to liberate natural philosophy from the dissent that stands in the way of its progress is the execution of

et effectus, ad pauca quaedam accidentia sensibilia communia, praecipue magnitudine, figuram et motum (in quibus tamen nulla est agendi virtus et efficacia) reiectis qualitatibus et formis substantialibus, in quibus omnis agendi virtus rerum naturalium continetur, solum referunt, atque ita et mutationes omnes, solo motu locali excepto, adeoque et alterationes ac generationes, e natura proscribunt; contra manifestam experientiam, quae qualitates, ut agendi virtutes in substantiis, atque ita etiam alterationes, corporum item subcoelestium generationes, adeoque et formas substantiales, inumeris experimentis comprobat. Ex horum numero fuerunt, inter Veteres quidem, Democritus, Leucippus atque Epicurus; ex recentioribus vero, Sebstianus Basso aliique nonnulli, et novissime Renatus Cartesius.'

[36] On a side note, it should be mentioned that de Neufville is already aware of the existence of Cartesian empiricists. However, their experimental abilities are not up to par. Cf. de Neufville, *Physiologia*, praef., [8f]: 'Non sufficiunt autem hic pauca quaedam et vulgaris, licet varia et ex omni rerum genere desumpta, experimenta, eaque sapenumero, neque certo comperta, nec diligenter examinata et pensitata: cujusmodi, in naturae arcanis scrutandis, plerosque ex iis, qui rationalem seu dogmaticam philosophiam profitentur, solummodo arripere ab experientia, reliqua vero in speculatione seu meditatione et agitatione mentis ponere, deprehendimus.' On Cartesian experimental philosophy cf. *Cartesian Empiricisms*, eds. Mihnea Dobre, Tammy Nyden (Dordrecht, 2013).

[37] Cf. de Neufville, *Physiologia*, praef., [10]: 'Multo minus hic sufficiunt experimenta unius generis solum, quantum vis selecta et accurate examinata: e quibus plurimi universam philosophiam naturalem educere conati sunt, reliqua, quae ad illud genus, unde desumpta sunt ista experimenta, non pertinent, miris modis ad ea detorquentes.' On the roots of this argument in Bacon cf. Gaukroger, loc. cit., 90.

[38] Cf. de Neufville, *Physiologia*, praef., [10]: 'Ex horum numero praecipue sunt Chymici, qui e fornaculis suis, id est chymicis solum experimentis, totius scientiae naturalis principia exstruere nituntur; ut ex Theophrasti Paracelsi, Petri Severini, Oswaldi Crollii, Henrici Nollii atque aliorum scriptis cognoscere licet.'

[39] Cf. de Neufville, *Physiologia*, praef., [10f]: 'Eadem ratione etiam Guilhelmus Gilbertus Anglus solis experimentis magneticis, et Robertus Fludd seu de Fluctibus solis fere experimentis rarefactionis et condensationis corporum a calore et frigore, naturalis scientiae principia constituere simulque fulcire et stabilire conati sunt. Thomas etiam Campanella, eiusque antecessor Bernardinus Telesius, licet, duce sensu philosophandum esse, contendant; ex solis tamen caloris frigorisque (quae cum materia faciunt prima corporum omnium principia) actionibus, omnia fere in naturali scientia derivare annituntur: idque non duce sed reclamante experientia.'

experiments through all genera of natural things, thereby removing the limitations on empirical investigations of nature imposed by the *empirici*.[40] We must then use induction to derive from these experiments generalised principles of particular domains that are irrefutable, because they are based on experiential input. We must adhere to the program laid out by Bacon e.g., in *Instauratio magna*.[41] But Bacon's approach must be emendated. De Neufville brings forward four objections. Three of them concern the compatibility of Baconian natural history with an Aristotelian model of science as proof-based substantiation of causal relations. In discussing these problems, de Neufville envisions a Baconian *philosophia nov-antiqua* that fuses Aristotelian logic and theory of science and a Baconian theory of experiential justification. The fourth objection concerns the pragmatic context of teaching natural philosophy. De Neufville pleads to retain teachings of the ancients, if they are at least probable, i.e., if they do not evidently contradict experience.

In his first objection, de Neufville complains that Bacon is concerned only with the investigation of definitions (in Bacon's terminology 'forms'). But natural philosophy requires with equal urgency a method for the investigation of causes.[42] And the second objection makes clear that such an investigation of causes must be based on syllogisms. Bacon had claimed that Aristotelian logic leads to error and tempts us to introduce fictitious entities when attempting to explain nature.[43] But this is not the case.

---

[40] Cf. de Neufville, *Physiologia*, praef., [12]: 'Unicum igitur hoc tandem superest naturalis scientiae instaurandae remedium, ut omnis generis experimenta, circa res naturales quaslibet earumque causas et affectiones, hominum, praecipue doctorum, industria colligantur, atque ex iis naturalis historia plena et perfecta concinnetur, quae deinde sylvam et materiam suppeditare queat naturae inquisitori, ex qua veras certasque propositiones colligere et ad quam omnium quorumcunque philosophorum placita, circa rerum naturalium cognitionem, examinare et probare possit.'

[41] Cf. de Neufville, *Physiologia*, praef., [13]: 'Itaque satis laudari non potest Illustris et Generosi, Dn. Francisci Baconis B. de Verulamio etc. magni Anglie Cancellarii, Viri incomparabilis, industria et diligentia: qui, cum perspexisset, omnis incertitudinis et errorum, in rerum, praecipue naturalium, cognitione, potissimam et fere unicam causam hanc esse, quod homines non satis adhaereant observationi sensuum atque experientiae, sed abstractis mentis suae speculationibus nimis indulgeant, methodum excogitavit, non modo contexenda historiae naturalis, quae et evera ac certa et sufficientia experimenta contineret ad evolvendam rerum naturam, sed et per inductionem ex illis colligendi universalia axiomata seu propositiones, de quarum veritate, ob omnimodam earundem cum experimentis congruentiam, dubitare amplis non posset; uti in opere Instaurationis magnae, ab ipso evulgato, plenius videre licet.'

[42] Cf. de Neufville, *Physiologia*, praef., [14f]: 'Horum primum est, quod Organum hoc novum, ad formarum, uti Auctor appellat, h. e. definitionum inquisitionem, fere solum comparatum esse videam: quum tamen certum sit, methodum inquirendi seu investigandi causas, si non magis, certe non minus, ad naturalium praecipue rerum scientiam necessariam esse.'

[43] Cf. de Neufville, *Physiologia*, praef., [15]: 'Alterum est, quod solam inductionem sufficere putat Auctor, ad comparandam solidam rerum scientiam, excluso syllogismo; ideoque

Baconian induction that is meant to replace Aristotelian syllogistic states particular facts and generalises universal propositions from them. But it cannot show how single facts themselves cohere. It thus fails at the main task of natural philosophy.[44] De Neufville uses an analogy to make his point: the analysis of a simple notion based on apprehension does not in itself help us determine which of the properties surfacing in the analysis should be regarded as essential. For this we need more sophisticated logical instruments, namely the method of division. In the same way, induction provides us only with isolated facts. The connections between these facts can only be made explicit in syllogistic reasoning.[45]

The third objection concerns method more generally: if we limit ourselves to induction, we lose sight of the fact that scientific knowledge—in contrast to confused everyday knowledge—must always depend on an awareness of universals that we already know. In confused, sense-based perception particulars can be known more easily than universals. But the reverse is true in distinct, scientific knowledge: here, the universal is more readily knowable than the individual. Thus there is no perfect cognition of particulars or species without having a perfect cognition of the genera they belong to.[46] This means that Bacon lacks a valid method for the analysis of causal relations in science. For such an analysis to succeed we have to reintroduce syllogistic reasoning and to create a proper science of nature in

logicam, quae nunc in usu est, inutilem esse ad inventionem scientiarum, atque ad errores stabiliendos et figendos valere potius, quam ad inquisitionem veritatis, contendit'.

[44] Cf. de Neufville *Physiologia*, praef., [15]: 'Quum tamen inductio solam propositionis universalis, ex particularibus collectae, veritatem...nobis patefaciat; connexiones vero propositionum, quarum aliae ex aliis pendent et cognoscuntur,...in quo principaliter scientia consistit, haudquaquam monstret.'

[45] Cf. de Neufville *Physiologia*, praef., [15]: 'Ut enim, in simplici mentis apprehensione, per analysin simplicium notionum, plurimae quidem inveniuntur notiones seu termini simplices, qui ad rem subjectam referuntur et pertinent; attamen, quis inter illos ordo sit et nexus, et, quomodo ex illis seligi possint ii, quibus rei cujusque natura et essentia perfecte explicetur, aut causae investigentur, intelligi non potest, nisi adhibeantur alia instrumenta logica, videl.[icet] divisio et methodus definiendi atque investigandi causas: ita quoque, in cognitione judicativa, per quam integrarum propositionum veritas aut falsitas judicatur et cognoscitur, inductio, analysi respondens, plurimas quidem suppeditat propositiones veras: sed quarum nexus, adeoque ab illo nexu pendens scientifica cognitio, percipi non potest, nisi per alia instrumenta logica, syllogismum videl.[icet] et praecipue demonstrationem, tum a posteriori, tum a priori.'

[46] Cf de Neufville, *Physiologia*, praef., [15f]: 'Tertium est, quod gradatim progrediendum esse docet, a minus universalibus ad magis universalia: quum contra natura et experientia testentur, minus universalium perfectam cognitionem et scientiam, absque cognitione magis universalium, haberi non posse. Etsi enim cognitione confusa, minus universalia notiora nobis sint, et facilius cognoscantur, quam magis universalia; quod haec longius absint a sensibus, a quibus primo confusa cognitio derivatur: in distincta tamen cognitione, quae scientiam parit, contrarium accidit, ut nempe magis universalia minus universalibus prius et facilius cognoscantur, imo haec sine illis perfecte cognosci non possint'.

the Aristotelian sense. In this science, we learn the nexus of propositions that we derive inductively from experiences. In sum, these first three objections provide a sketch of a Baconian *philosophia nov-antiqua*. Its combination of a Baconian focus on experience with the conceptual tools of Aristotelian logic should finally achieve those goals that traditional Aristotelian natural philosophy could only aspire to and not deliver.

The fourth objection shows why such a fusion of traditional philosophical concepts and theories and Bacon's innovations is not only theoretically sound, but also superior on a pragmatic level. The objection concerns Bacon's views on *idola*. Bacon requires for the proper understanding (*interpretatio*) of nature a pure mind that has freed itself from all prejudices.[47] According to de Neufville, this demand can either be read innocuously or it can be understood in a way that renders Bacon's philosophy completely useless. Bacon may have meant that we should suspend our judgment, if the truth or falsity of a proposition cannot be derived from observations and experiments. This is unproblematic for de Neufville. Bacon is right in that premature judgment can lead into error.[48] But Bacon could also be understood as rejecting the tradition of natural philosophy in its entirety:

> But it is possible that the meaning of the statement is as follows: everything that until now has been invented regarding the cognition and knowledge of objects in nature through the work and industry of man and has been passed down [sc. to us] must be rejected indiscriminately and be excluded from our thinking. Then the human intellect is pure and free from all false and unsuitable concepts and opinions, so that it can renovate natural science through better instruments and aids than those used by man until now. After science has been built on the required foundations, the intellect can lead it to its planned perfection. [Sc. If this is what Bacon wanted to state,] we must reject it.[49]

---

[47] Cf. de Neufville, *Physiologia*, praef., [16]: 'Quartum et postremum, idque praecipuum est, quod idem Auctor, ad interpretationem naturae, requirit mentem puram, h. e. ab omnibus praeconceptis opinionibus seu idolis, ut loquitur, liberatam atque expurgatam'.

[48] Cf. de Neufville, *Physiologia*, praef., [17]: 'Quod si non haec solum, de cohibendo et moderando firmo mentis assensu circa ea, de quorum certa veritate, ex observationibus atque experimentis nondum constat, sint intelligenda; nihil est, quod in hac sententia improbare possimus: quandoquidem magni interest, ut, in inquirenda veritate, mens libera sit ab omnibus praejudiciis, quibus facile in errorem abduci potest.'

[49] De Neufville, *Physiologia*, praef., [16]: 'At si haec sit sententia, omnia ea, quae hucusque hominum labore atque industria inventa et tradita sunt circa rerum naturalium cognitionem et scientiam, absque ullo discrimine penitus rejicienda atque animo excludenda esse, ut intellectus humanus, purus et vacuus ab omnibus pravis et ineptis conceptibus atque opinionibus, naturalem scientiam melioribus praesidiis et auxiliis, quam quibus hactenus homines usi sunt, de integro instaurare atque a debitis fundamentis excitatam [sc. ad] adoptatum fastigium et perfectionem perducere queat; omnino eam probare neutiquam possumus.'

The difference between both stances seems to be minor: after all, in both interpretations Bacon is committed to the idea that the truth of a proposition in natural philosophy hinges on its empirical verifiability. And in both perspectives we must free our mind from prejudice in order to avoid premature judgment and error. But both readings differ in their understanding of prejudices: it either is or is not an a priori truth that all insights stemming from previous philosophers of nature must be discarded.

It may even be conceded that such a complete abandonment of the philosophical tradition could be the most advantageous path to knowledge about nature in principle. But it is nevertheless wrong for pragmatic reasons:

> For even if it would perhaps be possible to come closest to the envisioned goal [sc. of natural philosophy] taking this path of inquiry, this very same path is barely compatible with the principles of education, through which young people usually must be instructed in the cognition of things, and it is the cause of a lot of confusion in the future.[50]

De Neufville deems Bacon's proposal to be indefensible because it stands in the way of effective pedagogical practice. It would be completely unclear what to teach in schools and universities, while inquiry along Baconian lines proceeds. This question is particularly pressing because Baconian inquiry demands a concerted effort of many people over the course of several centuries.[51] In the end, the university as an institution conducting examinations and conferring grades would have to close down, if it has no longer a discernible rational basis.[52] De Neufville concedes that Bacon explicitly claims that he does not want to destroy existing practices in the arts and sciences, and paraphrases Aph. 128 of the *Novum Organon* accordingly.[53] But these protestations are less credible in view of Bacon's

---

[50] De Neufville, *Physiologia*, praef., [16f]: 'Nam licet vel maxime hac inquisitionis via ad scopum propositum tandem perveniri posset; eadem tamen institutioni scholasticae, per quam juventus ordinarie in rerum cognitione, erudiri debet et solet, minime est accommodata, maximarumque confusionum causa futura est.'

[51] Cf. de Neufville, *Physiologia*, praef., [17]: 'Hoc nam principio admisso, quid tandem erit, quod in scholis tradi possit, dum omnia longa et prolixa inquisitione, qua plurium hominum et seculorum continuatam industriam poscit, investiganda prius sunt, antequam de illis quidquam definiatur?'

[52] Cf. de Neufville, *Physiologia*, praef., [18]: 'Quaenam item futura est ratio examinis eorum, quibus testimonia Academica et dignitates seu gradus, ut loquuntur, conferendi sunt, ut eisdem, ad officia ac munera certa, quasi legitimentur et habiles pronuncientur?'

[53] Cf. de Neufville, *Physiologia*, 1645, praef., [18f]: 'Protestatur quidem Illustris Verulamius in Praefat. Organi novi et lib. 1. ejusdem aphor. 128. sibi minime propositum esse, artes et scientias, quibus utimur, destruere et demoliri; sed contra earum et usum et cultum et honores libenter amplecti: neque nullo modo officere, quin istae, quae invaluerunt, et disputationes alant, et sermones ornent, et ad professoria munera ac vitae civilis compendia adhibeantur et valeant, denique tanquam numismata quaedam, consensu inter

general appraisal of the validity of our methods to get to know the natural
world: if human reason is not well-equipped for the investigation of
nature, if our fundamental notions with regard to nature are erroneous—
based on a mixture of blind belief, accident, and notions we acquired in
our childhood—there is simply no conceivable justification to continue
such misguided epistemic practices and to teach them to the younger
generation. In such a situation a fresh start is not only beneficial, but the
only responsible option.[54] But then we cannot take seriously Bacon's
assurances to the opposite.

Even if we accept that past investigators of nature may have been prone
to error, the thesis that they were constitutively incapable of finding any
truth at all is less credible: after all, their speculations on nature started
from experience as well.[55] On the contrary, it is safe to assume that some
parts of the tradition in philosophy of nature are true.[56] We should not
abandon these truths, if they agree with observation and experience.[57] We
rather should submit all assumptions of previous centuries to experimental
verification, if their truth is under debate. This would remove all erroneous
doctrines from natural philosophy. So de Neufville's approach is evolutionary

homines recipiantur.' See Bacon, *New Organon*, book 1, Aph. 128, 99: 'But it would be
wrong even to entertain a doubt about whether we desire to destroy and abolish the philosophy, the arts and the sciences which we use; on the contrary, we happily embrace their use,
their cultivation and their rewards. We do not in any way discourage these traditional subjects from generating disputations, enlivening discourse and being widely applied to professional use and the benefit of civil life, and from being accepted by general agreement as a
kind of currency.'

[54] Cf. de Neufville, *Physiologia*, praef., [19]: 'Verum, si universa ista ratio humana, qua
utimur, quoad inquisitionem naturae, non bene congesta et aedificata sit, sed tanquam
moles aliqua magnifica sine fundamento; si errores omnes in primis notionibus radicati,
adeoque fundamentales sint; si ratio humana, quam habemus, ex multa fide et multo etiam
casu, nec non ex puerilibus, quas primo hausimus, notionibus, farrago quaedam sit et con-
geries, adeoque theoria et notiones illae communes penitus abolenda sint, ut intellectus
abrasus et aequus ad particularia de integro applicetur, ut diversis locis idem innuit: quid
attinet, nos iis excolendis tanto labore insudare, tantisque sumptibus conduci Professores et
Magistros, qui illas in scholis juventuti tradant atque instillent?'

[55] Cf. de Neufville, *Physiologia*, praef., [19f]: 'Verum enim vero, quanquam diffiteri non
possumus, uti supra quoque dictum fuit, scientiam naturalem maximis adhuc laborare
defectibus, plurimasque in eam invectas esse opiniones, quae naturae rerum atque experientiae penitus adversantur: nulla tamen ratione credibile sit, tot retroactis seculis, omnes,
quotquot naturalium rerum inquisitione occupati fuerunt, nihil penitus aut parum
admodum invenisse, quod verum sit; quum et ipsi ab iis quae sensu atque observatione
cognoscuntur speculationes suas orsi sint.'

[56] Cf. de Neufville, *Physiologia*, praef., [20]: 'Certe, in universa rerum naturalium scientia, plurima extant, superioribus seculis ab hominibus cognita, plurimaque indies detegun-
tur atque inveniuntur, quae certam atque evidentem veritatem habent, ita ut de ea nemo
iure dubitare possit.'

[57] Cf. de Neufville, *Physiologia*, praef., [20]: 'Quid igitur opus est, ea abjicere, si facto
examine, cum observationibus atque experimentis congruere deprehendantur?'

rather than revolutionary: it aims not at total destruction, but correction and emendation of established natural philosophy through an examination of existent knowledge and its compatibility with experience.[58]

However, such a gradual emendation of natural philosophy does not yet solve the question how to approach the task of teaching. De Neufville suggests to limit the material conveyed to students to those propositions that the learned accept because of a semblance of truth.[59] Only those parts of traditional natural philosophy should be discarded that can be proven to contradict experience.[60] In this case, the wrong proposition of traditional natural philosophy must be replaced with a correct formulation that does justice to our experiences. Those corrections can proceed step by step, while at the same time institutions conveying knowledge about nature, i. e., schools and universities, can continue to function with minimal interruptions.[61]

Clauberg on why natural philosophy should not follow Bacon

Clauberg discusses the views of his teacher in *Initiatio philosophi seu dubitatio Cartesiana*, published first in 1655. The text is part of Clauberg's extended dispute with Johann Revius.[62] But one chapter of the work is dedicated to a discussion of de Neufville's views and the relation between Cartesian and Baconian doubt. He quotes de Neufville's fourth objection

---

[58] Cf. de Neufville, *Physiologia*, praef., [20f]: 'Itaque naturalis scientiae instaurationem ita rectius procedere posse, mihi persuasum est, si elaborata plurimorum virorum, ingenio atque eruditione praestantium, coniunctis operis... historia naturali, quae non solum vera duntaxat certa atque explorata experimenta contineat, sed et plena sit atque omnibus partibus absoluta,... juxta illam deinde ea, quae de rebus naturalibus habemus, ab omni hominum memoria, hucusque ad nos devoluta placita, de quorum veritate dubitatur, et de quorum falsitate non certo constat, examini subjiciantur, ut ad rectae rationis, sensui, indeque per observationes deductis experimentis, rite innixae, normam ac regula explorentur, atque ita, quicquid in scientiam naturalem irrepsit falsarum opinionum, evellatur atque rescindatur'.

[59] Cf. de Neufville, *Physiologia*, praef., [21]: 'Interea vero, dum in naturali philosophia, hoc modo sensim instauranda et perficienda, laborabitur, retinendae et docendae erunt, in scholis praecipue, sententiae, ob majorem verisimilitudinem inter doctiores magis receptae'.

[60] Cf. de Neufville 1645, praef., [21]: 'neque ulla earum rejicienda erit, priusquam, facto legitimo examine, deprehenditur, ipsam cum experientia non consentire, atque ita falsam et erroneam esse'.

[61] Cf. de Neufville, *Physiologia*, praef., [21f]: 'quo in casu illis, quae hoc modo rejiciuntur, substituenda erunt aliae experimentis consonae et conformes, donec paulatim totum scientiae naturalis corpus, ab erroribus et defectibus, quibus adhuc scatet, expurgetur et liberetur. Atque hanc existimo esse viam tutissimam, simulque copendiossissimum, in recta praesertim juventutis institutione, pervenienda ad scopum propositum.'

[62] Cf. Verbeek, loc. cit., 198.

against Bacon in full and then discusses it in great detail. His main goal in this part of *Initiatio* is to show that Cartesian doubt, as he understands it, is not open to the kind of criticism brought forward by de Neufville against Baconian doubt. But at the same time, Clauberg also sets out to demonstrate that the vision of a slowly evolving *philosophia nov-antiqua* developed by de Neufville is misguided as well. So Clauberg does agree with Descartes and Bacon against de Neufville that there is no way around a radical and complete revolution in philosophy. He agrees with de Neufville against Bacon that, if we conduct such a revolution along Baconian lines, this would lead to an undesirable breakdown of traditional ways of instruction in philosophy. Yet, he also believes with Descartes against Bacon and de Neufville that the required revolution in philosophy can be effected without any profound change to methods of instruction, if it follows Cartesian precepts.

Clauberg motivates the comparison between Baconian and Cartesian doubt by pointing to Bacon's fame among the learned.[63] Hence, he gives an overview of the similarities between the Baconian and the Cartesian project. Both Bacon and Descartes require a 'pure mind' that is freed from prejudices. This requires the firm commitment to suspend judgment in all cases in which we have not yet examined the proposed content of the judgment.[64] Cartesian doubt appears to be a variety of the harmless doubt mentioned by de Neufville, as it does not force us to abandon traditional philosophy *per se*.[65] But this impression is misleading because Clauberg argues that de Neufville's claim that we can either subscribe to Bacon's project or to his own vision of a *philosophia nov-antiqua* is based on a false dichotomy: we can accept Baconian radicalism without the negative consequences that de Neufville anticipated.[66] Clauberg provides three reasons for the spuriousness of de Neufville's dichotomy:

---

[63] Cf. Johann Clauberg, *Opera omnia* (Amsterdam, 1691), 1212, quoted as *Opera*.

[64] Cf. Clauberg, *Opera*, 1214: '1. Cartesiana Philosophia etiam requirit mentem puram, hoc est, ab omnibus praeconceptis opinionibus expurgatam; 2. Idque per suspensionem judicii et firmum animi propositum, nihil ex iis affirmandi vel negandi, quae olim affirmavimus vel negavimus, antequa ad novum et accuratum examen fuerint recovata.'

[65] Cf. Clauberg, *Opera*, 1214: 'Consistit igitur discipuli Cartesiani initiatio in eo solo, ut cohibeat et moderetur Philosophicum et firmum mentis assensum (debilis enim opinionibus assensus et quandoque etiam satis firmus in ordine ad vitam non idem denegatur) circa ea de quorum veritate nondum constat, et ab omnibus praejudiciis mentem suam liberet, hoc est, praecipitantiam in judicando et anticipationem vitet, uti vult praeceptum Cartesianae Methodi primum, quod primae Meditationi dedit originem. Ac proinde nihil est quod in tali Philosophi Cartesiani initiatione improbare possimus.'

[66] Cf. Clauberg, *Opera*, 1214: 'Quae deinceps enarrantur Verulamianae methodi incommoda, ea Certesianam minime commitantur.'

1. In Cartesian philosophy, doubt is only the initial stage of philosophising. It leads quickly to an understanding of one's own nature that is then followed by knowledge of God and of His creation.[67]

2. Cartesians do not need to investigate nature over the course of centuries, because they can rely on Descartes's own substantial findings.[68]

3. Cartesianism has proven its value in promoting advances across philosophical disciplines, namely in metaphysics, physics, mathematics, logic, and ethics.[69]

Clauberg comes to the conclusion that 'the Cartesian method is therefore compatible with education to the highest degree' (*Cartesiana methodus Scholasticae institutione maxime accommodata est*).[70] Its followers have professional success as pastors, professors, or doctors. However, those who want to have a successful career are still bound to obey the Cartesian maxim that they have always to suspend judgment when the questions to be answered are difficult and do not allow a certain answer.[71]

Of course the thesis that Cartesian doubt is less destructive than Baconian doubt and therefore compatible with being taught in a university needs further argument that does not only rely on Descartes's authority. And

---

[67] Cf. Clauberg, *Opera*, 1214: 'Nam 1. in Cartesiana dubitatione certitudo involvitur atque implicatur, qua dubitans suam illico naturam agnoscit, unde in Dei et porro in rerum a Deo creatarum notitiam devehitur.' See also Clauberg, *Opera*, 1132, where Clauberg points out that Cartesian doubt is intended to lead to knowledge gradually.

[68] Cf. Clauberg, *Opera*, 1214: '2. Neque hic relinquuntur omnia longa et prolixa inquisitione investiganda, sed jam a Cartesio investigata atque inventa traduntur.' In a similar vein, Clauberg, *Opera*, 1135, points out that Cartesian doubt comprehends only a short span in the intellectual biography of a student of Descartes's philosophy.

[69] Cf. Clauberg, *Opera*, 1214: '3. Et quidem dogmata Metaphysica, Physica, Mathematica, Logica, Ethica longe nobiliora, ac de quibusdam materiis etiam plura, quam ulla alia Philosophia proponat.' Clauberg adds that all these new findings can always be examined by anyone willing to do so. They may give rise to countless more discoveries and inventions, because Descartes has developed principles of philosophy. From these many new insights may be derived. Cf. ibid.: 'Et haec omnia Cartesius Lectori suo, per descriptam dubitationem initiato, eidemque maturo judicio praedito, examinanda tradit: in quo examine non modo vero consentanea ea deprehenduntur, verum etiam talia, ut ex iis alia innumera adhuc inveniri possint ac detegi, atque inde est quod librorum suorum maximum Principia Philosophiae inscripserit.' See also Clauberg, *Opera*, 1136, on the value of Cartesian philosophy for a career in politics.

[70] Clauberg, *Opera*, 1214.

[71] Cf. Clauberg, *Opera*, 1214: 'Ac proinde Cartesiana methodus Scholasticae institutioni maxime accommodata est, id quod ipsa experientia his annis comprobavit, dum tot Ecclesiarum pastores, Academiarum professores, Medici, Philosophi ex ea exsisterunt, quibus summo suo merito et gradus collati sunt et officia publica demandata. Quamvis hujusmodi argumenta a gradibus et dignitatibus petita, etc. non debeant ullo modo veritatis studiosum eo impellere, ut nimis in pronuncianda sententia festinet, non adhibita conveniente in rebus difficilibus judicii suspensione.'

Clauberg still has to show why de Neufville's plan of a gradual and evolutionary renewal of philosophy is misguided. Clauberg elucidates the productive role of Cartesian doubt in teaching through a comparison with Baconian doubt: Cartesian doubt is metaphysical in the sense that it relies on inferences (*ratiocinatio*) and 'intellectual attention', i. e., introspection. Baconian doubt is 'physical', i. e., it only concerns knowledge about nature. It requires observation and experiences or experiments. We find our way out of Cartesian doubt through an *a posteriori* demonstration of our existence and the existence of God. Baconian doubt can only be resolved through a long series of experiments that leads to defensible induction.[72] The Cartesian criterion for the successful resolution of a doubt is thus not the empirical verifiability of a proposition, but its agreement with reason. Observations and experiments have a role to play, at best, in natural philosophy, not in philosophy as a whole. So for anyone wanting to contribute to a possible renewal of philosophy, the Cartesian strategy is more promising than the Baconian, because it can be adopted easily without a huge investment of intellectual or other ressources.

The Cartesian model is superior to de Neufville's version of a *philosophia nov-antiqua* as well. Clauberg concedes that gradual transitions can be advantageous, both in nature and in politics: a sudden change from heat to cold, from deep shadow into glaring light can be a damaging experience. Augustus preserved republican institutions, so that the Roman people would tolerate his reign. A gradual reform of philosophy could have been helpful, too, increasing the acceptance of Descartes's ideas. But philosophy can only be reformed in its totality.[73] Philosophical convictions do not exist in isolation. The only defense against unexamined opinions is the suspension of judgment. The end goal of philosophy is a reform

---

[72] Cf. Clauberg, *Opera*, 1214: 'Porro Cartesiana dubitatio Metaphysica est, Verulamiana Physica: illa ratiocinatione et intellectuali attentione, haec sensuum observatione et experimentis, ex mente Authorum (Cartesii et Verulamii) tollitur: ab illa liberamur per brevem a posteriori demonstrationem (ut cum ex dubitatione percipimus nos dubitantes existere, et ex nostrae existentiae conservatione Deum existere probamus) ab hac per longam inductionem ex particularibus praemissis et experimentis.'

[73] Cf. Clauberg, *Opera*, 1215: 'Ut prioris qualitatis et formae nonnihil initio remaneat et paulatim aboleatur, utile est in mutatione Physica, quia valde noxium est corporibus nostris et valetudini adversum, si ab uno extremo ad aliud extremum subito transferantur, v. g. a summa calore ad summum frigus, ab obscurissimus tenebris illico ad clarissimam lucem, vide exemplum cap. 1. art. 10. Utile idem est in mutatione Politica (et ab Augusto Imperatore diligenter observatum) ne sentiat populus mutari formam reipublicae, ut aequire animo ferat imperium, etc. .... Et si simili modo vetus Philosophia a Cartesio potuisset reformari, forte minor fuisset strepitus, minor ad calumniandum ab adversariis inventa occasio. Sed non potuit eo modo, sensim et paulatim, Philosophia recte instaurari, quamvis alio qiudem sensu sensim instaurata dici potest.'

of one's mind, and this process can be impeded by false opinions; belief in only one absurdity can cause subsequent errors.[74]

Conclusion

I had set out to show how the adaptation of the 'new science' and its methodology was debated among university teachers. For de Neufville scholastic natural philosophy fails both in its doctrines and its method of teaching, i. e., disputations. But the 'reform movements' of *dogmatici* and *empirici* do not succeed either. The *dogmatici* have no other argument in disputes than the authority of Scripture or of reason. Yet, an appeal to authority cannot help to resolve disagreements. *Empirici* do not acknowledge that we need reason to supplement and to correct experiential evidence. De Neufville's objection that Bacon neglects Aristotelian logic and theory of science suggests that his brand of empirical natural history does not give enough weight either to the role of our higher intellectual capacities in scientific investigations.

This vision of a Baconian *philosopha nov-antiqua* would still be compatible with a complete disregard for the doctrinal content of traditional natural philosophy. We could start from a clean slate and apply Aristotelian tools to the results of the ongoing empirical investigation of nature. The inclusion of traditional doctrines in natural philosophy can only be justified pragmatically. De Neufville does have one substantial philosophical argument in favor of this: it is simply not credible that all previous investigations of nature were completely erroneous because some of their insights rely on experience. But the pragmatic argument carries more weight: we cannot simply shut down all universities, even if such a radical measure may in principle be desirable. This is why a philosophical stance that rests on a complete break with tradition and its institutions cannot be defended. Society is in need of philosophically-trained jurists, physicians, and theologians. The study of nature is an indispensable part of such instruction.

---

[74] Cf. Clauberg, *Opera*, 1215: 'Nam si reineantur opiniones aliquae nondum examinatae, nihil est proclivius, quam ut hae aliis se immisceant et justum earum examen impediant ac perturbent: et facillime tum recipiuntur opiniones illis nondum examinatis conformes ac similes. In multis aliis mutationibus id quod in principio mansit paulatim tolllitur et corrigitur, nec interim nocet reliquis; sed in Philosophica hac animi mutatione, si quid maneat nondum ad rectae rationis libellam appensum, id progressu temporis, multa incerta et falsa pariendo, reliquis noxium est, quoniam vel uno absurdo dato infinita sequuntur, ut testatur in vulgato verbo.'

This fundamental assumption is shared by both de Neufville and Clauberg. Clauberg, however, believes that in this respect Cartesianism is superior to de Neufville's Baconian *philosophia nov-antiqua*. Cartesianism can accommodate the pedagogical needs of the university as it exists; it allows for a clean break with the philosophical tradition without dubious invocations of the *consensus omnium* or a presumption of probability. This is the case because Cartesian doubt is not dependent on experience and the contingencies of prolonged investigations. It schools our intellectual capacities, inferences, and 'intellectual attention'. Clauberg concedes that de Neufville's suggestion of a gradual transition from old to new seems to be more agreeable and consonant with human nature. But unexamined opinions are a barrier to progress: no individual mind can undergo a successful process of reform while clinging to convictions that may, in the end, be false. At the same time, Cartesianism is also successful on a pragmatic level: its followers are successful professionals. It is thus the right answer to the educational needs of society.

School of Philosophy
HSE University Moscow, RF
shessbru@hse.ru

Domesticating Descartes, Renovating Scholasticism: Johann Clauberg and the German Reception of Cartesianism

Nabeel Hamid

Descartes in Germany

A century and a half ago, Francisque Bouillier observed that 'Cartesianism did not have as great an influence in Germany as in Holland or France.'[1] Descartes's appearance in Germany faced unique circumstances. It occurred in the midst of ongoing projects to craft distinct Protestant identities driven by the demands of religious apologetics in the closing years of the Thirty Years' War. It also had to confront a culture of university philosophy which had become deeply entangled in the religio-political disputes dividing German states. That Cartesianism did make gradual inroads there to become an important current by the late seventeenth century owed, above all, to the efforts of Johann Clauberg (1622–1665) in situating and disseminating Descartes's thought. The object of this essay is to understand the motivations and outcomes of those efforts. In particular, it asks why Clauberg preserved certain aspects of the prevailing Aristotelian framework even as he embraced many of Descartes's novelties. In the process, it examines the mediating role in this confluence of ideas of the educational culture of the early modern German Reformed community and, specifically, of the circumstances surrounding the creation of the University of Duisburg, where Clauberg taught and wrote.

The label 'Cartesian Scholastic' (and its variants) has been used to describe Clauberg's work at least since Josef Bohatec's *Die cartesianische*

---

[1] *Histoire de la philosophie cartésienne* (Paris, 1868), 405.

Nabeel Hamid, *Domesticating Descartes, Renovating Scholasticism: Johann Clauberg and the German Reception of Cartesianism* In: *History of Universities*. Edited by: Mordechai Feingold, Oxford University Press (2021).
© Oxford University Press.
DOI: 10.1093/oso/9780192893833.003.0003

Scholastik in der Philosophie und reformierten Dogmatik des 17. Jahrhunderts (1912). It has remained in use in recent scholarship.[2] The label arises out of an interpretive challenge presented by Clauberg's writings. On the one hand, he positioned himself as an ardent proponent of a bold new philosophy as superior to the traditional one in various respects. In a polemical juxtaposition of Cartesianism and school philosophy, *Unterschied zwischen den cartesianischer und der sonst in Schulen gebräuchlicher Philosophie* (1658; henceforth *Unterschied*), Clauberg underscores the distance between the two frameworks in dramatic terms. The Cartesian philosophy, he declares, is as different from the Scholastic or Jesuit as the Roman Catholic Church is from the Evangelical or Reformed.[3] More generally, Clauberg valorizes the difference and modernity of Cartesian thought and downplays its points of continuity with Scholasticism. Indeed, his defenses and elaborations of Descartes in titles such as *Defensio cartesiana* (1652), *Initiatio philosophi sive dubitatio cartesiana* (1655), and *Paraphrasis in meditationes cartesii* (1658) would introduce the next few generations of German intellectuals to Cartesianism and establish Clauberg's reputation as its key representative. G.W. Leibniz, notably, esteemed Clauberg as 'the most learned of the Cartesian sect' and as 'being clearer than the master'.[4] Christian Wolff similarly pronounced Clauberg as the best interpreter of Descartes, and credited him with having initiated an emendation of metaphysics which Leibniz further advanced.[5]

At the same time, Clauberg's systematic treatises such as *Metaphysica de ente* (1664) and *Disputationes physicae* (1664) retain much of the form, vocabulary, and substance of the scholastic tradition. His conception of metaphysics as a theory of being and its transcendental attributes, and his penchant for exhaustive conceptual distinctions has struck many readers as squarely in the tradition of school philosophy, the target of self-styled

---

[2] Eugenio Viola, 'Scolastica e Cartesianesimo nel pensiero di J. Clauberg', *Rivista di Filosofia Neo-Scolastica* 67 (1975), 247–66; Francesco Trevisani, *Descartes in Germania: La ricezione del Cartesianesimo nella facoltà filosofica e medica di Duisburg* (Milan, 1992), 97; Vincent Carraud, 'L'ontologie peut-elle être cartésienne? L'exemple de l'ontosophia de Clauberg, de 1647 à 1664: de l'ens à la mens', In *Johannes Clauberg (1622–1665) and Cartesian Philosophy in the Seventeenth Century*, ed. Theo Verbeek (Dordrecht, 1999), 13–38; Winfried Weier, 'Leibnitiana bei Johannes Clauberg', *Studia Leibnitiana* 32 (2000): 21–42; Andrea Strazzoni, 'The Foundation of Early Modern Science: Metaphysics, Logic and Theology', (Ph.D. Diss., Erasmus University Rotterdam, 2015).

[3] *Unterschied zwischen den cartesianischer und der sonst in Schulen gebräuchlicher Philosophie* (Duisburg, 1658), 4–6; (cited as *Unterschied*, by page number).

[4] *Sämtliche Schriften und Briefe.* ed. Berlin-Brandenburgische Akademie der Wissenschaften (Berlin, 1923-), II.1.112; II.1.15 (cited by series, volume, and page). It is worth noting that Descartes's complete works were not published in Germany until 1692.

[5] *Philosophia prima sive ontologia* (Renger, 1730), §7n. Wolff prominently cites Clauberg, alongside Aristotle, Descartes, and Leibniz, throughout the work.

intellectual revolutionaries such as Descartes. Indeed, Clauberg himself sometimes suggests that his work should be viewed as a synthesis, describing his *Logica vetus et nova*, for instance, as *'aristotelico-cartesiana'*. To some extent, he can plausibly be read as aligned with various mid-seventeenth century attempts to blend new and old philosophies, a project sometimes termed by its exponents as *novantiqua*. Several of Descartes's early followers and sympathizers, in fact, attempted to integrate his views with the reigning orthodoxy. Johannes de Raey, one of Clauberg's teachers in Holland, undertook such a project in his *Clavis philosophiae naturalis, seu introductio ad contemplationem naturae Aristotelico-Cartesiana* (1654). Not without good reason, the labels 'Cartesian Scholastic' and 'Cartesian Aristotelian'—since Aristotle's name was intimately tied to university or scholastic philosophy—intend to capture this dual character of Clauberg's self-presentation.[6]

In fact, a tension between narratives of rupture and continuity is evident even in Descartes's own presentation of his relation to the past. In concluding his account of material nature in *Principles of Philosophy*, for example, Descartes states that he has not used any principle 'which was not accepted by Aristotle and by all other Philosophers of all periods: so that this Philosophy is not new, but the oldest and most commonplace of all', a claim he repeats to the Jesuit Charlet.[7] On other occasions, however,

---

[6] The words 'Aristotelian' and 'Scholastic' are deeply entangled. For many early modern detractors of university philosophy, labels such as 'school philosophy', 'Aristotle', and 'Scholastic' are interchangeable terms of abuse connoting empty word-play, pedantry, or obstacles to the progress of knowledge. As we shall see in Section Four, Clauberg has a more nuanced view of the relationship between Aristotle, Descartes, and Scholasticism. To preview, Clauberg hopes to recover an Aristotle who is distinct in key respects from how the earlier scholastic tradition had understood him. On the topic of the varieties of Aristotelianisms in the Renaissance, see Charles B. Schmitt, 'Towards a Reassessment of Renaissance Aristotelianism', *History of Science* 11 (1973), 159–193. See also Edward Grant, 'Ways to Interpret the Terms 'Aristotelian' and 'Aristotelianism' in Medieval and Renaissance Natural Philosophy', *History of Science* 25 (1987), 335–358, who highlights the elasticity of the Aristotelian framework and its ability to absorb new challenges and influences as a feature of the tradition throughout its history: 'Aristotelianism often included conflicting earlier and later opinions simultaneously. There was always a domain of both traditional and innovative concepts and interpretations and was therefore inevitably elastic and absorbent' (352). See Stephen Menn, 'The Intellectual Setting', in *The Cambridge History of Seventeenth Century Philosophy*, eds. Daniel Garber and Michael Ayers, 33–86 (Cambridge, 1998), 38–47, for a survey of anti-Aristotelian trends in the sixteenth and seventeenth centuries. See Constance Blackwell and Sachiko Kusukawa, eds., *Philosophy in the Sixteenth and Seventeenth Centuries: Conversations with Aristotle* (New York, 1999), for treatments of Aristotle's continuing philosophical significance in the period.

[7] AT VIIIA.323, CSM I.286; AT IV.141, CSMK 238. Descartes's works are cited as [AT], by volume and page number: *Oeuvres de Descartes*. 2nd ed. 11 vols. ed. Charles Adam and Paul Tannery (Paris, 1964–1974); and [CSM(K)], by volume and page number: *The Philosophical Writings of Descartes*, 3 vols. eds. and trans. John Cottingham, Robert Stoothoff, Dugald Murdoch, and Anthony Kenny (Cambridge, 1984–1991).

Descartes declares that his new principles of physics 'destroy the principles of Aristotle'.[8] The autobiographical account in *Discourse on Method* confirms the image of Descartes as a lone intellectual revolutionary seeking the truth from the pure light of nature, unfettered by confusions transmitted through pedantry.[9] As Tad Schmaltz remarks, Descartes presented himself to his readers under two conflicting guises: 'The first of these was that of the innovator, someone who sets aside the study of the past in order to start afresh. But when it suited him, he could also wear the mask of the traditionalist, someone who is faithful to the views of the ancients, and of Aristotle in particular.'[10] Given Descartes's own ambivalence about his relation to the history of philosophy, contemporaries could fairly have characterized his thought as either preserving continuity with tradition or as a radical break.

I shall not call into question the plain fact that Clauberg drew on both Descartes and Aristotle. Instead, my specific interest lies in the reasons why, given his enthusiastic embrace of Descartes and the fact that his contemporaries and immediate successors saw him as a champion of Cartesianism, he borrowed foundational conceptions from Aristotle. My suggestion is perhaps disappointingly obvious: Clauberg found Aristotle philosophically valuable. Faced with the textual situation, many commentators have labeled Clauberg's work 'eclectical', and attributed that character of his writings to pressures of confessional politics, pedagogical convenience, or an isolated interest in Cartesian natural science. By contrast, this essay calls attention to Clauberg's attraction to the intrinsic philosophical merits of Aristotle's metaphysics considered purely as ontology. Clauberg initiates a project of embedding Descartes's first philosophy—a science of the first known beings, namely God and the human soul—within a more fundamental theory of being and its common attributes, a science of ontology considered as the doctrine of being *qua* being. One of the specific goals of Clauberg's metaphysics of being is to lay objective foundations for a Cartesian philosophy of nature on the principle of contradiction rather than on the experiential knowledge of God and the thinking self. With Clauberg, a new Aristotle—partly real, partly imagined—begins to appear in German philosophy.

Several intellectual and practical motivations underlie Clauberg's thought, from the question of reforming the arts curriculum to that of the relation between philosophy and theology. Accordingly, this essay first sets the cultural-historical stage, before turning to Clauberg's philosophical

---

[8] Letter to Mersenne, 28 January, 1641, AT III.298, CSMK 173.
[9] AT VI.7–8, CSM I.114–115.
[10] Tad Schmaltz, *Early Modern Cartesianisms* (New York, 2017), 64.

interest in uniting Descartes and Aristotle. The next section focuses on the early seventeenth-century situation in the German Reformed community, specifically in Duisburg, the site of a new university where Clauberg was appointed rector and where conditions were especially favorable for the pedagogical innovations he envisioned. Section Three considers several explanations for the ecumenical nature of Clauberg's work and finds them wanting. Section Four sketches the positive view, that Clauberg's ontology is designed to subsume the Cartesian theory of substance in general, and of created substance in particular, under a universal theory of being. Section Five concludes with some reflections on the continued use of labels such as 'Cartesio-Scholastic' and 'eclectical' to describe Clauberg's work.

Clauberg and Duisburg

Clauberg's philosophical fortunes are intimately tied to his brief career at the University of Duisburg, founded 1655. They are equally bound up with the pedagogical goals of the German Reformed (Calvinist) community, especially under the patronage of the Brandenburg electors after Johann Sigismund's conversion to Calvinism in 1613. As a result, Clauberg's contributions are central not only to Duisburg's association with German Cartesianism in the latter half of the seventeenth century but also with the link that German Cartesianism came to have with irenical theology, and with an emphasis on piety rather than doctrinal issues in religion.

Clauberg's familiarity with Descartes was acquired at close quarters. In 1644, after having studied in Solingen and Bremen, Clauberg moved to Groningen, where Cartesianism had recently won an important victory: the previous year, the Stadtholder of Groningen had ordered the Utrecht authorities to cease the suppression of Cartesian philosophy in the wake of the theologian Gisbert Voetius's efforts to have it condemned. Following extended stays in England and France (1646–1648), Clauberg returned to Holland to continue his studies with Johannes de Raey, an early convert to Cartesianism. Clauberg earned his place in Cartesian lore by drawing up a report of Descartes's conversation with Frans Burman at Leiden in 1648. The following year, he was appointed professor of philosophy and theology at the gymnasium in Herborn (Hesse-Nassau), an important center of Calvinist learning.[11] His tenure there, however, was an unhappy one.

---

[11] It was in Herborn in 1602 that Johannes Piscator (1546–1625) published the Reformed Church translation of the Bible. The Herborn academy served as a model for Calvinist schools in Central Europe. For a comprehensive study of the importance of the Herborn academy for German Calvinism during the Reformation, see Gerhard Menk, *Die hohe Schule Herborn in ihrer Frühzeit (1584–1660)* (Wiesbaden, 1981).

Besides the burdens of a heavy teaching load and not having his salary paid on time, Clauberg found the intellectual climate in Herborn unsatisfying. An emphasis on practical philosophy and theology, and a commitment to Aristotelian and Ramist logic as the only approved methods of instruction meant that Clauberg was not permitted to develop the new Cartesian logic, metaphysics, and natural philosophy he had learned in Holland.[12] Clauberg, along with his colleague and friend Christoph Wittich (1625–1687), left Herborn for Duisburg around Christmas 1651, bringing with him several students. He would spend fourteen highly productive years in the Rhineland until his death in 1665.

Already in the 1550s, the duke of Jülich-Cleves-Berg, Wilhelm the Rich, had proposed the founding of a new university in Duisburg. The right to confer degrees was granted to the duke by a papal bull and imperial privilege in the 1560s.[13] As originally envisioned, the university was to have a standing faculty of ten to eleven professors, including three for theology, three for law, two for medicine, and two to three for the humanities. When the university finally opened a century later, scarcity of funds meant that only half that number were appointed.[14] Importantly, Brandenburg's acquisition of the Duchy of Cleves in 1614 meant that the new university was established as a Reformed institution rather than as a Catholic one. Its creation thus accorded with the stated intent of the General Synod of the Reformed Church of Cleves to provide more academies for their youth in order to discourage them from leaving their community for the better-established network of Jesuit institutions.[15] After Friedrich Wilhelm became Elector of Brandenburg in 1640, the estates of Cleves wasted no time in impressing upon him the urgent need for new universities in Reformed territories.[16] The argument was a strong one: at the time, Brandenburg could count only one university—Frankfurt (Oder)—as an organ of the court's confession. Plans had advanced by the time Clauberg's move to the Duisburg gymnasium was announced in May 1651, and it is likely that he was apprised of the imminent creation of the university

---

[12] Günter von Roden, *Die Universität Duisburg* (Duisburg, 1968), 159–160; Theo Verbeek, 'Johannes Clauberg: A Bio-Bibliographical Sketch', in *Johannes Clauberg (1622–1665) and Cartesian Philosophy in the Seventeenth Century,* ed. Theo Verbeek (Dordrecht, 1999), 185–186.

[13] See Hubert Jedin, 'Der Plan einer Universitätsgründung in Duisburg 1555/64', in *Die Universität Duisburg,* ed. Günter von Roden (Duisburg, 1968), 1–32, for the initial plans, framed between 1555–1564, for the university.

[14] Werner Hesse, *Beiträge zur Geschichte der frühern Universität in Duisburg* (Duisburg, 1879), 17.

[15] August Tholuck, *Vorgeschichte des Rationalismus* (Halle, 1853), 246–247; Trevisani, *Descartes in Germania,* 19–20.

[16] Hesse, *Geschichte,* 13–14.

while still at Herborn.[17] On 14 October 1655, the university was inaugurated with much festivity. Clauberg, along with Martin Hundius (1624–1666) and Christopher Wittich, was declared doctor of theology and delivered the first rectoral address the following day.[18]

Circumstances in the wake of the Thirty Years' War meant that the new university was poised to become a leading center of higher learning in the Reformed community. It was also well-positioned to implement some of the pedagogical reforms that were being proposed around this time. The few Calvinist degree-granting institutions there had been in German principalities had suffered greatly during the war. Heidelberg's unparalleled status at the dawn of the seventeenth century as the most important center of Calvinist theology and philosophy came to an abrupt end in 1622 when Tilly's Catholic League army overran the city. The extensive Bibliotheca Palatina was handed over to Pope Gregory XV, and the once-distinguished university entrusted to the Bavarian Jesuits. Heidelberg was only reestablished as a Calvinist institution in 1652, and its subsequent recovery was slow.[19] Another important Calvinist university, that of Marburg, met a similar fate in 1624 as the forces of the Lutheran Ludwig V of Hesse-Darmstadt, an imperial ally, conquered the town. The university's entire professoriate was disbanded and replaced by professors from the Lutheran gymnasium at Gießen. Marburg would remain a Lutheran institution until 1653 after which it, like Heidelberg, would only slowly regain some of its earlier prestige.[20]

The Academia Viadrina in Frankfurt-on-the-Oder, meanwhile, enjoyed the protections that accompanied its status as the only university in Brandenburg confessionally aligned with the court. Immediately after his conversion to Calvinism, Johann Sigismund had begun to lean upon Frankfurt's theological faculty as an instrument for propagating his new faith. The elector's tight control over promotions and appointments quickly

---

[17] Trevisani, *Descartes in Germania*, 25.   [18] Hesse, *Geschichte*, 35–6.

[19] Peter Classen, and Eike Wolgast, *Kleine Geschichte der Universität Heidelberg* (Berlin and Heidelberg and New York, 1983), 24–5; Volker Press, 'Kurfürst Maximilian I. von Bayern, die Jesuiten und die Universität Heidelberg im Dreißigjährigen Krieg 1622–1649', in *Semper Apertus. Sechshundert Jahre Ruprecht-Karls-Universität Heidelberg 1386–1986*, ed. Wilhelm Doerr (Berlin and Heidelberg, 1985), 314–370; Notker Hammerstein, 'The University of Heidelberg in the Early Modern Period: Aspects of Its History as a Contribution to Its Sexcentenary', *History of Universities* 6 (1987), 118–120. Heidelberg's reputation rested on influential Calvinist thinkers such as Bartholomaeus Keckermann (1572–1608) and Abraham Scultetus (1566–1625).

[20] H. Hermelink and S.A. Kaehler, *Die Universität Marburg von 1527–1927* (Marburg, 1927), 220–222. Marburg had been home to notable academics such as Rudolph Goclenius (1547–1628) and Johann Hartmann (1568–1631), who held the first professorship in chemistry in Europe.

gave the university a Reformed identity.[21] Yet, perhaps because of the success of Brandenburg's so-called Second Reformation in Frankfurt, by mid-century the university came to express a high degree of ideological uniformity and stability. Under the patronage of the Brandenburg electors, the University of Frankfurt became the center of a Reformed theology of irenicism and its attendant political tendency toward religious toleration.[22] Irenicism emphasized doctrinal unity across confessional lines rather than the polemics of difference dominating theological writing in Germany. But, while a spirit of innovation persisted in Frankfurt's theological faculty, the university proved less hospitable to change in its philosophical curriculum. The case of Johannes Placentinus, a Bohemian-Polish mathematics professor and enthusiastic supporter of Descartes, underscores the rigidity in the arts curriculum. By encouraging his students to defend Cartesian and Copernican theses in natural philosophy, Placentinus incurred the anger of the philosophical faculty, which sought to have him censured. Only the intervention of Elector Friedrich Wilhelm quelled the controversy over Placentinus's continued appointment.[23]

Among the Reformed universities of Germany, then, Duisburg was uniquely prepared to institute wide-ranging educational reforms, especially with respect to the relationship between philosophy and theology. The polemical spirit of Protestant theology, which had prevailed in the sixteenth and early seventeenth centuries, had gradually co-opted philosophy for its traditional role of handmaiden to theology.[24] Lutheran theologians such as Christoph Scheibler as well as Calvinists such as Clemens Timpler found in traditional metaphysics powerful resources for the articulation and defense of theological doctrines, above all, of the increasingly sensitive

[21] Bodo Nischan, *Prince, People, and Confession* (Philadelphia, 1994), 128–130.

[22] For irenicism at Frankfurt and the concomitant rise of toleration in Brandenburg, see Nischan, *Prince*, ch. 10. For irenicism within the German Calvinist movement in the 1620s and 1630s, see Bodo Nischan, 'Reformed Irenicism and the Leipzig Colloquy of 1631', *Central European History* 9 (1976), 3–26. To be sure, irenicism gained adherents in Lutheran theology in this period as well, notably with the Helmstedt theologian Georg Calixt (1586–1656).

[23] See Pietro D. Omodeo, 'Central European Polemics over Descartes: Johannes Placentinus and His Academic Opponents at Frankfurt on Oder', *History of Universities* 29 (2016), 29–64, for Placentinus' career and the quarrel at Frankfurt between 1653–1656.

[24] The *ancilla theologiae* view of metaphysics is prominent in, for instance, Christoph Scheibler's influential *Opus metaphysicum*, which begins with an extended defense of the value of metaphysics for defending articles of faith; Christoph Scheibler, *Opus metaphysicum*, vol 1. In *Christian Wolff: Gesammelte Werke, Materialien und Dokumente*, III Abt., Bd. 142.1 (Frankfurt, 1665, reprint Hildesheim, 2015), Bk. I, Proemium, cII). Fittingly, Scheibler, known to the seventeenth century as the 'Protestant Suárez', would abandon a career as professor of metaphysics at Gießen in order to devote his energies to composing defenses of Lutheran orthodoxy.

issue of the interpretation of the Eucharist.[25] By contrast, irenicism did not have as much use for a well-defined metaphysics of substance and accident for its theses. Irenical theologians typically deemphasized metaphysical commitments entailed by one or another manner of receiving the sacraments and, instead, underscored the common significance each Church attached to the personal faith of the recipient.

The scholastic philosophical framework, accordingly, becomes less relevant for a conception of religiosity anchored more in piety than in doctrinal clarity. A turn toward lived faith figures prominently in the federalist or covenantal movement within Calvinism associated with Johannes Cocceius (1603–1669), the Leiden theologian whose version of pietistic Calvinism represents a sharp contrast to the scholastic Calvinism of Voetius.[26] Cocceian federalism marks a shift away from doctrinal issues and toward the practice of piety. For Cocceius, the proper Christian attitude toward revelation is one of devotion rather than the juridical one prevailing among theologians such as Voetius and at the synods. Cocceius's influence on Duisburg's theologians—Clauberg, Wittich, and Hundius— is well-attested, and a link between federalism and Cartesianism begins to emerge in Duisburg in the 1650s.[27] The anti-scholastic direction of Duisburg theology would align quite naturally with the natural philosophical orientation of Descartes's thought.

A shift toward pietism also features in prominent programs for educational reform in the period. The Moravian pedagogue Jan Amos Komensky's (1592–1670; Latin: Comenius) universalist vision of Christian education, for example, aims above all to prepare Christian youth for the afterlife through an efficient, practical curriculum. In four six-year periods, beginning with the 'mother school' of infancy and ending with the university, Comenius's *Magna didactica* lays out a comprehensive educational

[25] Perhaps no issue came to symbolize confessional identity in the period as much as the ritual and interpretation of the Lord's Supper. Lutherans insisted on the real presence of Christ in the sacrament, while Calvinists assigned an analogical or symbolic meaning to the elements. For the doctrinal details of the dispute, see Nischan, *Prince*, 138–40; and Cees Leijenhorst, 'Place, Space and Matter in Calvinist Physics', *The Monist* 84 (2001), 523–534.

[26] For a study of Cocceius's federalism, see Willem J. van Asselt, *The Federal Theology of Johannes Cocceius (1603–1669)* (Leiden, 2001). For Cocceius' influence in the Rhineland and his significance for the development of German pietism, see Heinz Schneppen, *Niederländische Universitäten und Deutsches Geistesleben* (Münster: Aschendorff, 1960), 85–92. Voetius, it will be recalled, had sought a broad condemnation of Cartesianism in the 1640s.

[27] Tholuck, *Vorgeschichte*, 248; Heinrich Heppe, *Geschichte der Evangelischen Kirche von Cleve-Mark und der Provinz Westphalen* (Iserlohn: J. Bädeker, 1867), 187; Trevisani, *Descartes in Germania*, 31; Schmaltz, *Cartesianisms*, 75–6. Schneppen, *Niederländische Universitäten*, 89, writes: 'After 1650 the anti-scholastic biblical theology of Cocceius and Leiden Cartesianism found in each other a common enmity toward the Aristotelian tradition.'

program through which 'the entire youth of both sexes...shall quickly, pleasantly, and thoroughly become learned in the sciences, pure in morals, trained in piety, and in this manner instructed in all things necessary for the present and future life.'[28] In particular, Comenius displays remarkable hostility toward classical learning. 'Christian schools', he thunders, 'should not resound with Plautus, not with Terence, not with Ovid, not with Aristotle, but with Moses, David, and Christ.'[29] For, if the new universal schools are 'to be truly Christian schools, the crowd of Pagan writers must be removed from them.'[30] Comenius's warnings against indulging in the subtleties of Aristotelian philosophy, in particular, echo the sentiment of earlier Calvinist pedagogues such as Johannes Piscator at the prominent Herborn gymnasium. Studies of scholastic intricacies rooted in the philosophy of Aristotle, for Piscator, 'are worthy of a free man and have their purpose; but they are for the most part more subtle than many can comprehend, and less learning than this seems necessary for understanding Christian doctrine.'[31] At the turn of the century, the Herborn academy, which served as the model for Reformed education in German territories, had effectively codified a turn away from classical humanism in favor of useful knowledge, toward praxis rather than theory.[32] On this conception, while an arts education is certainly valuable for cultivating civic morals, for learning languages needed for reading medical, legal, and theological texts, and for developing effective rhetorical skills, it should not be considered essential preparation for the defense of articles of faith.[33]

[28] *The Great Didactic*, ed. and trans. M.W. Keatinge (London: Adam and Charles Black, 1910), Title page.

[29] Comenius, *Great Didactic*, ch. XXIV, §20.

[30] Comenius, *Great Didactic* ch. XXV, §1. See Ulrich G. Leinsle, 'Comenius in der Metaphysik des jungen Clauberg', in *Johannes Clauberg (1622–1665) and Cartesian Philosophy in the Seventeenth Century*, ed. Theo Verbeek (Dordrecht, 1999), 1–12, for some sources of Comenius' influence on Clauberg via Tobias Andreae and the Dutch businessman Louis de Geer.

[31] Cited in Howard Hotson, *Johann Heinrich Alsted, 1588–1638: Between Renaissance, Reformation, and Universal Reform* (Oxford, 2000), 20–21.

[32] Hotson, *Alsted*, 22–3. It should be borne in mind, at the same time, that opinions on classicism and on scholastic metaphysics were not quite so uniform in Reformed schools at the turn of the century. We can note the example of the Steinfurt gymnasium, founded in 1588 on the model of Herborn, where Clemens Timpler (1563–1624) initiated a tradition of Protestant Scholastic treatises on metaphysics with his *Metaphysicae systema methodicum* (1604). For a detailed study of the development of scholastic metaphysics in the Protestant context between 1580 and 1640, see Ulrich Leinsle's *Das Ding und die Methode* (Augsburg, 1985).

[33] Comenius, *Great Didactic*, ch. XXII, §1, clearly takes an instrumental view of language education: 'Languages are learned not as forming in themselves a part of erudition or wisdom, but as being the means by which we may acquire knowledge and may impart it to others.'

Finally, the emergence of a policy of inter-confessional toleration in Brandenburg, resulting from a stalemate between the predominantly Lutheran estates and the Reformed court, further dulled the need for subtle theological dogmatics. The Hohenzollern court, beginning with Johann Sigismund's conversion, had at first hoped for a thorough reform of Brandenburg society along Calvinist lines. But, as they gradually discovered, Lutheranism had become deeply entrenched among the laity as well as among the greater part of Brandenburg and Prussian nobility. While the elector's envisioned reforms took root in places such as Frankfurt (Oder), the great majority of Brandenburg's population remained Lutheran and actively resisted court-backed efforts to supplant orthodox ritual practices with Calvinist ones. A policy of toleration resulted as a compromise following the court's recognition of the failure of Johann Sigismund's attempt to comprehensively reform Brandenburg.[34] By mid-century, the Great Elector Friedrich Wilhelm would more enthusiastically embrace a policy of inter-confessional toleration, a policy which favored more ecumenical attitudes toward philosophy and eventually led to the emergence of a common evangelical identity in Germany.[35]

In fact, pedagogical ease and a sharper separation of the spheres of faith and reason are two of the key virtues Clauberg attributes to Descartes. In *Unterschied* (1658), Clauberg lays out his clearest defense of Descartes's value in these respects. In the first place, the greater simplicity of Cartesianism rests for him in the fact that it is the product of a single mind. Using an extended urban planning metaphor (recalling Part 2 of Descartes's *Discourse on Method*), Clauberg applauds Descartes's individualism: whereas the scholastic philosophy is like a city built over a long period by many architects with varying tastes, so that lowly huts now stand beside grand palaces among crooked streets and winding alleys, the Cartesian system is like one that has been built from the ground up according to a single idea.[36] That it is the work of one individual is an advantage, for it frees Cartesianism from the confusions of past authors. Further, in contrast to the scholastic

---

[34] That toleration in Brandenburg resulted as a compromise in Brandenburg is Nischan's, *Prince*, 4, main thesis: 'In the end, the Hohenzollerns had to settle for a compromise that allowed their court Calvinism to coexist with the principality's popular Lutheranism; instead of calvinizing Brandenburg, toleration resulted'. While toleration was state policy, it did not easily gain acceptance among Brandenburg's Lutheran subjects. Notker Hammerstein, 'Zur Geschichte der deutschen Universitäten im Zeitalter der Aufklärung', in *Res Publica Litteraria: Ausgewählte Aufsätze zur frühneuzeitlichen Bildungs-, Wissenschafts- und Universitätsgeschichte*, eds. Ulrich Muhlack and Gerrit Walther (Berlin, 2000), 16, observes that 'Lutheran Orthodoxy' reigned in the decades after the Thirty Years' War with detrimental effects on the reconstruction of German universities.

[35] This climate was present at the time of the founding of the university in Duisburg; von Roden, *Universität Duisburg*, 157–158.

[36] *Unterschied*, 7–8. Cf. AT VI.11–12, CSM I.116.

method, Descartes employs fewer and simpler rules, such as the injunction to trust only clear and distinct perceptions, the analytic method of dividing any problem into parts, and the synthetic method of reconstituting parts by a step-wise, demonstrative procedure.[37] What's more, Cartesianism is based on only two substantial principles—mind and body—and eliminates the complicated system of faculties and substantial forms.[38] Further, Cartesian philosophy has the advantage of training the understanding and equipping it with general tools by which one can extend knowledge to new discoveries. The scholastic method, by contrast, only teaches one how to argue and dispute existing matters.[39] Finally, Clauberg claims, Cartesian philosophy is more succinct and economical in its terminology, more easily translated into the vernacular German, and thus better suited than the scholastic philosophy for dissemination.[40] That Clauberg composes this polemical tract in German is itself noteworthy and underscores the reader's sense that the author's concern in promoting Descartes is as much pragmatic as it is philosophical.

In the second place, Clauberg recognizes in Descartes an important loosening of the tie between philosophy and theology. Interpreting it as a break from an older conception of philosophy as *ancilla theologiae*, Clauberg embraces Descartes's restricted treatment of theological matters to only as much as is required for certainty in natural knowledge.[41] On this topic, he would have learned of Descartes's opinions first hand: to Burman, Descartes pointedly distinguishes the ethical and religious perspective from the metaphysical, and frames his discussion of God's mutability, and the nature of God's decrees, from the latter point of view. For articles of faith that depend on revelation, Descartes tells Burman, 'must not be subjected to our human reasoning'.[42] Indeed, Descartes even suggests eliminating formal theological studies altogether, asking Burman whether 'you need to spend all this effort on theology, when we see that simple country folk have just as much chance as we have of getting to heaven?'[43] To Mesland, similarly, Descartes declares: 'I keep away, as far as possible, from questions of theology'.[44]

In light of this confluence of philosophical and cultural factors, the conservative character of Clauberg's works is striking. Clauberg himself, as we have seen, sharply distinguishes Cartesian philosophy from Scholasticism and declares his preference for the former in no uncertain terms. We have also seen how conditions in Reformed Duisburg in the 1650s presented

---

[37] *Unterschied*, 15–17.   [38] *Unterschied*, 19–20.   [39] *Unterschied*, 49–51.
[40] *Unterschied*, 53–54.   [41] *Unterschied*, 58.
[42] AT V.166, CSMK 348; AT V.176, CSMK 350.   [43] AT V.176, CSMK 351.
[44] AT IV.119, CSMK 235.

Clauberg, educated in Holland and appointed rector of a brand new university, with the perfect opportunity to introduce curricular reform. In the post-war atmosphere of reconciliation and irenicism, Clauberg should not have felt such strong cultural pressures to toe intellectual lines established earlier in the century, whether that meant following Heidelberg Aristotelianism, or Herborn Ramism, for instance. That, despite his enthusiasm for Descartes's innovations and the favorable circumstances for educational reform, Clauberg chose to characterize his logic as *aristotelico-cartesiana*,[45] to hold the *Posterior Analytics* in highest regard,[46] or to conceive the subject matter of metaphysics in decidedly anti-Cartesian fashion as being *qua* being,[47] invite a question as to his motives. We turn now to some actual and possible explanations for the apparent conservatism of Clauberg's texts.

Cartesianisms (And Aristotelianisms) In Seventeenth-Century Germany

As Francesco Trevisani has observed, the so-called 'Cartesian Scholastic' in seventeenth-century Germany, or the various attempts to reconcile Descartes with school philosophy, was not a monolithic phenomenon. Different readers were drawn to Descartes for different reasons. Medical doctors found in Descartes's theory of motion and his corpuscularianism a promising new framework for the study of medicine. Others were drawn to Descartes's separation of theology and natural philosophy. Still others attempted to marry Cartesian metaphysics with that of Jesuit Scholasticism. In Germany, Trevisani emphasizes, Descartes showed different faces in different contexts so that no single intellectual phenomenon should be uniquely identified as 'Cartesian Scholasticism'.[48]

In this respect, the fortunes of Cartesianism mirror those of early modern Aristotelianism. Just as the medieval synthesis of Aristotelian philosophy with Catholic theology was transformed by the humanist and religious ideas of the sixteenth and seventeenth centuries, Descartes's

---

[45] *Initiatio philosophi sive dubitatio cartesiana*, Ad Lectorem, in Johann Clauberg, *Opera omnia*, 2 vols, ed. Johann Schalbruch (Amsterdam, 1691), cited as [OO] by volume and page.

[46] *Initiatio philosophi sive dubitatio cartesiana*, Prolegomena, §29, OO II.1128.

[47] *Met. de ente*, §1–2, OO I.283.

[48] Trevisani, *Descartes in Germania*, 15–16: 'The so-called Cartesian Scholastic is thus a less monolithic phenomenon as one might think. In particular, it is not so much a movement, if one understands by that an organized consciousness and a programmatic approach, which inclines to replace one scientific system, one vision by another system or another worldview.'

system underwent rapid fragmentation at the hands of his earliest followers. And, like the long history of Aristotle reception, the spread of Cartesianism inevitably involved deviation from the opinions of its namesake. In Protestant Germany and Holland, just as much as in Catholic France, Descartes's legacy displayed a complex interaction of socio-cultural factors and the putative deliverances of the light of reason. Three strains of Descartes reception in mid-seventeenth-century Europe furnish clues for understanding Clauberg's version of domesticated Cartesianism. These are, first, the attraction of Cartesian natural philosophy for medicine; second, a methodological conservatism which favored the retention of Aristotelian logic in the universities; and third, the need to bring Cartesian metaphysics to bear on theological questions.

As scholars have noted, in European academia Cartesianism made its most successful early forays in natural philosophy and medicine.[49] This fact should have met with Descartes's approval, for the application of corpuscular physics to medicine was among his most important philosophical ends: 'the principal aim of my studies has been the conservation of health.'[50] Descartes's mechanistic hypothesis of the human body as a hydraulic machine was received in the context of medical advances originating in the famed Paduan school in the sixteenth century. The corpuscular account of matter and the quantitative analysis of motion offered deeper cosmological foundations for the new medical research, from Andrea Vesalius's emendations of the Galenic theory of fluids, to William Harvey's model of the circulation of blood, to Franz de le Boë's chemical theory of digestion. By the late seventeenth century, doctors had situated Cartesian natural philosophy within medical research in the faculties at Louvain, Bern, Marburg, Halle, and Leiden.[51] It was Duisburg's doctors of medicine,

---

[49] Trevisani, *Descartes in Germania*, 16, identifies the promise of Cartesian mechanics for medicine as a key aspect of Descartes-reception: 'The corpuscular theory and the theory of motion symbolizes the best fruit of Descartes's thought, just as Sylvius' theory of digestion represents the best in biological research of the century.' And Schmaltz, *Cartesianisms*, 228: 'Though in the eighteenth century it was the engagement with Newtonian physics that was most prominent in the disputes over Cartesianism, initially issues concerning Cartesian medicine played an important role in the reception of Descartes.'

[50] Letter to Cavendish, October 1645, AT IV.329, CSMK 173–174. For the importance of medicine for Descartes's physics, see Thomas Steele Hall, 'Introduction', in *Treatise of Man,* ed. Thomas Steele Hall (Cambridge, 1974); Gary Hatfield, 'Descartes' Physiology and its Relation to his Psychology', in *Cambridge Companion to Descartes,* ed. John Cottingham (Cambridge, 1992), 335–370; Steven Shapin, 'Descartes the Doctor: Rationalism and Its Therapies', *British Journal for the History of Science* 33 (2000), 131–154; Annie Bitbol-Hespériès, 'Cartesian Physiology', in *Descartes' Natural Philosophy,* eds. Stephen Gaukroger, John Schuster, and John Sutton (London and New York, 2000), 349–382; Vincent Aucante, *La philosophie médicale de Descartes* (Paris, 2006).

[51] Bitbol-Hespériès, 'Cartesian Physiology', 375–377.

however, who paved the way for the second generation of Cartesian doctors in German universities such as Johann Jakob Waldschmidt (1644–1687) at Marburg, and Friedrich Hoffmann (1660–1742) at Halle.[52] Clauberg, while not himself a medical doctor, promoted the cultivation of Cartesian medicine in his influential capacities as doctor of theology and rector of the university.

At the same time, Clauberg's interest in Descartes extends beyond medicine to metaphysics. Unlike medical profesors in Frankfurt or Bern, who may have been content or compelled to bracket the more tendentious aspects of Descartes's system from those relevant to anatomy and physiology, Clauberg aspires to display the coherence of the system as a whole and to show how Cartesian mechanics and medicine are securely grounded in his metaphysics. In the context of Reformed learning, Clauberg's interest in Cartesian natural philosophy could reasonably be seen as a break from prevailing trends. Disaffection with Aristotle had already become widespread well before Descartes appeared on the scene, and Reformed authors in the first half of the seventeenth century had entertained several rivals to Aristotelian physics. Alsted's *Encyclopedia* gives an indication of some of these alternatives. He lists a Mosaic physics based on Genesis, a Rabbinical option founded on the Kabbala, an alchemical framework, and a 'poetical' physics consisting of interpretations of classical mythology.[53] None of these, however, are Clauberg's projects. For him, the true promise of Descartes's physics rests in its presentation of a systematic alternative to the study of nature that is not founded on speculative readings of scriptures or mythologies. But, if this is right, Clauberg's reliance on Aristotelian concepts appears even more puzzling. Despite enjoying relatively wide latitude for innovation in his institutional context, Clauberg nevertheless subordinates Cartesian physics to an orthodox metaphysical scheme, one which, while not founded in scriptural or magical traditions, remained

---

[52] See Trevisani, *Descartes in Germania*, chs. 2–3, for the introduction of Cartesian medicine in Duisburg's medical faculty.

[53] Hotson, *Alsted*, 36. Among the representatives of Mosaic physics at this time is Comenius, who develops in *Physicae ad lumen divinum reformatae* (1633) an account of nature rooted in a literalist reading of the Bible. See Ann Blair, 'Mosaic Physics and the Search for a Pious Natural Philosophy in the Late Renaissance', *Isis* 91 (2000), 32–58, for a study of Comenius' version of sacred physics. She notes the explicitly anti-Aristotelian motivations behind the genre: 'The specific expressions 'pious philosophy' and 'Christian philosophy,' however, became current in the Renaissance to designate philosophies opposed to Aristotelianism' (34). Alchemical and magical theories of nature also experience a revival in this time with authors such as Giordano Bruno (1548–1600), Michael Maier (1568–1622), and Robert Fludd (1574–1637). Frances Yates, *The Rosicrucian Enlightenment* (Trowbridge, 1972), 111–113, credits Marin Mersenne with having cleared the way for the rise of the Cartesian option through sustained attacks on Mosaic, Kabbalistic, hermetical, and magical approaches in natural philosophy.

vitalist at its core. Clauberg's systematic target, one gets the impression, is larger than natural philosophy, for which he returns to Aristotle.

A second explanation of Clauberg's continued reliance on tradition appeals to the pragmatic demands of education. On this account, it would simply have been too burdensome to overturn existing modes of teaching and learning in favor of a new, as yet untested method. Earlier in the century, in fact, the prominent Heidelberg philosopher and theologian Bartholomaeus Keckermann had defended an attitude of methodological conservatism on pedagogical grounds. Despite being a heterodox thinker on many issues, Keckermann upheld the use of scholastic methods in his textbooks for the reason that, '[it is] better to teach methodically ordered traditional positions, even if erroneous and questionable, than as yet unmethodized new theories, even if true.'[54] Clauberg, one suspects, might likewise have recognized the pragmatic value of pouring new wine in old bottles. Indeed, it is for such reasons that he defends the dry pedantry of his *Paraphrasis in meditationes cartesii*. While praising the *Meditations* as the worthiest (*dignissimis*) of all of Descartes's works, Clauberg acknowledges the critics' charges that its unusual method and structure render it obscure. To remedy the situation, he proposes to make Descartes's arguments more accessible by departing from the order and style of the original and adjusting it for use in the schools (*ad scholarum usum magis accommodato*).[55]

Methodological reasons, thus, appear as motives behind the apparent continuity with school philosophy of at least some of Clauberg's work. Yet, this cannot be the entire story either. For one thing, a great part of Descartes's philosophical legacy rests on his having provided a *systematic* alternative to scholastic orthodoxy. It was indeed common among Keckermann's generation of professors to weigh the substantive shortcomings of Aristotelian natural philosophy against the pedagogical ease of teaching a system of nature with well-elaborated cosmological foundations. But, as we have seen, by Clauberg's own reckoning, the appeal of Cartesian physics lies in its being an equally well-ordered, yet simpler and potentially more fruitful, alternative to the Aristotelian.[56] Despite this opinion, he persists with interpreting Cartesian physical concepts in Aristotelian language. While there is certainly evidence for a form of

[54] Cited in John Gascoigne, 'A Reappraisal of the Role of the Universities in the Scientific Revolution', in *Reappraisals of the Scientific Revolution*, eds. Robert S. Westman and David C. Lindberg (Cambridge, 1990), 214. For Keckermann's 'methodical Peripateticism' see Leinsle, *Ding und Methode*, 274–280, and Hotson, *Alsted*, 29–32.

[55] *Paraphrasis*, Praefatio ad lectorem, OO I.346.

[56] For this point, see Gascoigne, 'Reappraisal', 215–216.

methodological conservatism in Clauberg in keeping with earlier Calvinist professors, it sits uneasily with his modernizing aspirations.

The urgency of theological dogmatics has been offered as another possible explanation for Clauberg's adherence to tradition and, in particular, for his translation of Descartes into the idiom of Protestant school theology. In his path-breaking work, Bohatec submitted that the '*cartesianische Scholastik*' movement originated in a felt need to bring Descartes's ideas to bear upon theological debates current in seventeenth-century Germany.[57] His view suggests that any new philosophical system could only have entered German academic discourse by proving its relevance to the most divisive theological issues of the time. Given the long history of Aristotle's involvement in Christian theology, which persisted in Protestant metaphysics in the seventeenth century, it was inevitable that Descartes's novelties would only find an attenuated role in religious polemics, as supplementing, rather than supplanting, traditional modes of argument. On Bohatec's proposal, Clauberg's primary interest lay in doctrinal issues of German Protestantism, and the wider *cartesianische Scholastik* phenomenon to which he belonged should principally be regarded as an 'apology for conservatism and orthodoxy.'[58]

That the theological context was important to the reception of Descartes in Germany cannot be denied. This feature of early Cartesianism is also unexceptional—it resembles, for instance, the involvement of Cartesianism in disputes between Jansenists and Jesuits in France.[59] But, for our purposes, what bears emphasis is the particular conception of theology's relation to philosophy which Clauberg attributed to Descartes. This, as we saw in the previous section, was largely negative. Clauberg highlights a greater separation of philosophy and theology as an important virtue of Descartes's system. He interprets Descartes's restrictions on the involvement of natural reason in matters of faith as a demand for a minimalist rational theology: only as much appeal to God is legitimate as is needed for the possibility of certainty in knowledge of nature. Thus, for example, Clauberg embraces Descartes's invocation of God as the ground of the conservation of motion in the universe, an assumption needed for a realist interpretation of his physics, together with his admonition against seeking specific divine intentions in natural phenomena. But, unlike dogmatic theologians in both the Lutheran and Calvinist camps, Clauberg neither develops a full-fledged rational theology nor pronounces on important issues such as the interpretation of the Eucharist or the doctrine of

---

[57] Bohatec, *cartesianische Scholastik*, 4–5.   [58] Bohatec, *cartesianische Scholastik*, 20.
[59] See Tad Schmaltz, 'What Has Cartesianism to Do with Jansenism?' *Journal of the History of Ideas* 60 (1999), 37–56.

predestination. Responding in *Initiatio philosophi* (1655) to two of Descartes's theological critics, the Herborn professor Cyriacus Lentulus and the Leiden professor Jacob Revius, Clauberg praises Descartes's restrained treatment of theological matters both for its stance of intellectual humility and its being more conducive to piety.[60] In Descartes's separation of the domains of faith and reason, Clauberg would have found a view friendly to his own school of Calvinism, namely Cocceian federalism, with its emphasis on piety and suspicion of theological speculation.

Disentangling philosophy from school theology, in fact, was a goal Clauberg shared not only with Descartes but also with his teacher de Raey and with his colleagues Wittich and Hundius.[61] Clauberg's programmatic interest in the autonomy of philosophy from theology and, consequently, of the arts curriculum from the concerns of the theological faculty, cuts against Bohatec's opinion that Clauberg, and the German Cartesian Scholastic movement generally, proceeded from a perceived need to bring Descartes to bear positively on theological issues. Indeed, arts teaching in the first ten years of the University of Duisburg followed the humanist tradition. It combined an emphasis on classical philology, rhetoric, and a virtue theoretic orientation in ethics and politics with a studied avoidance of metaphysical topics commonly leveraged in theological discussions. The first chair of philosophy at Duisburg, Johann Schultingh (1630–1666, appointed 1655–1656), concentrated his teaching in rhetoric and classical literature. His successor, Johann Georg Graevius (1632–1703, appointed 1656–1658), was likewise known for philological and historical scholarship.[62] Given this relative disengagement of the Duisburg arts curriculum from the needs of doctrinal theology, Clauberg's positive metaphysical projects and his conciliatory natural philosophy should be understood independently of their significance for theology.

To be clear, I do not wish to suggest that theological concerns or motives of pedagogical convenience are entirely irrelevant for understanding Clauberg's blend of tradition and modernity. Still less should we expect to find a unique key which would cleanly unlock the various elements of Clauberg's system. As with any other *Rezeptionsgeschichte*, Descartes's legacy in seventeenth-century Germany is multi-faceted. It ought to be understood in terms of the social and institutional particularities of the time in addition to any generalities one might glimpse above the detail.

---

[60] *Defensio cartesiana* ch. V, OO II.955–959.

[61] De Raey, however, defended an even more radical separation, and in fact criticized Clauberg for leaving too much room for the intrusion of philosophical logic in the interpretation of Scripture; cf. Schmaltz, *Cartesianisms*, 77–83.

[62] Clauberg himself taught ethics and politics in the arts curriculum; see von Roden, *Duisburg Universität*, 222–224.

What I do wish to call attention to, however, is that one aspect of the German reception of Descartes has not been sufficiently appreciated: a sincere interest in recovering Aristotle and showing his harmony with Cartesianism. Clauberg stands in the early stages of a movement in German philosophy which aimed to unify a formal theory of being with a quantitative science of nature, as represented by Aristotle and Descartes respectively. In this movement, we may count Erhard Weigel (1625–1699) at Jena, Weigel's student Johann Christoph Sturm (1635–1703) at Altdorf, and, in a more advanced phase, Christian Wolff (1679–1754) at Halle. In the project of grounding the new natural science in a realist scheme of forms and essential powers, a conception of ontology borrowed from Aristotle plays a key role. Without discounting institutional and socio-logical reasons for the persistence of the Aristotelian tradition in even innovative German universities such as Duisburg, I propose that internal, philosophical reasons were also crucial for the continued relevance of Aristotle.[63]

Descartes, Aristotle, and a New School Philosophy

In concluding his defense of radical Cartesianism in *Unterschied*, Clauberg reveals his aspirations for an Aristotelianism purified of scholastic encrust-ations: 'I have contrasted [*entgegen gesetzet*] the Cartesian philosophy with the school philosophy, but not with the Aristotelian in and of itself…which in many basic respects agrees more with the Cartesian than with the school philosophy.'[64] Unlike many of the *novatores* at the time, for whom Aristotelianism and Scholasticism had become interchangeable labels for the common ills of academic learning, Clauberg aims to distinguish the two, and to retrieve the former for the project of constructing a new philo-sophical framework. We are naturally led to ask: what are these agreements between Descartes and Aristotle which Clauberg hopes to uncover? The systematic reason for Clauberg's synthesis of Descartes and Aristotle requires disambiguating three meanings of metaphysics in order to under-score Clauberg's interest in ontology as distinct from theology on the one hand, and from first philosophy on the other. Clauberg's ontology, or

---

[63] To this extent, I am in agreement with Pius Brosch, *Die Ontologie des Johannes Clauberg* (Greifswald, 1926), 9, that Clauberg deliberately bucked the anti-Aristotelian tendencies of his time.

[64] *Unterschied*, 65: 'Allein dieses muß ich noch einmahl dem Leser einschärffen, daß ich der Cartesianische philosophie der Schulphilosophie entgegen gesetzet, nit aber der Aristotelischen an und für sich selbst in massen beweißlich ist, daß diese in vielem haupt-stücken mehr mit der Cartesianischen als mit der Schulphilosophie übereinstimme.'

general theory of being, undergirds an objective science of created being, or natural philosophy.

Clauberg conceives ontology[65] as a *scientia Catholica,* a universal science which takes its subject matter as being *qua* being, or being considered apart from any particular thing or kind of thing.[66] The significance of this definition lies in its contrast with two other meanings of metaphysics available from Aristotle. In various places in the sprawling work which has come down to us under the title *Metaphysics*, Aristotle describes the object of the science as divine matters, thus as theology. But, in other places, it is to be a science of the principles requisite for knowledge in the special sciences such as biology or politics, a project Aristotle calls 'first philosophy'. These are apparently distinct from a third meaning, that of a science of being abstracted from all species of things, thus, of being insofar as it is being, or ontology.[67] Aristotle's attempts to define the sought-after, foundational discipline (which he never labels 'metaphysics') are equivocal. Even setting aside its meaning as a 'divine science' dealing with immaterial, unchangeable things—a meaning of great consequence for the development of medieval Scholasticism—it is unclear whether metaphysics is to be a general inquiry into being without reference to individual things or species of things, or whether it is instead to be a science of the special sciences, as general physics might stand with respect to mechanics or statics.[68]

In *Metaphysica de ente*, at any rate, Clauberg identifies the third of these senses, ontology, as its topic. With Clauberg, ontology gains currency as

---

[65] Clauberg is not the first to use the term 'ontology'. As early as 1606 Jacob Lorhard had used the term in his *Ogdoas Scholastica* as synonymous with 'metaphysics'. For a history of the origin of the term, see José Ferrater Mora, 'On the Early History of 'Ontology', *Philosophy and Phenomenological Research* 24 (1963), 36–47.

[66] *Met. de ente*, §1, OO I.283.

[67] *Met.* I.2 (Alpha) 982b29–983a12: 'For the science which it would be most meet for God to have is a divine science, and so is any science that deals with divine objects; and this science [i.e. metaphysics] alone has both these qualities.' And in *Met.* IV.2 (Gamma) 1003b19–1003b22, Aristotle describes metaphysics in the sense of ontology: 'Now for every class of things, as there is one perception, so there is one science, as for instance grammar, being one science, investigates all articulate sounds. Therefore to investigate all the species of being *qua* being, is the work of a science which is generically one.' A third sense, labeled 'first philosophy', in *Met.* IV.2 (Gamma) 1004a2–a9: 'And there are as many parts of philosophy as there are kinds of substance, so that there must necessarily be among them a first philosophy and one which follows this.' In *Met.* VI.1 (Epsilon) 1026a28–33, first philosophy seems to be synonymous with the science of being *qua* being. Aristotle's works are cited by title, book, chapter, and Bekker numbers. Translations are from *The Complete Works of Aristotle*, 2 vols., ed. Jonathan Barnes (Princeton, NJ, 1984).

[68] See Charles H. Lohr, 'Metaphysics', in *The Cambridge History of Renaissance Philosophy*, eds. Charles B. Schmitt, Quentin Skinner, Eckhard Kessler, and Jill Kraye (Cambridge, 1988), 537–638, for a history of the problem of defining metaphysics in the Medieval and Renaissance periods.

As early as 1606 Jacob Lorhard had used the term in his Ogdoas Scholastica as synonymous with 'metaphysics'.

general metaphysics, a science of the common predicates of being applied univocally to corporeal and incorporeal, to finite and infinite beings. He aims for a purity of ontology which surpasses that of Descartes's conception of first philosophy as the doctrine of the first known beings. Descartes's meditations on *prima philosophia* are directed toward knowledge of God and the immortality of the soul, as he makes clear in the dedicatory letter to the doctors of the Sorbonne.[69] In the Preface to the Reader to the Latin edition of the *Meditations*, Descartes equates treating the topics of God and the human mind with undertaking the 'whole of first philosophy'.[70] While modern scholars have sometimes emphasized the natural scientific motives of Descartes's *Meditations*, to a contemporary reader concerned to distinguish ontology from first philosophy, Descartes's prefatory remarks about the starting point of his philosophy could have suggested a conflation of two distinct subject matters.[71] In the terminology that would become standard in the next century, Descartes's conception of first philosophy could appear to run together the special metaphysics of psychology, cosmology, and theology with a general metaphysics of categories and principles. For a reader such as Clauberg, the science of ontology ought to be a universal discipline concerned with an analysis of being without regard to problems specific to uncreated as opposed to created, spiritual as opposed to material being. The being and attributes of God, the human mind, or the physical world are, for Clauberg, further topics to be treated under their distinct suppositions.[72] Ontology aspires to a plane of intelligibility unconditioned by, for instance, possible experience or the indubitable consciousness of one's own existence. It is a science of the categories of discursive thought prior to Cartesian first philosophy as an introduction to substantive metaphysics. As such, it is intended to furnish a common conceptual framework for discourse about any domain of reality. Jean École has described this feature of *Metaphysica de ente* as an attempt to 'secularize' ontology.[73] In the history of Aristotelianism, we might add that Clauberg's ontology represents also the recovery of a secularized Aristotle.

---

[69] *Meditations on First Philosophy*, AT VII.1, CSM II.3.

[70] *Meditations on First Philosophy*, AT VII.9, CSM II.8 (translation modified).

[71] An oft-cited piece of evidence for the primacy of natural science over metaphysics in Descartes comes from his remark to Marin Mersenne that his *Meditations* contain 'all the principles of my physics' (28 January, 1641, AT III.397–398, CSMK 173).

[72] In the Prolegomena to *Metaphysica de ente*, Clauberg pointedly distinguishes 'theosophia' or 'theologia' from 'ontosophia' or 'ontologia', the former being a special science of God and the latter as 'going over being in general' (*circa ens in genere versatur*) (OO I.281).

[73] 'La place de la *Metaphysica de Ente, Quae Rectius Ontosophia* dans l'histoire de l'ontologie et sa reception chez Christian Wolff', in *Johannes Clauberg (1622–1665) and Cartesian Philosophy in the Seventeenth Century*, ed. Theo Verbeek (Dordrecht, 1999), 66.

Aristotle's theory of categories provides Clauberg with the basis for a general concept of reality under which Descartes's novel approach to the concepts of God and the human soul can be treated. *Ontosophia*, thus, brings Descartes's notion of substance under a superstructure of possible being, or whatever can be the object of rational discourse. Clauberg identifies three significations of the term *ens*. In its most general signification, 'being is whatever can be thought or said', which includes discourse about non-being (*nihil*) as well as chimeras.[74] As Clauberg suggests with his examples, it is this sense of being that is expressed in the dialecticians' term 'theme' (*thema*) and is even sometimes meant by philosophers when they use the term *ens* without further specification.[75] In its widest range, the concept '*ens*' allows Clauberg to accommodate, and go beyond, a Cartesian identification of being with possible knowledge. For Clauberg, unlike Descartes, even non-being can be thought, even though it does not have positive, objective reality. Descartes himself, as Clauberg surely knew, objects to Burman that an 'idea of nothing is purely negative, and can hardly be called an idea.'[76] By contrast, Clauberg is willing to include in the scope of *ens* whatever can become the subject of rational discourse: fictitious entities, conventional objects of history or geography such as the 'the Middle Ages' or 'the Baltic Sea', and even *nihil*. Being extends, one might say, to the bounds of discursivity, not just to the bounds of possible objects of knowledge.

Narrowing the semantic range, Clauberg approaches the Cartesian conception of knowable reality. In his second sense, being signifies something (*aliquid*) that provides determinate content for thought, or that which does not involve logical contradictions such as 'four-sided circle' or 'leaden gold-coin'.[77] The domain of determinate being thus arises from a logical opposition between positive reality and what is purely privative, an opposition in which lies also the origin of the principle of contradiction. *Aliquid* excludes mere beings of reason (*entia rationis*) and concerns those contents which are objects of logical operations such as definition, division, or inference.[78] It is this sense of being that is proper to the mathematical sciences of arithmetic and geometry when, for example, one

---

[74] *Met. de ente*, §6, OO I.283: 'Ens est quicquid quovis modo est, cogitari ac dici potest. Alles was nur gedacht und gesagt werden kan. Ita *dico* Nihil, & cum dico *cogito*, *est* illud in intellectu meo.'

[75] As Strazzoni, 'Foundation of Early Modern Science', 67, notes, in the *Logica vetus et nova*, Clauberg identifies ideas with *themata*, either simple or complex propositions. Being in the most general sense, thus, can exclude from its sphere concrete objects in a narrower sense.

[76] 'Conversation with Burman', AT V.153, CSMK 338.

[77] *Met. de ente*, §38, OO I.289.   [78] *Met. de ente*, §40, OO I.289.

contemplates the essence of a triangle or a chiliagon and discovers their immutable properties. For Clauberg, as for Descartes, there are primary truths which can be known with certainty simply by considering the meanings of the terms in which they are expressed, or by reducing propositions to identity statements. *Aliquid* signifies the domain of determinate possibilities. Thus, it is narrower than the sphere of the merely thinkable and sayable, yet broader than that of the actual.

Finally, in its strictest sense (*magis propria significatione*), being coincides with Descartes's idea of substantial reality. In this third Claubergian sense, being signifies thing (*res*) or real being (*ens reale*), as when one thinks of a substance as distinct from its modes, such as a mind distinguished from its faculty of thought, or a body from its extension.[79] Clauberg defines substance in agreement with the Aristotelian and Cartesian senses of something which is not lacking for its existence and is the subject of accidents.[80] In its meaning as *res* or *substantia*, being applies to the essences of both created and changeable, and uncreated and unchangeable substances. It thus captures the subject matter of the sciences of nature on the one hand and of theology on the other.[81] Under this threefold understanding of the core concept of general metaphysics, and especially under its third sense as substantial being, Clauberg builds a familiar apparatus of the common attributes of beings such as essence and existence, sameness and difference, whole and part, truth and falsity, and goodness and evil, as well as their relational attributes such as cause and effect and sign and signified. While abstracting away from every special discipline, Clauberg's *ontosophia* aims to serve as a universal conceptual scheme for each one of them, whether belonging to the book of material nature or to the book of the human mind. Indeed, it leaves open the possibility of a science of a perfect or infinite mind, or a rational theology, of a substance in the most proper sense insofar as God is considered as the absolutely self-sufficient source of all reality.[82]

Yet, ontology does not demand the elaboration of a divine science any more than it compels the articulation of a science of nature. Clauberg's actual projects in the latter domain and conspicuous silence on the former indicate a systematic upshot of this way of relating Descartes's substance-mode metaphysics with Aristotelian category theory. Using Clauberg's

[79] *Met. de ente*, §42, OO I.290.

[80] *Met. de ente*, §44, OO I.290: '*Substantiae*, id est, rei quae ita existit, ut aliquo ad existendum subjecto non indigeat, opponitur *Accidens*, quod in alio existit, tanquam in subjecto.'

[81] *Met. de ente*, §45, OO I.290.

[82] *Met. de ente*, §164, OO I.310: 'Deo multo magis definitio & nomen adeoque idea Substantiae convenit, quam Creaturae.'

framework, one may certainly choose to undertake a special metaphysics of rational theology. But, within the same conceptual scheme, one may instead direct one's energies to physical science or psychological science, as Clauberg does in his *Disputationes physicae,* for instance. For his part, what Clauberg stresses as the positive value of Cartesianism has to do with its application to the study of nature and of the human mind. Its negative value consists in its restrictions on rational theology to only as much as is required to support first principles relevant to the study of creatures. To the extent that a broadly Aristotelian framework for understanding nature as an ordered, changeable reality can accommodate the principles of Cartesian science, we can make sense of Clauberg's enigmatic claim that Aristotle and Descartes have more in common than meets the eye. Indeed, his explication of Cartesian science in Aristotelian terms initiates a fruitful program in German natural philosophy of reinterpreting the new, quantitative science of nature under the strongly objectivist character of his ontology. For Clauberg, the basic categories of physical nature are not drawn from a divine guarantee of the veracity of clear and distinct perceptions delivered to an indubitably existing self but rather from a primitive opposition between being (*ens*) and non-being (*nihil*). The objectivity conferred by the discovery of the nature of the self and the certainty of its ideas lies at a further remove from the absolute objectivity lent by a general conception of being founded upon the principle of contradiction. This Aristotelian ontological scheme, as Trevisani rightly notes, has as its principal goal the secure development of natural science in the context of the arts curriculum and in medicine, unimpeded by theological considerations.[83]

To be sure, the envisioned marriage of Descartes and Aristotle is not without philosophical problems. As an objective science of nature considered as a structured totality, Clauberg's ontology presumes the reality of forms and qualities in the created world. We can treat the problem of the forms of natural bodies, of the variety of species commonly found in *res extensa*, as a lens through which the putative harmony of Aristotle and Descartes gets strained. Whereas Descartes prefers to characterize matter geometrically in terms of quantitative extension, Clauberg readily identifies extension with the quality of impenetrability borrowed from Aristotelian physics. Extension as impenetrability becomes synonymous here with *materia prima* which, in scholastic physics, designates the first requisite to constitute a body as a substance. *Materia secunda*, by contrast, is that which is the subject of accidents of corporeal substances and, thus,

---

[83] Trevisani, *Descartes in Germania*, 90.

designates matter together with a definite form or species.[84] It is controversial, to say the least, whether such an interpretation of extension would be acceptable to Descartes, who objects vigorously to the Aristotelian treatment of bodies as unities of matter and structured sets of qualities, or substantial forms, which determine them as instances of oaks or swallows or any other natural kind. While Clauberg agrees with Descartes's charge that substantial forms are unintelligible, occult notions, he nonetheless remains committed to the reality of species in virtue of the existence of individuals of those kinds.[85] The Aristotelian principle that natural reality is organized into fixed species characterized by stable, real qualities and causal relations continues to underpin Clauberg's interpretation of Descartes's quantitative conception of corporeal being.[86] The problem of corporeal forms, or of how the concept of body considered essentially as continuous quantity could be differentiated into objective species forms, was never fully resolved by Descartes. Three-dimensional, movable extension was to be the essence of all bodies, while the sensible qualities associated with them were conceived as relational properties partially dependent upon suitably positioned human observers. In Descartes's picture, since all bodies, from trees to birds to chairs, are characterizable as differently shaped parcels of geometrical extension, it is difficult to treat oaks and swallows as essentially distinct kinds of bodies, their distinct, characteristic appearances notwithstanding.

Clauberg was only the first of German philosophers of the early modern period to appeal to Aristotle's concepts of form and matter to address problems in Descartes's cosmology. Attempts to bring Aristotle to bear on Descartes, and vice versa, assumed various guises, of which space permits me to offer only the briefest of sketches. Erhard Weigel, professor at Jena, for instance, takes a rather different interpretation of Cartesian extension. Where Clauberg begins with an identification of quantitative extension with the quality of impenetrability, Weigel instead conceives Cartesian extension itself as prime matter, and form as a passive modification of the latter. But extension, for Weigel, is not an independently existing substance at all. Instead, extension, for him, is identical to space considered as an aptitude (*aptitudo*) of the mind to receive the forms of finite things.[87]

---

[84] *Disp. phys.* IV, §§15–17, OO I.58.   [85] *Disp. phys.* XII, §§3–4, OO I.80.

[86] See Christia Mercer, 'Johann Clauberg, Corporeal Substance, and the German Response', in *Johannes Clauberg (1622–1665) and Cartesian Philosophy in the Seventeenth Century*, ed. Theo Verbeek (Dordrecht, 1999), 147–159, for a more detailed treatment of Clauberg's response to the problem of corporeal substances in Descartes.

[87] *Philosophia mathematica, Theologia naturalis solida* (Jena, 1693), 11: 'Patet itaque, quod Spatium utrumque veluti materialiter (substantialiter) sit nihil; sed formaliter sit aptitudo conceptibilis'.

Weigel, like Clauberg, remains committed to the reality of universal species of bodies. But, unlike Clauberg, his path to the reality of forms is an
idealistic one grounded ultimately in God's mind as the source of the
mathematical conceptions received in human minds.[88] Weigel's student
Johann Christoph Sturm, professor at Altdorf, adopts a similarly conciliatory stance between Descartes and Aristotle through creative reinterpret-
ations of both. Sturm's physics begins with the Aristotelian principles of
form, matter, and privation, but also incorporates distinctively Cartesian
theses such as a rejection of final causes in physics and an occasionalist
model of causation.[89] He construes the actuality-conferring substantial
forms and real qualities of the Latin Aristotelian tradition as heuristics, or
subjective means for conceiving changes in bodies but not as constituting
the essences of material substances. Aristotle's prime matter, for Sturm, is,
remarkably, not merely potential being but actual being, which he identifies with the concept of body, a position that should be acceptable to
neither Aristotle nor Descartes.[90] By the time Christian Wolff would
compose his treatises on physics and cosmology in the 1720s and 1730s,
such collocation of Aristotelian and Cartesian ideas in German university
philosophy had become the norm rather a sign of innovation. Clauberg can
justly be seen as standing at the origin of a movement of furnishing general
ontological foundations to Cartesian physics, of underlaying Descartes's
theological and psychological points of departure with a general theory
of being.

Clauberg A Cartesio-Scholastic?

Undeniably, Clauberg and those in his milieu drew on elements of
Cartesian as well as of Aristotelian thought. A century ago, this circum-
stance led Bohatec to coin the label *cartesianische Scholastik* to describe this
phenomenon in seventeenth-century German universities. But, while the
label may render a hermeneutical convenience for the purposes of situating Clauberg within larger intellectual currents of the seventeenth century,
it becomes less useful once we treat him seriously as a thinker in his own
right. If we wish to read Clauberg for his substantive philosophical views
rather than as an instance of an intellectual-historical type, approaching
his texts as a mere reconciliation between Aristotle and Descartes is

---

[88] Weigel, *Philosophia mathematica*, 52.
[89] *Physica conciliatricis* (Nürnberg, 1687), 9–10; 11–12.
[90] See Bohatec, *cartesianische Scholastik*, 130–34.

misleading.[91] For one thing, his thought contains aspects of not just Descartes and Aristotle but a host of other cultural and intellectual movements of the period. For another, it deviates in crucial respects from each thinker. Clauberg rejects, for instance, the hylomorphist theory of substance central to Aristotle and also undermines the foundational status of Descartes's *cogito*. By focusing on how well Clauberg's thought approximates that of other authors, we risk losing sight of his distinct philosophical ends.

More importantly, the 'Cartesio-Scholastic' label suggests the kind of lack of originality and systematicity connoted by the much-abused term 'eclectic'. The latter is sometimes applied not just to Clauberg but also to the larger context of philosophy in seventeenth- and eighteenth-century German universities.[92] Designating an author 'eclectic' typically implies their interest in summarizing the views of past thinkers, a polemical position of non-sectarianism, or an intellectual attitude of non-dogmatism. Each of these are modes of being fragmented or derivative. A thorough examination of the label 'eclectic', whether as an actors' category or as an analytic one, would take us too far afield. What I hope to have communicated in this essay is that Clauberg's uses of Descartes and Aristotle defy treating his thought as eclectical in these senses. He embraces neither figure simply for polemical ends or for the sake of signaling an intellectual attitude. He was neither a mere apologist for institutional tradition nor an uncritical importer of exotic views. Rather, he had systematic motivations of providing a new conception of nature as divided into radically distinct mental and physical domains with unified, objective foundations which are neither ideal nor material but cognitively prior to both. Clauberg initiates a project in German universities of the late-seventeenth and early-eighteenth centuries of constructing a common ontological framework, Aristotelian in origins, for the new philosophy of nature. This project is both distinctive in the history of early modern philosophy and self-consciously systematic. We should view its exponents, from Clauberg to Wolff, as representing an original current of modern thought rather than as holdovers from an earlier time, or as epigones of a few inspired minds such as Descartes or Leibniz (or Aristotle). Such an approach would reveal the still-understudied context of early modern German university philosophy as not simply a repository of medieval orthodoxy but rather

---

[91] Massimiliano Savini, *Johannes Clauberg: Methodus cartesiana et ontologie* (Paris, 2011), 9–10, notes this feature of Clauberg scholarship and advocates with his work a different approach.

[92] École, 'La place', 69; Helmut Holzhey, 'Philosophie als Eklektik', *Studia Leibnitiana* 15 (1983), 19–29; Ulrich Johannes Schneider, 'Eclecticism Rediscovered', *Journal of the History of Ideas* 59 (1998), 173–182.

as a site of innovative responses to emerging problems of European modernity.[93]

Deparment of Philosophy
Concordia University
nabeel.hamid@concordia.ca

[93] I would like to thank audiences at the Oxford Seminar in Early Modern Philosophy at Mansfield College, March 13–14, and at the conference, 'Teaching the New Science: The Role of Academia in the Scientific Revolution', at the University of Groningen, June 15–17, 2017. For helpful questions and comments, I especially wish to thank Paul Lodge, Julia Borcherding, Eric Schliesser, Julie Klein, Lisa Shapiro, Roger Ariew, Helen Hattab, Stefan Heßbrüggen-Walter, Andrea Sangiacomo, Tad Schmaltz, Gary Hatfield, Karen Detlefsen, Devin Curry, and an anonymous referee for *History of Universities*.

Methods of Teaching or Discovery? Analysis and Synthesis from Zabarella to Spinoza

Helen Hattab

Introduction

Nowadays we draw a sharp line between the context of discovery and the context of justification. In teaching the sciences, the context of discovery is treated as irrelevant. For instance, high school students never learn by what insights and processes of reasoning Isaac Newton came to discover his laws of motion. Even at the higher levels of education, the theoretical justification of these laws is neatly separated from the historical method by which Newton came to discover and prove them. But for proponents of new sciences in the seventeenth century, matters are not this clear cut. Early proponents, like Francis Bacon, Galileo Galilei, and René Descartes were cognizant of the fact that in advancing new philosophies of nature they were also introducing new methods and approaches to investigating nature. Hence they eschewed communicating their discoveries by the standard Scholastic Aristotelian teaching methods of textual commentary and syllogistic disputation of questions. Instead they attempted to instruct their readers by leading them through their own thought processes by means of aphorisms, dialogues, autobiographies, and even fables. By the mid-seventeenth century, however, proponents of highly controversial philosophies were appropriating more familiar didactic genres to convey their radical doctrines. Most notably, the first book of Thomas Hobbes's *De Corpore* follows the familiar order of topics of standard Scholastic Aristotelian logic textbooks, and Benedict de Spinoza's *Ethics* famously emulates Euclid's *Elements*, by presenting astounding conclusions about nature, substance, and extension *more geometrico*.

Helen Hattab, *Methods of Teaching or Discovery? Analysis and Synthesis from Zabarella to Spinoza* In: *History of Universities*. Edited by: Mordechai Feingold, Oxford University Press (2021). © Oxford University Press.
DOI: 10.1093/oso/9780192893833.003.0004

The question arises whether these appropriations of more familiar teaching formats merely concede the need to lower the resistance of potentially hostile readers and students by repackaging new ideas in more familiar formats, or whether there is also a shift in the method of inquiry and discovery that accompanies this revival of older means of justification. The question is especially difficult to answer with respect to Spinoza's *Ethics,* inspiring a long-standing debate among scholars regarding whether the geometrical method of synthesis Spinoza employs is intended as a method for demonstrating and arriving at new truths or merely as a form of presentation that bears no relation to Spinoza's method of philosophical inquiry. This essay aims not so much to definitively answer this question, as to shed light on the issue through an examination of previous accounts of the methods of synthesis and analysis found in philosophers of Spinoza's context. I begin with Jacopo Zabarella's influential Scholastic Aristotelian account before making connections between Spinoza's method in the *Treatise on the Emendation of the Intellect* (henceforth TIE) and the views of three philosophers that form part of his immediate intellectual context, namely, Franco Burgersdijk, René Descartes, and Thomas Hobbes.

Zabarella on method

Zabarella's logical works were reprinted throughout Europe, and were much cited and paraphrased by philosophers at both Catholic and Protestant universities well into the seventeenth century. However, Zabarella spent his entire academic career, from student to professor, at Padua, and taught there first logic and then natural philosophy. The University of Padua was founded in 1222. By the sixteenth century it, along with the rest of the Veneto region, had emerged as the premier centre for the study of Aristotelianism, drawing students and physicians from all over Europe, including, as Suitner has recently documented, Antitrinitarian Reformers.[1] As Schmitt cautions, one must be careful not to overstate Padua's uniqueness, as there was a great deal of curricular similarity among renaissance Italian universities.[2] However, Schmitt also highlights that only Padua

---

[1] Riccarda Suitner, 'Radical Reformation and Medicine in the Late Renaissance: The Case of the University of Padua', *Nuncius* 31 (2016): 11–31.

[2] The universities at Pisa, Ferrara and Bologna had equally distinguished traditions in the fields of medicine and natural history, and by the 16th century, faculty at all Italian universities benefited from the new humanist translations of Greek texts as well as the writings of Averroes that became available in print in the Giunta edition of 1550–1552. Charles Schmitt, 'Aristotelianism in the Veneto', in Charles Schmitt, *The Aristotelian Tradition and Renaissance Universities* (London, 1984), 109–113.

combined all features that contributed to the success of renaissance Italian universities. As he puts it succinctly: 'The combination of distinguished philosophical medicine, a wide-ranging tradition of Aristotelian studies (covering the spectrum from Scotist metaphysics to the careful study of Averroes and to philological investigations of the Greek text), and a flourishing printing industry combined to make the Veneto the most important centre of Aristotelian studies in Italy.'[3]

Padua, like Bologna, also counted as one of the most renowned medical universities from the thirteenth to seventeenth centuries. Correspondingly, logic and philosophy were considered preparatory to medical studies proper. Although the mathematical arts, Greek and Latin literature, moral philosophy, and metaphysics were also taught, the core of education, institutionalized by the statutes of the University of Padua in the late fifteenth century, was logic, followed by natural philosophy, followed by medicine. Correspondingly, the typical career progression of the successful professor was from teaching logic, to teaching natural philosophy, and finally to teaching medicine. Medical professors were paid more and enjoyed a higher social status than philosophy professors, though philosophy was considered beneficial to medical studies, as well as important in its own right.[4] Finally, Padua counted several important mathematicians among its faculty, including Pietro Catena, Guiseppe Moleto, and Galileo Galilei himself. They not only lectured on the traditional topics of astronomy, geometry, and geography, but also optics, the *pseudo* Aristotelian questions on mechanics, anemography, hydrography, and military fortifications.[5] The institutional context may thus explain Zabarella's concern to account for the order found in Euclid's *Elements of Geometry*.

According to Zabarella's *De Methodis,* analysis and synthesis are methods for ordering knowledge so that it is more easily grasped and taught. Like other Aristotelians, Zabarella holds that synthesis proceeds from the more simple, i.e., from the universal or genus, to the species and from there to particular attributes of the object of knowledge. For instance, in teaching physics, one would proceed from the genus of motion, to the kinds of motions, and finally to their properties. Analysis, which was often attributed to practical disciplines, starts from the end to be accomplished and works its way back from there, to the means and finally to the starting points of the process of production. Analysis and synthesis are not, as commonly thought, methods of demonstration for Zabarella and should

[3] Ibid, 109.
[4] Charles Schmitt, 'Aristotle Among the Physicians', in *Reappraisals in Renaissance Thought*, ed. Charles Webster (London, 1989).
[5] Schmitt, 'Aristotelianism in the Veneto', 115.

not be confused with the resolutive and compositive phases associated with a type of proof known as the *regressus*.

In *De Methodis*, Zabarella aims to give an account not of method in mathematics or natural philosophy, but rather of the nature of method. He defines method in this broad sense as: 'an instrumental *habitus* of the intellect, which aids us in attaining knowledge of things.'[6] Next, Zabarella divides method, taken broadly, into order and method properly speaking. The task of method in the proper sense is to lead us from a known thing to knowledge of another, unknown thing, as when we are led from substantial change to knowledge of prime matter or, from eternal motion to knowledge of an eternal unmoved mover. The *regressus*, a particular form of scientific proof, falls under this second sense of method.[7] Extensive study of Zabarella's theory of the *regressus* has resulted in both comparisons and contrasts to the forms of demonstration used by Galileo Galilei, William Harvey, and René Descartes, but the relationship between early modern methods and the other branch of Zabarella's method is relatively understudied.[8] My focus in this paper will not be on the *regressus*.

The sense of 'method' that interests me in relation to the teaching of the new science is method as order. As Zabarella notes, method as order does not cause us to infer one thing from another, but rather arranges

---

[6] 'Ideo eam diximus esse habitum intellectus instrumentalem, quo ad rerum cognitionem consequendam iuuamur'. Jacopo Zabarella, *De Methodis*, in *Opera Logica* (Cologne, 1597) I.ii, 136.

[7] In his *Liber De Regressu*, Zabarella gives a rather succinct example, taken from the first book of Aristotle's *Physics*, of the three parts of the demonstrative *regressus*. The first is the resolutive phase, by which we deduce confused knowledge of the cause from our confused knowledge of the effect. The second phase consists in the mental consideration of the cause known confusedly, so as to know it distinctly. The third phase consists in composition, by which the effect is deduced from the cause, now known distinctly. In the example Zabarella takes from Book I of Aristotle's *Physics*, we start from our confused knowledge that there is a certain effect: the generation of a substance. We then reason back to the more fundamental principle, i.e., the cause of this generation. This is the *demonstratio quia* or τό ὅτι proof from what is more known to us to what is prior by nature. Jacopo Zabarella, *De Regressu*, in *Opera Logica* (Cologne, 1597), ch. iv, 484–86.

[8] Studies in connection with Galileo's and Descartes's methods include: William Wallace, 'Galileo's Regressive Methodology: Its Prelude and Its Sequel', in *Method and Order in Renaissance Philosophy of Nature*, eds. Daniel Di Liscia, Eckhard Kessler and Charlotte Methuen (Aldershot, 1997), 229–22; Benoît Timmermans, 'Descartes's Conception of Analysis', *Journal of the History of Ideas* 60 (1999): 433–47; J.N.Watkins, relying on Randall and one passage from Harvey's *On Generation of Animals* connects Harvey's method back to Zabarella's *regressus*. J.N. Watkins, *System of Ideas* (London, 1973), 64. This connection is, however, contradicted by more in-depth studies revealing that Fabricius, under whom Harvey studied medicine at Padua, drew heavily on Aristotle's biological writings in his method rather than Zabarella's writings on method. Andrew Cunningham, 'Fabricius and the 'Aristotle Project' in Anatomical Teaching and Research at Padua', in *The Medical Renaissance of the Sixteenth Century*, eds. A.Wear, R.K. French and I.M. Lonie (Cambridge, 1985), 211.

[*disponere*] the things to be treated, as when the order of teaching demands that we first discuss the heavens and then the elements. In other words, it arranges the parts of a discipline.[9] Order takes precedence because one must divide a discipline into parts, before one can articulate the method that will lead us from the known to the unknown that is sought within each part.[10] For example, one must first treat of living things in general, then each individual species of living thing; and finally seek methods to treat what is common to animals, to understand the nature of a particular animal and its accidents.[11]

Zabarella adds that one must not state that the order is made randomly without any reason and internally by our choice: there has to be some certain reason or certain, necessary norm by which the correct disposition and appropriate ordering is taken up.[12] At the same time, Zabarella denies earlier views that ordering must always proceed from one thing, either a principle, medium, or end, and that correspondingly, there are three types of order: compositive, definitive, and resolutive.[13] He thus rejects the view that traces back to Galen. Rather, Zabarella follows Averroes, claiming that the procedure for ordering the sciences and all disciplines is found not in the essence of the objects sought, but in the manner of knowing things that is best and easiest for us. When a science is ordered in one way rather than some other, it is so ordered because it shall be learned more easily and effectively this way, not because of a natural order that exists outside the mind.[14]

Next Zabarella addresses the problem of whether the proper order is always from the universal to the particular, as *per* Aristotle. Zabarella affirms this on the grounds that we always investigate the essence or nature

---

[9] Zabarella, *De Methodis*, I.iii, 139.

[10] Zabarella holds that one must treat of order first because it appears to be something more general, extending more widely than method, for it regards *scientia* as a whole and compares its parts. Method proper, by contrast, consists in the investigation of a single sought thing without any comparison to other parts of *scientia*. Zabarella, *De Methodis*, I.iii, 139.

[11] ' Zabarella, *De Methodis*, I.iii, 139.

[12] Zabarella, *De Methodis*, I.iv, 140. Following the distinction between order and method, Zabarella amends the common interpretation of the order of a discipline as an instrumental *habitus* or mental instrument, by means of which one is taught to appropriately arrange the parts of a doctrine.

[13] Zabarella, *De Methodis*, I.v, 140–141.

[14] He points out, if the suitable order within each discipline were found in the natural order of its objects, then the compositive order would be the only valid one since the simples and the principles of nature are prior by nature to the composites. Zabarella, *De Methodis*, I.vi, 142. However, the suitable order is the order by which we know more easily and more effectively, as seen by the fact that Aristotle often follows the resolutive order in his works (e.g., in Book VII of the *Metaphysics* and also the *De Anima* and *N.E.*). Zabarella, *De Methodis*, I.vi, 142. Nonetheless, sometimes a given order of learning will coincide with the natural order, which accounts for how some come to confuse the natural order with the order of knowing. Zabarella, *De Methodis*, I.vi, 144.

of a thing or its proper accidents. To know the nature of a thing we must know its species, and this is only possible once we know the nature of the genus. Likewise, we know the accidents of the species when we know the accidents of the genus. Therefore, the easiest and most effective order of learning is from knowledge of the genus, or the more universal, to the species and thence to accidents of the species.[15] This is the method of synthesis.

The Renaissance revival of Euclid's works presents a counter-example to this standard Aristotelian method of teaching. Most notably, the ordering of the books of Euclid's *Elements* does not conform to the proper order of teaching from universal to particular. As Zabarella points out, Euclid deals with lines and surfaces in the first four books of the *Elements* and only then turns to magnitude, taken broadly, in Book V. Euclid does not even give his definition of magnitude, taken broadly, in Book V, but simply states the names of some of the accidents of magnitude he will demonstrate. Zabarella characterizes the whole of Book V as being about the accidents of magnitude, taken broadly, without any mention of the substance and nature of magnitude. In other words, Euclid's *Elements* violate the proper synthetic order from the more universal to the less universal; from the nature of the genus to its accidents; and then onto the nature and accidents of the species.[16] To accommodate this apparent counter-example to the suitable order, Zabarella spells out two criteria one has to meet to dispense with the order from the most universal to the less universal:[17] the nature of the genus must be known *per se,* and hence not require explanation, and the accidents of the species cannot be species of the accidents of the genus.

In fact, mathematics meets both criteria. First, Zabarella points out, the subject treated by Euclid possesses magnitude, taken most broadly, but abstracted by the mind from every sensible thing. The nature of

---

[15] Zabarella, *De Methodis*, I.iii, 139.   [16] Zabarella, *De Methodis*, I.xiii, 156–57.

[17] In some cases, the property of the species being taught is also the species of the property of the genus. For example, motion away from the center of the earth is a property of a species of natural body known as light body. At the same time, motion away from the center of the earth is also a species of a property of the genus, the genus being natural body, with this kind of motion being a species of motion, a property of natural bodies. Zabarella reasons that in such cases, it is easier to learn that motion away from the center of the earth is a property of light bodies, if we first understand what natural bodies are (this is the genus); that motion is a property or accident of this genus; and that there are certain species of motion that are accidents particular to certain species of natural bodies. Then we can advance to understanding the nature of light bodies, as a species of this genus, and see that the species of motion belonging to them is motion away from the center of the earth. But there are other cases, where knowing the genus and its property will not make it easier to learn that a certain property belongs to a species. For example, heat is also a property of light bodies, but heat is not a species of the property of the genus, as heat is not a species of motion on the Aristotelian view (and presumably not of any other generic property). So for this case, the order of teaching need not begin with a treatment of the genus, its nature and accidents.

magnitude, taken broadly, need not be expressed as a definition because everyone knows that magnitude is that which is measured out, by something. When we define mathematical entities, our definitions are advanced as principles 'since they are heard and understood at the same time, and are known *per se*.'[18] This is because things like 'line' and 'surface' are simple accidents, so the declaration of merely the word suffices to signify the essence. In other words, in mathematics, nominal and essential definitions of the object coincide; thus, in mathematics, one has a perfect definition once one obtains a nominal definition. This view was shared by some seventeenth-century mathematicians, e.g., the Jesuit Josephus Blancanus, who claims that most mathematical definitions bear the advantage of being both nominal and essential definitions. Blancanus notes, 'when it is said that an equilateral triangle is one having three equal sides, at once you see the cause for both the name and the thing.'[19]

Blancanus's work is cited in Marin Mersenne's early publications, making it quite likely that both Descartes and Hobbes were exposed to Blancanus's mathematical theory, via the Mersenne circle. On this theory, the definitions of mathematical objects carry the distinct advantage that their names concurrently tell you how the object is caused. Consequently, one need not define in terms of genus and differentia to attain a full understanding of the object's nature, i.e., one need not first treat the genus to which a mathematical object belongs in order to understand its definition and demonstrate its properties from this definition. And this accounts for why the order of teaching and learning in mathematics need not proceed from most universal to the particular. In sum, to accommodate the case of Euclid's *Elements*, Zabarella introduces considerable flexibility as to the exact order that synthesis, the method for teaching theoretical matters, follows. In particular, he makes room for starting points other than genera in the synthetic ordering. This, in turn, allows proponents of the new science who reject Aristotelian universals, to nonetheless present their novel theories using the familiar method of synthesis.

Burgersdijk's adaptation of Zabarella

Zabarella's writings on method were incredibly influential and made their way into numerous Aristotelian textbooks on logic, including Bartholomeo Keckermann's *Systema Logicae* and Franco Burgersdijk's *Institutionum*

---

[18] Zabarella, *De Methodis*, I.xiv, 159.
[19] Josephus Blancanus, *De Mathematicarum Natura Dissertatio*, Appendix to *Aristotelis Loca Mathematica*, trans. Gyula Klima, in *Philosophy of Mathematics and Mathematical Practice in the Seventeenth Century*, ed. Paolo Mancosu (Oxford and New York, 1996), 181.

Logicarum Libri Duo, two widely-used works in the Protestant North. I will briefly lay out Burgersdijk's adaptation of Zabarella's influential views on method before turning to Descartes and Hobbes's uses of analysis and synthesis in relation to Spinoza's. Burgersdijk (1590–1635) was a Dutch Calvinist philosopher. He was appointed professor at the University of Leiden in 1620 where he first taught logic and physics, and then metaphysics.

The University of Leiden was established as a Calvinist academy in 1575 by the rebel government of William of Orange, at the heels of the Dutch revolt against Spanish rule. Initially its degrees were considered suspect, given that the established European universities were largely Catholic and sanctioned by pope and emperor. The humanist leanings of the early curators of the Academy of Leiden meant that, unlike the focus on Calvinist theology at its sister Academy in Geneva, the emphasis at Leiden was on wisdom. Any form of Calvinist theocracy was opposed.[20] Although founded as a Calvinist institution, the university statutes were soon revised, releasing all students but students of theology from taking an oath to adhere to Calvinist doctrine. The student body was correspondingly diverse, including Catholics, Jews, Socinians, and members of the Eastern Orthodox church. This policy of religious tolerance, combined with a series of strategic hires, probably contributed to the University of Leiden's growing reputation as one of the premier universities in seventeenth-century Europe (the University of Leiden hired renowned philologists Justus Lipsius and Josephus Justus Scaliger as research faculty, as well as the famous botanist Carolus Clusius).[21] In January 1597, just before the Toleration Edict at Nantes, King Henry IV of France granted his privilege to recognize degrees in philosophy and law from Leiden, thus securing the academy the status of an international university in Europe.[22] The fledgling academy at Leiden thus quickly established itself as the flagship university of the newly-founded Dutch Republic.[23]

The curriculum at Leiden was innovative in several respects. Owing to the initial humanist emphasis on wisdom, philosophy and philology were

[20] Willem Frijhoff, 'University, academia, Hochschule, college: Early modern perceptions and realities of European institutions of higher education' [abbreviation: 'University, academia'], In *Zwischen Konflikt und Kooperation: Praktiken der europäischen Gelehrtenkultur (12.-17. Jahrhundert),* eds. Jan-Hendryck de Boer, Marian Füssel and Jana Madlen Schütte, *Historische Forschungen Band 114* (Berlin 2016), 67–88, 76.

[21] Eduard Grant Ruestow, *Physics at Seventeenth and Eighteenth-Century Leiden* (The Hague, 1973), 4–6.

[22] Frijhoff, 'University, academia', 77.

[23] Eduard Grant Ruestow, *Physics at Seventeenth and Eighteenth-Century Leiden* (The Hague, 1973), 2–3. Given its excellent faculty in this field, the university was known for classical and philological studies, which included not only Greek, Latin and Hebrew but also Arabic.

considered the core disciplines and this led to a different curricular structure. Rather than taking its traditional place in subordination to the higher faculties of theology, law, and medicine, the faculty of arts became an independent faculty of philosophy, liberal arts, and mathematics, on the same footing as the faculties of theology, civil and canon law, and medicine.[24] By the early seventeenth century, under pressure from students who insisted on familiarity with the works of Aristotle taught at other European universities, Scholastic Aristotelian philosophy, primarily derived from Suarez's *Metaphysical Disputations*, was incorporated into the philosophy curriculum. The emphasis on educating students in Scholastic Aristotelian philosophy persisted into the seventeenth century.[25]

The University of Leiden was also the successor to the University of Padua in medical studies. After constructing an anatomical theatre in 1597, Leiden successfully established clinical instruction in medicine from 1638 onwards—something that had been tried unsuccessfully at Padua.[26] Despite the international reputation the University of Leiden gained through its policy of religious tolerance and curricular innovations, this was not without backlash from conservative Calvinist theologians.[27]

---

[24] Frijhoff, 'University, academia', 76.

[25] As J.B.M. van Rijen notes, a series of complaints from different sources about the lack of uniformity in textbooks and curricula causing too much diversity in background knowledge among university students, finally led to the School Order of 1625 requiring the Latin Schools in the provinces of Holland and West Friesland to adopt a uniform curriculum. The School Order also assigned to Franco Burgersdijk, the task of writing a new logic handbook, modeled after the logic of Calvinist philosopher, Bartholomeo Keckermann. It was published a year later. Designed to prepare students for university studies, it represents an eclectic compromise consisting mostly of Scholastic Aristotelian logic. J.B.M. van Rijen, 'Burgersdijk, Logician or Textbook Writer?', in *Franco Burgersdijk (1590–1635): Neo-Aristotelianism in Leiden*, eds. E. P. Bos and H. A. Krop (Amsterdam, Atlanta GA: Editions Rodopi B.V., 1993), 17–20. J. A. van Ruler points out that Philosophy Professors at Leiden Petrus Bertius and Gilbert Jack follow Suarez on key metaphysical matters. Bertius follows Suarez's *Metaphysical Disputations* almost step by step in his discussion of divine concurrence, and Gilbert Jack taught based on his abstract of Suarez's *Disputations*. J.A. van Ruler, 'Franco Petri Burgersdijk and the Case of Calvinism Within the Neoscholastic Tradition', in *Franco Burgersdijk*, 46–47. H. A. Krop shows that Gilbert Jack's proof of God's existence follows the same progression as Suarez's and that Burgersdijk's treatment in his metaphysics text is also heavily influenced by Suarez. H. A. Krop, 'Natural Knowledge of God in Neo-Aristotelianism: The Reception of Suarez's Version of the Ontological Argument in Early Seventeenth Century Leiden', in *Franco Burgersdijk*, 76–77.

[26] Eduard Grant Ruestow, *Physics at Seventeenth and Eighteenth-Century Leiden* (The Hague, 1973), 5–7. In 1634 a medical student by the name of Franciscus de le Boe Sylvius defended John Harvey's theory of the circulation of the blood in his medical disputation at Leiden. He returned to Leiden in 1638 after further studies at Padua, and in 1658 became a Professor of Medicine at the University. Sylvius won his Professor of Medicine at Leiden, Adrianus Walaeus, over to Harvey's theory and Walaeus was a friend of Descartes'.

[27] Mistrustful of the theological education provided at the University of Leiden, the Reformed Church established its own theological college next door and only recognized its own exams. Frijhoff, 'University, academia', 77.

Conflicts between more liberal and more orthodox theology faculty at Leiden University came to a head during the Arminian crisis.[28] By 1619 this prolonged theological crisis had resulted in a schism within Calvinism when the Arminians, who questioned divine predestination, were branded as heretics at the Synod of Dordrecht.[29] To preserve political stability and unity, Prince Mauritz sided with the orthodox Calvinists. The Remonstrants who took up Arminius's cause after his death in 1609 were forced into hiding and exile in 1619, the same year Descartes left the Netherlands the first time. However, after the death of Mauritz in 1625, the Remonstrants returned, and controversial writings attributed to Arminian sympathizers and Socinians continued to circulate in the following decades.[30] A suspected connection between Descartes's teachings and the writings of David Gorlaeus—a Theology student, proponent of atomism, and suspected Arminian/Socinian sympathizer at the University of Leiden at the time of the crisis—became the basis for Gijsbert Voetius's accusations against Descartes, prompting what is commonly referred to as the Utrecht quarrel.[31]

Burgersdijk's *Institutionum Logicarum* was the standard logic textbook used at the University of Leiden after it adopted a Scholastic Aristotelian curriculum and was widely reprinted and adopted at many other Dutch universities. Moreover, Spinoza owned a copy. Hence, I will focus on this text as representative of how Zabarella's view of the methods of analysis and synthesis was developed in this context. Burgersdijk defines order or method as 'the apt arrangement [*dispositio*] of the things pertaining to it in order that they are most easily and optimally understood and that they inhere most tenaciously in memory.'[32] He reserves the term 'method' for 'order', pointing out that Zabarella's other sense of method encompasses

---

[28] The crisis was exacerbated by the hire of Theology Professor Conradus Vorstius. Vorstius was Arminius's replacement at the University of Leiden until, after only half a year, accusations of Socinianism from, among others, James I of England forced him to relinquish his position in 1612. Christoph Lüthy, 'David Gorlaeus' Atomism, Or: The Marriage of Protestant Metaphysics with Italian Natural Philosophy', in *Late Medieval and Early Modern Corpuscular Matter Theories*, eds. Christoph Lüthy, John E. Murdoch, William R. Newman (Leiden: 2001), 274–275.

[29] What started out as a theological dispute between Jacob Arminius (1560–1609), member of the Theology faculty at the University of Leiden, and his more orthodox colleague, Franciscus Gomarus (1563–1641), grew into a political crisis due to the close connection between religious and political concerns that existed in the loose federation of Dutch provinces at this time.

[30] *Descartes and the Dutch*, 1–4. Theo Verbeek points to interesting parallels between the threat that Cartesianism posed to Orthodox Calvinists, and the earlier threat of Arminianism. *Ibid*, 5.

[31] Theo Verbeek, *La Querelle d'Utrecht: René Descartes et Martin Schoock* (Paris: Impressions Nouvelles, 1988).

[32] Franco Burgersdijk, *Institutionum Logicarum* (Leiden,1626), 375–376.

the logical instruments, namely, definition, division, and syllogism which are not properly classified as arrangements. Burgersdijk distinguishes between a natural method, which is the didactic method that gives us distinct knowledge, and an artificial method used to persuade and delight the common folk. To the question of whether the didactic method should begin from things prior by nature or prior to us, Burgersdijk responds: 'I deem both to be true, Method is to be taken both from nature and our easier cognition.... Now in fact, the same things are prior by nature which are more known to us, as far as distinct cognition goes. For that cognition is distinct which corresponds to the things themselves and the order of nature.'[33]

He then defines 'analysis' and 'synthesis' in the context of discussing the natural method. First Burgersdijk describes the natural method as follows:

> *The natural method ought to always progress from the universals to the particulars; in this progression all the parts are connected by apt chains of transition.*
>
> 1. (*From the universals*) of course, because universals are not only more known than particulars as far as distinct cognition (goes); but they also contribute to the acquiring of distinct cognition of particulars: since they are contained in their definition. Progress from universals to particulars would be through division. The parts of the same division are to be connected by an apt transition. This connection consists in this or similar form; *And these things suffice concerning this said thing, it follows from the instituted order* & c. which formulae of the things read, by incredible repetition, please a great deal.[34]

This method is further divided into a total and partial natural method, with analysis and synthesis comprising the total method:

> *VIII. The total method is that by which some entire discipline is arranged.*
> *IX. It is either Synthetic or Analytic* [e. I.Eth.c.23].
> *XI. The Synthetic method is that which progresses from the most simple principles towards those which are composed from those principles.*
> *XI. The speculative discipline is treated by this method.*
> *XII. The Analytic method is that which with the beginning made from the end, progresses to the proximate media, and from these to other more remote ones, until it has arrived at the first and most simple.*
> *XIII. The arts and practical disciplines are treated by this method.*[35]

---

[33] '...Methodus ita instituenda est, ut inserviat distinctae rerum propositarum cognitioni facilius acquirendae. Iam verò, quae nobis notiora sunt, quoad cognitionem distinctam eadem priora sunt naturâ. Cognitio enim distincta est, quae rebus ipsis respondet & ordini naturae.' Burgersdijk, Theorem IV, 1.§, 378.
[34] Burgersdijk, 380.   [35] Burgersdijk, 380–381.

Burgersdijk follows common Aristotelian uses of these terms as found in Zabarella, but appears to erase the distinction between what is prior by nature and what is prior to us in the sense that it is more easily known to the human mind. Rather synthesis begins from distinct cognitions that are both better known by us and prior by nature. Once one rejects the syllogism and other instruments of Aristotle's logic, what remains is a natural method, starting from distinct cognitions by which one can learn, retain, and teach the true order of nature. With Aristotle's logic of demonstration placed squarely outside the domain of method, the distinction between method as order and method as a process of demonstration for deriving new knowledge also threatens to collapse.

Burgersdijk's optimism about our ability to know the true natures of things is echoed by Descartes in the *Discourse on the Method* when he proclaims that: 'the power of judging well and of distinguishing the true from the false... is naturally equal in all men, and consequently that the diversity of our opinions does not arise because some of us are more reasonable than others but solely because we direct our thoughts along different paths and do not attend to the same things.'[36] In other words, we are all capable of distinct cognitions such that as long as we attend to the same things and apply the right method, we will all arrive at the same truth. But Descartes rejects Burgersdijk's view that synthesis is the appropriate natural method for theoretical matters. Instead, he characterizes synthesis as a method more suitable for compelling belief and analysis as the proper method of discovery.

Descartes and Hobbes

In his *Rules for the Direction of the Mind*, Descartes indicates that his method of analysis is inspired by the secret art of analysis used by ancient mathematicians; but despite many attempts to make sense of this, it is still not clear how Descartes's philosophical senses of analysis and synthesis are supposed to conform to mathematical definitions and uses of these methods.[37] Descartes's fullest statements on the nature of analysis and synthesis occur in his reply to Mersenne's request, in the Second Set of

[36] René Descartes, *Discourse on the Method,* in *The Philosophical Writings of Descartes,* trans. John Cottingham, Robert Stoothoff, Dugald Murdoch, and Anthony Kenny, 3 vols. (Cambridge, 1985–1991), vol. 1: 111. [Henceforth CSM I]

[37] See, for instance, Athanassios Raftopoulos 'Cartesian Analysis and Synthesis', *Studies in History and Philosophy of Science* 34 (2003), 305 and Doren Recker, 'Mathematical Demonstration and Deduction in Descartes' Early Methodological and Scientitic Writings' *Journal of the History of Philosophy*, 31:2 (April 1993): 223–244.

Objections, that Descartes present the arguments of his *Meditations on First Philosophy* in geometrical fashion. Descartes begins by distinguishing between 'two matters [*res*] in the geometrical manner of writing: namely, the order and the procedure of demonstrating [*rationem demonstrandi*]'.[38] Similar to Zabarella, Descartes considers the order in question to be an order that facilitates learning: 'The items which are put forward first must be known entirely without the aid of what comes later; and the remaining items must be arranged in such a way that their demonstration depends solely on what has gone before.'[39] Descartes adds that he tried to carefully follow this order in his *Meditations*.

However, unlike Zabarella, Descartes draws the distinction between analysis and synthesis within the context of demonstration instead of the context of order, stating: 'Of demonstrating, however the procedure [*rationem*] is twofold, one namely through analysis, the other through synthesis'.[40] Descartes finds synthesis, the procedure of demonstrating normally used in the writings of ancient geometers, less satisfying because instead of showing how the discovery was made:

> It demonstrates the conclusion clearly and employs a long series of defin-
> itions, postulates, axioms, theorems and problems, so that if anyone denies
> one of the conclusions it can be shown at once that it is contained in what
> has gone before, and hence the reader, however argumentative or stubborn
> he may be, is compelled to give his assent.[41]

Descartes characterizes this kind of proof as more of an *a priori* proof (from cause or principle to effect or consequence), but he also confusingly states that in synthesis the search is *a posteriori* as it employs a method that is directly opposite to the *a priori* way of analysis. Analysis,

> [s]hows the true way by means of which the thing in question was discovered
> methodically and as it were *a priori*, so that if the reader is willing to follow
> it and give sufficient attention to all points, he will make the thing his own
> and understand it just as perfectly as if he had discovered it for himself.[42]

In this particular passage the term 'a priori' rather than referring to reasoning from cause to effect, appears to designate a procedure that begins from what is prior or better known relative to us, in the sense that we must take certain preliminary steps before we can gain perfect knowledge of

[38] René Descartes, *Meditationes de Primâ Philosophia*, in *Oeuvres de Descartes*, eds. Charles Adam and Paul Tannery, 12 vols. (Paris, 1996), 8:155. [Henceforth AT] (translation mine).

[39] René Descartes, *Meditations on First Philosophy*, in *The Philosophical Writings of Descartes*, trans. John Cottingham, Robert Stoothoff, Dugald Murdoch, and Anthony Kenny, 3 vols. (Cambridge, 1985–1991), vol. 2: 110. [Henceforth CSM II]

[40] AT VII, 155.   [41] CSM II, 111.   [42] CSM II, 110.

principles, which are absolutely prior. Descartes elaborates that the 'a priori' analytic way is more suitable to metaphysics than the synthetic way used in geometry, because the primary metaphysical notions, unlike geometrical notions, are not in accordance with our senses and hence are not readily accepted by everyone. Analysis thus appears to be the way we must follow in metaphysics in order to overcome obstacles posed by human cognition, as it enables us to rid ourselves of preconceived notions and make 'our perception of the primary notions clear and distinct'.[43]

Unlike Burgersdijk who holds that there is one natural order from most universal to least, Descartes agrees with Zabarella that the proper order must take whatever path most facilitates cognition in the subject. Furthermore, although the analytic procedure of demonstration fails to compel assent from the 'argumentative or stubborn reader', it is, according to Descartes, 'the truest and best way of instruction' because it follows the path of discovery.[44] When it comes to the best way to proceed, the path to acquiring or discovering knowledge and the order of teaching coincide for Descartes. The same is true of Thomas Hobbes, who in *De Corpore* characterizes synthesis, which he equates with composition, as both the method of demonstration and the method of teaching.

We know that Spinoza owned a copy of Hobbes's *De Cive* and Spinoza's political writings also indicate that he read the *Leviathan*. Whether or not Spinoza read the first part of Hobbes's *De Corpore*, which comprises his logic and a chapter on method, is less clear as the first Dutch edition was printed after the usual dating of the TIE. But there are some textual parallels between Hobbes's chapter 'On Method' and the TIE, and given that we cannot be certain when the TIE was written, they merit close scrutiny. Ernst Cassirer was the first to emphasize the striking parallel between Spinoza's discussion of genetic definitions in the TIE and Hobbes's account and examples of definitions in *De Corpore*.[45] In light of this, the theory of definitions, which forms part of Hobbes's method for attaining *scientia simpliciter,* merits our attention.

For Hobbes, definitions are the only proper principles. As he stresses in chapter 6, section 4 of *De Corpore* devoted to method, definitions give us the causes of individual natures, which we discover by extracting universals from our conceptions of individual things through the method of analysis or resolution. Hobbes's use of the term 'universal' is confusing

[43] CSM II, 111.   [44] AT VII, 156.

[45] Karl Schuhmann, 'Methodenfragen bei Spinoza und Hobbes: Zum Problem des Einflusses', *Studia Spinoziana* 3 (1983): 47–86, 71. Another allusion to *De Corpore* I, i, 8 was noted by Alexandre Koyré; see Benedict de Spinoza, *Treatise on the Emendation of the Intellect* in *The Collected Works of Spinoza*, trans. Edwin Curley, 2 Vols. (Princeton, 1985), vol. 1: 31, note 52. [henceforth TIE Curley]

here, as he had already claimed, in chapter 2, sec.9 of *De Corpore* that so-called Aristotelian universals, like human, stone or spirit, can never be universal. Only the corresponding words, which are names common to many things, can be named 'universal'. Like Spinoza, Hobbes considers the conceptions raised in our mind when someone utters these common names to be products of the imagination. He characterizes them as:

> the images and phantasms of several living creatures or other things. And therefore, for the understanding of the extent of an universal name, we need no other faculty but that of our imagination, by which we remember that such names bring sometimes one thing, sometimes another, into our mind.[46]

Hobbes then distinguishes between the more common names, which are called the genus or general name, and the less common names which are called the species or special name. The difference lies merely in the fact that the more common names are names of more things.

The strict nominalism implied by the discussion in chapter 2 appears to directly contradict the method Hobbes proposes in chapter 6 for obtaining knowledge of 'universals' and their causes. One way to resolve the apparent contradiction is to read Hobbes's claim that universals are nothing but common names in chapter 2 to be limited to Aristotelian universals, i.e., species and genera. By contrast, in chapter 6 Hobbes, seems to invoke a different type of universal conception that takes the place of Aristotelian genera and species in definitions. His twofold method of analysis and synthesis is designed to discover and then compound these universal conceptions into definitions and scientific demonstrations.

Hobbes provides two examples of the purely analytical method used to attain the universals necessary to understand things indefinitely or *simpliciter*. Analysis, or resolution, is used to extract these universals or accidents which he claims are both contained in individual natures and common to all material things. Then, in a second step, the causes of these universals or accidents are discovered.

Example 1. One begins with an idea of individual thing [*Idea rei singularis*], e.g., idea of a square.
Step (i): this idea is resolved into 'plain, terminated with a certain number of equal and straight lines and right angles. Thus we have these universals or things agreeable to all matter: line, plain (which includes superficies), terminated, angle, straightness.'[47]

---

[46] Book I, ch.2, sec.9, 12. In Ch.6, sec.11 he again states 'every universal denotes the concept of infinite singular things.' Thomas Hobbes, *Elementorum Philosophiae, Sectio Prima De Corpore* (London, 1655), 49. (translation mine) [henceforth DC 1655]

[47] DC 1655, 43.

Step (ii) 'If we can find out the causes of these, then we may compound them together into the cause of the square.'[48]

Note that the example makes little sense if the universals, line, plane, etc., are merely common names. For how would one extract these words from an idea? And even if one could, would this then not result in a different analysis in each language? For example, a German speaker would extract 'Linie' and 'Ebene' not 'line' and 'plane' from her idea of a particular square. Finally, how are we to compound the causes of these words, which are artefacts of convention, to find the cause of the square? Hobbes seems to understand these universals to be some type of conceptual parts that make up our particular ideas and map on to the common accidents of matter.

Paradoxically, Hobbes also claims that these conceptual parts are particular but makes it clear that they are not sensory images of particular parts of the object. In an earlier example found in section 2 of the same chapter, Hobbes writes that reason gives us knowledge of the particular ideas of a man being figurate, animate, and rational. Scientific knowledge consists in knowing the causes of the parts, and compounding the cause of the whole, out of the causes of the parts. Hobbes then clarifies that by parts, he means not the man's shoulders, arms, head, etc., but his figure, quantity, motion, sense, reason, etc. Hobbes calls these parts 'accidents', stating that when they are compounded, they constitute the whole nature of a man, but not the man himself.

Now let us relate this to Hobbes's second example of analysis. There Hobbes begins with the concept of a natural object, that gold, and resolves his conception of the individual nature of that gold to arrive at the cause of its common or universal nature.

Example 2. *Individual Nature:* Conception of gold.
(i) resolved into ideas of solid, visible, heavy (the universals or common accidents of gold).
(ii) 'which [i.e., the ideas of solid, visible, heavy] they may resolve again, till they arrive at the most universal.'[49]

This example is, unfortunately, very cryptic. Hobbes fails to spell out what the universals at the top-most level of resolution would be, but he indicates that gold's solidity, visibility, and heaviness would eventually reduce to types of motion, stating that motion is the most universal cause which requires no method to be known. So perhaps the ultimate causes of the

[48] DC 1655, 43.   [49] DC 1655, 43.

conceptual parts of the individual gold (i.e., the ideas of solid, visible, and heavy) would be certain types or patterns of motion.

What is clear is that the purely resolutive part of the method takes us only to the universals or common accidents of matter. It is only when we employ synthesis to compound the abstract names we attach to these common accidents that we gain causal demonstrative knowledge. For instance, by compounding 'solidity', 'visibility', 'heaviness', and other abstract terms attached to common accidents extracted from our individual idea of gold, we arrive at the definition of 'gold' and this gives us causal knowledge of the individual nature of gold. Hobbes later defines a cause as: 'the sum or aggregate of all such accidents, both in the agents and the patient, as concur to the producing of the effect propounded; all of which existing together, it cannot be understood but that the effect existeth with them; or that it can possibly exist if any one of them be absent.'[50] Scientific knowledge is thus built up when we compose names into propositions using the copula 'is', and then compose propositions into syllogisms. Hobbes specifies that the first principles by which we know the causes of things are definitions, not axioms, for the latter are not really simple and can be proven. He defines definitions as, 'nothing but the explication of our most simple [*simplicissimum*] conceptions.'[51] Hobbes is adamant that 'Besides definitions, there is no other proposition that ought to be called primary, or (according to severe truth) be received into the number of principles.'[52]

In addition to the explicative definitions, like the ones of our simplest conceptions of place and motion, synthesis also relies on definitions that describe how things are generated. For example, Hobbes explains: 'a line is made by the motion of a point, superficies by the motion of a line, and one motion by another motion, etc.'[53] Close to the end of the TIE, Spinoza employs the very same examples to illustrate how the intellect, having perceived the idea of quantity through a cause, then forms determinate ideas from it.[54] Based on these genetic definitions, Hobbes envisions the gradual synthesis of a unified structure of sciences, or *scientia simpliciter*. *Scientia simpliciter*, which consists in attaining as much knowledge of the

---

[50] Thomas Hobbes, *Elements of Philosophy, The First Section Concerning Body* (London, 1656), 56. [Henceforth DC 1656]

[51] For example, place is, 'that space which is possessed or filled adequately by some body.' Motion is, 'the privation of one place, and the acquisition of another.' DC 1655, Ch.6., 44.

[52] DC 1656 Ch.6, sec.13, 59; DC 1655, 50.

[53] This is preceded by 'next we have...' DC1656 Ch.6, sec.6, 52; DC 1655, 44. In this chapter, Hobbes presents this as the next step, implying that you start with stipulative definitions and then move to generative definitions. This appears to contradict the next passage where he talks of the method of teaching, which is entirely synthetic.

[54] TIE, Curley, 43–44.

causes of things as possible, starts from the causes of the simple objects of geometry, i.e., lines or lengths generated from points in motion, and surfaces generated from long bodies. These, once demonstrated, are composed to generate the more complex phenomena of the science of motion, itself produced by the effects of one body's motion on other bodies. Now, the science of motion provides the starting points for demonstrating the phenomena of physics, which are produced by the motions of the parts of bodies, including our sense organs. In like manner, Hobbes thinks that we can progress all the way up to moral philosophy, which considers the motions of the mind, i.e., the passions, and civil science.[55] The demonstrative knowledge of all sciences, including politics, will necessarily rest on geometrical definitions. Scientific reasoning thus builds upon first principles, namely definitions, including genetic ones that give us the causes of our conceptions. From these we syllogistically deduce even more complex wholes, i.e., the effects of these causes, which consist in more complex ideas and conceptions of the differentiating accidents of individual natures, including the nature of civil society.

Spinoza

As stated, Spinoza was familiar with the writings of Burgersdijk, Descartes, and Hobbes. With this background in hand, we are ready to turn to the question whether Spinoza's use of the geometrical method is merely a method of teaching, a method of discovering and demonstrating new knowledge, or both. As we know, despite his misgivings about using the method of synthesis in metaphysics, Descartes ends up fulfilling Marin Mersenne's request and in his Replies to the Second Objections gives his 'Arguments proving the existence of God and the distinction between the soul and the body arranged in geometrical fashion.'[56] This becomes the inspiration for Spinoza's first publication: *The Principles of Philosophy Demonstrated in the Geometric Manner* which presents a large portion of the arguments in Descartes's *Principles of Philosophy*, following the same method of synthesis Descartes employs in his reply to Mersenne. Given that the *Ethics* takes the same format, it raises the distinct possibility that

---

[55] Though Hobbes adds that there is a short cut in that one can sever Civil Philosophy from Moral Philosophy, given that the motions of the mind can be known by introspection as well as ratiocination. Moreover, one can arrive at knowledge of whether an action is just or unjust by analysis by resolving unjust into 'fact against law' and law into 'the power of him or them that have coercive power to the end they may live in peace...' From there one can then compound to the determination of the justice or injustice of any action. DC, 1656, 54.

[56] CSM II, 113.

Spinoza directly applies Descartes's synthetic procedure of demonstrating. This is confirmed by Spinoza's friend, Lodewijk Meyer, who highlights in his Preface to Spinoza's *Principles* that Spinoza came to put Part II and some of Part III of Descartes's text in this form when he was tutoring a student who had difficulty mastering Cartesian philosophy. Meyer characterizes Spinoza's endeavour as arranging 'in synthetic order what Descartes wrote in analytic order'.[57] He emphasizes that Spinoza 'has simply given Descartes's opinions and their demonstrations just as they are found in his writings, or such as should validly be deduced from the foundations laid by him'.[58] He adds that Spinoza's own views differ from Descartes's on several points.

If Meyer accurately presents Spinoza's aims,[59] then the geometrical order of Spinoza's *Principles* would be only a way to give an account demonstrating the conclusions that is suitable for teaching an untalented student, nothing more. At best then Spinoza, following Descartes, initially regarded synthesis as the most effective method for instructing argumentative and stubborn readers. Of course, none of this precludes that, by the time Spinoza presented his own original philosophy in the *Ethics*, he also diverged from Descartes by adopting the synthetic method as a proper method for the discovery of metaphysical truths. But it does mean we must be careful not to assume, at the outset, that the Euclidean form Spinoza adopts to present his philosophy in the *Ethics* necessarily represents his method of discovery and demonstration rather than a method of instruction.

Given his familiarity with Burgersdijk and Hobbes, there is an alternative reading, namely, that Spinoza regarded synthesis as a natural method that is both didactic and reveals the true order of nature. In other words, the mere fact that Meyer claims Spinoza adopted the synthetic order so as to teach Descartes's *Principles* does not preclude the possibility that the Spinoza may have also, *contra* Descartes, regarded synthesis as the proper method of inquiry into the true natures of things. In other words, Spinoza might have held with Descartes that when it comes to the best method, the method of teaching and discovery coincide, while agreeing instead with Burgersdijk that synthesis is the best method because it follows the natural order of things. Moreover, given that Zabarella's influence looms large in this context, it would also have been reasonable for Spinoza to suppose that, as in Euclid's *Elements*, there need not be a strict deductive progression starting from genera and advancing to particulars for the

[57] Baruch Spinoza, *Spinoza Complete Works*, trans. Samuel Shirley (Indianapolis, 2002), 117–118 [henceforth CW].

[58] CW, 119.

[59] Aaron Garrett presents evidence that he does. Aaron Garrett, *Meaning in Spinoza's Method* (Cambridge, 2003), 116.

Ethics to follow the method of synthesis. One could begin with the simple accidents that are known *per se,* as Euclid does with point and line, and then progress to the more universal concepts such as magnitude, or in Spinoza's case, *Deus sive Natura.*

So far, what has been established is that this alternative reading of Spinoza's procedure in the *Ethics* is possible. Is it also likely? To answer this, let's turn to Spinoza's unpublished treatise on method, the *Treatise on the Emendation of the Intellect* to see if it contains any clues regarding what type of method he uses in the *Ethics.* The explicit aim of the TIE is to emend the intellect so that it becomes capable of understanding things in the way required to attain union with nature and the highest joy. In order to reach his aim, Spinoza thinks we must come to know the nature of things to the extent necessary to a) make correct inferences regarding their differences, agreements, and oppositions; b) correctly conceive what they can and cannot undergo; and c) compare the nature of things with the nature and power of man.[60] In order for the requisite knowledge of nature to be attained, the intellect must be emended and purified so that it is up to this task.[61] In particular, the intellect requires a method for obtaining the fourth kind of knowledge, namely intuitive knowledge. This leads Spinoza to examine what method is, and what would be the most perfect method.[62] The first part of the TIE is devoted to these questions and the method advanced there appears to be broadly Cartesian in its orientation.

Spinoza observes that, even though the intellect has inborn tools to obtain knowledge of its union with nature, it must first fashion further tools for discriminating between true ideas and the rest before it can begin to realize its potential for this kind of knowledge. Spinoza here draws on Descartes's analogy in Rule 8 of the *Rules for the Direction of the Mind* between his method and the procedure of the blacksmith, who must first fashion his anvil and hammer from natural resources, like rocks, before he can proceed to make horseshoes.[63] This suggests that what Spinoza advances in the TIE is a meta-method in the Cartesian sense, rather than

---

[60] TIE, Curley, 15 [25]).   [61] TIE, Curley, 11–16, [16]-[29])

[62] TIE, Curley,18–22, [37]-[48].

[63] Spinoza, drawing on the same analogy, writes: 'But just as men, in the beginning, were able to make the easiest things with the tools they were born with (however laboriously and imperfectly), and once these had been made, made other, more difficult things with less labor and more perfectly, and so, proceeding gradually from the simplest works to tools, and from tools to other works and tools, reached the point where they accomplished so many and so difficult things with little labor, in the same way the intellect, by its inborn power, makes intellectual tools for itself, by which it acquires other powers for other intellectual works, and from these works still other tools, or the power of searching further, and so proceeds by stages, until it reaches the pinnacle of wisdom.' TIE, Curley, 17.

a method for retaining and teaching scientific knowledge, which is Burgersdijk's concern. This reading is confirmed by Spinoza's claim that:

> Method is not the reasoning itself by which we understand the causes of things; much less the understanding of the causes of things, it is understanding what a true idea is by distinguishing it from the rest of the perceptions; by investigating its nature, so that from that we may come to know our power of understanding and so restrain the mind that it understands, according to that standard.[64]

The overarching approach and method of the TIE thus echoes Descartes's endeavours in the *Rules* and *Discourse*. This suggests that the overall method Spinoza lays out in the TIE may be closer to a Cartesian analysis, designed to free us from our preconceived notions so as to identify the true ideas, rather than telling us anything about the method of synthesis on display in the *Ethics*.

However, the link to Descartes's method turns out to be anything but straightforward as Spinoza diverges from Descartes in articulating a very different view of truth. Whereas he affirms with Descartes that 'before all else there must be a true idea, in us, as an inborn tool…' Spinoza insists that truth requires no sign.[65] Unlike Descartes, Spinoza denies that a separate act of judgment affirming an idea is needed for truth and he continues to maintain this view in the *Ethics*. As Spinoza puts it in the TIE, 'to understand the essence of Peter, it is not necessary to understand an idea of Peter, much less an idea of an idea of Peter.'[66] Rather, all that is required for me to be certain that I know Peter is that I have the objective essence of Peter, which Spinoza defines as the mode by which I am aware of Peter's formal essence. For Spinoza, certainty is to have an adequate idea of a thing, and an adequate idea is nothing but the objective essence of the thing, or my awareness of the thing's formal essence.

In developing this account of truth, Spinoza stresses the difference between an idea and its object.[67] For example, the idea of a circle is not something that has a periphery and a center. From the fact that an idea is something different from its object, Spinoza takes it to follow that an idea is also something intelligible in itself, that is, it can be understood *qua* idea. As he notes, the formal essence of an idea can itself be the object of another objective essence—in other words, I can be aware of and take as object of my thought the nature of an idea, rather than what the idea is of. The objective essence in this case will be the adequate idea of my idea, *qua* idea. Now this objective essence of my idea, just like the objective essence

---

[64] TIE, Curley, 18–19 [37].   [65] TIE, Curley, 19 [39], 17 [36].
[66] TIE, Curley, 18.   [67] TIE, Curley, 17–18 [34].

of Peter or the circle, will in turn be something real and intelligible, regarded in itself *qua* idea. This is the case for all our ideas of ideas, *ad infinitum*. Since ideas are real and intelligible in and of themselves, truth is also an intrinsic feature of ideas.

Having laid out his account of truth, Spinoza then defines the true method as the way that truth itself, or the objective essences of things, or the ideas (he says that these all mean the same thing) should be sought in the proper order.[68] The proper order for Spinoza, as for Burgersdijk, is the true order of nature. Spinoza spells out that method is nothing but reflective knowledge, which he clarifies as an idea of an idea. A good method is one which shows how the mind is to be directed according to the standard of a given true idea. Spinoza is explicit that the idea is object-ively the same way its object really is.[69] For Spinoza then, the true idea, in the sense of the objective essence, or the mind's awareness of the thing, reveals the true order of nature. It is by reflecting on the given true idea, as the standard, that the intellect will understand more things and perfect itself.[70] How can a mere idea do this? It can because the given true idea is none other than the idea of the most perfect Being.

Spinoza explains this point with the following cryptic reasoning:

i) The relation/proportion [*ratio*] between two ideas [in the sense of their objective essence] is the same as the relation/proportion between the formal essences of those ideas.
ii) Given i) the reflective knowledge of the idea of the most perfect Being will be more excellent than the reflective knowledge of any other ideas.[71]

Later on Spinoza elaborates as follows: since an idea must agree with its formal essence, in order for the human mind to reproduce completely the likeness of nature, it must bring all of its ideas forth from that idea which represents the source and origin of the whole of Nature so that the idea is also the source of other ideas. The idea of God or nature is thus the true given idea from which all other ideas flow just as what it represents is the source of the causal order of nature.

After discussing how true ideas are to be distinguished from all other perceptions and how to restrain the mind from the latter, Spinoza, in the second part of the TIE, aims to 'teach rules so that we may perceive things unknown according to such a standard.'[72] In this part of the TIE, he turns to the correct way of investigating things. It is in this section where com-mentators like Martial Gueroult and Herman De Dijn have detected an

[68] TIE, Curley, 17 [36].   [69] TIE, Curley, 20 [41].   [70] TIE, Curley, 19 [39].
[71] TIE, Curley 19 [38].   [72] TIE, Curley, 22–23 [49].

affinity to the type of method found in Burgersdijk and Hobbes.[73] According to Spinoza, we must avoid making inferences from abstractions, and instead draw our conclusion from a true and legitimate definition.[74] Spinoza here lays out a method of inquiry amounting to synthesis:

> So the right way of discovery is to form thoughts from some given defin-ition. This will proceed the more successfully and easily the better we have defined a thing. So the chief point of this second part of the Method is concerned solely with this: knowing the conditions of a good definition, and then the way of finding good definitions.[75]

There are two main requirements that a good definition of a created thing must meet for Spinoza: first, the definition must include its proximate cause, and second, all the thing's properties must be deducible from the concept or definition considered alone.[76] Spinoza gives the following def-inition of a circle as one that fulfils both conditions: 'it is the figure that is described by any line of which one end is fixed and the other movable.'[77] This definition includes the proximate cause of the circle, i.e., it is a genetic definition which describes how the circle can be generated. Second, we can deduce from it the property of a circle that all the lines drawn from the center are equal.

Hobbes, in the second part of chapter 6 'On Method' which deals with the method of teaching (as stated, for him, this is identical to the synthetic method of discovery), gives the same example to illustrate the definitions of names that have a conceivable cause. According to him such definitions: 'must consist of such Names as express the cause or manner of their gen-eration, as when we define a Circle to be a Figure made by the circumduc-tion of a straight line in a Plaine, etc.'.[78] This example, together with Hobbes's description in *De Corpore* of a unified structure of sciences, rest-ing on genetic definitions of mathematical objects, from which more and more complex natural wholes are constructed by synthesis, is congenial to Spinoza's method. In particular, Spinoza appears to advocate a similar procedure when he claims that true progress of the intellect requires that it proceed, as far as possible, according to the series of causes, from one real being to another, always drawing inferences from or to real things, never passing over to abstractions and universals. For both Spinoza and Hobbes, reason, starting from genetic definitions, must construct true knowledge

---

[73] See, for instance, Martial Gueroult, *Spinoza*, 2 Vols. (Paris, 1968), I: 12–13 and Herman de Dijn, 'Conceptions of Philosophical Method in Spinoza: Logica and Mos Geometricus', *Review of Metaphysics* 40:1 (Sept 1986): 68.
[74] TIE, Curley, 38–39 [92]-[93].   [75] TIE, Curley, 39 [94].
[76] TIE, Curley, 39–40 [96].   [77] TIE, Curley, 40 [96].
[78] DC 1656, Ch.6, sec.13, 59.

of the natures of things by deriving their properties not from static universals or axioms, but from the dynamic progression of their causes of generation. But Spinoza does not share Hobbes's view of truth. For Hobbes, truth is merely a property of speech, and so only propositions can be true or false. For Spinoza, truth is a feature of complete or adequate ideas, and in fact, he proposes to begin his synthesis from the idea of the most perfect being, which he characterizes as the maximally true idea.

With this new theory of truth, and a method in hand, the second part of Spinoza's method aims,

> to have clear and distinct ideas, i.e., such as have been made from the pure mind, and not from fortuitous motions of the body. And then, so that all ideas may be led back to one, we shall strive to connect and order them so that our mind, as far as possible, reproduces objectively the formal character of nature, both as to the whole and as to the parts.[79]

To fulfil this aim, Spinoza must conceive things through their essences or proximate causes. To accomplish the latter, he must have genetic definitions, of the same kind sought out by Hobbes. This, in turn, will enable Spinoza to mentally reproduce the order of nature:

> As for order, to unite and order all our perceptions, it is required, and reason demands, that we ask, as soon as possible, whether there is a certain being, and at the same time, what sort of being it is, which is the cause of all things, so that its objective essence may also be the cause of all our ideas, and then our mind will (as we have said) reproduce Nature as much as possible. For it will have Nature's essence, order, and unity objectively.[80]

The second part of Spinoza's method thus tracks the natural order by connecting all our perceptions by means of an orderly progression, from our clear and distinct knowledge of the most fundamental and general principle, to the clear and distinct cognition of complex particulars. This part of Spinoza's method resembles Burgersdijk's method of synthesis, with the difference that, following Hobbes's critique of Aristotelian universals, Spinoza rejects such universals as the proper starting points for subsequent deductions of particulars:

> From this we can see that above all it is necessary for us always to deduce all our ideas from Physical things, *or* from the real beings, proceeding as far as possible, according to the series of causes, from one real being to another real being, in such a way that we do not pass over to abstractions and universals, neither inferring something real from them, nor inferring them from something real. For to do either interferes with the true progress of the intellect.[81]

---

[79] TIE, Curley, 38.   [80] TIE, Curley, 41.   [81] TIE, Curley, 41.

A few pages earlier in the TIE, Spinoza had described knowledge of a thing's real essence as follows:

> the latter [the intimate essence of things] is to be sought only from the fixed and eternal things, and at the same time from the laws inscribed in the former things [singular mutable things], just as in their true codes, according to which all singular things both come to be, and are ordered. Indeed these singular mutable things therefore depend so intimately, and (so to speak) essentially, on those fixed things that they can neither be nor be conceived without them. Whence these fixed and eternal things, though they would be singular, nevertheless, because of their presence everywhere, and widest power, will be to us as it were universals or genera of the definitions of singular, mutable things, and the proximate causes of all things.[82]

In this passage, Spinoza seeks to replace the problematic Aristotelian species and genera, from which Burgersdijk starts his synthesis, with fixed and eternal things on which the series of changeable things coming into being in nature depends essentially. At the same time, to avoid the nominalism implied by Hobbes's approach, Spinoza ties these fixed and eternal essences to the true codes which can be read off from the laws, inscribed in singular mutable things. These laws govern the coming into being and order of natural things. Even though Spinoza emphasizes that these fixed and eternal things are singular, since they are present everywhere, they function like Aristotelian universals and genera in the definitions of singular, mutable things. In other words, there is no shared essence of humanity for Spinoza that gets defined by predicating the genus 'animal' and differentia 'rational' of 'human being'. But there is something like an eternal essence. These essences are codified when inscribed as laws in singular changing things determining their order. The fixed and eternal things, despite being singular, are ever present, and take the place of genera in definitions, such as the genus 'animal' in the definition of a human being.

What these codes are and how these genus-analogues form part of definitions remains mysterious, as Spinoza's focus in the TIE is on the method for acquiring knowledge of these true, fixed, and eternal essences and causes of mutable things, rather than on their nature. How are we to even begin to deduce one real or physical thing from another without knowing what these codes are? One possibility is that, in reflecting on our ideas, we do not need to know what the codes operating at the level of formal essences of things are. For if we reflect on our ideas by following the correct method, starting from the maximally true idea and connecting all other true ideas back to it in orderly fashion, then we will have an order of

---

[82] TIE, Gebhardt, 36–37. (translation mine)

objective essences that mirrors the causal order of formal essences, and this in turn will purify the intellect and put us on the path to eternal joy. On this reading, the *Ethics* could be the implementation of the method for attaining blessedness that Spinoza proposes in the TIE.

In sum, to the extent that the first part of Spinoza's method is designed to identify those innate ideas of the intellect, which are the proper starting points for true knowledge of nature, Spinoza's procedure in the TIE seems closer to Cartesian analysis even though he differs from Descartes in his account of truth. Like Descartes, Spinoza characterizes such ideas as the inborn tools of the mind from which further tools, e.g., the rules for forming definitions to which he turns in the second part of the TIE, are then fashioned. However, the second part of Spinoza's method is quite different from the rules Descartes constructs from the inborn tools of his mind in the *Rules*. Descartes's rules are ultimately rules for solving particular problems, including simple mathematical problems and the complex problems of physics, such as the nature of the magnet.[83] The second part of Spinoza's method, by contrast, aims 'to connect and order them [clear and distinct ideas] so that our mind, as far as possible, reproduces objectively the formal character of nature, both as to the whole and as to the parts.'[84] To fulfil this aim, Spinoza must conceive things through their essences or proximate causes. To accomplish the latter, he must have genetic definitions, of the same kind sought out by Hobbes. This, in turn, will enable Spinoza to mentally reproduce the order of nature. As seen, this component of Spinoza's method resembles Burgersdijk's view of synthesis more than anything else. Consistent with Burgersdijk's account of the natural method, the second part of Spinoza's method tracks the natural order by connecting all our perceptions by means of an orderly progression, from our clear and distinct knowledge of the most fundamental and general principle, to the clear and distinct cognition of complex particulars. Only Spinoza, following Hobbes's critique of Aristotelian universals, rejects Burgersdijk's appeal to Aristotelian universals as the proper starting points for subsequent deductions of particulars.

Although this unpublished, incomplete work by Spinoza does not definitively show that the method of the *Ethics* is meant to be both a method of discovery and teaching, the fact that the second part of the TIE incorporates crucial elements of Burgersdijk and Hobbes's methods makes this likely. As seen, Spinoza there advocates a Hobbesian style method of

---

[83] Aaron Garrett further argues that Spinoza's rejection of Descartes' distinction between the will and intellect also leads to a rejection of Cartesian analysis. Garrett, *Meaning in Spinoza's Method*, 121.
[84] TIE, Curley, 38.

synthesis that provides knowledge of the natures of things by constructing them from genetic definitions. However, Spinoza also incorporates a Cartesian style of analysis aimed at fashioning intellectual tools that will securely ground the rules of his method in the ultimate standard of the given true idea of the most perfect being. In this way, I take it, Spinoza seeks to avoid the potentially subjective nature of the mathematical definitions which Hobbes takes as the starting points of his synthesis. With the idea of *Deus sive Natura* as his ultimate foundation, Spinoza can be assured that his application of the method of synthesis will, as *per* the requirement of Burgersdijk's natural method, reproduce the true order of nature by reflecting on the order by which objective essences logically follow from the given true idea.

If I am correct in my conclusion that Spinoza's method is most likely not just a method of instruction but also a method of inquiry, then what are the implications for Spinoza's project in the *Ethics*? At least three possibilities spring to mind. First, Spinoza could be completing the project of the TIE by developing a methodological procedure to perfect the intellect by engaging in reflective study of the natures of things. This is suggested by the ultimate goal of perfecting the intellect and attaining union with God/nature, which carries over from the TIE to the *Ethics*. Although the broader aim of attaining perfection and union with God is continuous with the TIE, the *Ethics* does not appear to focus heavily on the epistemological concerns of Spinoza's early treatise on method nor does it begin with an examination of the properties of the intellect with which the TIE breaks off. So this way of reading the *Ethics* is problematic.

Second, Spinoza could be engaging in a metaphysical inquiry into formal and objective essences. In other words, he may have abandoned the TIE because he realized that in order to methodically reflect on the nature of the intellect and expand its power, one must first know how the intellect and its ideas fit into the order of formal essences, and that requires that one unpack the corresponding objective essences, in an orderly fashion, from one's idea of the most perfect being. It is worth investigating further whether the *Ethics* can be read this way.

Finally, it is also possible that Spinoza gave up entirely on the project of the TIE and embarked on a different project in the *Ethics*. Whether and how the method of the TIE relates to the *Ethics* is as yet unclear. However, we can conclude from this exploration of prior senses of analysis and synthesis that the method Spinoza lays out in the TIE certainly contains elements of Hobbes's use of mathematical genetic definitions as principles, Descartes's meta-method of analysis, and the synthesis by which Burgersdijk orders distinct cognitions to track the order of nature. In the TIE Spinoza appears to have developed various methods he encountered in his immediate intellectual environment into an amalgamated method for investigating and teaching the order of nature that is uniquely his own.

Department of Philosophy
University of Houston
hhattab@central.uh.edu

Caspar Langenhert's Parisian 'School of Egoists' and the Reception of Geulincx's Physics, from Occasionalism to Solipsism

Michael Jaworzyn

Introduction: Egoism, Occasionalism, and Langenhert's 'New Philosophy'

Given his obscurity today, it may come as a surprise that for a brief period after his death Caspar Langenhert (1661–*c*.1730) seems to have been reasonably widely remembered as a controversial, if peculiar, thinker—the 'leader' of a 'bizarre system of *egomets* or egoists', as one source put it.[1] The only genuinely contemporary report regarding Langenhert's attempt to start a school in Paris, in the February 1702 edition *of Nouvelles de la République des Lettres*, was a little more restrained in its evaluation, though; concerning his philosophical thought, it references only his claims to novelty. 'A certain Dutch philosopher named Langenhert',[2] it tells us, had been holding regular weekly conferences in Paris, teaching 'a new Philosophy founded on Principles unknown to Philosophers, ancient as much as modern, and which overthrow, as he claims, all systems which have been advanced up until now'.[3] In addition to these meetings, Langenhert's 'new philosophy' was to be published as a series of dialogues in both Latin and French; the first instalment had by that point already appeared. As for the school he attempted to found, however, he was very soon supposed to have given up on it, and on his philosophical innovations, in the face of an anonymous *Dissertatio Critica*. Langenhert, we are told, never responded

---

[1] J.F. Adry, 'Catalogues des Ouvrages de Malebranche', in *Oeuvres complètes de Malebranche. Tome XI. Traité de Morale*, ed. A. Robinet, 20 vols. (Paris, 1958–76), 11: x–xii (xi).
[2] Jacques Bernard, 'Article VII, Extrait de diverses Lettres', *Nouvelles de la République des Lettres* (Feb. 1702), 230–1 (230).
[3] Bernard, 'Article VII', 230–1.

Michael Jaworzyn, *Caspar Langenhert's Parisian 'School of Egoists' and the Reception of Geulincx' Physics, from Occasionalism to Solopsism* In: *History of Universities*. Edited by: Mordechai Feingold,
Oxford University Press (2021). © Oxford University Press.
DOI: 10.1093/oso/9780192893833.003.0005

to the critical dissertation, and even ceased to hold his weekly meetings as a result.

This latter part of the story seems unlikely. Langenhert at least continued his writing: there were three further dialogues, whose content is continuous with the first, and which mention that he had been criticized.[4] And while it is possible that he had to give up on his public teaching, not much later there emerged quite different accounts of the reasons he did so. Lefèbvre de Beauvray, in particular, reports that the impression Langenhert made in Paris was such that the government, alarmed by the 'noise' and 'bad effect' of his school, asked him to teach elsewhere.[5] Either way, Langenhert's school was short-lived.

Langenhert's views, however, seem to have become recognizable enough to be afforded the standing of a (slightly disreputable) school of thought in the following years. Lefèbvre de Beauvray, for example, would characterize Langenhert's teachings as one of the more unconvincing strands of metaphysical thinking of the period: 'some, who believe themselves more reasonable than the others [idealists and materialists] and who are even less, admit of no other reality than their own proper and individual being. This last system under the name of egoism has been maintained in our times, even in Paris, quite publicly by a Dutch sophist named Langhner [*sic*].'[6] Similarly, a review of Rousseau's *First Discourse* suggests that what the reviewer calls Rousseau's 'animalism' be added to a list of modern sophisms including Berkeley's 'spiritualism', La Mettrie's 'machinism'—and more unexpectedly, Langenhert's 'egoism'; the brief account it gives of Langenhert's views accuses him of holding that the only thing one could prove was '*l'Egoïté*', one's own existence—'*ego existo*'. [7] Still others would later characterize Langenhert's views in almost exactly the same way.[8] According to these later reports, Langenhert was supposed to have been what we might refer to nowadays as a solipsist.[9]

---

[4] Caspar Langenhert, *Novus Philosophus, Le Nouveau Philosophe* (Paris, 1701–2). Henceforth: NP followed by dialogue number, Latin then French pagination respectively. The translation, by Regnier-Desmarais, indicates the well-placed allies Langenhert had in Paris; on this, as well as the fact that Langenhert openly discussed Spinoza's work, albeit critically, see Paul Vernière, *Spinoza et la pensée française avant la Révolution* (Paris, 1954), 235–40. Across the four dialogues various characters take the role of Langenhert's representative and his interlocutor; neither character is supposed to be entirely familiar with Langenhert's own views. The *Dissertatio Critica* did exist, but the only remaining copy seems to be bound with the rest of the *Novus Philosophus* in the held by the University of Glasgow (Sp Coll BC2-i.29). Though Langenhert was clearly aware of it, whether he genuinely responded to it is a different question.

[5] Claude-Rigobert Lefèbvre de Beauvray, 'Métaphysique', in *Dictionaire social et patriotique* (Amsterdam, 1770), 328–34 (328).

[6] Lefèbvre de Beauvray, 'Métaphysique', 328.

[7] Élie Fréron, 'Lettre VII', *L'Année Litteraire* VII (1755), 145–167 (166–7).

[8] E.g., Prosper Wartel, *L'Atheisme Dévoilé* (1763), 8.

[9] I will usually refer to egoism rather than solipsism—this is the term used by Langenhert's near-contemporaries; no ethical view is intended. There is an important distinction between

These accounts have more recently been questioned. Sébastien Charles has argued that Langenhert's published work did not conform to the picture they paint; Langenhert should not be counted among the egoists, if there even were any.[10] As Charles emphasizes, far from denying the existence of the external world, Langenhert affirmed it, albeit as a hypothesis in physics rather than as a metaphysical truth. And although Langenhert did claim that the existence of the external world could not be shown, this was argued according to Descartes's principles rather than his own. Charles, then, takes Langenhert to be engaging in the polemics surrounding Cartesianism in France at the time as a critic of Descartes and Descartes's occasionalist followers.

It seems to me, however, that Langenhert's views do in fact resemble crucial aspects of what has become known as occasionalism: for Langenhert, finite creatures do not bring about any changes, only God does.[11] God

those who account our own minds the source of what seems to be the world—this is what I generally have in mind when referring to genuine solipsism—and those who give God responsibility for engendering such thoughts in us. Langenhert is the latter. In what follows, I will usually refer to the external world, and sometimes to the physical or corporeal world, in the context of the discussion of Cartesianism—God is not included among the things of the external world. Langenhert refers to *corpora extra nos* (bodies outside us) in his arguments against Cartesian accounts of causation and representation of the external world, but it will turn out that these are applicable to any finite substances in Langenhert's own system. Referring to the 'world' is supposed to remain indifferent to the question of how many corporeal substances there might be in the various Cartesian systems, as are references to 'body' without an article.

[10] Similar accounts of Langenhert's supposed egoism are given in the following: Sébastien Charles, *Berkeley au Siècles des Lumières: Immaterialisme et Scepticisme au XVIIIe Siècle* (Paris, 2003), 57–9; Sébastien Charles, 'Du 'Je Pense, Je Suis' au 'Je Pense, Seul Je Suis': Crise du Cartésianisme et Revers des Lumières', *Revue Philosophique de Louvain* 102 (2004), 565–582 (574–5); Sébastien Charles, 'Skepticism and Solipsism in the Eighteenth Century: Revisiting the Egoist Question', in *Skepticism in the Modern Age*, eds. José R. Maia Neto, Gianni Paganini, and John Christian Laursen (Leiden, 2009), 325–42 (330–3).

[11] Some care is needed when applying a term like 'occasionalism', particularly given Langenhert's idiosyncratic understanding of the term 'occasional cause'. Langenhert takes the occasional cause to be the cause which actually operates or produces the requisite effect, and the patient to provide the occasion for the occasional cause to act on it (NPIV 29–30/73); more usually, however, occasional cause or occasion are synonymous, and not in the patient—though Langenhert does follow contemporaneous usage in not necessarily taking the cause which actually exerts causal power as having to be God. Steven Nadler has rightly pointed out in 'Descartes and Occasional Causation', *British Journal for the History of Philosophy* 2 (1994), 35–54—that occasional causation is a wider concept, which need not amount to occasionalism as loosely defined below; for example, some movement in body can be an occasional cause for the mind to produce some sensation in itself (God might be involved in other ways, e.g., in the institution of nature which allows for the coincidence in the first place). Nevertheless, it seems to me that, with certain caveats, Langenhert's views at every point of his career can be aligned with various accounts of occasionalism. If occasionalism is taken only to involve the negative claim that finite creatures have and exercise no causal powers, and the positive claim that God alone does, and it is recognized that one can be either a full occasionalist (where these theses apply in the various domains of interaction which are considered in a broadly Cartesian thought, e.g., body-body, body-mind,

alone is the source of all modifications and any changes in the human mind; all things—bodies or minds—other than God are for various reasons causally inefficacious. Langenhert's was, nevertheless, an unusual form of occasionalism—one primarily based on the metaphysical claim that no individual thing has anything in common with any other thing. And despite sharing the occasionalists' views regarding God's power and creature's lack of it, Langenhert's metaphysics eventually did away with the appeal to causally inefficacious occasions in the physical world; in the case of our thoughts, where occasionalists take the 'occasion' for God to act on the mind to be in the external world, for Langenhert it is in the mind itself. Inasmuch as it seems to cast doubt on any role played by the external world, this looks as though it might commit Langenhert to a kind of solipsism.[12]

mind-body, mind-mind) or a partial occasionalist (where the two theses apply to only some kinds of interactions), it is indisputable that Langenhert throughout his career is an occasionalist with respect to at least some kinds of alleged interactions. But the increasing attention in recent years to the various possible scopes of and arguments for occasionalism—while wholly applicable to Langenhert since he does not come close to mentioning mainstays of occasionalist argumentation such as the lack of a necessary connection between cause and effect or the radicalization of the doctrine of continuous creation—has often coincided (as in Nadler, ibid.) with the claim that occasionalism is not a particular (ad hoc) solution to the mind-body problem, but a systematic view with other motivations such as exalting God's omnipotence by making him play the role of sole cause in nature (e.g., Alfred Freddoso, 'Medieval Aristotelianism and the Case against Secondary Causation in Nature', in *Divine and Human Action: Essays in the Metaphysics of Theism*, ed. Thomas V. Morris (Ithaca, NY, 1998) 74–118). It strikes me, however, that the early Langenhert's views approach the traditional view (God is invoked in order to explain the otherwise impossible mutual action and passion of mind and body). Langenhert in the *Novus Philosophus* would count as a full occasionalist: as all states which ordinarily might be said to be the result of some kind of interaction in his system are directly and solely brought about by God, although Langenhert admits of fewer kinds of interactions than most occasionalists—the existence of bodies cannot be proven in metaphysics, and they are not needed to serve as occasions for God's action. Equally, the motivation for invoking God again is not so much a systematic commitment to emphasizing the role of God's action in nature as the need to explain change in the mind (this time not an apparent mutual interchange of action and passion, but simply the fact that our minds do change, and neither we nor bodies could be responsible). Of course, further specifications can be made to the definition of occasionalism, such as Bardout's stipulation that the positive thesis involves God acting in a law-like, determinate way on the basis of occasions as 'sufficient reasons' (Jean-Christophe Bardout, 'Occasionalism: La Forge, Cordemoy, Geulincx', in *A Companion To Early Modern Philosophy*, ed. Steven Nadler (Oxford, 2002), 140–51 (150); something in the vein of Bardout's additional condition makes historical sense, but do not mean that Langenhert's views are not akin to and developed from occasionalism: the possibility that the occasions occur in the very thing being changed does not seem to be considered by scholars of occasionalism (such that, for Langenhert, particular modifications of the mind follow from one another in a determinate law-like way, but owing to God alone). Though I will discuss all this in passing here, I will provide a more detailed philosophical reading of Langenhert's account of divine action elsewhere.

[12] Since this seems, in metaphysics at least, to commit Langenhert to the existence of minds and God alone, one could also ascribe to Langenhert a form of immaterialism in a Berkeleyan vein. Langenhert's trajectory to immaterialism from an unusual Cartesianism

A better comparison, however, would be the account of the term *egomet* given in the *Dictionaire de Trévoux*. Where solipsists are often taken to make themselves the source of what they seem to perceive of the external world, for the *egomet*, 'there is nothing real outside us, and our sensations do not presuppose that there necessarily is something outside us, because God can produce them in our soul by himself, & without the aid of any object existing outside us'.[13] Still, although Langenhert is not entirely forthcoming regarding how God 'does everything in everything',[14] it seems clear enough that he thinks neither bodies nor our minds—which are unable to bring about changes in themselves—could produce the various modifications of our minds. Even though we cannot have a metaphysical explanation of how God brings about particular modifications of our minds, we can know by elimination that he is the only possible source of change in us.[15]

As unusual as Langenhert's variety of occasionalism is, his theoretical proximity to occasionalism in general can be corroborated historically by looking at his philosophical development from the context of his earlier work in the Dutch Cartesianism at the University of Leiden. It can be observed in the changes in his views from his 1685 Leiden *Disputatio Philosophica Inauguralis*,[16] to his ambivalent 1688 commentary on the physics of Arnold Geulincx (1624–1669)—best known as a particular kind of occasionalist, who spent the latter part of his career as an unsettled,

---

would then constitute an alternative version of the account given in Charles J. McCracken, 'Stages on a Cartesian Road to Immaterialism', *Journal of the History of Philosophy* 24:1 (1986), 19–40. One could claim, then, that there is a Cartesian road to immaterialism more specific to the University of Leiden than the general story McCracken tells.

[13] 'Egomet', in *Dictionnaire universel françois et latin, vulgairement appelé dictionnaire de Trévoux*. 8 vols. (Paris, 1771), 3: 948–9. Not everything else in the entry in question corresponds to Langenhert's views (the proof it claims the *egomets* provide, following Descartes, of God's existence does not have any analogue in Langenhert's work, for example.) As we will see, Langenhert also denies the distinction between sensations and ideas (usually spelled out in terms of representation), so what is here said about sensations applies to all thoughts for Langenhert. Still, *egomet* is here accounted a synonym for egoist, and elsewhere, 'egoism' is limited to denying other creatures (bodies, minds) rather than God, as in the famous (uncredited) review of Berkeley's *Principles* in *Mémoires de Trévoux*, (May 1713), 921–2 (922); Charles may have been too hasty in denying the status of egoist to Langenhert.

[14] NPIV 44/85: 'Deus... omnia in omnibus operatur'. For a caveat, see NPI 80/81: 'Res generalis ea est, *quae multis rebus aliis est communis*'.

[15] My purpose here accordingly does not include giving an account of exactly how God acts on us; Langenhert strictly circumscribes the role of metaphysics, and his position clearly excludes such things, theological matters, from metaphysics, even if his characters in the dialogues are not always as careful to observe the distinction between disciplines as they might be.

[16] Caspar Langenhert, *Disputatio Philosophica Inauguralis*, (Leiden, 1685); no pagination— citations given by section and thesis number. The only discussion of this I know of is a brief mention in Wiep van Bunge 'Langenhert', in *The Dictionary of Seventeenth and Eighteenth-Century Dutch Philosophers* eds. Wiep van Bunge et al., 2 vols. (Bristol, 2003) 2:587–9.

and according to some accounts comparatively minor, figure in Leiden—
in the *Compendium Physicae*,[17] to the later Parisian teachings of the *Novus
Philosophus*. Langenhert's development is, on the one hand, clearly a move
away from the Cartesianism (still somewhat unorthodox, depending on
what takes to be definitive of Cartesianism generally) of his early time at
the University of Leiden; on the other hand, it is a move which also draws
on a different strand of Cartesian occasionalism which was also present in
Leiden: that presented in Geulincx's physics. As a result, I suggest that,
while it is not inconceivable that Langenhert's move to Paris put him into
contact with the Cartesian and occasionalist views he opposed in the
Novus Philosophus, it is the complicated situation of his earlier years at or
around Leiden which best allows us to understand Langenhert's philosophical path—and for which, unlike whatever he may have picked up
once he moved to the French context, there is published evidence.

The intention in this essay is to illustrate these points by focusing on
one particular case: the way Langenhert's accounts of whether and how
mind and body interact changed, and the consequences regarding how
our minds can relate to the physical world, if at all.[18] All through his career

---

[17] Arnold Geulincx, *Compendium Physicae. Illustratum a Casparo Langenhert. Accedit
hujusce Brutum Cartesianum* (Franeker, 1688), hereafter CP, followed by part number
and page.

[18] This focus means that, other than indicating why his arguments against any metaphysical proof of the external world commit him just as much to the form of occasionalism
I ascribe to him, I will tend to set aside addressing in too much detail the reconstruction of
Langenhert's own views on causation. Equally, although the question of the role heterogeneous natures of mind and body is one useful way of understanding Langenhert's philosophical development in the context of the University of Leiden, there are other possible
avenues. Two particularly noteworthy cases which will not receive the attention they war-
rant here are i) Langenhert's reference in both the early works discussed to what he seems to
take as a principle or axiom, 'nothing is changed by itself', and ii) Langenhert's relegation of
the existence of the external world to a hypothesis in physics in the *Novus Philosophus*. The
former is primarily mentioned to rule out the possibility—sometimes adopted by various
Cartesians and more recent scholarly readings of Descartes—that the mind may in some
respect contribute to bringing about its own (passive) perceptions, but taken more generally,
if the bringing about of active modifications of the mind, such as volitions or judgements,
counts as the mind changing itself, then these too would be beyond the mind's own power.
The principle in question is also ascribed by Langenhert to Spinoza in his unpublished
manuscript arguing against Spinoza's *Ethica*, with the consequence that he thinks no change
whatsoever is possible in Spinoza's system: see Miguel Benitez, 'Une réfutation inédite de
l'*Ethica* de Spinoza', in *Materia actuosa. Antiquité, Age classique, Lumières. Mélanges en
l'honneur d'Olivier Bloch* eds. Miguel Benitez, Antony McKenna, Gianni Paganini and Jean
Salem (Paris, 2000), 327–41. The reasons Langenhert takes Spinoza to be committed to the
principle, however, I would suggest also apply to Langenhert's own work in the *Novus
Philosophus*, with one difference: their respective accounts of God, which Langenhert thinks
allows him a possible source of change not open to Spinoza. The point regarding hypotheses
is of interest as a possible vector of Geulincx's influence. No mention is made of hypotheses
in Langenhert's Leiden disputation, in physics or otherwise; in Geulincx's work, however,
Langenhert would have read that while the possibility of motion can be shown in

Langenhert took it as a given that mind and body are of wholly different natures to one another; they have nothing whatsoever in common. But at different stages Langenhert spells out the consequences of this claim differently. In the *Disputatio*, it indicates that God must intervene to make mind and body interact, but they do actually then interact; in his commentary on Geulincx it indicates that they do not interact, but that God brings about the relevant changes in the mind only when given occasion to do so by the relevant changes taking place in the body; in the *Novus Philosophus* it indicates not only that those who subscribe to the heterogeneity of mental and physical substances cannot know that the external world (bodies) exist—our ideas of the world cannot represent it—but also that our ideas of it are not caused by it, and do not even require it to provide the occasions for God to produce those ideas in the mind. Although in this final stage the argument is primarily against Cartesians who hold that mind and body have nothing in common and yet think that their various sensations or thoughts originate in the external world, Langenhert's own view is that no two substances have anything in common, so the same reasoning he mobilizes against the Cartesians is something he too is committed to. Behind this sequence of views there are a number of changes in Langenhert's situation and academic context; this case is one where Langenhert seems to directly make use of material drawn from various Cartesian traditions at Leiden. In particular, his engaging with Geulincx's work coincides with his advocating a stricter occasionalism, and later leads to his adapting to his own ends arguments he had previously agreed with Geulincx in rejecting. Geulincx's work, then, provides a crucial pivot for understanding how he came to his unusual later views from the Cartesianism of his early work. But I would also tentatively suggest that in addition to owing his view of the heterogeneous natures of mind and body to the earlier Leiden context, Langenhert's willingness to adapt his views over the course of his career is an indication that the variety of Cartesianism he defended in the Leiden disputation was a less dogmatic Cartesianism than Cartesians of the decade prior—including actual students of Geulincx—had exhibited.

This also makes Langenhert's work an interesting example of the reception of Geulincx's views in the early modern period. Geulincx may not have been one of the more influential thinkers of the period in question—though perhaps more influential than is nowadays generally recognized—but even those who knew of his work quite well interpreted it quite differently. The

metaphysics, its actual existence is a hypothesis required to explain the phenomena; in the *Novus Philosophus*, the very existence of the external world is a hypothesis of physics. Still, even if Langenhert does not make use of hypotheses in his *Disputatio*, that does not mean he could not have picked it up from Descartes or elsewhere in either Leiden or Paris rather than from Geulincx.

Compendium Physicae would have been one of the conduits of Geulincx's thought beyond his immediate context,[19] but it was one of two editions appearing in the same year, and differed in a number of respects from its rival. Geulincx's supporters agreed that his physics was broadly Cartesian, but they also emphasized the crucial addition of a kind of occasionalism based on an epistemic condition on causation.[20] Nevertheless, where others influenced by Geulincx, such as Johannes Swartenhengst (1644–1711) or Cornelis Bontekoe (*c.*1644–1685), differed regarding the extent of Geulincx's occasionalism and the consequences of his adherence to the epistemic condition on causation, Langenhert held that Geulincx did not develop his occasionalism consistently.[21] In fact, Langenhert seems only

[19] This edition, whose provenance is unknown, is sometimes quite different to other editions of Geulincx's physics; the edition published in the same year with works of his student Cornelis Bontekoe—Arnold Geulincx, *Physica Vera. Quae Versatur Circa Hunc Mundum. Opus Posthumum* (Leiden, 1688)—seems more complete and more polished. C. Louise Thijssen-Schoute, *Nederlands Cartesianisme* (Utrecht, 1989), 208–10, discusses Langenhert's edition of Geulincx's physics, though she does not mention the points regarding causation at issue here. It was reviewed in *Acta Eruditorum* 3 (1688), 623–4, and Bayle's mention of the *Brutum Cartesianum*, a text Langenhert appended to the *Compendium Physicae,* indicates that he would have known of the edition too—and he seems to assign the *Brutum Cartesianum* to Geulincx. See Pierre Bayle, *Dictionaire historique et critique*, 2 vols. (1697), 2/2:957. Since the epistemic condition on causation was one of Bayle's favoured arguments for occasionalism, as pointed out in Todd Ryan, *Pierre Bayle's Cartesian Metaphysics: Rediscovering Early Modern Philosophy* (New York, 2009), 71–3, and Bayle was certainly not someone who hid his erudition, we might expect Bayle to have exhibited more familiarity with Geulincx than he did. Accordingly, Geulincx was probably not the source of his use of the *quod nescis* principle.

[20] Geulincx's occasionalism has been—alongside the connection to and comparison with Spinoza—one of the things for which he is best known; it is the subject of a full-length study: Alain De Lattré, *L'Occasionalisme d'Arnold Geulincx* (Paris, 1967), though there were prior attempts not to deny but to downplay Geulincx's occasionalism by H.J. De Vleeschauwer, 'Occasionalisme et *Conditio Humana* Chez Arnold Geulincx', *Kant-Studien* 50 (1958), 109–24; some recent discussions of the principle usually taken as the basis of Geulincx's occasionalism—the called variously the 'no-knowledge' argument, the epistemic condition on causation, or the principle *quod nescis quomodo fiat, id non facis* [that which you do not know how to do, you do not do] include Stephen Nadler, 'Knowledge, Volitional Agency and Causation in Malebranche and Geulincx', in *Occasionalism: Causation Among the Cartesians* (Oxford, 2011), 74–87; Emanuela Scribano, "Quod Nescis Quomodo Fiat, Id Non Facis'. Occasionalism against Descartes?', *Rinascimento* 51 (2011), 63–86; Andrea Sangiacomo, 'Defect of Knowledge and Practice of Virtue in Geulincx's Occasionalism', *Studia Leibnitiana* 46 (2014), 46–63. Geulincx's physics seem to be less well served by scholarship than other areas of his thought, especially with regard to their role in his occasionalism and its transmission, though Thijssen-Schoute, *Nederlands Cartesianisme*, Gotthelf Gronau, *Die Naturlehre Geulincx' und ihr Zusammenhang mit die Naturlehre Descartes'* (Wolfenbüttel, 1911), and Edward G. Ruestow, *Physics at Seventeenth and Eighteenth-Century Leiden: Philosophy and the New Science in the University* (The Hague, 1973) also address various aspects of his physics.

[21] Ester Bertrand takes Swartenhengst's reading of Geulincx's occasionalism to exhibit an asymmetry between mind-to-body and body-to-mind causation, and not always to make use of the *quod nescis* principle when expected to do so—see Ester Bertrand, 'Johannes Swartenhengst (1644–1711): A Dutch Cartesian in the Heat of Battle' (Ph.D. Diss.,

sporadically to recognize Geulincx as an occasionalist at all, and as a consequence—as I will point out in the course of this article—often seems to think that Geulincx's words need various kinds of elaboration, clarification or supplementing. In this respect, even if he may have had a role in downplaying the originality of Geulincx's thought, perhaps to the detriment of Geulincx's reputation, Langenhert would have played a role in passing on ideas derived from Geulincx's work or developed as a response to it.

From here we will proceed as follows: in the first part, we will look at the views Langenhert advanced in his earlier works, providing contextual information about the background at Leiden which will contribute to an understanding of the changes in his views mentioned above. The second part will examine his positions in the *Novus Philosophus*, showing that his criticisms of Descartes's accounts of our knowledge of the external world depend on his reducing ideas and sensations to modifications of the mind, neither of which need an occasion in the external world for God to produce them in us. The third part briefly indicates that Langenhert's own views commit him to precisely what he accuses the Cartesians of—and hence to being something comparable to an *egomet*.

Langenhert before the Move to Paris

Langenhert's Leiden Disputio Philosophica Inauguralis.

There is no evidence that while in Leiden, Langenhert considered the possibility of relegating the existence of the external world to a mere hypothesis in physics. He did, however, in his *Disputatio Philosophica Inauguralis* briefly indicate that, despite the fact that the respective natures of mind and body should rule it out, there is a *conjunctio* of the two which, as he puts it, involves their mutual action and passion. Of course, it is difficult to establish with any certainty whether Langenhert genuinely held the precise views he put forward in the *Disputatio*. And as we will see shortly, there were crucial details which Langenhert changed his mind about soon after; if institutional constraints of the Leiden context, the disputation format—or indeed the general atmosphere—pressured Langenhert to adopt views he did not really believe in, this could certainly explain why he was so willing to do so.

University of Edinburgh & Free University of Brussels, 2014). Bontekoe, it seems to me, extended his occasionalist views to our bringing about our own thoughts (e.g., volitions) too, and hence was a more thoroughgoing occasionalist than even Geulincx—see Cornelis Bontekoe, *Metaphysica* (Leiden, 1688), 14–5.

This particular early disputation of Langenhert's took place with Wolferd Senguerd (1646–1724) presiding; Senguerd, for his part, was appointed—in the wake of Cartesian disruption to teaching at Leiden—as a 'Peripatetic' counterpart to a thinker who was considered more inclined to Cartesianism, Burchard to Volder (1643–1709). After the founding of the *Theatrum physicum* in Leiden (1675), however, both Senguerd and De Volder became just as well known for their use of experiments in teaching as for their adherence to particular philosophical schools. And both made use of the disputation format in ways which mean we cannot necessarily understand the views expressed as exactly those of anyone involved.[22] Yet while Langenhert's disputation is not unwaveringly Cartesian,[23] it is also undoubtedly more Cartesian than anything else. Scholastic Aristotelian principles are dismissed, and the kind of ideologically noncommittal reference to experimentation one might expect plays no role. So it seems unlikely that Senguerd, unlike what was sometimes the case with other *praeses*, exerted much influence over the content of the disputation from this perspective.

With respect to the issue guiding this essay, what Langenhert defends certainly looks like a form of Cartesianism. Here is the crucial sequence of theses, which seem to form a chain of argumentation:

20. Nothing is changed by itself.

21. We recognize nothing beyond God, minds, bodies, and their attributes.

22. The mind... by its nature cannot act on body, nor body on mind.

23. Whence the conjunction of mind & body, which is nothing other than mutual action & passion, clearly demonstrates the existence of God a posteriori.[24]

---

[22] See Gerhard Wiesenfeldt, 'Academic writings and the rituals of early modern universities', *Intellectual History Review* 26:4 (2016), 447–60. Senguerd is mentioned as someone who published a series of disputations over the course of which he changed his mind, in this instance in the light of results of experimentation carried out during the course. The extent of De Volder's Cartesianism in the years after his founding the *Theatrum physicum* is a matter of debate; see, e.g., Wiep van Bunge, 'Dutch Cartesian Empiricism and the Advent of Newtonianism', in *Cartesian Empiricisms*, eds. Mihnea Dobre and Tammy Nyden (Dordrecht, 2013), 89–104, for a view which emphasizes De Volder's continuing Cartesianism despite his adherence to experimental philosophy; see also Tammy Nyden, 'De Volder's Cartesian Physics and Experimental Pedagogy', in *Cartesian Empiricisms*, eds. Mihnea Dobre and Tammy Nyden (Dordrecht, 2013), 227–49.

[23] Van Bunge, 'Langenhert', 588, suggests that the disputations are for the most part 'completely loyal' to Descartes: in their claims about the mind, body and causation this is not the case, nor is it with Langenhert's account of the will, which 'follows' the intellect, nor in his rejection of Descartes's principle of inertia, however.

[24] Langenhert, 'Ex Metaphysicâ', *Disputatio*, Th.20–3: '20. Nulla res mutatur à se./21. Praeter Deum, mentes, corpora, eorumque attributa, nihil novimus./22. Mens (animam rationalem alii vocant) suâ naturâ non potest agere in corpus, nec corpus in mentem./23.

The disputation format does admittedly make the reasoning, and some-times what precisely Langenhert is claiming, somewhat opaque—all we have are the theses, without the defence they would have received on the occasion, and there was no need for either the presiding teacher or the student to have believed what was argued. In this instance, though, Langenhert seems to have taken ownership of the views, while at the same time indicating that he was prepared to change them. So we can say that, at this time, for Langenhert the very fact that there is mutual action and passion between mind and body is used as an indication that God both exists and brings about their conjunction. The possibility that mind and body bring about the relevant changes in themselves by themselves, such that the mutual action and passion are merely coinciding or concomitant changes of each (which nevertheless appear as if there was interchange between the two) is ruled out by the claim that nothing is changed by itself. Without further clarification, however, we cannot be sure what kind of involvement Langenhert has in mind for God in the interaction of mind and body. It could be, among other possibilities, that God somehow enables mind and body to act on one another themselves despite their intrinsic inaptness for doing so, perhaps either by somehow elevating their natures such that the interaction can occur, or by using them as instru-ments; or it could that God solely brings about the respective changes which are only loosely referred to as mutual action and passion. My suspi-cion is that Langenhert's terminology suggests one of the former options. In any case, the key point of doctrine here is that Langenhert takes the mutual action and passion of mind and body as a given, a plain fact which can only be explained by God because the natures of mind and body themselves cannot.

Langenhert's Annotations to the Compendium Physicae and Geulincx's Physics at Leiden.

Roughly three years later, in his annotations to Arnold Geulincx's physics in the *Compendium Physicae*, Langenhert seems to have entirely adopted what we might call a genuinely occasionalist view—and in passing to have downplayed Geulincx's own occasionalist views by taking Geulincx him-self to have allowed for certain kinds of interaction of mind and body. The way Langenhert expresses the denial of the mutual action and passion of mind and body in the *Compendium Physicae* is clearly a departure from the *Disputatio* where he had allowed for it, albeit with divine intervention of

Unde conjunctio mentis & corporis, quae nihil est, quam mutua actio & passio existentiam Dei à posteriori clare demonstrat.'

some sort. It is of course not unprecedented for thinkers to change their minds, even over quite brief periods. But this abrupt shift, and the way parts of the *Compendium Physicae* seem to prefigure the claims of both the characters in the dialogues of the *Novus Philosophus* who are supposed to be representing Langenhert and those he does not agree with, together indicate the importance of this work and the engagement with Geulincx in Langenhert's trajectory.

Langenhert's annotations in the *Compedium Physicae* came about as a result of his teaching a young nobleman, Alexander Zoete de Laeke van Villers. But the very fact that Langenhert chose to use Geulincx's physics is itself a little unexpected.[25] Langenhert's own lauding of Geulincx's work in the preface, which might serve as some justification for making use of it, is somewhat undermined when only a few lines later he goes on to say that it is quite often obscure, and that while he has attempted to explain Geulincx's views for the most part there are times when he could not resist giving his own opinions. Still, the existence of the *Compendium Physicae* may well constitute evidence that Geulincx's teaching of physics— which is not one of the areas he has since been best remembered for— remained influential in Leiden for some years, even after his death.[26]

Van Ruler has pointed out that Geulincx's followers often operated outside academia; this was not always entirely by choice.[27] Two of Geulincx's most enthusiastic students, Bontekoe and Swartenhengst, were heavily involved in the anti-peripatetic troublemaking at Leiden, and were sanctioned in various ways by the curators, eventually leading to their being banned and dismissed.[28] Langenhert's adopting Geulincx's work for instructional purposes almost ten years after these events suggests, though,

[25] A further fact, that *Compendium Physicae* was published in Franeker, and Langenhert's dedication signed in there, does not shed much light on what Langenhert had in mind. Nothing else is currently known about his time there. It is also unclear to what extent Langenhert's time as deputy head [*conrector*] of the Latin school in Zwolle prior to his move to Paris in 1697 can be demonstrated to have played a role in the development of his philosophical thought. The most detailed account of Langenhert's position in Zwolle and move to Paris is C. Louise Thijssen-Schoute, 'Een Notitie over Caspar Langenhert', in *Het Spinozahuis. Acht-en-Vijftigste Jaarverslag* (Leiden, 1956), 31–3.

[26] As mentioned before, Geulincx's situation at Leiden never seems to have really stabilized, and though he had his defenders in the Leiden faculty—most prominently the theologian Abraham Heidanus (1597–1678)—he remained beset with difficulties both financial and with the authorities at Leiden. See Han van Ruler, 'Arnold Geulincx', in *The Dictionary of Seventeenth and Eighteenth-Century Dutch* Philosophers eds. Wiep van Bunge et al., 2 vols. (Bristol, 2003), 1:322–9.

[27] Van Ruler, 'Arnold Geulincx', 328.

[28] A detailed account of these events can be found in Ester Bertrand, 'Swartenhengst', 52–60. Both were eventually allowed to reenroll, although it appears only Bontekoe did. Both were popular with their students, who joined in the troublemaking by 'shouting, banging their feet, and throwing beans' (Bertrand, 'Swartenhengst', 59).

that the actions of Geulincx's more unruly followers did not mean he was wholly forgotten, at least as a teacher, at the University of Leiden.[29] Nevertheless, as we will soon see, the *Compendium Physicae* would not have done much to advance the views Geulincx himself held. While Langenhert recognises, and seems to endorse, Geulincx's application of an epistemic condition to causation—the principle 'what we do not know how to do is not our action'—he does not seem to always recognize Geulincx's occasionalism.

Langenhert's own views at the time, however, are presented clearly enough. He gives a more detailed account of why mind and body cannot interact than in the very brief theses of the earlier *Disputatio*. He also mentions that even God's cooperation could not elevate bodies to cause states of our minds, as well as explicitly making use of the terminology of occasions rather than causes. Finally, he encounters Geulincx himself mooting the possibility that God would be no less of a deceiver in using an 'instrument' without any similarity to our perceptions to produce them than if he brought those sensations about himself directly.

For Geulincx, what is at issue in the relevant passages is the hypothesis of the existence of motion. Although one can give a metaphysical account of its possibility, the actual existence of motion cannot be demonstrated by reason alone; the senses are necessary too. Geulincx points out initially that we have certain sensations of which we cannot be the source (and to support this, Langenhert cites the principle, which he had also made use of in the *Disputatio*, that 'nothing is changed by itself', claiming that we are changed [*mutamur*] to the extent that we have perceptions, but that we could not be the source of changes in ourselves).[30] Geulincx continues: God alone could not bring sensations about without being a deceiver; nor could body, which of itself is at rest and 'without any action'; all that remains, then, is body in motion.[31] The fact that we have sensations is, accordingly, reason to posit the existence of motion as a hypothesis in physics. Geulincx concedes the lack of similarity, proportion, or force between the mind and motion in body; hence, the way that our perception depends on motion is obscure, but suggests nevertheless that it is what God willed. Langenhert's second contribution here is to ground the lack of proportion in a metaphysical account of substance and mode: the point he makes is that the modes differ in as much as the respective substances which they modify differ, because a mode is just the way a particular

---

[29] Another possible reason for making use of Geulincx's physics is that the teachings of the more recent Leiden professors, involving public demonstrations of experiments, were less easily transferred from the University to smaller-scale undertakings.

[30] CPIV 124, n.5.   [31] CPIV 125–6.

substance is modified;[32] the obscurity of the supposed connection between body in motion and our perceptions he takes up later.

Geulincx then presents as a possible objection to his own views the idea that God could by himself [*se solo*]—'immediately', as Langenhert glosses the passage—bring about our perceptions without the use of some kind of instrument.[33] Given the fact, the objection goes, that there is 'no proportion' between the supposedly necessary bodily instruments and the resultant mental perception, God would be no more a deceiver were he to bring about those perceptions in us without them than if he were to do so using such instruments. This, as we will see shortly, is a key point which Langenhert makes in his own name in the *Novus Philosophus*. Geulincx's own response is initially to say that God 'has infinite power, and could move body in as many ways as suffice to excite in us all those perceptions',[34] and hence we should rightly say that he excites in us those perceptions. On the other hand, though, Geulincx tells us secondly that we apprehend 'as if by a natural instinct'[35] that those perceptions come forth to us [*provenire*] from body in motion. But, he concludes, because either of these ways of explaining our perceptions is possible for God, we should believe the possibility which seems to us 'easier and more natural'.[36] Here, though he does not say it explicitly, this could well mean we should follow that natural instinct. As Langenhert points out, though, this is to believe something on the basis of something obscure and confused;[37] Geulincx had already conceded another point which Langenhert would go on to use in his arguments against our having any knowledge of the external world: we clearly and distinctly perceive that our sensations are modes of our mind, but we do not have similar certainty that they come from or otherwise depend on a really existing modifications of body.[38]

Langenhert is ambivalent about this line of thinking in Geulincx in other ways. He suggests that for the first part of Geulincx's response—which he takes to be what Geulincx endorses—there must be for Geulincx, in fact, some unknown 'proportion or commonality' between the motions of body and the perceptions in the mind because of the latter's use of terms implying such a relation.[39] Langenhert, however, claims not to know what that would be; motion itself, even if infinite force were employed by God, would never suffice to excite such thoughts in us. Very soon after he

---

[32] CPIV 126–7, n. 14.   [33] CPIV 128; ibid. n. 16.

[34] CPIV 128–9: 'Deus habeat vim infinitam & possit corpus movere tot modis, quot sufficiunt ad omnes illas perceptiones in nobis excitandum'.

[35] CPIV 129.   [36] CPIV 130.   [37] CPIV 129, n. 20.

[38] Only in the *Compendium Physicae* version of Geulincx's physics is the 'natural instinct' invoked.

[39] CPIV 128, n. 18. He presumably means 'as many as suffice' [*tot...quot sufficiunt*] quoted n. 31.

quibbles, too, with Geulincx's way of putting this first point—bodies excite perceptions in us, Langenhert tells us, only as occasions, and not as causes. And he certainly does not approve of Geulincx's entertaining the possibility that our perception could really come from body in motion, at least if by this Geulincx means as from a cause. The footnote claiming this expresses almost word for word the view Langenhert would take as the position of his interlocutor—but also, for that reason, the standard view, the view against which his own 'new philosophy' is opposed—in the *Novus Philosophus*: we finally do not know what the particular causes of our thoughts are; all we apprehend is that given the presence of certain 'determinations' in body certain determinate thoughts come to us (and in the *Novus Philosophus* his own view denies even this coincidence). Likewise, where in the *Disputatio* Langenhert had mentioned a conjunction of mind and body involving mutual action and passion, in his commentary in the *Compendium Physicae* he is more circumspect, describing it in these same terms of the presence of respective determinations of each on various occasions;[40] he can be quite dismissive of Geulincx when the latter seems to suggest there is interaction between the two.[41] And Langenhert seems more generally to view Geulincx not so much as someone who denied that the mind could act on body at all, but as someone who held the mind could only 'determine'—roughly, change the direction of—motion in very specific contexts, without being able to increase or diminish its quantity.[42] Langenhert takes these views of Geulincx's as being incompatible with positions he ought to have held: that the respective natures of mind and body having nothing in common, and the substance-mode metaphysics that rules out any mode of one being a mode of the other—both of which would play important roles in Langenhert's arguments in the *Novus Philosophus* too. But the brief reference in the *Compendium Physicae* to what is often considered the most crucial point of Geulincx's occasionalism— the principle *quod nescis quomodo fiat, id non facis* (roughly, what you do not know how to do is not your action)—receives positive commentary

---

[40] See e.g. CPV 147, n. 1, CPVI 201, n. 4.   [41] See e.g. CPVI 208–9, n. 26.

[42] CPIII 114. See e.g., Peter McLaughlin, 'Descartes on Mind-Body Interaction and the Conservation of Motion', *The Philosophical Review* 102:2 (Apr. 1993), 155–82 for discussion of this view in Descartes. Geulincx does say we 'use' [*utimur*] motion here, but there is no evidence that he meant the specific view of determination Langenhert suggests, and the point of the passage in Geulincx is that what we will in the physical world comes about only because of God's action. That Geulincx in many respects was not as consistent—or perhaps as overt—about the extent of his denial of interaction between mind and body in the *Compendium* may explain this misunderstanding. The version of Geulincx's physics on which Langenhert was commenting lacks explicit statements of many of Geulincx's views; equally, Langenhert seems either not to have noticed, or to have intentionally downplayed various of Geulincx's more distinctive positions.

from Langenhert, including a slightly more detailed restatement of the argument.[43]

It is possible, then, that what Langenhert perceived as weaknesses in Geulincx's views led him to advocate something closer to strict occasionalism in the *Compendium Physicae* than in his earlier *Disputatio*, particularly when it came to interaction between the mind and body. And in fact, the positions staked out in the commentary in response to Geulincx would be very close to the views Langenhert would argue against in the *Novus Philosophus*. The sometimes unexpected starting points in the *Novus Philosophus*—particularly those which Langenhert seeks to move beyond—make a good deal more sense if the *Compendium Physicae* is taken to express more or less what Langenhert later takes to be the most compelling alternative to his own views. Likewise, key positions—such as his endorsing mutual action and passion of mind and body—had clearly changed compared to the *Disputatio*. Whether they changed because of his engaging with Geulincx's work, or whether the commentary was only an opportunity to express these thoughts, we cannot know. Still, it is clear that key points brought up by Geulincx are echoed in Langenhert's later views.

But regarding the wider reception of Geulincx's work, Langenhert's commentary would—intentionally or otherwise—have diminished the perceived extent of Geulincx's occasionalism still further than Geulincx's own ambiguous main text might have done. It could be that the more controversial, unorthodox aspects of Geulincx's teaching had been forgotten with the departure of his most outspoken students; or it could be that their lingering reputation led Langenhert to downplay Geulincx's eccentricities.[44] But in choosing, almost twenty years after Geulincx's death, to use Geulincx's physics as the basis of his instruction, he remained within the domain of Leiden—albeit a Leiden from before his own time as a student. In any case, Langenhert's edition of the *Compendium Physicae*

---

[43] CPIII 110; Ibid., n. 47

[44] One such case concerns Geulincx's particular account of the mind; when Geulincx here says that when using reason we are 'beyond the world and before God' (CPV 148) he presumably is alluding to the view he elsewhere expresses by claiming human minds are modes of the one, eternal divine mind. This was one of the aspects of Geulincx's thought which would have been very controversial if it was known, since it sounds suspiciously close to Spinozism; on this aspect of Geulincx's thought and the connection to Spinoza, see Han van Ruler, 'Substituting Aristotle: Platonic themes in Dutch Cartesianism', in *Platonism at the Origins of Modernity: Studies on Platonism and Early Modern Philosophy*, eds. Sarah Hutton and Douglas Hedley (Dordrecht, 2007), 159–175 (171). Langenhert, though, takes this not in the metaphysical sense Geulincx probably had in mind, but only to mean that we are partaking of the intellectual life (CPV 148, n. 6). Whether this is because again Geulincx is not as direct as he was elsewhere, or because he was seeking to cover over Geulincx's more dangerous tendencies (Langenhert makes multiple negative references to Spinoza throughout his work), is again hard to say.

remains vital to understanding the views he would adopt after his departure from the United Provinces for Paris.

Langenhert's Parisian Teachings and the *Novus Philosophus*

The Cartesian Background and the External World.

Based on just the fourth dialogue, it is easy to see why recent scholars have not taken the early reports of Langenhert's being an *egomet* to be correct.[45] For my part, I think that Langenhert's historical background in Leiden Cartesianism and occasionalism suggests that there is more to these reports than might initially seem to be the case, and the hypothesis that Langenhert taught more freely in person might explain the apparent discrepancy. To establish this, we will proceed as follows: we will see that Langenhert's rejection of Descartes's proof of the existence of the external world is part of a broader picture, taking in various respects in which Cartesians would appeal to it, including both representing it, and requiring certain occurrences in it as occasions for our sensations. It turns out, though, that the question of the existence of the external world is brought up in order to defend an appeal to causally inefficacious occasions in the physical world as the foundations of our sensations, which Langenhert had already argued were redundant. In the following section, we will see that the same lines of argumentation Langenhert employs against the Cartesians apply all the more to his own views.

By the end of the fourth dialogue of the *Novus Philosophus*, Langenhert claims to have shown that according to Cartesian principles, 'no bodies exist outside us, that is outside our minds, or we cannot know that they exist'.[46] And, crucially, a few lines later he adds that no metaphysical demonstration of the existence of bodies whatsoever can be given. Langenhert faults the Cartesian position not because it cannot show there is an external

---

[45] There are further reasons why Langenhert's views are comparable to those of an *egomet*. Langenhert's admitting bodies as a hypothesis in physics does not amount to saying anything about the existence of bodies outside the mind: for Langenhert, every science exists only in the intellect, and the 'truth' of that science is identical with the science itself, not dependent on something outside the mind—See NPI 54/55. I further discuss this claim elsewhere. Equally, *pace* Alan Charles Kors, *Atheism in France 1650–1729, Volume I: The Orthodox Sources of Disbelief* (Princeton, 1990), 376, Langenhert's is not a sceptical position, firstly because he outright denies it, since he has a 'system' (NPI 14/15), and secondly because although we cannot know if there is an external world, we can know that according to Langenhert's account of causation it could not cause anything in us; this is an explicit metaphysical view, rather than a suspension of judgement.

[46] NPIV 47/87: '*corpora nulla extra nos*, id est, mentem nostram, *existere*; vel *nos ea extra nos existere scire non posse*'.

world, then, but because it claims it can. But even in his discussion of the apparently Cartesian views, Langenhert also has a broader metaphysical aim in mind than the target of Descartes's account of the external world: it is not just our ability to represent the external world that is in question, but the latter's causal role too. Langenhert's final argument regarding the external world is the culmination of a longer train of thought, which (mostly implicitly) had taken a more sophisticated approach to the various Cartesian reasons one might refer to the existence of bodies.

Roughly speaking, Langenhert had treated two aspects of what having a thought related to body or the external world is supposed to involve: such a thought can be understood as an operation of the mind occasioned by something happening in the physical world, or it can be understood in terms of the fact that it is supposed to be of or about the physical world—to represent it, that is to say. In Langenhert's work these correspond roughly—despite his dismissive attitude to the terminology—to what the Cartesians would refer to as the formal and objective reality of ideas respectively.[47] Different explanations can be provided for both aspects; each can potentially be explained by reference to the external world, so Langenhert has to rule out both. Of course, these two aspects of an idea may be closely connected in practice too: in fact, a crucial part of Langenhert's approach is to reduce both the operation of mind and its representative being to their status as modifications of the mind. He does, however, endeavour to treat the issues arising from both separately. Whether and what modifications of the mind are supposed to represent is, it seems, besides the point when attempting to understand them merely as operations of the mind, because for Langenhert—in line with what he took to be the standard Cartesian view of the time—there are examples of modifications of the mind which do not purport to represent anything in physical reality: sensations, in a broad sense including secondary qualities such as colours and sounds. And the causal history of an idea, when an idea is understood as a modification of mind which is supposed to represent something in external reality, can be bracketed when looking at what is intrinsic to the experience of it—for Langenhert, an idea's seemingly being of a particular thing is explained by (or just is) the fact that the mind is modified one way rather than another.

Langenhert's strategy is to address these aspects in turn. Both come into consideration, in particular, in the fourth dialogue of the *Novus Philosophus*. There, Langenhert discusses two closely related issues: i) the question of

[47] Of course, how precisely to spell out these times was a matter of disagreement both implicit and explicit, then as now. Here I will not enter into those debates, but present the terms as Langenhert does.

whether the 'foundation' of a colour can be in bodies even if colours themselves are not, and ii) the question of whether Descartes had successfully provided a metaphysical demonstration of the existence of bodies 'outside us'. Ultimately, both kinds of being ascribed to ideas are reduced by Langenhert to the mind's being modified a particular way. In turn, this will mean both that they cannot resemble, and hence cannot represent, anything in external reality, and that they cannot have a cause in some external physical reality; positing a causally inefficacious occasion for them is consequently superfluous.

Langenhert's Case against the Representation of Bodies.

Langenhert's most clear-cut statement as to why a Cartesian could not prove the existence of 'bodies outside us' comes as the result of his discussion of the possibility that our ideas of extension really do represent extension. His interlocutor claims that the idea we have of extension, in representing extension—or containing objectively what is formally contained in extension—is something which must have come to us not from God or from ourselves, but from extension itself. And Langenhert's representative does concede that he has an idea of three-dimensionally extended matter, and that he can conceive of or has ideas of the various parts, figures, and motions it has or might have. Though they are not extension, motion, or figure themselves, these ideas are, Langenhert's interlocutor initially urges, 'entirely similar' [*omnino similis*] to the them.[48] It is this purported similarity which Langenhert's representative denies, and without which he thinks they could not represent extension—to the point where he will deny that the idea we seemingly have of extension can tell us anything about extension, even that it exists. According to Langenhert, the various ways of accounting for the similarity necessary for representation—and hence reason to suppose that our having an idea of extension means that it really exists—can each be ruled out. There is no similarity in the genuine sense of some kind of agreement in nature, nor is there any resemblance in a 'metaphorical' sense. Nor does Langenhert think that what he considers his interlocutor's most sophisticated response, claiming that the very same extension formally existing outside the mind is contained in the mind objectively, allows us to say that our idea of extension represents it, and hence that it must exist.

This latter possibility is that, as his interlocutor puts it, it is 'one and the same [extension] which is said to be contained formally in body and

[48] NPIV 32/75.

objectively in the mind.'[49] To this Langenhert responds that the extension formally in body and objectively in the mind are not so according to the same respect: extension is 'in body formally and thus indeed such that it constitutes its nature, such that it is body itself,' whereas it is merely 'objectively in the mind, not constituting its nature, but a modification'.[50] Although Langenhert does not dwell on it, it is crucial that the idea of extension—or any other idea—can be reduced to being a particular modification of the mind. If, as we saw above in the case of sensations, what it means for the mind to have a particular thought is for the mind to take on that modification, then if the same extension that was formally in the world was supposed to be objectively in the mind, the mind itself would have to be extended. For mental modifications with no real counterpart in the physical world, such as sensations, it is not quite so problematic for the mind to be modified that way, as long as we do not take them to actually represent anything in the external world; for things which are supposed to have the properties of extended matter, it would either contradict the nature of mind or else lead us to say that the mind is identical to extension. Even claiming the identity of extension taken formally and objectively cannot, according to Langenhert, save the suggestion that our ideas can represent extension.

The particular conception of what it is to be a modification of the mind Langenhert is using is one which reflects his own views, and is not necessarily shared by Descartes himself. Equally, Langenhert took a different view of how to understand the 'objective' of objective extension; some later Cartesians might have understood the objective being of (say) extension to be nothing over and above the particular act by which extension is represented (with the clarification that there is something about the act itself which makes it about extension rather than something else), but Descartes likely took it to be something additional in the mind.[51] Langenhert, however, does not allow for any such further extension in the mind. His dismissal of the suggestion that there is a metaphorical similarity between the extension apparently in the mind and that in the world leads his interlocutor to admit that it was not 'two' extensions that Descartes had meant, but that the same formal extension was also contained objectively in the mind.

[49] NPIV 37/79: 'unam enim eandemque formaliter in corpore, objectivè in mente contineri dicit'.

[50] NPIV 37–38/79: 'in corpore formaliter & ita quidem, ut naturam ejus constituat, ut sit ipsum corpus; in mente objectivè, naturam ejus non constituens, sed modificationem'.

[51] Cf., e.g., the account of Arnauld's reinterpration of the Cartesian term 'objective being' in Han Thomas Adriaenssen, *Representation and Scepticism from Aquinas to Descartes* (Cambridge, 2017), 162–4.

It is less clear why Langenhert thinks he can dispense with that 'additional reality' quite so easily, though. Perhaps it stems from his understanding of thoughts as mere modifications of the mind, not really distinct from it, and taking Cartesians to do the same; there is no place in his ontology for the kind of additional reality such an account would call for. On the other hand, if Descartes is taken to have been closer to an account of objective extension where it is not something beyond the modification of the mind, then the problems we have already seen Langenhert raise for the Cartesian return: there is no way in which the extension in the mind and that in the world can really be said to be the same. If extension taken objectively actually is extension itself, then it cannot be instantiated in the mind, even in a different mode of being; their natures are wholly different, and hence there is no way those two natures could be modified such that the same thing could be in each. If extension taken objectively is a modification of the mind, all it can have in common with the formal extension it is supposed to represent is the name extension. Neither way can there be the similarity needed for representation.

Accordingly, for Langenhert there is nothing about objective extension which makes it represent formal extension; it is a particular modification of mind and no more. This suggests that it has particular intrinsic features or characteristics which distinguish it from other ideas, but it does not have these either in virtue of being a modification of the mind instantiating what is supposed to be its formal counterpart, or by having something extra, as it were, contained in the mind. This means that the idea of extension has roughly the same status as a sensation: it is a particular modification of the mind, one which is presumably involved in a succession of such modifications. This succession of modifications needs some kind of explanation—since, as with sensations, it does not come from us—but not one in terms of what is purportedly represented.

Langenhert's final statement that if one subscribes to Descartes's principles one cannot show the external world exists follows easily enough from this account of the inability of our ideas to represent bodies. According to Descartes, Langenhert says, extension and its modes are wholly different from us, that is from our minds. Extension itself and our minds have nothing in common, no connection whatsoever, either with respect to their entire natures or with respect to any of their affections or modifications. This being the case, the idea we supposedly have of extension—objective extension, according to Langenhert's rendering of the Cartesian terminology—is a only an idea, a modification of mind, and can have nothing in common with the extension of the physical world, i.e., extension taken formally. It cannot, therefore, represent it, since according to Langenhert representation requires similarity. Hence our having an idea of the external world can tell us nothing about the existence of bodies outside us.[52]

Our ideas of extension—and hence of the external world generally—amount to modifications of the mind; they have no intrinsic similitude to extension itself. There is no useful way in which one might appeal to body to explain the kinds of thoughts which are supposed to be representations of it. All this is based partly on what Langenhert takes to be a Cartesian point—that mind and body, and their modifications, have nothing in common—and partly on taking the objective extension in our minds as nothing more than a modification of our minds, and partly on the claim that the modifications of the mind are not distinct from the mind itself. This last point is likely more than Descartes would agree to, since he is willing to consider distinctions other than real ones, and it probably is not one he needs to make the claim that mind and body have nothing in common—but it is something Langenhert requires for his own metaphysical system.

Langenhert's Case against Bodily Occasions for Sensations.

The question of the external world's existence actually arises in the course of Langenhert's argumentation as his interlocutor's last resort for saying that certain modifications of the mind are occasioned—though not caused—by particular occurrences in the external world. Langenhert's discussion of the existence of the external world, then, comes about not only for its own sake, but also serves as a path to arriving at Langenhert's view that God is the only cause or condition of the modifications of our minds, other than perhaps our minds themselves. And as we've seen, Langenhert's arguments against the Cartesian claim that there is an external world involve saying that the ideas purportedly representing it are mere modifications of the mind, which do not resemble it and hence cannot represent it. As such, as we will now see, they have the same status as sensations. But even in the case of non-representative modifications of the mind, the possibility that they are occasioned by certain occurrences in the external world remains. So we turn now to Langenhert's criticisms of the appeal to occasions in the external world, and how, accordingly, Langenhert's interlocutor was initially pressured to introduce the Cartesian proof of its existence.

---

[52] Charles suggests that Langenhert simply takes up Foucher's sceptical critique of Descartes here; an influential treatment of Foucher is Richard A. Watson, *The Downfall of Cartesianism 1673–1712* (The Hague, 1966), 36–9. Langenhert nevertheless has different ends to Foucher.

The discussion of non-representative states of mind occurs when the question of the supposed 'foundations' of our sensations of colour is raised in the fourth dialogue. Sensations in general—according to Langenhert, but also among Cartesians of the period—were not taken to have the similarity to extension and its modifications necessary to be representations. To be sure, in the case of Descartes himself there has been much recent discussion of whether and in what way sensations might be representational.[53] For Langenhert, though, there is no question: sensations are mere modifications of mind, with nothing in common with extension. Colours, and indeed all sensations, are 'certain modes of thinking,' which have as their subject thinking substance; they are said to inhere in (*inesse*) or to modify a mind.[54] Langenhert seems to take this in a quite particular way, but one bearing comparison to other Cartesians of the time.[55] In an earlier dialogue, Langenhert had referred to the view that the mind itself, and not any body, is properly speaking what is said to be coloured: 'bodies, not minds, are said to be coloured, while minds actually are coloured, not bodies: common speech forbids saying that the soul is green & gold; Philosophy commands one to think the soul is green & gold.'[56] We clearly and distinctly perceive, we are told, that there can be nothing in body other than 'extension, motion, rest, figure, and the disposition of parts',[57] and this exhausts what they are; there is nothing coloured in them. Since, however, we really do experience colours (even if they do not represent anything in the world), if they cannot have body as their subject, they must be modifications of the mind. But the modifications of mind and the modifications of body have nothing in common. Consequently, as Langenhert's representative will go on to emphasise, they seem to have no connection by which they could either be understood by means of one another or by which one could be said to be cause or effect of the other.[58]

---

[53] See, e.g., Alison Simmons, 'Are Cartesian Sensations Representational?', *Noûs* 33:3 (1999), 347–69 for a good recent account.

[54] NPIV 6/54: 'Colores nempe nihil aliud sunt quàm certi quidam cogitandi modi; sive sensationes, quae substantiam cogitantem subjectum suum habent, utpote in quâ clarè & distinctè percipiuntur'. Although *modi cogitandi* need not necessarily mean (kinds of) modifications of the mind (it can also refer to something equivalent to beings of reason), Langenhert clearly opts for the former. Langenhert uses the terms nature and essence interchangeably, and attribute, affection, mode, and modification equivalently.

[55] Desgabets and Malebranche, for example, both made similar-sounding claims: see, e.g., Tad Schmaltz, *Malebranche's Theory of the Soul* (Oxford, 1996), 82–4.

[56] NPIII 62/116: 'cum tamen corpora, non mentes, dicantur colorata, mentes autem coloratae reverâ sint, non corpora: viridem animam dicere & flavam lingua communis vetat; viridem animam esse & flavam Philosophia cogitare jubet'.

[57] NPIV 6/54.

[58] NPIV 8/55: 'cum quibus tamen nihil quicquam commune habent, quique adeò nec intelligi per se invicem possunt, neque sui invicem vel causae esse vel effectûs, nullam penitùs cum se invicem connexionem habentes'.

Nevertheless, when initially pressed to be clearer about what is meant by 'foundation' and 'cause', Langenhert's interlocutor tells us that 'the foundation of colour and its occasional cause are one and the same thing, namely the figure, motion, & the disposition of parts which are in body. As for the foundation of any particular thing whose explanation you ask of me, it is that without which the thing can neither be nor be conceived.'[59] This definition of foundation strikes Langenhert as difficult to uphold. In fact, after negotiating through various possible ways it could be spelled out, Langenhert's interlocutor concedes it is best put in a more modest counterfactual way: the presence, absence, or change of one state of the mind to another concurs with the presence, absence, or change of certain motions in the body.[60] This, in fact, is precisely the view Langenhert had himself taken in the *Compendium Physicae*, to the point of reprimanding Geulincx for not having done so clearly enough himself.

Having conceded that there is no strict causal connection between the various modifications of mind and body, Langenhert's interlocutor appeals to 'everyday experience' to convince us that these coincidences of the two very different modifications nevertheless really happen, with one as the foundation of the other, despite there being nothing in their respective natures or modifications to explain why. He soon admits, though, that all such experience can really tell us is that the modifications of mind and body, respectively, occur simultaneously.[61] But without some respect in which they are comparable—something in common—there is no principled way of drawing up an ordering between the two so that one could be said to be the foundation of the other; two things are entirely capable of occurring simultaneously with no causal or other relation to one another. For Langenhert, the supposed occasions do not necessitate God's production of a particular determinate effect, and we are perfectly capable of having sensations without the requisite bodily motions anyway.[62] And this, Langenhert thinks, means the simultaneity of the two modifications is not sufficient to draw any conclusions about one being the cause or foundation of the other.

For Langenhert's interlocutor to claim that the relevant modifications of body are the foundation for a particular sensation, and not the other way around, he accordingly has to appeal to what he refers to as the 'order of nature.' But this must, we are told, be the order of our ideas—as we have seen, since they have nothing in common, every appeal to the natures of

---

[59] NPIV 12/59: 'Fundamentum colorum, & causa eorum occasionalis, una eodemque res est; nempe figura motus, & partium dispositio quae sunt in corpore. Quantùm vero ad rei alicujus fundamentum cujus à me explicationem quaeris, hoc id est, sine quo res ea nec esse, nec concipi potest.'
[60] NPIV 9/55–6.   [61] NPIV 14–5/60–1.   [62] NPIV 28/71; NPIV 19/65.

the two respective things themselves and their modifications cannot tell us about their relation to one another. When it comes to the order of our ideas, however, to claim, as Langenhert's interlocutor does, that we conceive the modifications of body prior to colours is mistaken: the mind, Langenhert thinks, is familiar first of all with its modes. In fact, it is precisely the belief in the existence of body which leads to this mistake regarding the order of ideas:

> Not only their [the modes of mind] essence, but also their existence was clearly and distinctly perceived by you before you knew any body existed; at that time figure, motion, and the disposition of parts were neither the foundation nor the cause of the existence any more than the essence of colours, at that time modes of the mind went prior in the order of cognition; after, however, you came upon a demonstration of the existence of a modified body outside your mind, that is to say, all of this was made different, and the names changed.[63]

The belief in the existence of body, therefore, not only inverts the natural order of our ideas, but worse: it does so without any metaphysical justification. There is, Langenhert asserts, no good proof that the external world exists. So why appeal to something which—though usually believed—is not known with anything like the certainty we have of our own sensations as modifications of our minds?

This is why Langenhert's interlocutor eventually brings up Descartes's proof of the existence of the external world, quoting Descartes almost word for word.[64] The intention is to make the existence of bodies plausible enough to sustain the case that they could be occasions for sensations. This too, however, is found wanting by Langenhert: he takes the Cartesian argument for the existence of the external world to depend on the impossibility of God's being a deceiver—but God, he thinks, would no less be a deceiver in bringing about our sensations by means of an occasion wholly different to those sensations than he would be if he brought them about immediately himself. This is almost exactly the objection that Geulincx had raised, and apparently answered, against his own work in the *Compendium Physicae*. Now, however, it is presented as Langenhert's own

---

[63] NPIV 17/63: 'Separabiles numquid etiam sunt & corporis & mentis modi? Non essentia tantùm, sed & existentia eorum à vobis clarè & distinctè percepta fuit, antequam sciebatis ullam corpus existere; tunc nempe figura, motus & dispositio partium tam non existentiae, quam non essentiae colorum neque fundamentum erant neque causa, tunc mentis modi cognitionis ordine priores ibant; postquam verò demonstrationem existentiae corporum modificatorum extra mentem vestram invenistis, scilicet, omnia haec facta fuerunt alia, & nomina mutarunt.'

[64] NPIV 21–2/66–7; René Descartes, *Oeuvres de Descartes*, eds. Charles Adam and Paul Tannery, 13 vols. (Paris, 1897–1913, rev. 1964–76), VIIIA: 40–1.

considered view. And this is the point where Langenhert's interlocutor suggests turning to the idea of extension instead. If we can be persuaded that there is such a thing, then there is also reason to think that what it represents could serve as the occasional cause for sensations too. But we have already seen that for Langenhert ideas, too, are reducible to modifications of the mind. Once again, the point that mind and body have nothing in common serves to reaffirm that there is no reason to appeal to the external world to provide the occasions for our sensations, or indeed our ideas; God is entirely responsible for bringing them about himself.

The Impossibility of Creaturely Causation and Representation in Langenhert's Metaphysics

Langenhert takes the crucial Cartesian view for showing Descartes's inability to prove that there is a physical world, that our ideas can neither represent it nor be caused by it, to be that mind and body have nothing in common. But Langenhert's own view—which is what he intends with an extended denial of the existence of universals, even in the mind—is that no two things whatsoever have anything in common. The first three dialogues of Langenhert's *Novus Philosophus* are largely dedicated to arguing this; it is beyond what can be covered here to discuss the numerous examples of putative universals he addresses. But it means that the things Langenhert claims the Cartesian accounts of causation and the external world are committed to are deliberately reflected in his own metaphysical views too.

In the first dialogue, it was announced that '[Langenhert] denies that there are *Universals* in things; moreover... he says that they are not even certain affections of our minds, but mere chimeras & mere words.'[65] Similar declarations are made throughout the dialogues, with the effect of ruling out any basis not just for identical or shared essences, but even for any common traits, properties or modifications whatsoever. A universal or general thing, as Langenhert understands it, is anything 'common to many other things',[66] but whatever is 'in one thing, whether it be essence, or a mode of an essence, is not in another thing in the same way.'[67] When it comes to individuals, then, Langenhert puts it as follows: 'a singular thing is nothing other than its nature or essence modified, if you will, with its

---

[65] NPI 32/33. '*Universalia* dehinc negat noster rebus inesse; immò, quod mireris, ne mentis quidem nostrae certis ea quasdam affectiones esse ait, sed meras chimaeras & verba mera.'

[66] NPI 80/81. 'Res generalis ea est, *quae multis rebus aliis est communis*'.

[67] NPI 82/81: 'quod in unâ est, sive sit essentia, sive sit essentiae ejus modus, id non itidem est in aliâ'.

affections.'[68] These modifications or affections have nothing in common with any other modifications; every modification of one thing differs really from every modification of any other thing, apparently because they are modifications of the particular thing they exist in. There is, to use Langenhert's example, no fluidity common to oil and water. The fluidity of the oil is a particular way of being of the oil and that of the water likewise; each is a singular determination of a singular substance, with nothing in common save the word.[69] But as for why Langenhert thinks the natures of things also have nothing in common with one another, he could be more explicit; he does at one stage seem to assert that two things being posited as existing means that they 'therefore' [*ergo*] have different natures, and hence that there is nothing which is in both in the same way and at the same time [*itidem et simul*].[70]

Accordingly, if Langenhert's arguments against Cartesian and occasionalist appeals to, or proofs of, the existence of the physical world all depend on the fact that our minds have nothing in common with it, then the fact that for Langenhert nothing has anything in common with anything else rules out both causation and representation between finite things altogether in his own metaphysics. Where the argument against Descartes is based on the different kinds of nature had by mind and body (though Langenhert's ascription of his own reductive account of modifications to Cartesians seems to figure into his argumentation too), in Langenhert's own case the very fact that two things really differ is enough to say that they have nothing in common. But the same reasoning applies; causation and representation between two things require those things have something in common.

Since Langenhert in the *Novus Philosophus* does not even consider the possibility that our own minds could be responsible for bringing about even some aspects of their own states, God is the only remaining candidate for cause. The result, in fact, is not unlike what Langenhert had expressed in Thesis 23 of the *Disputatio* mentioned above. Now, however, rather than the fact to be explained being the mutual action and passion of mind and body, it is simply that our minds undergo various successive modifications. And for this to be the case, God must exist, and be able to bring about what is otherwise inexplicable. Saying more than that, however, would take us beyond metaphysics; Langenhert is always circumspect in

[68] NPI 82/81: 'res autem singularis nihil aliud est quàm natura sive essentia sua modificata, si vis, affectionibus suis.'

[69] NPIII 14/73.

[70] NPII 18–19/85–6. Immediately after Langenhert also rejects the relevance of a merely numerical distinction to the question, since—with Descartes as his authority—he claims that 'number' does not inhere in things themselves.

expressing God's ways of acting for just that reason. But at one stage, he puts it as follows: 'God certainly, by his omnipotence, with a single and most simple operation with respect to himself, created both mind and body, and conserves them, and performs everything in all things, but not even the most subtle intellect can either comprehend, or understand that operation.'[71]

A final note about all this in the context of Langenhert's earlier work: Langenhert's positions in the *Novus Philosophus* are couched as self-consciously 'new'—but it is the Cartesians rather than the Aristotelians whose combination of terminological obscurity and doctrinaire outlook Langenhert disapproves of and seeks to replace. He takes, in effect, the same attitude towards the Cartesians as the they had towards the Aristotelians. Now his attitude towards Cartesianism here could be taken as an indication that the more-or-less Cartesian views defended in his earlier *Disputatio* had been adopted as the result of external pressures. But, as we have seen, that disputation was presided over by a professor hired as an Aristotelian, and with a bent towards experimental work; if there were any such pressures, they would more likely have come from Cartesian students than from above—and even then, by the time of Langenhert's disputation such disturbances seem to have died down. Likewise, the positions Langenhert himself seemed to later take up in the *Compendium Physicae* are still Cartesian: occasionalists too are, and were recognized as, broadly Cartesian. Indeed, the views Langenhert refers to as Cartesian in the *Novus Philosophus* are far closer to the occasionalist views Langenhert himself put forward in the *Compendium Physicae*. I am not so sure, then, that Langenhert was insincere in his early Cartesianism. My suspicion, although it is difficult to really say on the basis of the available texts, is that the Cartesianism of his Leiden period had not been of an aggressively rigid variety, but that he was well aware that Cartesianism could take such forms because of its history in Leiden.[72] In any case, if Langenhert can be taken as an example, some Cartesians educated in Leiden were sincerely open to correcting their views not only in the cases which could be settled by experimentation, but also when metaphysical reasoning was in question. Langenhert's form of occasionalism, one which seems to have dispensed even with occasions in the external world for God's actions on our minds,

[71] NPIV 44/85: 'Deus quidem omnipotentiâ suâ, unâ & simplicissimâ operatione respectu sui & mentem & corpus creavit, easque conservat, atque omnia in omnibus operatur, sed ne subtilissimus quidem intellectus operationem eam comprehendit, neque intelligere eam potest'. Note that the reference to God creating the body too is a concession to his interlocutor specific to this argument.

[72] Because he does not mention any French Cartesians, it is hard to say whether his new Parisian context could have been equally responsible cementing the negative view of Cartesianism he exhibits in the *Novus Philosophus*.

can be seen as one particular result of such a process—even if it may not have been one that other Cartesians would have foreseen.

Conclusion

There is good reason to read Langenhert's work as an outgrowth of occasionalism, in both a theoretical and historical sense. God alone remains a viable cause in Langenhert's later metaphysical system, even if how he acts cannot be explained. And Langenhert seems to have developed some of his views if not drawing directly on Geulincx's work, then at least as an amendment and supplement to it. This much is suggested by the changes between the earlier theses defended in Leiden and the views expressed in his commentary on Geulincx's physics. So although in the *Novus Philosophus* he was a critic of the appeal to occasions or occasional causes in the external world, his own views had more in common with his opponents in the dialogues than with even the more orthodox Cartesians who admitted the interaction of mind and body; he was, then, an internal critic of Cartesianism.

As a reader and interpreter of Geulincx, Langenhert's outlook was ambivalent. Nevertheless, his efforts in the *Compendium Physicae* would have resulted in greater visibility for Geulincx's own specific vision of philosophy and physics, if not exactly how Geulincx would have presented it. Likewise, Langenhert's use in the *Novus Philosophus* of views Geulincx had discussed in his writings indicates that his influence may have been felt in a small way in France, where his work is not generally taken to have been very well known at all. Still, influence might not be the best word when Langenhert remains more obscure than Geulincx himself, and Geulincx would hardly recognize his work in Langenhert's later views.

Compared to other adherents of more or less Geulingian views, Langenhert seems not to have been particularly dogmatic, and hence willing to adapt his views in the light of either circumstances or, as might well be the case here, his encountering or working out new lines of metaphysical reasoning. In this respect, perhaps he really was a product of a period in Leiden in which both supposedly Cartesian and Aristotelian professors exhibited a tendency towards eclecticism and a willingness to amend their views. In this way Langenhert carried—albeit in an oblique fashion—the teachings of more than one era of professors of the University of Leiden into his own idiosyncratic school. All this underlines that both Cartesianism at Leiden and the varieties which could be said to stem from Geulincx were far from being unitary phenomena. There were different strands, with varying degrees of intransigence, and there were those who would go on to attempt to make something ostensibly quite different of it.

Langenhert's venture, however ill-fated it may have been, was something of the latter kind.

Finally, a few points have been mentioned in passing which might indicate that we cannot entirely dismiss the possibility that Langenhert remains a less-than-complete occasionalist. In particular, he gives almost no indication of what he takes to be happening when it comes to what Cartesians would call the actions of the mind or will, which we experience as originating in us. A hint might be found in the fact that Langenhert makes use of the principle 'nothing is changed by itself' in both the earlier works discussed here. Even so, it would still have to be established that in the *Novus Philosophus,* too, he thought that the mind could not bring about any changes in itself. But whatever Langenhert's views about these kinds of thoughts, it is clear enough that any of the thoughts a Cartesian would usually classify as passions—perceptions, sensations, etc.—could only be brought about by God. And this means that, regardless of the extent of his occasionalism, Langenhert fits the term *egomet* quite well. This is not as explicitly phrased as it might be in the *Novus Philosophus,* though—to see it, some reconstruction of Langenhert's views certainly helps. It is enough to make one wonder whether the seemingly exaggerated reports of Langenhert's work were based not so much on the somewhat sketchy accounts of his views given by his characters in the dialogues of the *Novus Philosophus* as on what he taught in person, where he might have felt more able to voice his own views freely.[73]

Department of Philosophy
KU Leuven
michael.jaworzyn@kuleuven.be

[73] Thanks to Lydia Azadpour and Can Laurens Löwe for their comments on drafts of this essay, and to the participants at the Teaching the New Science conference in Groningen for their useful questions and patience with a very early version. Research on this essay was supported by the Fonds Wetenschappelijk Onderzoek (FWO), Flanders.

'Following No Party But The Truth': Petrus Van Musschenbroek's Rhetorical Defence Of '(Newtonian) Experimental Philosophy'

Pieter Present[1]

Introduction

The Dutch Republic played a pivotal role in the spread of Newton's ideas on the Continent.[2] Eric Jorink and Huib Zuidervaart have argued that Dutch Newtonianism was on the one hand 'an elaboration of an already existing tradition of empirical research', and on the other hand 'a philosophical—and to a certain extent social—construction, created for and adapted to specific local problems and circumstances'.[3] The most important of these 'local problems and circumstances' was the perceived threat of the ideas of Spinoza and his followers, which were regarded as an atheist attack on established religion.[4] What made the problem of Spinoza's

[1] Research for this paper was funded by the Research Fund—Flanders (project: G.0271.15N). I am indebted to Steffen Ducheyne and Jip van Besouw for comments on earlier drafts of this paper, as well as to the Special Collections Department at Leiden University Library for permission to quote from the material in their care. Many thanks to Colin Rittberg and Andrew Morris for going through the final version.

[2] For a discussion of the reception of Newton's ideas in the Dutch Republic, see Eric Jorink and Ad Maas, eds., *Newton and the Netherlands: How Isaac Newton was fashioned in the Dutch Republic* (Amsterdam, 2012).

[3] Eric Jorink and Huib Zuidervaart, "The Miracle of Our Time': How Newton Was Fashioned in the Netherlands', in *Newton and the Netherlands*, eds. Eric Jorink and Ad Maas (Amsterdam, 2012), 14.

[4] Jorink and Zuidervaart, "The Miracle of Our Time", pp. 18–19. On the role of religion in the spread of Newtonianism in the Dutch Republic, see Ernestine G.E. van der Wall, 'Newtonianism and Religion in the Netherlands', *Studies in History and Philosophy of Science* 35 (2004), 493–514. On the circle of people responsible for the earliest propagation of

Pieter Present, *'Following No Party But The Truth': Petrus Van Musschenbroek's Rhetorical Defence Of '(Newtonian) Experimental Philosophy'* In: *History of Universities*. Edited by: Mordechai Feingold, Oxford University Press (2021). © Oxford University Press.
DOI: 10.1093/oso/9780192893833.003.0006

philosophy even more pressing was that he presented his ideas as resulting from geometrical demonstrations, and thus as having mathematical necessity. In this context, Newton was presented as not only a pious man and Christian, but also as a brilliant mathematician, who provided a philosophy in which mathematics was correctly used in order to frame a natural philosophy that was able to point at the existence of God as creator and ruler.[5] The use of the term 'Newtonianism' as an analytical concept, however, has been problematized.[6] In the context of the Dutch Republic, being a 'Newtonian' did not mean that one subscribed to a certain set of ideas which were shared by all Newtonians.[7] In the so-called *vis viva* controversy, for example, 's Gravesande and van Musschenbroek sided with Leibniz against other 'Newtonians' such as Samuel Clarke.[8] Therefore, in the literature, the 'Newtonianism' of 's Gravesande and van Musschenbroek has been qualified as being 'methodological'.[9] This is understood as meaning that 'Newtonianism to their mind meant adhering to Newton's method rather than clinging all too literally to his notions'.[10] Recent scholarship has also mitigated this view. The methodological views of 's Gravesande and van Musschenbroek have been shown to differ from those of Newton in certain respects. Both men were influenced by sources other than

Newton's philosophy and their religious and social context, see Rienk Vermij, 'The Formation of the Newtonian Philosophy: The Case of the Amsterdam Mathematical Amateurs', *British Journal for the History of Science* 36 (2003), 183–200.

[5] Jorink and Zuidervaart, "The Miracle of Our Time", 23.

[6] Rod Home, 'Out of the Newtonian Straightjacket: Alternative Approaches to Eighteenth-century Physical Science', in *Studies in the Eighteenth Century, Vol. 4: Papers presented at the Fourth David Nichol Smith Memorial Seminar*, eds. Robert F. Brissenden and John C. Eade (Canberra, 1976), 235–49; Simon Schaffer, 'Newtonianism', in *Companion to the History of Modern Science*, eds. Robert C. Olby, Geoffrey N. Cantor, John R. R. Christie, and Michael J. S. Hodge (London, 1990), 610–26.

[7] A recent discussion of Dutch 'Newtonianism' (including the problematic nature of the term) can be found in Steffen Ducheyne and Jip van Besouw, 'Newton and the Dutch 'Newtonians': 1713–1750', in *The Oxford Handbook of Newton*, eds. Eric Schliesser and Chris Smeenk (Oxford, 2017).

[8] For a recent treatment of the *vis viva* controversy, see Mary Terrall, 'Vis Viva Revisited', *History of Science* 42 (2004), 189–209. A specific analysis of van Musschenbroek and 's Gravesande's position can be found in Jip van Besouw, 'The Wedge and the Vis Viva Controversy: How Concepts of Force Influenced the Practice of Early Eighteenth-Century Mechanics', *Archive for History of Exact Sciences* 71 (2017), 109–56.

[9] Robert E. Schofield, *Mechanism and Materialism, British Natural Philosophy in the Age of Reason* (Princeton, 1970), 140; van der Wall, 'Newtonianism and Religion in the Netherlands', 495; Kees de Pater, "The Wisest Man to whom this Earth has as yet given Birth': Petrus van Musschenbroek and the Limits of Newtonian Philosophy', in *Newton and the Netherlands: How Isaac Newton was fashioned in the Dutch Republic*, eds. Eric Jorink and Ad Maas (Amsterdam, 2012), 140.

[10] Van der Wall, 'Newtonianism and Religion in the Netherlands', 495.

Newton, and refined their methodological views throughout their career.[11] At the same time, both 's Gravesande and van Musschenbroek explicitly presented themselves as following 'Newton's method of philosophizing' in several contexts. Despite the problematic nature of the term, Fokko Jan Dijksterhuis has therefore argued that at least in the context of the Dutch Republic and the early spread of Newton's ideas there, 'the term 'Newtonian' acquires actual historical significance and was indeed an actor's category'.[12] Although Dijksterhuis agrees that the term 'Newtonianism' is problematic as an analytic category, he does see historiographical value in it when it is understood 'as the ideological label in the way the Dutch Newtonians used it'.[13] In this paper, I will concern myself with 'Newtonianism' in this sense, i.e., as an actor's category and ideological label.

More specifically, I will focus on Petrus van Musschenbroek (1692–1761) and the rhetoric he used in his attempts to introduce and defend '(Newtonian) experimental philosophy' and/or 'Newton's method of philosophising' in the institution of the university. I will show how van Musschenbroek's rhetoric relates to the specific nature of the early modern Dutch university and its place in society. To do this, I will analyse on the one hand van Musschenbroek's academic orations, which he delivered at key moments in his academic career.[14] On the other hand, I will look at

---

[11] Steffen Ducheyne, 'W. J. 's Gravesande's Appropriation of Newton's Natural Philosophy, Part II: Methodological Issues', *Centaurus* 56 (2014), 97–120 and Steffen Ducheyne, 'Petrus van Musschenbroek and Newton's *vera stabilisque Philosophandi methodus*", *Berichte zur Wissenschaftsgeschichte* 38 (2015), 279–304. 's Gravesande's interest and activities in natural philosophy have moreover been shown to predate his acquaintance with Newton's work: Jip van Besouw, 'The Impeccable Credentials of an Untrained Philosopher: Willem Jacob 's Gravesande's Career before His Leiden Professorship, 1688–1717', *Notes and Records: The Royal Society Journal of the History of Science* 70 (2016), 231–249.

[12] Fokko Jan Dijksterhuis, 'Low-Country Opticks: The optical pursuits of Lambert ten Kate and Daniel Fahrenheit in early Dutch 'Newtonianism'", in *Newton and the Netherlands*, eds. Eric Jorink and Ad Maas (Amsterdam, 2012), 174.

[13] Dijksterhuis, 'Low-Country Opticks', 174.

[14] I will limit myself to the orations in which van Musschenbroek explicitly defends or mentions '(Newtonian) experimental philosophy'. These orations have all been put to print. The Special Collections department of Leiden University Library contains two manuscripts of orations which have never been printed (MS BPL 240.6, MS BPL 240.7). Both orations deal with the topic of astronomy. The first manuscript (MS BPL 240.6) contains the text of an oration delivered in September 1726 (cf. f. 1ʳ: 'Oratio habita mense Septembri 1726'). The other oration (MS BPL 240.7) bears the title 'Oratio de astronomiae praestantia et utilitate quam aliis scientiis assert', and was delivered on 6 October 1732. Van Musschenbroek gave this oration when he accepted the professorship of astronomy. This position, accompanied by a rise in salary, was given to him after he had declined an invitation to Copenhagen. Van Musschenbroek was also given permission to buy extra scientific instruments. (Cf. Gerhard Wilhelm Kernkamp, *Acta et decreta senatus: vroedschapresolutiën en andere bescheiden betreffende de Utrechtse Academie*, 3 vols. (Utrecht, 1936–1940), 2: 325). A.J. van der Aa further mentions an oration given by van Musschenbroek at the occasion of becoming professor of medicine at Duisburg in 1721. This oration was titled 'Oratio de conjungenda medicina

the prefaces of the different editions of his textbooks, in which he defends or presents a certain picture of '(Newtonian) experimental philosophy'. Both the prefaces and the orations provide the perfect material to analyse van Musschenbroek's defence of '(Newtonian) experimental philosophy' in relation to the university and its place in Dutch society.[15] Academic orations had a public character, and played a role in the self-presentation of both the individual professor and the academic institution in which he worked.[16] Both the local elite and the university board were present at these occasions, which thus connect university and society.[17] A key element of oratory is of course the adaptation of one's message and style to the time, and the expectations and sensibilities of one's audience. For this reason, acadamic orations can be expected to take rhetorical advantage of contemporary ideas on the nature of the university and its tasks.

Like academic orations, textbooks also played a role in the self-presentation of the professor and the university. Universities expected their professors to dedicate their textbooks to them and to provide the correct affiliation and titles. Failures to do so were reprimanded.[18] Owing

cum philosophicis scientiis' (A.J. van der Aa, *Biographisch woordenboek der Nederlanden. Deel 12. Tweede stuk* (Haarlem, 1869), 1181). Unfortunately, van der Aa does not provide any references, and I have not been able to find a copy of this oration, nor a manuscript.

[15] On the use of orations and prefaces as source material, see Dirk van Miert, *Humanism in an Age of Science: The Amsterdam Athenaeum in the Golden Age, 1632–1704* (Leiden/Boston, 2009), 7.

[16] For a discussion of the function and nature of academic orations in the seventeenth century Dutch Republic, see Dirk van Miert, 'Retoriek in de Republiek. Vormen en functies van academische oraties in Amsterdam in de zeventiende eeuw', *De Zeventiende Eeuw* 19 (2003), 67–78. As van Miert himself points out, literature on the function of the academic oration is unfortunately extremely scarce. The existing literature focusses mostly on the rhetorical and literary character of the orations, for example E. Kegel-Brinkgreve, 'De Rol van de Retorica in Boerhaaves Orationes', *Batavia Academica* 2 (1984), 25–34. An exception to this is an article by Gerhard Wiesenfeldt which, whilst it focusses on disputations, also contains a discussion of the nature and role of academic orations in the early modern university: Gerhard Wiesenfeldt, 'Academic writings and the rituals of early modern universities' *Intellectual History Review* 26 (2016), 447–460.

For a more general assessment of rhetoric in seventeenth century Dutch culture and public discourse, see Arthur Weststeijn, *Commercial Republicanism in the Dutch Golden Age: The Political Thought of Johan & Pieter de La Court* (Leiden/Boston, 2012), 69–140. On rhetorical education in the seventeenth century Dutch Republic, see Dirk van Miert, *Humanism in an Age of Science*, 161–63, 188–90.

[17] Academic orations were very ritualised social events. The members of the public had to be addressed in a specific order, starting with members of the local government. The burgomasters of Leiden refused to attend the celebrations of the *dies natalis* of the university for a period of eight years because in 1725 the rector had addressed the university senate before the city magistrates (Willem Otterspeer, *Het Bolwerk van de Vrijheid: De Leidse Universiteit in Heden En Verleden* (Leiden, 2008), 37).

[18] Willem Otterspeer mentions the case in which a professor was reprimanded by the city council for putting 'Academia Batavia' instead of 'Academia Lugduno-Batava' on his title page (Otterspeer, *Het Bolwerk van de Vrijheid*, 43). In turn, good behaviour was

to the public and dedicatory character of these textbooks, their prefaces also had a rhetorical character and authors did their best to create a positive image of themselves and their work.

In this paper, I will show how van Musschenbroek on the one hand indeed explicitly presents himself to Newton as someone propagating the 'Newtonian philosophy'. Van Musschenbroek's early textbooks are likewise presented as teaching a 'Newtonian philosophy'. Newton himself is brought forward as a pious philosopher. Thus, in the case of van Musschenbroek, 'Newtonianism' is indeed an actor's category. However, I will also show that van Musschenbroek is not consistent in presenting himself and his philosophy as 'Newtonian'. In some contexts, van Musschenbroek explicitly stated that he should *not* be seen as a *follower* of Newton. In those contexts, Newton is no longer presented as someone who introduced a new philosophy, but rather as the best (but not the only) example of someone following the method of experimental philosophy. In general, I aim to demonstrate that van Musschenbroek's rhetoric can and should be understood against the background of the early modern university.

The outline of my paper will be as follows. Before turning to van Musschenbroek's texts, I will discuss the nature of the university in the Dutch Republic. More specifically, I will show how views on the nature and aim of the university were at play in the controversies on Cartesianism at the time of its introduction in Dutch universities. Hereafter, I will turn to van Musschenbroek's defence of '(Newtonian) experimental philosophy'. Van Musschenbroek, I will show, takes rhetorical advantage of the criticism that had been levelled at Cartesianism in order to argue for its replacement by '(Newtonian) experimental philosophy'.

My discussion of van Musschenbroek's presentation and defence of '(Newtonian) experimental philosophy' has three parts. First, I discuss van Musschenbroek's emphasis on the stabilising nature of this method and the agreement among those who follow it. I show how van Musschenbroek consistently contrasts this stability and agreement with the instability and disagreement found in Cartesian philosophy. I argue that van Musschenbroek in this way incorporates existing anti-Cartesian rhetoric in his defence of '(Newtonian) experimental philosophy'. Whereas the introduction of Cartesian philosophy in the university caused disorder and discord, the introduction of '(Newtonian) experimental philosophy' will foster a philosophy of harmony and agreement inside the university

---

rewarded. During van Musschenbroek's time at Utrecht for example, the senate consistently thanked him (and other professors) when he published a book with the proper dedications (Kernkamp, *Acta et decreta senatus,* 291, 331).

walls, according to van Musschenbroek. However, some critics tried to turn the tables on van Musschenbroek and argued that the Newtonians were themselves just another sect in natural philosophy, and therefore the cause of discord and sedition. In reaction to this, van Musschenbroek turned away from presenting his views as 'Newtonian', and put more emphasis on the method of experimental philosophy as an impartial method. Second, I will show how van Musschenbroek grounds the view on '(Newtonian) experimental philosophy' as a stabilising force in his conception of the laws of nature. I will also show how he uses this conception to further criticise Cartesian philosophy and to present experimental philosophy as parallel to and in harmony with the study of Scripture. Where theologians study the word of God as it is contained in Scripture, natural philosophers study His will as it is expressed in creation. Third, I discuss the way van Musschenbroek defends the usefulness of the teaching of '(Newtonian) experimental philosophy' within the institution of the university, by showing how it prepares students for their study in the higher faculties of theology, law, or medicine. In all these three sections, I will show how van Musschenbroek's rhetoric relates to the nature of the early modern Dutch University, its organisation, and its aims. In each case, van Musschenbroek incorporates existing anti-Cartesian arguments into his defence of '(Newtonian) experimental philosophy' by showing how his approach to natural philosophy succeeds where Cartesianism had previously failed.

The University in the Dutch Republic and the Controversies over Cartesianism

During the sixteenth century, secular authorities increasingly took the initiative to found universities. This was linked to the growth of the state apparatus of these authorities and the need for well-educated state officials. Universities were also seen as instruments to attain more societal cohesion and to maintain religious orthodoxy.[19]

---

[19] In his work on the history of Leiden University, Ronald Sluijter puts the founding of the university in this broader European context: Ronald Sluijter, *'Tot Ciraet, Vermeerderinge Ende Heerlyckmaeckinge Der Universiteyt': Bestuur, Instellingen, Personeel En Financiën van de Leidse Universiteit, 1575–1812* (Hilversum, 2004), 17–18. In 1765, four years after van Musschenbroek's death, an anonymous writer in the journal *De Denker* lamented the deplorable state of science in the Dutch Republic and looked back to its glory days at the beginning of the eighteenth century: 'Newton gave us 's Gravesande and Musschenbroek, and both of those have given us men who still today excel in the government of the state, and at our universities' (quoted in Jorink and Zuidervaart, "The Miracle of Our Time", 48).

The birth of the first university in the Dutch Republic is inextricably linked with the birth of the state (and later Republic) itself. Plans to found a university emerged during the period of the Dutch Revolt, and were motivated by the desire to gain independence from Spain. The first Dutch university was the university of Leiden, founded in 1575. The motives for the founding of a new university are summarised by Ronald Sluijter as 1. the defence and the spread of the 'true' faith 2. increasing unity and societal stability 3. schooling future civil servants.[20] As we will see, van Musschenbroek uses these goals of the university in the defence of his philosophical programme. He stresses Newton's piety and the complementarity of experimental philosophy with theology; argues that his way of doing philosophy was characterised by stability and unity; and emphasises its utility for society.

In the controversies on Cartesianism in the Dutch universities during the seventeenth century, these views on the nature and aim of the university can be seen to play a crucial role. It was at the University of Utrecht that, around 1639, the first clashes on Cartesianism occurred in the Dutch Republic.[21] These first clashes centred around the person of Henri de Roy (Regius) (1598–1697), a Cartesian who had become professor of theoretical medicine and botany in 1638, and Gisbertus Voetius (1589–1676), professor of theology. The conflict started owing to disputations on atheism being defended by students under Voetius's supervision, with allusions being made to Cartesian philosophy.[22] Regius rose to the defence of Descartes's views, but was instructed by the academic senate in 1642 to limit himself to his own domain of medicine. In the university statutes of the following two years, it is explicitly mentioned that all philosophical instruction should be restricted to the philosophy of Aristotle. As motivation, both the protection of Church doctrine as well as students intending to study in one of the higher faculties (i.e., law, medicine, or theology) were mentioned.[23] With regard to the latter, in his analysis of the controversy on Cartesianism at the University of Utrecht, Jan van Ruler has shown how Voetius's attack on this new philosophy was also motivated by

---

This comment shows that the idea of the university as a training ground for government officials was still at play in the middle of the eighteenth century.

[20] Sluijter, '*Tot Ciraet, Vermeerderinge Ende Heerlyckmaeckinge Der Universiteyt*', 17–18.

[21] An elaborate treatment of the 'Querelle d'Utrecht' is given in Han A. Van Ruler, *The Crisis of Causality: Voetius and Descartes on God, Nature, and Change* (Leiden/New York/ Köln, 1995).

[22] On these early accusations of Cartesianism leading to atheism, see Theo Verbeek, 'Descartes and the Problem of Atheism: The Utrecht Crisis', *Nederlands Archief Voor Kerkgeschiedenis/Dutch Review of Church History* 71 (1991), 211–23.

[23] Edward G. Ruestow, *Physics at Seventeenth and Eighteenth-Century Leiden: Philosophy and the New Science in the University* (The Hague, 1973), 35–36.

pedagogical concerns and the institutional organisation of the university. Given the neo-scholastic nature of the theology teaching, students needed to have a background in Aristotelian theory and terminology. Cartesian philosophy could not provide students with this necessary background.[24]

The controversies on Cartesianism were not limited to the strife between Regius and Voetius, but also spread to Leiden University. There, they were even more vehement, leading to heavy polemics between professors and even student uproar. In 1656 matters had gotten out of hand to such a degree that the States were asked to intervene, after which they issued a decree 'against mixing theology with philosophy and abusing the freedom of philosophizing to the prejudice of the Scripture'.[25] Despite these quarrels, and despite interventions from university faculties and governments, in the end most universities in the Dutch Republic adopted a pragmatic policy of dividing chairs between Cartesians and adherents of the Aristotelian philosophy.[26]

Alexander Douglas has linked the concerns on the teaching of Cartesianism within the university to the university's relation to society. Critics of Cartesianism regarded it as a philosophy with impious implications. As we have seen, in the early modern period, the main aim of the university was to train government officials and to guarantee religious orthodoxy. Thus, in the eyes of the critics, the introduction of the teaching of Cartesian philosophy in the preparatory faculty of arts and philosophy meant that it 'threatened to spread beyond a handful of academic philosophers and into the hearts and minds of ecclesiastical and civil bureaucrats in training'.[27]

Some Cartesians in turn tried to defend themselves by putting forward what Douglas has called a 'separation thesis'. (Cartesian) philosophy was strictly separated from 'common experience'. Both were two completely different ways of knowing. The disciplines taught in the higher faculties based themselves on this 'common experience', of course with the additional guidance of Scripture. By strictly separating (Cartesian) philosophy from theology and the higher faculties, these Cartesians tried to disarm critics who argued that the teaching of Cartesian philosophy would have impious effects.[28] Through this strategy, however, they also disarmed

---

[24] Van Ruler, *The Crisis of Causality*, 28–31.

[25] Ruestow, *Physics at Seventeenth and Eighteenth Century Leiden*, 46.

[26] Wiep van Bunge, *From Stevin to Spinoza: An Essay on Philosophy in the Seventeenth-Century Dutch Republic* (Leiden/Boston, 2001), 44.

[27] Alexander X. Douglas, *Spinoza and Dutch Cartesianism: Philosophy and Theology* (Oxford, 2015), 37.

[28] On the 'separation thesis' and responses to this strategy from critics of Cartesianism, see Douglas, *Spinoza and Dutch Cartesianism*, 37–62. For a discussion of the strict distinction between 'philosophical' and 'normal knowledge' made by the Cartesian Johannes de

themselves by making the teaching of philosophy in the preparatory faculty irrelevant for those interested in the teaching provided in the higher faculties. We will see how van Musschenbroek plays into this by explicitly commenting on the usefulness of '(Newtonian) experimental philosophy' for the disciplines taught in the higher faculties.

Cartesian philosophy also spread beyond the university walls and became a cultural phenomenon in the Dutch Republic. The contents of non-academic Cartesian tracts demonstrate the entanglement of questions of philosophy, theology, politics, and epistemic authority.[29] These authors used Cartesian philosophy to tackle questions of social order and the organisation of the state, argued for the separation of philosophy and theology, and criticised attempts of Calvinist ministers to gain political power. More radical writers, such as Lodewijk Meyer in his anonymously published *Philosophia Sancta Scripturae Interpres* (1666), even argued that since religious strife arose as a consequence of different readings of the Bible, interpretation of the Bible should be done by philosophers, rather than by theologians. Meyer used the certain character of Cartesian philosophy (it being 'vera, certa, ac indubita') to argue for its unifying potential.[30] Van Bunge sees this belief in the unifying potential of Cartesian philosophy as an explanation for the appeal of Cartesianism to non-academic thinkers. The Cartesian stress on certainty appealed to thinkers who longed for political stability and coherence. As Cartesianism led to certain knowledge in the realm of natural philosophy, applying Cartesian principles to political philosophy could only lead to indubitable insight into the best way to organize the state.[31] Wiep van Bunge reads these appeals against the background of the emphasis on (the need of) coherence and unity in seventeenth-century Dutch intellectual and political life.[32] In his treatment of discussions on religious toleration in the eighteenth-century Dutch Republic, Joris van Eijnatten demonstrates how this emphasis is still present in van Musschenbroek's time.[33]

Raei (a student of Regius), and its use in anti-Spinozist polemics, see van Miert, *Humanism in an Age of Science*, 243–244.

[29] Van Bunge, *From Stevin to Spinoza*, 74–93.

[30] Van Bunge, *From Stevin to Spinoza*, 95–96.

[31] Van Bunge, *From Stevin to Spinoza*, 93–96.

[32] Van Bunge, *From Stevin to Spinoza*, 18–26.

[33] Joris van Eijnatten, *Liberty and Concord in the United Provinces: Religious Toleration and the Public in the Eighteenth-Century Netherlands* (Leiden/Boston, 2003), 1–70. In the selling catalogue of van Musschenbroek's library, numerous works of the figures discussed by van Eijnatten occur, e.g. Salomon van Til, Taco Hajo and Joan van den Honert, Hieronymus van Alphen, Johannes van Herwerden, Franciscus Fabricius, Albert and Jan Jacob Schultens, Nicolaaas Holtius, Berhardinus de Moor, Campegius Vitringa, Bénédict Pictet ([Anon.], *Bibliotheca Musschenbroekiana, Sive Catalogus Librorum Viri Celeberrimi Petri van Musschenbroek, Dum Vivebat* (Leiden, 1762)).

The appearance of Baruch Spinoza on the Dutch intellectual scene posed a problem for Cartesians making this argument. After its publication in 1667, Spinoza's *Tractatus Theologico-Politicus* caused general outrage in the Dutch Republic, being perceived by most critics as a shameless expression of downright atheism.[34] The publication of the *Opera posthuma* (1670), which included his *Ethica* in which he famously equated God and Nature, did not help to dispel this impression. Anti-Cartesian critics saw Spinoza's philosophy as a confirmation of their judgment on the danger of Descartes's philosophy: Cartesianism in the end entailed Spinozism and therefore atheism.

In this way, Spinoza's philosophy formed a pressing problem for Cartesian philosophers, who were obliged to defend themselves against these accusations. They therefore vehemently criticised Spinoza's philosophy, while at the same time defending Cartesian philosophy against accusations of atheism. The controversy is neatly summarized by the titles of two tracts published in the context of a polemic between Ruardus Andala (1665–1727) and Johannes Regius (1656–1738). In 1719 Regius, an Aristotelian professor of philosophy at the University of Franeker, wrote a tract entitled *Cartesius verus Spinozismi Architectus* or 'Descartes, the true architect of Spinozism'.[35] This led Andala, a Cartesian and professor of theology at the same institution, to respond with a tract entitled *Cartesius verus Spinozismi Eversor* or 'Descartes, the true destroyer of Spinozism'.[36] Andala had also attacked fellow Cartesians such as de Volder and Geulinx for being closet-Spinozists.[37] Douglas refers to Johannes de Raei as another example of a Cartesian condemning fellow Cartesians in order to

[34] For an overview of contemporary reactions to Spinoza, see van Bunge, *From Stevin to Spinoza*, 108–121; Douglas, *Spinoza and Dutch Cartesianism*, 91–146; Susan James, *Spinoza on Philosophy, Religion, and Politics: The Theologico-Political Treatise* (Oxford, 2012); Michiel Wielema, *The March of the Libertines: Spinozists and the Dutch Reformed Church (1660–1750)* (Hilversum, 2004); Theo Verbeek, *Spinoza's Theologico-Political Treatise: Exploring 'The Will of God'* (Aldershot: 2003).

[35] Johannes Regius, *Cartesius Verus Spinozismi Architectus* (Franeker, 1719). For a discussion of the Andala-Regius debate, see Jonathan Israel, *Radical Enlightenment: Philosophy and the Making of Modernity 1650–1750* (Oxford, 2001), 482–485. This text was not the first one written by Regius on the subject. In 1714 he had already written a Dutch tract with the title *Kartezius Spinoza Voorlichtende* (This was published as an addition to the Dutch translation of his *Principia Philosophiae Theoreticae*: Johannes Regius, *Beginselen der Beschouwende Filozofy* (Rotterdam, 1714)). An extended overview of the polemics between Andala and Regius, including a chronology of the publications, can be found in Sybrand H. M. Galama, *Het Wijsgerig Onderwijs Aan de Hogeschool Te Franeker: 1585–1811* (Franeker, 1954), 70–76.

[36] Ruardus Andala, *Cartesius Verus Spinozismi Eversor* (Franeker, 1719).

[37] Israel, *Radical Enlightenment*, 480–481; Han van Ruler, 'The Shipwreck of Belief and Eternal Bliss: Philosophy and Religion in Later Dutch Cartesianism', in *The Early Enlightenment in the Dutch Republic: 1650–1750*, ed. Wiep Van Bunge (Leiden/Boston, 2003), 110.

safeguard his own position.[38] Despite all promises of providing a philosophy which could finally provide certainty and social stability, Cartesianism thus ended up being torn up by criticism coming from both the inside and the outside. We will see how van Musschenbroek uses this in his defence of '(Newtonian) experimental philosophy'.

Thus, in the end, Cartesianism was the cause of controversies and strife both within and outside of the universities. Enemies of Cartesian philosophy did not fail to make use of this fact. In *Het Vergift Van de Cartesiaansche Philosophie Grondig Ontdekt* ('The poison of the Cartesian philosophy thoroughly unmasked'), published in 1692, Jacobus Koelman uses the example of the uproar that Cartesian philosophy had caused in the universities to criticise the philosophy of Descartes and his followers.[39]

In the dedication, Koelman explicitly states that it is his aim to destroy Cartesianism root and branch, since atheistic ideas like those of Spinoza will keep surfacing if their source, i.e., Cartesianism, still exists.[40] He also adds that the work is specifically written

> for parents (be it those who have studied themselves, or those who haven't) who would like to send their children to Academies, in order that they would have some knowledge of this philosophy, and of Descartes and Cartesians, and that they would know, how and on what grounds, based on [the opinions of] all kinds of scholars, and also of entire Synods, [people have] fought against this philosophy, so that they would not let their children get into the hands of Cartesian Professors, who now have [spread] from Amsterdam to Franeker[.][41]

Koelman lists several reasons why Aristotelian philosophy should be retained and taught. The first is that through the ages and through the Reformation, Aristotelian philosophy had itself been 'reformed' and purified from its heterodox elements. Therefore, 'she conforms well to orthodox theology'.[42] Aristotelian philosophy is, moreover, 'not only an orthodox, but also a subservient philosophy, that can settle itself in the service of all higher faculties; she is not like a master, but submissive, and rightly suited to serve theology'.[43]

---

[38] Douglas, *Spinoza and Dutch Cartesianism*, 60.

[39] Jacobus Koelman, *Het Vergift van de Cartesiaansche Philosophie Grondig Ontdekt. En Meest Historischer Wijze, Uit de Schriften van Des Cartes Zelfs, En van Andere Schrijvers, Zo Voor Als Tegen Hem, Getrouwelijk Aangeweezen. Op Gestelt, Tot Een Grondt van de Wederlegging van Bekkers Betooverde Wereldt* (Amsterdam, 1692).

[40] Koelman, *Het Vergift*, 'Aan den Leeser', p. 5 of unnumbered preface.

[41] Koelman, *Het Vergift*, 'Aan den Leeser', pp. 22–23 of unnumbered preface. Unless mentioned otherwise, all translations of Dutch and Latin citations are my own.

[42] Koelman, *Het Vergift*, 144.   [43] Koelman, *Het Vergift*, 144.

Reiterating the comments on the purification of Aristotelian philosophy and its usefulness for the higher faculties, Koelman now also adds the danger of introducing discord in the university by introducing a new philosophy:

> Because it would be a way of causing a lot of discord and bitterness between professors and students, if one would allow a new philosophy alongside an old one in the academies, given that the old one has been well-tried for so many years, so that it has been purified and reformed, and is therefore exceptionally useful for all the faculties[:] theology, law and medicine.[44]

The 'discord and bitterness between professors and students' was not a hypothetical situation. In Leiden, Cartesian students had resorted to harassing professors and disrupting disputations, even leading to fist fights.[45] Further on in the chapter, when Koelman argues against the introduction of Cartesian philosophy, by reiterating the same arguments used for retaining the Aristotelian philosophy, he indeed explicitly refers to these incidents.[46]

I will now turn to van Musschenbroek's defence of '(Newtonian) experimental philosophy'. In the next section, we will see how van Musschenbroek takes up this idea of Cartesian philosophy as characterised by strife, and in turn emphasises the stabilising and harmonious nature of '(Newtonian) experimental philosophy'.

A 'True and Stable Method of Philosophising (*Vera Stabilisque Methodus Philosophandi*)'

During his academic career, van Musschenbroek occupied positions at the university of Duisburg (1719–1723), Utrecht (1723–1739), and finally Leiden (1740–1762).[47] In the early days of his professorship at Utrecht, van Musschenbroek wrote a letter to Newton in which he made his intentions explicit:

> Being an admirer of your wisdom and philosophical teaching, of which I had experience while in Britain in familiar conversation with yourself, I thought it no error to follow in your footsteps (though far behind), in embracing and propagating the Newtonian philosophy. I began to do so in

---

[44] Koelman, *Het Vergift*, 145.
[45] Ruestow, *Physics at Seventeenth and Eighteenth Century Leiden*, 45–46.
[46] Koelman, *Het Vergift*, 159.
[47] For more biographical details, see Kees de Pater, *Petrus van Musschenbroek (1692–1761), Een Newtoniaans Natuuronderzoeker* (Utrecht, 1979); de Pater, "The Wisest Man to Whom This Earth Has as Yet Given Birth", 140–143.

two universities, where the triflings of Cartesianism flourished, and met with success, so that there is hope that the Newtonian philosophy will be seen as true in the greater part of Holland, with praise of yourself. It would flourish even more but for the resistance of certain prejudiced and casuistical theologians. I have prepared a compendium for beginners with which, if it does not displease you greatly, I shall be well satisfied. I shall always endeavour to serve the wisest man to whom this Earth has as yet given birth. Utrecht, 23 February 1726.[48]

The 'compendium for beginners' mentioned in the letter refers to the first edition of van Musschenbroek's textbook. In the preface to this textbook, van Musschenbroek implicitly attacks the Cartesian way of doing philosophy and explicitly presents the book as following the 'Newtonian method of philosophising'. He contrasts the method followed in the book with a method which works by 'explaining singular phenomena of bodies from some assumed hypotheses', and which engages itself 'in a useless investigation of primary causes'.[49] He then argues that physics has been held captive by this method and puts forward Newton as a crucial turning point. According to van Musschenbroek, Newton introduced a new method of doing physics:

> The disease of this way of reasoning however became so strong, that from its beginning up until the time of Newton, physics was full of hypotheses constructed by second-rate intellects to explain the phenomena. This man [however], who had a stunning intellect and a divine penetration in physics and mathematics, first rejected all hypotheses, and taught a more virtuous method of reasoning, through which a certain physics could be obtained, by assuming nothing that could not in the most clear way be demonstrated by experiments and mathematical demonstrations, and he left behind an inimitable example in [his] *Principia Philosophiae* and [his] *Optica*.[50]

Van Musschenbroek explicitly refers to this method as 'Newton's method of philosophising (*Newtoni philosophandi methodus*)', and mentions his fellow countryman Bernard Nieuwentijt as someone who tried to follow this method.[51] Following the rhetoric of presenting Newton's philosophy

---

[48] A. Rupert Hall, 'Further Newton Correspondence', *Notes and Records of the Royal Society of London* 37 (1982), 32.

[49] Petrus van Musschenbroek, *Epitome elementorum physico-mathematicorum conscripta in usus academicos* (Leiden, 1726), 'Praefatio', 3b-4a.

[50] Van Musschenbroek, *Epitome*, 'Praefatio', 4.

[51] Van Musschenbroek, *Epitome*, 'Praefatio', 4b. On Nieuwentijt's use of Newton against Spinoza, see Steffen Ducheyne, 'Curing Pansophia through Eruditum Nescire: Bernard Nieuwentijt's (1654–1718) Epistemology of Modesty', *HOPOS: The Journal of the International Society for the History of Philosophy of Science* 7 (2017), 272–301. For a comparison of Nieuwentijt and van Musschenbroek's views on the proper use of mathematics in natural philosophy, see Steffen Ducheyne, 'Constraining (Mathematical) Imagination by

as an antidote to atheism, van Musschenbroek adds that 'only atheists, or those who try to hide [their] evil mind under a mask of piety, could bad-mouth, taunt, or render suspect the doctrines of both men'.[52]

The method of philosophising exemplified by Newton, and its contrast with the *a priori* method favoured by the Cartesians, formed the subject of an oration that van Musschenbroek had given three years prior to the publication of this textbook. This oration was delivered at the start of his academic career in Utrecht, when he took up the position of professor of philosophy and mathematics. The oration bore the title 'On the certain method of experimental philosophy'.[53] In this oration van Musschenbroek puts forward the claim that only a physics which is based on the experimental method is 'true, certain, and firm'.[54] Van Musschenbroek, however, not only wanted to *defend* this method, he also intended to *attack* the *a priori* method favoured by the Cartesians. The philosophy based on the *a priori* method is contrasted with the 'firm and certain' nature of experimental physics and is presented as being 'uncertain, infirm, [and] fleeting'.[55] The certainty and 'firmness' of experimental physics is a recurrent theme in the rest of the oration, as is the contrast with the uncertain and fleeting character of physics based on *a priori* reasoning. This theme also reoccurs throughout van Musschenbroek's oeuvre. [56]

Experience: Nieuwentijt and van Musschenbroek on the Abuses of Mathematics', *Synthese* (Online First, April 2017), 1–19 (URL=<https://doi.org/10.1007/s11229-017-1392-1> [accessed February 14 2018]). For a general account of Nieuwentijt's thought, see Rienk H. Vermij, *Secularisering En Natuurwetenschap in de Zeventiende en Achttiende Eeuw: Bernard Nieuwentijt* (Amsterdam, 1991).

[52] Van Musschenbroek, *Epitome*, 'Praefatio', p. 4b-5a.

[53] Petrus van Musschenbroek, *Oratio de Certa Methodo Philosophiae Experimentalis* (Utrecht, 1723).

[54] Van Musschenbroek, *Oratio de Certa Methodo*, 8.

[55] 'I will first try to show, that we owe [*deberi*] [our] ideas of bodies and their attributes to the experiences of [our] senses. Then [that] those [ideas] that we possess so far are not sufficient for us to be able to a priori infer a lot from them through reasoning about the nature of bodies, or their attributes: Next, [I will demonstrate that] they are so insufficiently known, and [insufficiently] clear and evident, that whatever we know, should be called mere ignorance as it were, if we take into consideration all the things unknown. [I then demonstrate that] the reasonings of the philosophers which are deduced out of those things, as if they would a priori demonstrate the workings of nature are uncertain, infirm, [and] fleeting. Finally, I will demonstrate that the only firm and certain physics is built solely on experiments which are accurately observed, and sparse reasoning on the basis of them' (Van Musschenbroek, *Oratio de Certa Methodo*, 10).

[56] In all the other orations delivered by van Musschenbroek, the theme of the firmness and stability of experimental physics reoccurs. I will treat those passage in my main text when discussing those orations. In *Physicae experimentales*, van Musschenbroek character-ises the 'new science' based on experiments as 'stable and unshakable knowledge (*scientiam, stabilem & inconcussam*)' (Petrus van Musschenbroek, *Physicae Experimentales, et Geometricae, de Magnete, Tuborum Capillarium Vitreorumque Speculorum Attractione, Magnitudine Terrae, Cohaerentia Corporum Formorum Dissertationes: Ut et Ephemerides Meteorologicae*

The stability and firmness of the method of experimental physics also reflects back on the community of practitioners. Where the community of philosophers using the *a priori* method is characterised by strife and disagreement, the community of experimental philosophers is described by van Musschenbroek as being 'free from all disputations and controversies'.[57]

In the section on the controversies surrounding Cartesianism, we have seen how Cartesianism caused strife and even violence within the university, and how the threat of Spinozism caused discord within the Cartesian camp. This was put to use by adversaries of Cartesianism in their critique. Van Musschenbroek capitalises on this in his introduction of the 'Newtonian philosophy' in the University of Utrecht by presenting the followers of the experimental method of Newton as characterised by concord and unity.

Van Musschenbroek was not the first to use this strategy. In a similar vein, Boerhaave, in his oration 'On the Achievement of Certainty in Physics' delivered at the University of Leiden in 1715, had mocked the 'inconstancy of slippery doctrine' found in physics which works by reasoning from some assumed first principles.[58] Bernard Nieuwentijt, in his turn, concluded his *Gronden van zekerheid* ('Grounds of Certainty') as follows:

> [W]hen all disputes which are only based on human reason, are taken away, at least everyone who has practised these sciences will have to observe, that large parts of those [disputes] which until now have taken place amongst Christians, and burning disagreements, will be extinguished. May the Almighty God give His blessing to this![59]

On 27 March 1730, van Musschenbroek handed over the function of rector of the University of Utrecht. On this occasion, he delivered an oration

---

Ultrajectinae (Leiden, 1729), 'Praefatio', 3b). In *Tentamina*, he writes that the philosophers working at the Academia del Cimento had provided 'the foundations of a true physics, which will stand firm in all eternity (*verae Physicae, quae in omne aevum firma staret, fundamenta*)' (Petrus van Musschenbroek, *Tentamina Experimentorum Naturalium Captorum in Academia Del Cimento* (Leiden, 1731), 'Praefatio', 2a). A bit further in that same work, he mentions Newton as the 'British Oracle' who had shown how 'a true and stable knowledge could be obtained (*quomodo... vera stabilisque Scientia comparari queat*)' (Van Musschenbroek, *Tentamina*, 'Preafatio', 3b). In the second edition of the *Elementa Physicae*, van Musschenbroek refers to the method of physics followed by him as 'the true and stable method of philosophizing (*vera stabilisque Philosophandi methodus*)' (Petrus van Musschenbroek, *Elementa Physicae Conscripta in Usus Academicos* (Leiden, 1741), 'Praefatio', 4a).

[57] Van Musschenbroek, *Oratio de Certa Methodo*, 42.

[58] Herman Boerhaave, 'Discourse on the Achievement of Certainty in Physics' in *Boerhaave's Orations*, trans. and ed. E. Kegel-Brinkgreve and A.M. Luyendijk-Elshout (Leiden: 1983), 173.

[59] Bernard Nieuwentijt, *Gronden van zekerheid, of de regte betoogwyse der wiskundigen: ter wederlegging van Spinosaas denkbeeldig samenstel en ter aanleiding van eene sekere sakelyke wysbegeerte* (Amsterdam, 1720), 458.

on the subject of 'the method of performing physical experiments'.[60] He now delivers the oration in a completely different position than in 1723. No longer the new professor presenting himself and his programme, he has become a well-known figure who has just occupied a prestigious position in the university. Unlike the previous one, this oration is not aimed at a defence of experimental philosophy, but contains an exposition on the proper method of designing and conducting experiments.

There are, however, some polemical passages to be found. Some of the themes and issues which we encountered in the previous oration, reoccur. Throughout the oration, van Musschenbroek repeatedly emphasises the stability of experimental physics.[61] The main adversaries are still those 'who judge that only reason is to be consulted, and that this [reason] is the only instructress of philosophy'.[62]

In the same oration, van Musschenbroek also mentions critics who say that he and his fellow Newtonians are 'only mindful to attraction, because [they] follow a faction in philosophy, applying this [term] only thanks to the Britons, who have not doubted to use this word very frequently in their disciplines'.[63] We can understand this criticism as an attempt to turn the tables on van Musschenbroek. In his first oration at Utrecht, van Musschenbroek had argued that experimental philosophy was characterised by consensus and stability, in contrast with physics based on *a priori* reasoning which was characterised by strife and a constant stream of ideas and fashions. The critics argue that it is the Newtonians using the term 'attraction' who are forming sects within philosophy and thereby causing discord. Van Musschenbroek defends the use of the term 'attraction' by emphasising that its use is based on observation and experimentation, unlike the philosophy of those who take offence in the use of the word 'attraction', but who 'only think about bodies in their study... but never bring their hand to experimental physics, never accurately examine any phenomenon, explore bodies in different ways, caste off prejudices, think sharply'.[64]

Van Musschenbroek was clearly troubled by this accusation of partisanship.[65] Although in the preface to the 1734 edition of his textbook,

---

[60] Petrus van Musschenbroek, 'Oratio de Methodo Instituendi Experimenta Physica' in *Tentamina Experimentorum Naturalium Captorum in Academia Del Cimento* (Leiden, 1731), I–XLVIII.

[61] Van Musschenbroek, 'Oratio de Methodo', IX, XIV, XIV, XXIII.

[62] Van Musschenbroek, 'Oratio de Methodo', X.

[63] Van Musschenbroek, 'Oratio de Methodo', XXXIII.

[64] Van Musschenbroek, 'Oratio de Methodo', XXXIII–XXXIV.

[65] In his personal copy of the book containing a printed version of the lecture, van Musschenbroek added marginal notes on the necessity of 'casting of prejudices (*deponere praejudicia*)' and 'favouring no sect (*sese nulli sectae addictum gerere*)'. Being a prejudiced

he still presents the work as part of the same tradition of teaching 'Newtonian philosophy (*Newtoniana philosophia*)' as that of Desaguliers and Pemberton,[66] he subsequently becomes more cautious and starts to increasingly emphasise impartiality in his rhetoric.

In the preface to the Dutch 1736 edition of the textbook, van Musschenbroek incorporates into his defence against accusations of sectarianism the image of philosophers only thinking about things in their study, but not doing any experimental work:

> I have never followed any sect; those who try to accuse me of doing so, are doing a great injustice to me: embracing the truth is my only goal, no matter who has found her. My using the terms 'attracting (*aantrekken*)' and 'attractive force (*aantrekkingskracht*)' is not a sign that I have surrendered myself to some sect, as some scholars feel I do, but on the contrary a true sign, that I am not doing any such thing, and am only taking into consideration the phenomena of nature, observing her with accuracy and effort, devoting my time to making many experiments; but not producing some chimeras in my study, nor trying to squabble about phenomena from vain presuppositions. Somebody is following a sect, when he accepts certain presuppositions which have been invented by others without proof, and builds upon these. But he who builds on solidly proven truths, or clear and simple grounds, which are experiments and observations in physics, [he] is not committed to any sect.[67]

Van Musschenbroek's disclaimers were however to no avail. In 1738, Nicolaus Engelhard, professor of philosophy at Groningen University (under a pseudonym) publishes a tract containing criticism of van Musschenbroek's 1736 book.[68] As part of his attack, Engelhard accuses van Musschenbroek of blindly following Newton's opinion because of his 'deference for everything that comes across the sea from that direction [i.e., England]'.[69]

---

follower of Newton is put on the same footing as being a Cartesian or Aristotelian: 'the same thing is looked upon in another way by an Aristotelian, in another way by a follower of Descartes, in another way by one who is a servant to the opinions of Newton or Stahl (*alio modo eandem rem intuetur Aristotelicus, alio Cartesii sectator, alio qui Newtoni alio qui Stahlii placitis est addictus*)' (Leiden University Library, Special Collections, MS BPL 240.59, Recto side of folio glued to p. XI). Unfortunately, I have not been able to date the note.

[66] Petrus van Musschenbroek, *Elementa Physicae Conscripta in Usus Academicos* (Leiden, 1734), 'Praefatio', 4b.

[67] Petrus van Musschenbroek, *Beginselen Der Natuurkunde Beschreeven Ten Dienste Der Landgenooten* (Leiden, 1736), 'Voorreden', 5a-5b.

[68] For a summary of this criticism, and an overview of the polemics (by proxy) that followed, see Kees de Pater, 'Nicolaus Engelhard (1696–1765) en zijn kritiek op de Beginselen der Natuurkunde van Petrus van Musschenbroek (1692–1761): Wolffianisme versus Newtonianisme', *Tijdschrift Voor de Geschiedenis Der Geneeskunde, Natuurwetenschappen, Wiskunde En Techniek* 13 (1990), 141–62.

[69] Daniel Coste van Hessom, *Nodige Dog Korte Aanmerkingen over de Beginselen Der Natuurkunde van Den Heer P. Musschenbroek, Hoogleeraar in de Wysgeerte En Wiskunde in de Universiteit t'Utrecht* (Groningen, 1738), 91.

In 1740, van Musschenbroek leaves the University of Utrecht and takes up a professorship at his *alma mater* Leiden University. His inaugural oration at Leiden was no longer a polemical defence of Newtonian philosophy, as were his orations at the University of Utrecht. Instead, it treated the philosophical question of the mind's knowledge of itself.[70] The notion of a 'true' philosophical method proscribing hypotheses and turning away from *a priori* reflection is mentioned in passing as the only proper way to arrive at 'true and firm demonstrations' on the nature of the mind.[71] However, this method is no longer presented as specifically 'Newtonian', nor is Newton's name connected to it.

Near the end of this oration, van Musschenbroek again takes up the theme of concord and harmony, but this time in order to apply it to his own person. He asks his new colleagues 'to cheerfully accept [this new] colleague, who very much loves peace and tranquillity, and who is most foreign to all discord, tricks, and meanness'.[72] After that, he singles out 's Gravesande and addresses him specifically. Having praised him and having commented on their longstanding friendship, van Musschenbroek concludes that he wishes to 'venerate and follow [him], although with unequal steps and far behind, as ['s Gravesande] had [done with] Newton'.[73]

In 1741 a second edition of the 1734 Latin version of van Musschenbroek's textbook appears. In the 1734 edition, as we have seen, van Musschenbroek still presented the work as part of the tradition of teaching 'Newtonian philosophy'. In the 1741 edition the 'true and stable method of philosophizing' takes centre stage, and is decoupled from the figure of Newton: 'A true and stable method of philosophizing has been found, through which one can obtain the certain and the true in physics, and purify science from fictions'.[74]

Van Musschenbroek then repeats that he 'follows no party, but the truth'.[75] To emphasise this point, the vehement anti-Cartesian adds

---

[70] Petrus van Musschenbroek, *Oratio Inauguralis De Mente Humana Semet Ignorante* (Leiden, 1740).

[71] Van Musschenbroek, *Oratio Inauguralis De Mente*, 23–24.

[72] Van Musschenbroek, *Oratio Inauguralis De Mente*, 25.

[73] Van Musschenbroek, *Oratio Inauguralis De Mente*, 26.

[74] Petrus van Musschenbroek, *Elementa Physicae Conscripta in Usus Academicos* (Leiden, 1741), 'Praefatio', 4a.

[75] 'Nullius partes sequor, nisi Veritatis' (Van Musschenbroek, *Elementa* (1741), 'Praefatio', 4b). This can be seen as a variation on the wide-spread saying 'Amicus Plato, amicus Aristoteles, magis amica Veritas'. Newton had written this as a motto on his personal notebook. For a discussion of the history and spread of this saying, see Henry Guerlac, 'Amicus Plato and Other Friends', *Journal of the History of Ideas* 39 (1978), 627–33. An example of the use of this saying in the Dutch Republic, in combination with the assertion of 'not following any sect' can be found in the 1648 oration of Senguerdius Sr.: 'Nulli Philosophorum sectae nos emancipemus, sed eo sequamur, quo nos veritas &

that he 'has retained the things which the very intelligent Descartes has demonstrated well'.[76] He also mentions that he has added several of the discoveries of Newton in his book, but immediately adds that he follows the opinion of Leibniz in what we now call the *vis viva* controversy.[77]

On 8 February 1744, van Musschenbroek stepped down as rector of the University of Leiden and on this occasion gave his last academic oration. The theme of this oration was 'divine wisdom', and the oration itself consists of a long exercise in natural theology.[78] As in the 1740 oration, the notion of a 'method of philosophising' is only mentioned in passing. At the beginning of the text, van Musschenbroek says that the fact that philosophers like Democritus, Epicurus, and Lucretius have lapsed into atheism can partly be explained by the fact that 'they did not know the rules to reason well'.[79] Newton is again mentioned, but only as an exceptional genius. Although van Musschenbroek still believes that 'when it comes to advancing the true and stable philosophy and mathematics, no period in time has produced somebody equal [to him]', the 'great glory of Britain' is no longer presented as somebody who has introduced a specific method in philosophy.[80]

To summarize, in this section I have shown how van Musschenbroek used the (already existing) idea of Cartesian philosophy as a philosophy characterised by strife as a starting point for both his criticism of this philosophy, and his defence of the experimental method of Newtonian philosophy. The latter was characterised by harmony and consent. Van Musschenbroek's critics, however, tried to use his own rhetoric against him, by arguing that the Newtonians were just a new sect in natural philosophy, trying to introduce notions like 'attraction'. This led van Musschenbroek to increasingly emphasize the notion of the method of experimental philosophy as a neutral method, not linked to any doctrinal position or natural philosophical sect.

---

rationem ducunt pondera' (Arnold Senguerd, *Oratio de Vero Philosopho* (Amsterdam, 1648), 23). On Senguerdius and this oration, see van Miert, *Humanism in an Age of Science*, 229–230. In the beginning of the seventeenth century, the Remonstrant Simon Episcopius had also used a variant of the saying in his plea for toleration and debate within the church, cf. Jacobus Arminius and Simon Episcopius, *De Arminiaanse Vredeskerk: Redevoeringen van Jacobus Arminius (1606) en Simon Episcopius (1618) over de Onderlinge Verdraagzaamheid der christenen*, trans. and ed. Simon Vuyk (Hilversum, 2015), 86.

[76] Van Musschenbroek, *Elementa* (1741), 'Praefatio', 4b.
[77] Van Musschenbroek, *Elementa* (1741), 'Praefatio', 4b-5a.
[78] Petrus van Musschenbroek, *Oratio de Sapientia Divina* (Leiden, 1744).
[79] Van Musschenbroek, *Oratio de Sapientia Divina*, 5.
[80] Van Musschenbroek, *Oratio de Sapientia Divina*, 13.

Law and Order

In this section I will show how van Musschenbroek links the idea of experimental philosophy as characterised by harmony and consensus with a specific conception of 'laws of nature'.[81] His specific take on the nature of these laws and their dependence on the will of God will provide him with an argument in favour of the stability of the method of '(Newtonian) experimental philosophy'. At the same time, it will show why the method of *a priori* philosophy favoured by the Cartesians is intrinsically flawed, and can, by default, only lead to disorder and disagreement.

The notion of a 'law of nature' played a crucial role in the natural philosophy of Descartes.[82] In his *Principia Philosophiae*, Descartes puts forward three 'laws of nature (*leges naturae*)', which he derives from the immutability of God, and from which he in turn derives laws of motion.[83] In *Le Monde*, the notion of 'laws of nature (*loix de la nature*)' is taken up again. There, at the end of the chapter on laws of nature, Descartes states that these laws allow one to derive all known phenomena from them *a priori*.[84]

The concept of a 'law of nature' is also utilised by Spinoza. The controversy surrounding his work was partly caused by his necessitarian metaphysics, in which God was presented as being bound by the laws of his own nature. In the *Ethics*, Spinoza concluded that '[*t*]*hings could have been produced by God in no other way, and in no other order than they have been*

---

[81] I will only discuss the role of this concept in van Musschenbroek's defence of the method of '(Newtonian) experimental philosophy'. For an in-depth discussion of van Musschenbroek's views on 'laws of nature' and their development, see Steffen Ducheyne and Pieter Present, 'Pieter van Musschenbroek on Laws of Nature', *The British Journal for the History of Science* 50 (2017), 637–656.

[82] The history and development of this concept is a complex issue, and has been the subject of numerous studies. More recent ones include Sophie Roux, 'Les Lois de La Nature À L'âge Classique: La Question Terminologique', *Revue de Synthèse* 4 (2001), 531–76; Eric Watkins, ed., *The Divine Order, the Human Order, and the Order of Nature: Historical Perspectives* (Oxford, 2013); Lorraine Daston and Michael Stolleis, eds., *Natural Law and Laws of Nature in Early Modern Europe: Jurisprudence, Theology, Moral and Natural Philosophy* (Aldershot, 2008). The work of René Descartes played an important role in the spread and use of this concept in natural philosophy. John Henry even goes as far as saying that Descartes was 'effectively responsible for single-handedly introducing the notion of laws of nature into natural philosophy' (John Henry, 'Metaphysics and the Origins of Modern Science: Descartes and the Importance of Laws of Nature', *Early Science and Medicine* 9 (2004), 73–114).

[83] René Descartes, 'Principia Philosophiae' in *Oeuvres de Descartes*, ed. Charles Adam and Paul Tannery (Paris, 1905 [1644]), 8: 62.

[84] René Descartes, 'Le Monde', in *Oeuvres de Descartes*, ed. Charles Adam and Paul Tannery (Paris, 1909 [1677]), 11: 47.

produced'.[85] As we have seen, anti-Cartesians had argued that Spinoza's impious ideas were the natural consequence of Descartes's philosophy. In his *Cartesius Verus Spinozismi Architectus*, which was introduced above, Johannes Regius explicitly invokes Descartes's conception of 'laws of nature' as laying the foundations for Spinoza. One of the sub-chapters in this work reads: 'The laws of nature invented by Descartes completely make God into a thing acting out of necessity'.[86] As I have shown above, Dutch Newtonians used this image in their rhetoric, presenting their programme as a pious alternative to Cartesianism and Spinozism.[87]

In Newton's own work, there were already passages where a certain conception of laws of nature was used in a polemical way. Especially in the second edition of the *Principia*, which proved to be instrumental in the spread of Newton's ideas in the Dutch Republic, one already finds arguments levelled against Cartesianism which will be taken up by the Dutch Newtonians in their fight against Spinoza and his followers.[88]

In the preface to the second edition of the *Principia*, Roger Cotes, the editor of this second edition, distinguishes three classes of practitioners of natural science: Aristotelians, Cartesians, and experimental natural philosophers.[89] Whereas the Cartesians were right in turning away from Aristotelianism and in looking for simple principles governing all things, they were wrong in 'tak[ing] the foundation of their speculations from hypotheses, even if they then proceed most rigorously according to mechanical laws'.[90] Experimental philosophers, including Newton, do not make this mistake and 'assume nothing as a principle that has not yet been thoroughly proved from phenomena'.[91] So although both Descartes

[85] Benedictus de Spinoza, *The Collected Works of Spinoza*, trans. and ed. Edwin Curley (Princeton, 2016), 1: 436. In a series of lectures, van Musschenbroek had explicitly criticised Spinoza's necessitarian metaphysics. For a discussion of this criticism, see Steffen Ducheyne, "Celeberrimus Atheismi Patronus Praecedentis saeculi:' Petrus van Musschenbroek's Anti-Spinozism Unveiled' *Lias, Journal of Early Modern Intellectual Culture and Its Sources* 41 (2014), 173–97.

[86] '*Leges naturae a Cartesio inventae omnino faciunt Deum agens necessarium*' (Regius, *Cartesius Verus Spinozismi Architectus*, 170, emphasis in original).

[87] A more general take on the role of the concept of laws of nature, and especially its use in debates on the status of the Bible in the defence of Newton's ideas in the Dutch Republic can be found in Rienk Vermij, 'Defining the Supernatural: The Dutch Newtonians, the Bible and the Laws of Nature', in *Newton and the Netherlands*, ed. Eric Jorink and Ad Maas (Amsterdam, 2012), 185–206.

[88] On the importance of the second edition of the *Principia* for the spread of Newton's ideas in the Dutch Republic, see Jorink and Zuidervaart, "The Miracle of Our Time", 25–31.

[89] Roger Cotes, 'Editor's Preface to the Second Edition' in Isaac Newton, *The Principia: Mathematical Principles of Natural Philosophy*, trans. and ed. I. Bernard Cohen and Anne Whitman (California, 1999), 31.

[90] Cotes, 'Editor's Preface', 31.

[91] Cotes, 'Editor's Preface', 31.

and Newton (according to Cotes) share a commitment to the use of laws to deduce phenomena from, Cotes explicitly points out the difference between the epistemic foundation each provides for the laws they put forward. Cotes then links this to theological issues. Because the laws of nature depend on the 'perfectly free will of God, who provides and governs all things':

> [W]e should not seek these laws by using untrustworthy conjectures, but learn them by observing and experimenting. He who is confident that he can truly find the principles of physics, and the laws of things, by relying only on the force of his mind and the internal light of his reason should maintain either that the world has existed from necessity and follows the said laws from the same necessity, or that although the order of nature was constituted by the will of God, nevertheless a creature as small and insignificant as he is has a clear understanding of the way things should be.[92]

Cotes is confident that Newton's work will convince any honest reader of the supremacy of the experimental method. Because of this, 'Newton's excellent treatise will stand as a mighty fortress against the attacks of atheists; nowhere else will you find more effective ammunition against that impious crowd.'[93] In the General Scholium, Newton gives further remarks on his theological views, especially emphasising the dominion of God and his ruling all things, for which he is known as Lord God *Pantokrator*.[94] Denying God's dominion, according to Newton, would lead to the kind of necessitarianism against which Cotes had already warned in the Preface:

> For a god without dominion, providence, and final causes is nothing other than fate and nature. No variation in things arises from blind metaphysical necessity, which must be the same always and everywhere. All the diversity of created things, each in its place and time, could only have arisen from the ideas and the will of a necessarily existing being.[95]

To summarize, with regard to laws of nature, the second edition of the *Principia* contains the message that these laws cannot be discovered through *a priori* reasoning, as Descartes thought; that they can only be found through observation and experimentation. Moreover, these laws are not metaphysically necessary or a consequence of the nature of God, but rather the outcome of an act of will by God.

In 1726, in the preface to his first textbook, van Musschenbroek explicitly introduces Newton as a pious philosopher, quoting a passage from Newton's General Scholium: '[Newton] demonstrates, how this universe, this most elegant construction of the sun, planets, and comets, could not

---

[92] Cotes, 'Editor's Preface', 43–44. [93] Cotes, 'Editor's Preface', 44.
[94] Newton, *The Principia*, 586. [95] Newton, *The Principia*, 588.

have been fabricated mechanically, nor from a random concurrence of atoms, but only through the "design and the dominion of an intelligent and powerful being".'[96]

In the first chapter of the textbook, van Musschenbroek clarifies to his readers what he takes to be the nature of the discipline of physics, and its proper object of study.[97] The proper object of physics, van Musschenbroek says, is 'body and motion (*Corpus et Motus*)'.[98] Immediately after this, van Musschenbroek introduces 'mechanics (*Μεχανική*)' and defines it as 'the part of physics, which teaches according to which laws of motion bodies are being altered, or act and are moved'.[99] A 'law' is then defined as being '*a rule*, according to which God wanted that in the most constant manner phenomena of a certain kind would happen in such kind of conditions of bodies'.[100] In the next paragraph, van Musschenbroek emphasises that 'we can only learn these kinds of laws from our sensory observations'.[101] These laws, he further adds, allow us to make predictions about the future. If this would not have been the case, we would have been condemned to a life of perpetual experimentation, and our reasoning would not have any stable ground.[102]

In the second edition of the textbook, published in 1734, van Musschenbroek expands these paragraphs on laws of nature, making explicit certain assumptions. He repeats that we can only learn these laws through sensory observation, but now explicitly contrasts this with the *a priori* method favoured by the Cartesians: 'Not even the wisest of mortals has been able to discover any [law] a priori, even less so does he find an innate idea of any [such law] to be innate in his mind'.[103] Van Musschenbroek then links this criticism of *a priori* philosophy to the dependence of these laws on God's will, a point that is also made more explicit than in the first edition:

> Truly all [these laws] depend on the most free will of the Creator, which established that certain motions would always be executed on the same occasions.... By his infinite power, God could have constituted all these things differently, if he had wanted. Why he has however ordained those things thus, we only perceive minimally: it suffices for us to see, that all these things are ordered most wisely. Therefore, the reason and cause of these laws are unknown to us. They are truly most constant, because the divine will has ordained it thus.[104]

---

[96] Van Musschenbroek, *Epitome*, 'Praefatio', 4b. The original can be found in Newton, *The Principia*, 586.

[97] Van Musschenbroek, *Epitome*, 1

[98] Van Musschenbroek, *Epitome*, 5.

[99] Van Musschenbroek, *Epitome*, 5.

[100] Van Musschenbroek, *Epitome*, 3.

[101] Van Musschenbroek, *Epitome*, 3.

[102] Van Musschenbroek, *Epitome*, 3–4.

[103] Van Musschenbroek, *Elementa* (1734), 4.

[104] Van Musschenbroek, *Elementa* (1734), 4.

In the next edition of the textbook, published in 1741, the last sentence is slightly reworked to make the point even more explicit: 'These [laws] are truly most constant, because the divine will is most constant'.[105]

To summarize, van Musschenbroek puts forward the view that the laws of nature are regularities that are imposed on nature by a divine act of will. God acted completely freely when imposing laws on his creation; he 'could have constituted all these things differently, if he had wanted'. Epistemologically, van Musschenbroek thus undercuts a direct access by means of reason to the laws of nature. In the 1723 oration 'On the certain method of experimental philosophy', van Musschenbroek starts with a criticism of the possibility of there being innate ideas and their serving as the basis of knowledge.[106] Therefore, the only means left for us to access the laws of nature is by experimentation on and observation of nature itself. In the same oration, van Musschenbroek mentions a possible criticism which could be made at this point. Are not the senses known to be deceptive? Has it not been shown that they do not provide a basis for certainty, which only reason can provide?[107] Here, van Musschenbroek first replies by arguing that the senses can only deceive us if we do not take care to employ them correctly.[108] Moreover, our senses are given to us by God, about whom all will agree that he is the 'source of all truth (*omnium veritatum fons*)'.[109] God is not only the source of truth and the guarantee for the reliability of our senses but also, as we have just seen, the source of the laws which he has imposed on nature by an arbitrary decree of his will. At the end of his 1723 oration, van Musschenbroek uses this view on the origin of the laws of nature to drive the point home against the Cartesians. As we have seen in the previous section, van Musschenbroek presented the method of experimental philosophy as being characterised by harmony, stability, and consensus. At the end of his oration on the certain method of experimental philosophy, this stability is premised on the constancy of the divine will and the dependence of the laws of nature thereupon:

> For has there ever been an experiment which, after being accurately observed with an eye on all its circumstances, been discovered as being false? It could not happen, unless the entire order of things would be inversed, and bodies would now be subject to other laws than they were earlier, which without the new creation of other [laws], and the abolition of those, which exist now, cannot happen ... because of this the greatest harmony [exists] between philosophers who perform experiments, and accurately take note of the

105 Van Musschenbroek, *Elementa* (1741), 5.
106 Van Musschenbroek, *Oratio de Certa Methodo*, 10–19.
107 Van Musschenbroek, *Oratio de Certa Methodo*, 19.
108 Van Musschenbroek, *Oratio de Certa Methodo*, 19–20.
109 Van Musschenbroek, *Oratio de Certa Methodo*, 20.

phenomena of nature: because whatever effects of nature are being produced, they are truly given and produced from their causes, which always
remain the same, as they are established as a law by God.[110]

At the beginning of the oration, van Musschenbroek had stated that the
order of nature was both created and maintained 'by the incomprehensible power (*vi incomprehensibili*)' of God.[111] Because of this incompre-
hensibility, trying to rationally discover these laws is to no avail. The only
option left is to observe nature and to discover the regularities occurring
there. Because of the constancy of God's will, we can be sure that the
regularities found in nature also have a stable character. Therefore, sensory observations can provide a solid foundation for philosophy. In
turn, a community of philosophers who observe nature's constancy
(an expression of the divine will) can only be constant and harmonious
itself. Philosophers only using *a priori* reasoning in their philosophy
deprive themselves of the only available foundation for certain knowledge.
This, for van Musschenbroek, explains 'the inconstancy of the dogma
of reason'.[112]

At this point, we might seem to have ventured far away from the institution of the university into the dark waters of epistemology and metaphysics. Van Musschenbroek's polemical use of this conception of laws of
nature is linked, however, to the nature of the institution of the university
and the struggles discussed above. Given the fact that the early modern
Dutch university was conceived first and foremost as a training ground for
the country's political and spiritual elite, the teaching of Cartesian philosophy in the preparatory faculty of arts and philosophy was seen as a
threat. It could not, the critics argued, provide the right preparation for
studies in the higher faculties of theology, law, or medicine. Moreover, it
could have a corrupting effect on the people who would soon occupy key
positions in Dutch society. We also saw how the introduction of Cartesian
philosophy had led to discord within the university, a fact emphasised by
critics of Descartes philosophy. In this section, I have shown how van
Musschenbroek used his conception of laws of nature and their dependence on the will of God to ground his rhetoric on the community of
experimental philosophers as a group characterised by harmony and consensus. Rhetorically, his conception of laws of nature allowed him to do
more than just provide divine grounds for the stability of experimental
philosophy. It also turned natural philosophy into a pious examination of

---

[110] Van Musschenbroek, *Oratio de Certa Methodo*, 42–44.
[111] Van Musschenbroek, *Oratio de Certa Methodo*, 9.
[112] Van Musschenbroek, *Oratio de Certa Methodo*, 44.

the will of God as expressed in nature.[113] This resonated with the idea of nature as the second book of God, an idea which was common in Dutch Calvinist Orthodoxy, and could even be found in the Belgic Confession, which was one of its foundational texts.[114] In the same way as the reading of Scripture allows us to learn the moral and religious laws which God has imposed on us, empirical investigation allows us to discover the laws he has imposed on nature. Whereas Cartesians were sometimes criticised for not accepting any authority but their own reason,[115] van Musschenbroek could present '(Newtonian) experimental philosophy' as a humble and pious reverence for the authority of God: one reads the laws of nature as they are inscribed in the Creation by God himself. Natural philosophy can thus again perform its role as a preparatory study fit for the training of the country's elite.

Moreover, while the Cartesians had put forward a principled distinction between philosophy and theology, but failed to prevent others criticising their philosophy for its pernicious theological implications, the idea of the two books also allowed van Musschenbroek to present the search for laws in natural philosophy as in synergy with theology. Cartesianism had been involved in heavy debates on the status of miracles as described in the Bible, especially after Spinoza had argued that the notion of a miracle is inconsistent with the notion of a law of nature.[116] From the second edition of his textbook onwards, van Musschenbroek explicitly presents the search for laws in natural philosophy as not only compatible with theology, but even helpful: 'By way of these laws we understand what happens naturally, and what happens miraculously: because miracles happen, when phenomena occur which are contrary to [these] laws'.[117] At the end of the introductory chapter, van Musschenbroek devotes a paragraph to the utility of physics. Here, he includes the fact that it 'eradicates superstition, and

---

[113] In the 1732 oration on astronomy (cf. supra note 14), van Musschenbroek presents empirical astronomy as instilling reverence for the immense power of God, and protecting people from lapsing into absurd opinions on God, such as 'that God is extended or a space capable of all things', which people like Spinoza or Joseph Raphson think ('Deum esse extensum aut Spatium omnium rerum capax cum Raphsono, et aliquomodo cum impio Spinoza statueret', MS BPL 240.7, fol. 11').

[114] For an elaborate discussion of the idea of the Book of Nature, see Eric Jorink, *Reading the Book of Nature in the Dutch Golden Age, 1575–1715* (Leiden/Boston, 2010).

[115] Van Bunge, *From Stevin to Spinoza*, 107.

[116] A general take on these debates, the role of the concept of laws of nature, and the spread of Newtonianism can be found in Vermij, 'Defining the Supernatural', 193–200. The issue of the relation between miracles and the laws of nature was also hotly debated outside the Dutch Republic. See for example Peter Harrison, 'Newtonian Science, Miracles, and the Laws of Nature', *Journal of the History of Ideas* 56 (1995), 531–53.

[117] Van Musschenbroek, *Elementa* (1734), 4.

puts divine miracles in the clearest light'.[118] This will, with certain additions, be repeated in all subsequent versions of the textbook.

At the University of Utrecht, van Musschenbroek's rhetoric was taken over in the self-presentation of the institution. In 1736, when van Musschenbroek was still a professor there, the university celebrated its centennial jubilee. On this occasion, the professor of history and rhetoric Arnold Drakenborch (1684–1748) gave a panegyric oration. Drakenborch mentioned the theatre for experimental physics and presented it as a place of pious observation of God's creation: 'In order that those who teach philosophy could better educate the studious youth in all parts of this discipline, a theatre was built, where the miracles, which the infinite power of God had put into nature, could be investigated'.[119]

The utility of physics will be the topic of the following section. In the beginning of this paper, I discussed how Cartesians argued for a strict distinction between philosophy and theology. Philosophy dealt with certain knowledge, which had nothing to do with the kind of practical knowledge that was used in theology, but also in law and medicine. This strategy however had the unintended result that it severed the link between the teaching in the preparatory faculty of arts and philosophy and the teaching in the higher faculties of theology, law, and medicine. In the end, it made philosophical knowledge irrelevant for those interested in the learning presented in the higher faculties. Here, also, we will see how van Musschenbroek defends '(Newtonian) experimental philosophy' by showing how it succeeds where Cartesianism had failed. Both in his textbooks and in his orations, van Musschenbroek explicitly emphasises the usefulness of his teaching for the disciplines taught in the higher faculties.

'Utilitas Physicae Ingens Est'

At the end of the introductory chapter of his textbook, van Musschenbroek presents arguments in favour of the utility of his teachings. As we saw in the previous section, one of the things van Musschenbroek emphasized was the theological utility of natural philosophy based on the method of

[118] Van Musschenbroek, *Elementa* (1734), 6.

[119] Arnoldus Drakenborch, *Oratio Panegyrica in Natalem Saecularem Academiae Traiectinae* (Utrecht, 1736), 37. At the end of his oration, Drakenborch explicitly expresses the idea of the university as a 'nursery for church and state': 'may the Academy of Utrecht never fail in being a nursery for the state and the church, out of which daily come forth, those who, being advanced to the government of the country, keep liberty unharmed; [and] those who, being given the authority of directing your church, hand over the invaluable shield of religion, purged from every stain of superstition, without blemish, to [our] descendants!' (Drakenborch, *Oratio Panegyrica*, 57).

'(Newtonian) experimental philosophy'. Knowledge of the laws of nature helped one show how the miracles contained in the Bible were indeed miracles, i.e., events contradicting these laws.[120] Van Musschenbroek provided more reasons why experimental philosophy was theologically useful.

In an article giving an overview of the development of the thinking on laws of nature in seventeenth-century England, Peter Harrison shows that the Cambridge Platonists saw problems in Descartes's deductive approach to the discovery of the laws of nature: 'Combined with Descartes's denial of final causes, the *a priori* approach to God's existence ruled out a species of design argument much cherished by English natural philosophers'.[121] Theo Verbeek has likewise pointed out that the fact that Descartes ruled out cosmological arguments in favour of God's existence played a role in his philosophy being accused of leading to atheism.[122]

In van Musschenbroek's work, we find both an emphasis on the re-introduction of teleology in natural philosophy, and on physico-theology, the attempt to show the providence and design of God as they manifest themselves in nature. From the third edition of the textbook onwards (1741), teleology is explicitly mentioned as a sub-discipline of philosophy.[123] In the paragraph on the utility of physics, the investigation of nature is presented as leading directly to a proof of the existence of God: '[Physics] leads us directly to the knowledge and proof of the existence of God, and gives us an optimal understanding of several of his attributes'.[124]

From the third edition onwards, van Musschenbroek adds the clarification that physics leads us to a knowledge and proof of God's existence and providence, and an understanding of the attributes of power, wisdom, and goodness more specifically.[125] At the beginning of his oration on the certain method of experimental philosophy, van Musschenbroek also presents the latter as starting with the collection of observations, and ending with a 'demonstration of the first cause, with infinite power, most wise, out of whose immense generosity, [and] incomprehensible power all things flow forth, and through which they remain, and conserve the most elegant

---

[120] In the last edition of his textbook, published posthumously, this link to Biblical miracles is made explicit by references to stories from the Bible, cf. Petrus van Musschenbroek, *Introductio ad philosophiam naturalem* (Leiden, 1762), 8, 21–22.

[121] Peter Harrison, 'Laws of Nature in Seventeenth-Century England: From Cambridge Platonism to Newtonianism', in *The Divine Order, the Human Order, and the Order of Nature: Historical Perspectives*, ed. Eric Watkins (Oxford, 2013), 138.

[122] Verbeek, 'Descartes and the Problem of Atheism', 216.

[123] Van Musschenbroek, *Elementa* (1741), 2.

[124] Van Musschenbroek, *Elementa* (1734), 6.

[125] Van Musschenbroek, *Elementa* (1741), 8.

order perfectly in all their parts'.[126] In 1744, as we have seen, he even devoted an entire oration to the subject of physico-theology.[127] Theology was, however, not the only thing van Musschenbroek had in mind when he commented on the 'utilitas physicae'. In his textbook, van Musschenbroek indicated at the utility of physics in 'finding and amplifying conveniences in human life'.[128] Already in his first public defence of '(Newtonian) experimental philosophy', van Musschenbroek had appealed to its broader use for society, contrasting it again with the *a priori* search for causes:

Aside from the unshaken certitude of this science, [the] method [of experimental philosophy] is recommended by [its] extraordinary utility, because the experiments that are done can serve infinite human uses in civil life, either by chance, or because one already had that goal in mind [when doing the experiment]... [but] the subtle search for causes has never brought something good. Indeed: if what we do is not useful, glory is foolish.[129]

The valuation of the practical applicability of knowledge changed throughout the history of the Dutch Republic. In the early days of the Republic, from the end of the sixteenth century until the middle of the seventeenth century, utility and practical application were highly emphasised.[130] In the second half of the seventeenth century, up until the first decades of the eighteenth century, the emphasis on utility declined heavily.[131] In the first part of the eighteenth century, partly owing to the emergence of Newtonian experimental philosophy, utility and practical applicability gained importance.[132] These shifts were caused and entwined in a complex way with socio-economic, political, technological, and ideological developments.[133]

[126] Van Musschenbroek, *Oratio de Certa Methodo*, 9.

[127] Van Musschenbroek, *Oratio de Sapientia Divina*.

[128] Van Musschenbroek, *Elementa* (1741), 8.

[129] Van Musschenbroek, *Oratio de Certa Methodo*, 44.

[130] Van Bunge, *From Stevin to Spinoza*, 1–9; C.A. Davids, 'Universiteiten, Illustre Scholen en de verspreiding van technische kennis in Nederland, Eind 16e—Begin 19e Eeuw', *Batavia Academica* 8 (1990): 4–8. On the role of the valuation of the practical utility of knowledge in the foundation of the Illustrious School in Amsterdaam, see van Miert, *Humanism in an Age of Science*, 35–40.

[131] Van Bunge, *From Stevin to Spinoza*, 55–56; Davids, 'Universiteiten, Illustre Scholen en de verspreiding van technische kennis in Nederland', 8–10.

[132] Davids, 'Universiteiten, Illustre Scholen en de verspreiding van technische kennis in Nederland', 11–23.

[133] An overview of the technical developments in the Dutch Republic in this period and their social and economical context can be found in Karel Davids, *The Rise and Decline of Dutch Technological Leadership: Technology, Economy and Culture in the Netherlands, 1350–1800* (Leiden/Boston, 2008). For a reading of the spread of 'Newtonianism' in relation to (ideas of) practical utility, cf. Margaret C. Jacob and Larry Stewart, *Practical Matter: Newton's Science in the Service of Industry and Empire, 1687–1851* (London/Cambridge MA, 2004).

Van Musschenbroek can thus be seen as part of the early eighteenth century tendency to revalue utility. In a rhetorical context, van Musschenbroek used this again as a way to demonstrate that '(Newtonian) experimental philosophy' should replace Cartesian philosophy in the institution of the university. When it comes to providing useful results for society, it is again the method favoured by van Musschenbroek that succeeds where Cartesianism had failed.

Van Musschenbroek also explicitly emphasises the educational utility of natural philosophy within the university. As we have seen, the teaching of philosophy took place in the preparatory faculty of arts and philosophy and prepared students for an education in the higher faculties of theology, law, and medicine. Whereas the Cartesians had separated philosophy from the teaching in the higher faculties, van Musschenbroek never tires of explicitly emphasizing the usefulness of physics for the students in the higher faculties. In his textbook, van Musschenbroek stressed that physics is useful 'in all the human arts, and also for the advancement, explanation, and understanding of other disciplines, but especially in medicine'.[134] In the oration given at the start of his career at Leiden University in 1740, van Musschenbroek ends by addressing the students and convincing them of the utility of the teaching provided in the arts and philosophy faculty. Using the words normally reserved for experimental philosophy, van Musschenbroek tells his students that 'the true and certain foundations of your studies depend on the exercise and knowledge of the liberal arts and philosophy'.[135] He then addresses the future theology, law, and medicine students separately. Theology students will benefit from the study of pneumatics and metaphysics, but also from learning 'how the existence of a supreme Divinity is demonstrated from the works of nature'.[136] Prospective law students will benefit most from the study of logic. Students wanting to study medicine, in their turn, will benefit from knowing 'the principles of mechanics and physics' and also the 'clear, certain, and unshakeable foundations, on which the art of chemistry rests'.[137] The experimental method thus not only provides the certain and unshakeable foundations of philosophy, but experimental philosophy in turn provides the student with a stable foundation for his further studies. Where the Cartesian philosophers upholding the 'separation thesis' had unintentionally separated themselves institutionally from the teaching provided in the higher faculty, van Musschenbroek is able to defend the place of '(Newtonian) experimental philosophy' in the educational framework of the university.

[134] Van Musschenbroek, *Elementa* (1741), 8.
[135] Van Musschenbroek, *Oratio de Mente*, 26.
[136] Van Musschenbroek, *Oratio de Mente*, 27.
[137] Van Musschenbroek, *Oratio de Mente*, 27–28.

Summary and Conclusion

In this paper, I have discussed van Musschenbroek's defence of '(Newtonian) experimental philosophy'. More specifically, I have read his rhetoric against the background of the early modern Dutch university. In a letter to Newton, van Musschenbroek presented himself as someone with the aim of combatting the Cartesian philosophy in the universities and replacing it by Newtonian philosophy. Since its introduction in Dutch universities, Cartesian philosophy had been subject to severe criticism. Some, if not most, of this criticism was linked to views on the nature and goal of the university as an institution. Given that the main aim of the university was to train the political and religious elite of the Dutch Republic, critics argued that introducing Descartes's impious philosophy in the university posed a danger for Dutch society at large. Critics also pointed at the discord that the introduction of Cartesianism had caused in several universities, in order to argue that it was inherently destabilising. Although some Cartesians had themselves presented Cartesian philosophy as a stabilising force, this argument became less convincing when they succumbed to internal strife owing to the threat of Spinozism. In an attempt to shield themselves against the accusation that Cartesian philosophy had impious theological implications, some Cartesian philosophers started to uphold what Alexander Douglas has called a 'separation thesis', arguing for a strict separation between the kind of knowledge provided by philosophy and the kind of knowledge that was used in theology and other disciplines. This, however, had the unintended consequence of making the philosophy taught in the preparatory faculty of arts and philosophy useless for those wanting to study in the higher faculties of theology, law, and medicine.

Reading van Musschenbroek's rhetoric, we see how he took rhetorical advantage of this criticism and consistently tried to show how '(Newtonian) experimental philosophy' succeeded where Cartesian philosophy had failed. Van Musschenbroek presented experimental philosophy as an enterprise built upon a stable foundation of observations and experiments, and the community of experimental philosophers as characterised by harmony and consensus.

This harmony and consensus was both explained by, and grounded in, a certain conception of the laws of nature. By emphasising the fact that the laws of nature depended on an act of will by God, which was not accessible through reason, he undercut Cartesian appeals to knowledge of these laws by *a priori* reasoning. By emphasising the constant character of God's will, he could explain why observations of natural regularities provided a stable and certain basis for natural philosophy. This also allowed him to explain the harmony and consensus in the community of experimental philosophers.

Presenting experimental philosophy as the search for laws in the natural world also allowed van Musschenbroek to present it as a pious endeavour, in a symbiotic relationship with theology. Where theologians studied the book of scripture, experimental philosophers studied the book of nature. Trying to discover the laws of nature and study its design also helped to provide arguments for the existence of God. In this way, experimental philosophy had its place in the university conceived of as an institution which should help in stabilising the nation and maintaining its godliness. Van Musschenbroek also emphasized the utility of physics *within* the institution of the university, arguing that it fulfils its role as preparatory study for students going on to study in the higher faculties of theology, law, and medicine.

In general, this discussion of van Musschenbroek's rhetoric both aligns with, but also refines, the existing understanding of the defence of Newton's views in the Dutch Republic. Van Musschenbroek's rhetoric fits the general picture of Newton being introduced as an antidote against Spinozism and atheism. Newton himself was presented as an exemplar of piety, and the theological potential of his natural philosophy in providing evidence for the existence and design of God was heavily emphasised. These elements are also present in van Musschenbroek's presentation of Newtonian philosophy. However, as Spinozism was never institutionalised, van Musschenbroek's main target was Cartesianism. Moreover, although all the editions of his textbooks contained a discussion of Newton's *regulae philosophandi*,[138] and in his last oration he still presented himself as following in the footsteps of Newton, in some contexts van Musschenbroek moved away from the emphasis on the persona and doctrine of Newton. This, I have shown, was linked to the criticism levelled at him: the Newtonians were just another sect in natural philosophy. Given the heavy emphasis on consensus, impartiality and stability in his rhetoric, this was an accusation that van Musschenbroek had to take seriously. In reaction, van Musschenbroek presented himself as an impartial follower of the experimental method, even accepting certain views of Leibniz or Descartes if they turned out to be right.

Department of Philosophy and moral sciences
Ghent University
Belgium
pieter.present@ugent.be

[138] For a discussion of van Musschenbroek's take on Newton's *regulae* and its development, cf. Ducheyne, 'Petrus van Musschenbroek and Newton's 'Vera Stabilisque Philosophandi Methodus'', 279–304.

Speculative Philosophy
at the Berlin Academy

Christian Leduc

Introduction

The creation of the class of speculative philosophy at the Berlin Academy in the 1740s is remarkable for at least two reasons: on the one hand, it is the only major academy at the time to include the study of disciplines like metaphysics, logic, and moral philosophy, which were grouped together under the name of speculative philosophy. Other comparable institutions, such as the London and Paris academies, did not comprise these domains of thought, for they were normally studied in the universities. At its inception in 1700, the Berlin Academy was similar to other such institutions and was exclusively concerned with the experimental sciences, mathematics, and belles-lettres. Its founder, Leibniz, did not see a reason for including philosophy and metaphysics, although, as we know, he was more than inclined to such fields of research, to which he made significant contributions.[1] The changes made by Frederick II and the new generation of academicians are thus innovative even for the Berlin Academy. On the other hand, the use of the expression speculative philosophy raises many questions: speculating about metaphysics and practical philosophy was often perceived at the time in a pejorative way. For instance, Hume, as many others in the eighteenth century, most often associates speculative knowledge with abstract and uncertain opinion.[2] Speculation was thus conceived of as a useless and even damaging sort of reasoning for philosophy in general, and this would

---

[1] On Leibniz's views about academies, see: Eberhard Knobloch, 'Die Leibniz'sche Akademiekonzeption', in *Leibniz heute lesen*, hrsg. von Herta Nagl-Docekal (Berlin-Boston, 2018), 143–160. Hans Poser, *Leibniz' Philosophie*, hrsg. von Wenchao Li (Hamburg, 2016), 408–445.

[2] David Hume, *Treatise of Human Nature*, I, I, IV and VII, I, III, ed. by Peter H. Nidditch (Oxford, 1978), 13, 18 and 138–139.

Christian Leduc, *Speculative Philosophy at the Berlin Academy* In: *History of Universities*. Edited by: Mordechai Feingold, Oxford University Press (2021). © Oxford University Press. DOI: 10.1093/oso/ 9780192893833.003.0007

certainly be the case in the context of an academy tasked with increasing our knowledge and contributing to the common good.

Some scholars have mentioned the particularity of the class of speculative philosophy, but no studies have sought to explain this unique theoretical situation in any detailed manner.[3] In this paper, I would like to address the following matters: first, I will examine the notion of speculative philosophy in the eighteenth century in order to show the originality of the Berlin Academy's conception. There are good reasons for maintaining that the academicians of the 1740s proposed a quite novel definition of speculative philosophy. A comparison with other conceptions, above all those of Boyle, Locke, and Wolffian-inspired thinkers such as Baumgarten and Meier, will help us to understand its originality. This point is especially important for understanding the evolution of such a notion in the history of German institutions and universities during the second half of the eighteenth century. Second, I would like to analyse some key *mémoires* in which academicians attempted to determine the nature and relevance of speculative philosophy in their institution. An important source is Maupertuis, who, as president, explains his views on the division of classes and on the advantages of undertaking such research in an academy. But there are other subsequent contributions, in particular those of Formey, who, as secretary, wrote papers on these questions. These considerations were raised at distinct periods and express different ways of conceiving of the production of academic scholarship. Most importantly, their understanding of speculative philosophy will change, to the extent that some will come to believe that it should be studied outside of the academy. Garve maintains this position, which clearly departs from Maupertuis and Formey. We note that his interpretation is concomitant with a gradual disappearance of speculative reflections in the Berlin Academy. It is also interesting to note that Kant, Fichte, and Hegel, who were prominent figures of the German academic world at the turn of the century, reinvest speculative philosophy with new theoretical tools.

What is Speculative Philosophy?

During the early modern period, the terms speculation and speculative philosophy obviously possessed different meanings at different times. One

---

[3] Christian Bartholmèss, *Histoire philosophique de l'Académie de Prusse depuis Leibniz jusqu'à Schelling* (Paris, 1855); Adolf Harnack, *Geschichte der Königlich Preussischen Akademie der Wissenschaften zu Berlin* (Berlin, 1900); Werner Hartkopf, *Die Berliner Akademie der Wissenschaften: Ihre Mitglieder und Preisträger 1700–1900* (Berlin, 1992); Conrad Grau, *Die Preussische Akademie der Wissenschaften zu Berlin* (Heidelberg, 1993); Christian Leduc and Daniel Dumouchel (eds.), *La philosophie à l'Académie de Berlin au XVIIIe siècle*, in *Philosophiques*, 41/1, 2015.

of the first meanings of the word appeared in the seventeenth century in the context of the discussion on scientific methodology. Thinkers who considered themselves experimental philosophers had cast doubt on principles and arguments that were not grounded on *a posteriori* validation, and therefore on those associated with a certain kind of contemplation. Bacon often uses the term '*speculatio*' in a depreciative way and seems to understand it as signifying an inadequate manner of observing or imagining, akin to an irregular mirror that distorts and corrupts our knowledge of things.[4] Bacon also claims that 'nature is much subtler than are our senses and intellect; so that all those elegant meditations and human speculations and excuses are unsound things'.[5] In this sense, speculative reasoning belongs to those cognitive efforts that exceed the capacities of both sensation and understanding. This meaning of the word will also appear later in many investigators who give priority to experimentation over *a priori* and more theoretical explanations; among them, Boyle is certainly the most influential. From the 1660s onward, he not only begins to use experimental tools, mostly in chemistry, but he also clearly takes a stance against speculative methodologies in natural philosophy.[6] Many other thinkers share this view in that period, Hooke and Cavendish, for example.[7] For them, as for Bacon and Boyle, natural philosophy should rely on experimentation and avoid what could be called *a priori* reasoning. Later, Newton and many Newtonian philosophers, such as Roger Cotes, will come to profess a similar position and defend experimentation against more hypothetical approaches. Speculation is thus associated with hypothetical and metaphysical knowledge that has no basis in empirical induction. In the preface to the second edition of Newton's *Principia mathematica*, Cotes maintains that: 'those who take the foundation of their speculations from hypotheses, even if they then proceed most rigorously according to mechanical laws, are merely putting together a romance'.[8] At least theoretically, and following Newton's famous *hypotheses non fingo*, the Newtonian tradition will often criticize metaphysical speculation and oppose it to true experimental science.

This distinction, between experimental and speculative philosophies, has been well documented, and I do not wish to further analyse it here.[9]

---

[4] Francis Bacon, *Novum Organum*, I, 41.   [5] *Ibid.*, I, 10.

[6] Robert Boyle, *Some Considerations touching the Usefulness of Natural Philosophy* (Oxford, 1664), II, 5.

[7] Robert Hooke, *Micrographia* (London, 1665); Margaret Cavendish, *Observations upon Experimental Philosophy* (London, 1666).

[8] Roger Cotes, Preface to the Second Edition, *The Principia*, ed. by I. Bernard Cohen (Berkeley, 1999), 386.

[9] In particular, see: Peter Anstey, 'Experimental versus Speculative Natural Philosophy', in *The Science of Nature in the Seventeenth Century* (Dordrecht, 2005), 215–242; Michael

But for the sake of the present study, it might be useful to mention that this division was still quite vivid in the mid-eighteenth century, in particular for the *Encyclopédie* authors who used it on many occasions. Like Bacon and other natural philosophers, the Encyclopaedists appear to generally favour experimentation over speculation. According to d'Alembert, experimentation allows us to establish physics on the basis of facts, and when associated with geometry, it is sufficient for discovering the truths of natural philosophy.[10] It is interesting to see just how doctrines and approaches, which obviously pose many challenges, are qualified as speculative. For instance, some entries discuss the characteristics of speculative medicine and theology, while others those of speculative atheism and eclecticism.[11] These usages are not necessarily negative, but they seem to make reference to positions that avoid or minimize recourse to empirical knowledge. As had been previously maintained, speculation is understood here as a kind of reasoning that proceeds independently of *a posteriori* sources.

Yet there is another important sense of the term that can certainly be traced back to antiquity: speculative principles or truths are often opposed to practical and moral ones. At first sight, speculative could mean theoretical in the Aristotelian sense since it deals with contemplative notions and arguments, while practical knowledge would refer to truths that concern intentional and voluntary perceptions, the effects of which are manifest in our actions. This association is probably accurate and could certainly describe the way in which many thinkers have distinguished between the reflexive and normative realms of learning.

Let us give an account of two influential positions in the eighteenth century. On many occasions, Malebranche clarifies the distinction between speculative and moral truths.[12] The first kind concerns judgments exclusively, while the second also incites motion in the soul. But two further points are relevant for the present analysis. On the one hand, Malebranche associates these truths with two kinds of relations: speculative truths concern relations of magnitude, whereas moral ones formulate relations of perfection.[13] In order to illustrate this distinction, he gives the following examples: two plus two equals four is a speculative proposition because it

---

Ben-Chaim, *Experimental Philosophy and the Birth of Empirical Science. Boyle, Locke, and Newton* (London-New York, 2016).

[10] Jean le Rond d'Alembert, 'Expérimental', *Encyclopédie ou dictionnaire raisonné des sciences, des arts et des métiers* (Paris, 1751–1780), 6, 299–300.

[11] See in *Encyclopédie*: 'Athéisme', 1, 802; 'Eclectisme', 5, 272; 'Empirisme', 5, 587; 'Théologie', 16, 249.

[12] Perhaps Malebranche borrowed this distinction from Descartes who employs it in the *Discours de la méthode*: AT VI, p. 61–62.

[13] Nicolas Malebranche, *Entretiens*, VIII, 13. See also: *Traité de morale*, I, I, VI–VII.

does not cause any motion in the soul. In contrast, truths that concern the passions, such as love and hate, are thought to have a moral content, and are thus considered expressive of levels of perfection. The proposition according to which men are more valuable than animals is not only a theoretical judgment, but it also incites the soul to adhere to the love and esteem of humanity. On the other hand, Malebranche maintains on some occasions that disciplines can be identified on the basis of such a distinction: astronomy, music, and mechanical sciences belong to the speculative sort of learning, since they all rely on measures of magnitude and extension.[14] In contrast, we could certainly maintain that ethical and political domains, which deal with relations of perfection and explain how the soul reacts to such and such an idea, would be comprised of moral knowledge. This also suggests that moral truths are theoretical as well, since they enunciate judgments of knowledge, except that they also produce motions in the soul owing to their normative reach. The status of metaphysics and theology, which would be later discussed later at the Berlin Academy, is not clear in Malebranche's framework; but these could most certainly be associated with practical truths, since knowledge of God and of spiritual beings contributes to determining virtue and moral conduct.[15]

An even more influential view held by eighteenth-century philosophers is probably the distinction that Locke offers in his *Essay concerning Human Understanding*, which is similar to Malebranche's in a number of ways. As is well known, the first book concerns the refutation of innatism and is organized according to the distinction between speculative and practical principles. On this occasion, Locke describes what these kinds of knowledge mean. His main criterion pertains to the causal effect that they can produce: while a speculative truth only incites consent, for here we either approve of some judicable content or not, a practical truth also provokes action, insofar as we can either act in conformity with a moral rule or not.[16] Locke establishes another interesting epistemological distinction as a consequence of this criterion: whereas speculative principles are self-evident, such as the principles of identity or non-contradiction, practical ones require reasons or motives in order to be understood. In other words, in order to agree to act in conformity with a rule of action, we need to know the reasons why we ought to behave in a particular way. Of course, the fact that they produce a certain effect is an additional reason, for Locke, to reject their supposedly innate nature.[17]

---

[14] Nicolas Malebranche, *Recherche de la vérité*, 6, 4, 3.
[15] Nicolas Malebranche, *Traité de morale*, I, I, XIX.   [16] John Locke, *Essay*, 1. iii. 3.
[17] *Ibid.*, 1. iii. 4.

Locke comes back to this distinction at the very end of the *Essay* in order
to establish a new division of the sciences that is particularly relevant for
the purposes of this study. Because they require the 'skill of applying our
own powers and actions in the right way for the attainment of things that
are good and useful',[18] practical disciplines are identifiable on the basis
of a rather classical distinction; this realm is mostly interested in ethical
reasoning, which seeks to understand the rules of human action and hap-
piness. The situation is, however, different with regard to speculative
sciences, since Locke provides an unusual definition of speculative truth:

First, the knowledge of things as they are in their own beings—their constitution, properties and operations. I am including here not only matter and body,
but also spirits, which also have their proper natures, constitutions, and operations. This, in a slightly enlarged sense of the word, I call *physike*, or natural
philosophy. This aims at bare speculative truth, and anything that can give the
mind of man any such truth belongs to natural philosophy, whether it concerns God himself, angels, spirits, bodies, or any of their states or qualities.[19]

Here Locke broadens the scope of speculative truth to the entire realm
of natural philosophy; even more, he holds that any proposition that
addresses the nature of God, spirits, or bodies must belong to natural
philosophy and thus contain speculative principles. Put differently, if a
science does not explain the relations between norms and actions (like
ethics) or the use of signs (like logic), but rather enables us to contemplate
the nature of things, this knowledge can be characterised as speculative.
This means that Locke's conception includes many disciplines that were
not encompassed by speculative knowledge before, namely, theology and
psychology, which are now considered to be in the same category as
sciences such as physics and physiology.[20]
   Many philosophers in the eighteenth century relied on this general
distinction between speculative and practical truths and principles. It is
used in a very similar way in the *Encyclopédie*.[21] In the early German tradition, however, very few seem to have placed emphasis on it: to my knowledge, neither Thomasius, Leibniz,[22] nor Wolff make this distinction, even
though they would most likely have agreed with Malebranche and Locke
on the necessity of differentiating kinds of truth according to their practical causal power. We find a trace of it later in German scholars, notably
in the 1740s and 1750s, by the time the division of classes is established

---

[18] *Ibid.*, 4. xxi. 3.   [19] *Ibid.*, 4. xxi. 2.
[20] See: Peter Anstey, *John Locke and Natural Philosophy* (Oxford, 2011).
[21] In the *Encyclopédie*: 'Spéculatif', 15, 448; 'Pratique (Philos.)', 13, 264.
[22] Leibniz employs the distinction in the *Nouveaux Essais sur l'entendement humain*, but
obviously on the basis of Locke's doctrine: 1. 3. 3.

at the Berlin Academy. For example, Baumgarten, in his *Metaphysica*, speaks in a similar manner to Malebranche and Locke:

> Whoever desires or averts intends the production of some perception. Hence, the perceptions containing the ground of this sort of intention are the impelling causes of desire and aversion, and thus they are called the *Incentives of the mind*. *Knowledge*, insofar as it contains the incentives of the mind, is *Moving* (affecting, touching, burning, pragmatic, practical, and, more broadly, living), and insofar as it does not contain these incentives, it is *Inert* (theoretical and, more broadly, dead) and when this knowledge is otherwise perfect enough, it is called *Speculation* (speculative, empty, hollow).[23]

A distinction between two sorts of knowledge is made on the basis of what Baumgarten calls perceptions of incentives of the mind. Practical knowledge is moving and takes desire and aversion into consideration, while speculation is deprived of any volitional aspects. Baumgarten specifies further details: practical knowledge relies on the intuitive perception of pleasure and pain, since these have a motive power; speculation, on the other hand, keeps the mind in a state of indifference. In this account, we already note that the mind derives more benefit from practical knowledge than from purely speculative knowledge because of its utility for human conduct. This idea is supported by other passages in which speculative truths seem to belong to a lower level of perfection: in the section devoted to the concept of God (§ 873), Baumgarten characterizes divine knowledge, which is the most extended and ordered, as deprived of any ignorance and errors. But most importantly, God is also incapable of any inert or speculative cognition. His understanding and wisdom are incompatible with the sort of knowledge that humans have, namely, symbolic and purely contemplative truths. This kind of cognition appears here to be incomplete and proper to finite human faculties.

We find this distinction in Meier's *Vernunftlehre*, in which speculative philosophy is also largely depreciated. This work was clearly influenced by Baumgarten's views, since Meier uses the very same terms and distinction, and it seems to have become a common distinction in German institutions. Significantly, Meier devalues the search for speculative knowledge and radicalizes the positions expressed in the *Metaphysica*. It should be mentioned that Meier published the *Vernunftlehre* in 1752, two years after Maupertuis had publicly read his paper on the division of classes and on his conception of speculative philosophy at the Berlin Academy.[24] The

[23] Alexander Gottlieb Baumgarten, *Metaphysica*, § 669, trans. by Fugate and Hymers (London, 2013), 241–242.

[24] Pierre Louis Moreau de Maupertuis, 'Des devoirs de l'académicien', in *Histoire de l'Académie des sciences et belles-lettres* (Berlin) [abbrev. *HAB*], 1753). The *mémoires* were first

contrast between both conceptions is elucidating and I will come back to it later. For the moment, let us see what Meier's criticisms of speculative cognition are. Before Tetens later made his contribution[25], this was, I believe, one of the most extensive contributions to the characterization of speculative philosophy in the German world.

It seems that, after Malebranche and Locke, the distinctness and certainty of speculative knowledge was not called into question. Meier admits that speculation can attain a certain level of perfection, and can thus express the order of things in an adequate way. Therefore, many propositions and doctrines in logic, mathematics, physics, and metaphysics, although considered speculative, are deemed true. But we readily note, Meier observes, that speculative cognition is flawed when compared with practical domains. First, when a truth is pursued for the sake of contemplation alone, and not for some utility, it necessarily lacks motivation. Meier claims that seeking truths that neither have any impact on our life nor concern our perfectibility is simply useless and should be avoided. He gives some examples of speculative theories, for instance, determining how monads are articulated with respect to one another or how a point is situated in empty space, which clearly refers to purely metaphysical reasoning.[26] According to Meier, such interrogations, as is the case in any other discussions about fundamental and non-applicable reflections, must be left aside owing to their lack of practical consequences. Practical knowledge is more perfect than speculation because it enables us to improve upon our faculties:

> It is undeniable that by means of a merely speculative knowledge the understanding, the power of knowledge, never improves to the same degree, as happens with practical knowledge. The latter knowledge, besides improving the power of desire in a noticeable manner, something that speculative knowledge is not in a position to do, gives the power of knowledge one more perfection than the speculative. For it is certainly a perfection of the understanding when it masters and governs the will.[27]

In other words, practical knowledge not only contributes to the perfection of our cognitive capacities, but also articulates the relationship between the understanding and the will so that our actions become more virtuous. More precisely, Meier distinguishes between three categories of speculative

read at the assembly and then published, most of the time two or three years later. We indicate here the date of publication.

[25] Johann Nicolas Tetens, *Über die allgemeine speculativische Philosophie* (1775), (Berlin, 1913).

[26] Georg Friedrich Meier, *Vernunftlehre* (Halle, 1752), § 247, 364.

[27] *Ibid.*, § 249, 365–366.

truths: first, there is knowledge whose utility is so minimal that it should be considered speculative, for instance, fundamental discussions about geometrical entities such as points, lines, etc. Second, many works are simply deprived of any practical consequences and must also be set aside. Meier gives examples of historiographical studies, classified under belles-lettres at that time, whose goal was often the dating of a classical text or discovering its author.[28] This means that speculative knowledge is not characterized by the kind of cognition it employs, but again by its lack of applicability. Third, and finally, Meier identifies approaches that are not only irrelevant for practical life, but also even damaging for virtuous conduct. Someone who spends his whole life thinking about fundamental problems of metaphysics, physics, and logic is no wise person, but only a speculative mind.[29]

Let us summarize our analysis of speculation so far. There seem to be two primary ways of characterizing speculative philosophy in terms of a dichotomy: on the one hand, speculative philosophy is opposed to experimental learning, since it purports to establish truths *a priori* or primarily through reasoning. This first meaning emerged in a theoretical context that conceived of speculation as detrimental in order to favour *a posteriori* and inductive methods. On the other hand, speculation is contrasted with practical approaches and is thus clearly understood as theoretical. According to the different sources, speculative knowledge was more or less criticized, Meier being the most unfavourable to such learning. However, despite the former opposition, that is, to experimental philosophy, it does not appear that kinds of cognition are implicated here: for example, Locke believes that both theoretical and practical principles have their origin in the same empirical sources of knowledge. The main criterion is that practical knowledge has an impact on our will and behaviour, while speculative cognition is deprived of any such influence. Finally, attempts were made to associate various disciplines and scientific realms with speculative knowledge. Generally, domains such as metaphysics, physics, mathematics and logic, at least when they address fundamental questions, belong to speculative philosophy. The case of theology is less clear, since knowledge of God obviously has consequences for our virtue and actions. This signifies that some theoretical principles belong to practical knowledge, as is the case with truths concerning the divine being.[30] However, purely theoretical doctrines, dealing with the foundations of metaphysical or geometrical principles, are inevitably speculative and, according to many at the time, damaging to philosophy.

---

[28] *Ibid.* § 258, 378.   [29] Ibid., § 258, 379.
[30] Meier claims exactly this point: *Ibid.*, § 248, 364.

The class of speculative philosophy

As previously mentioned, the establishment of a class of speculative philosophy in an academy was quite unique. When the Berlin Academy was created in 1700, there were already four classes, including (1) physics and medicine, (2) mathematics, (3) philology and oriental studies, and finally (4) German history and language.[31] The first two were quite standard subjects for a scientific academy and were included in Leibniz's planning from the beginning. Philology and German history were often studied in a distinct institution, such as the Paris Académie des Inscriptions et des Belles-Lettres, but were integrated into the Berlin Academy, notably for educational reasons.[32] In any case, these subjects were traditionally discussed in academies and their inclusion in Berlin was therefore not unusual. The modifications of the 1740s would essentially preserve three out of the four of the classes; however, the creation of a class of speculative philosophy in the academy, a field that is traditionally studied in universities, was unorthodox.

In the documents pertaining to the foundation and modifications of the Berlin Academy from the 1740s onward, very few reasons are provided that explain this addition. The rules simply include a list of four classes and succinctly describe the content of speculative philosophy. Instead of limiting the academy to the study of empirical and mathematical objects, Frederic II decided to include speculative disciplines. Perhaps he wanted to compensate the lack of a university in Berlin, which will only be established in the beginning of the nineteenth century by Wilhelm von Humboldt.[33] As indicated in the rules, the class of speculative philosophy aims to study logic, metaphysics, and moral philosophy.[34] This is of course a surprising decision. Even Leibniz, who was a major contributor to these fields, did not wish to include metaphysical or logical subjects, since they did not seem to contribute directly either to virtue, education, or healthcare.[35] These topics are obviously related to the sciences, but they did not seem to be suited to an academic environment.

---

[31] 'Histoire de l'Académie' in *HAB*, 1748, 2; Samuel Formey, *Histoire de l'Académie royale des sciences et des belles-lettres depuis son origine jusqu'à present* (Berlin, 1752), 31 and 49.

[32] See Leibniz's positions: Samuel Formey, *Histoire*, 1752, 23.

[33] However, his memoirs do not give us any information in this regard: *Œuvres posthumes de Frédéric II, roi de Prusse*, (Berlin, 1788).

[34] Samuel Formey, *Histoire*, 1752, 99.

[35] *Ibid.*, p. 22. It is however interesting to note that Leibniz, and his successor, Jakob Paul von Gundling, were praised for their philosophical accomplishment and thus deemed suitable for the presidential function: *Ibid.*, 28 et 59.

Before analysing what the academicians had to say about the inclusion of speculative philosophy in their institutions, let us raise some points of comparison between the Berlin classification system and the previous considerations. The following are the rules concerning the four classes:

The Academy will remain as it is, divided in four classes. 1. The class of experimental philosophy will contain chemistry, anatomy, botany and all the sciences that are grounded in experience. 2. The class of mathematics will contain geometry, algebra, mechanics, astronomy, and all the sciences that have as their object abstract extension, or numbers. 3. The class of speculative philosophy, will apply to logic, metaphysics, and morality. 4. The class of Belles-Lettres will encompass antiquity, history and languages.[36]

The main points worth mentioning here concern the place of speculative philosophy within the classification system, which can be contrasted with the three others. (1) Speculative philosophy does not seem to produce knowledge based on experience alone, as is the case with experimental philosophy. Speculative disciplines are not like chemistry or anatomy, which necessitate observation and experimentation. This does not mean that speculative knowledge can be conceived of independently of any experience. On the contrary, many academicians who made contributions in speculative philosophy had recourse to empirical concepts and truths. For instance, Mérian maintains that the true method of metaphysical investigation relies on empirical analysis.[37] Like empiricists such as Locke and Condillac, Mérian believes that the only way to elaborate philosophical and metaphysical positions is through recourse to experience. Closer to the Wolffian movement, Formey and Sulzer also agree that empirical knowledge is a necessary component of philosophy, even if the understanding can surpass it. At the very least, most contributors would concur with the opinion that empirical knowledge must be taken into account in establishing metaphysical and moral principles. At the same time, experimental philosophy clearly employs *a posteriori* tools of investigation that are not made use of in speculative domains. Many papers presented within the class of experimental philosophy and physics cite experiments in chemical separation and dissolution as well as on anatomical observations and dissections. Furthermore, it appears that the experimental sciences must stick to sensible data and never surpass them.[38] In sum, without having to completely dismiss empirical knowledge, speculative philosophy can exceed the limits of sensible properties, and thus discuss intelligible

[36] 'Règlement de l'Académie', in *HAB*, 1748, 3–4.
[37] Jean Bernard Mérian, 'Mémoire sur l'aperception de sa propre existence', in *HAB*, 1751, 443.
[38] Pierre Louis Moreau de Maupertuis, 'Des devoirs de l'académicien', in *HAB*, 1753, 514.

principles; also, it does not proceed by experimental methods and seems to be satisfied with common and inner experiences. In comparison with what was discussed earlier, this distinction between the experimental and speculative philosophies is, in the end, a legacy of the division that is found in Bacon, Boyle, Newton, and many others. The constitution of a new class of philosophy obviously emerges from its comparison with domains like anatomy and chemistry.

(2) Its relationship with the class of mathematics is instructive as well. Both classes consider things and properties more independently of sensible characteristics and thus enable us to exceed this kind of cognition. The objects of mathematics are abstract extension and numbers, and are understood here in the more traditional sense, which includes not only geometry and arithmetic, but also astronomy and mechanics. Generally, mathematical matters, in comparison with both experimental and speculative ones, are the object of quantification and measurement. One interesting aspect of the Berlin Academy is its general criticisms of the use of geometrical methods in philosophy. Even though mathematical and mechanical domains exceed sensible explanations, their methods are considered to be the opposite of speculative ones. Once again, Mérian seems to express a quite common position: mathematical abstractions are certainly useful for many sciences, including astronomy and mechanics, but are nonetheless detrimental to speculative demonstrations:

> This affection for the geometrical method has done infinite damage to speculative sciences: it has often spread ridicule upon the most respected truths. And indeed a great number of these demonstrative proofs, drawing their force from the prestige of definitions alone, demonstrate only the proud weakness of the human understanding.[39]

Therefore, both their objects and methods distinguish mathematical and speculative knowledge. This point would of course require more analysis, since it was the object of many debates at the Berlin Academy. Let us then simply mention the 1763 *Preisfrage* on evidence in mathematics and metaphysics, for which Mendelssohn received the first prize and Kant honourable mention.[40] Some academicians were also favourable to reconciling the mathematical with the metaphysical, or more precisely, to establishing a methodology common to both. Lambert's approach is certainly an undeniably illustration of the attempt to see the fruitful relationship

[39] Jean Bernard Mérian, 'Discours sur la métaphysique', in *HAB*, 1767, 460.
[40] Moses Mendelssohn, *Abhandlung über die Evidenz in metaphysischen Wissenschaften*, (Berlin, 1764). See: Tinca Prunea-Bretonnet, 'La méthode philosophique en question. L'Académie de Berlin et le concours pour l'année 1763', in *La philosophie à l'Académie de Berlin au XVIIIe siècle*, 2015, 107–130.

between geometry and philosophy. At the same time, he agrees that they must be distinguished according to their specific objects.[41]

(3) The comparison with the belles-lettres is worth mentioning for one important reason: it appears, according to the general rules, that history and literature do not belong to philosophical considerations. Again, this aspect deserves greater attention since many philosophers at that time, especially in the eclectic tradition of thinkers like Thomasius and Brucker, held that the history of philosophy is a part of philosophy. Besides, other academicians maintained the same idea and published mémoires on the history of philosophy in the class of speculative philosophy. François-Vincent Toussaint even claimed that philosophy and belles-lettres should be understood together.[42] However, the division of classes suggests that speculative philosophy should restrict its general reflections to metaphysics, logic, and morality rather than to the history of such disciplines.

Apart from this classification, there is at least one textual source that gives an official account of the creation of the class of a speculative philosophy. The preface to the first volume of the renewed series of mémoires, published in 1746, clarifies a number of points. Formey, the new secretary of the Berlin Academy, wrote the preface and begins by acknowledging that speculative questions are not usually addressed in academic publications. His justification is the following: first, metaphysics is the mother of all other sciences and should therefore be discussed in the academy in order to provide the first principles as a foundation for all our certainties. This explanation must be made sense of within its historical context: as long as metaphysics was under the yoke of scholasticism, it was perfectly understandable that scientists wished to avoid it. This is why the first academies, such as those in London and Paris, did not include speculative philosophy as a field of research. Now that metaphysicians were free of superstition and knew the boundaries between reason and faith, it was high time to reintroduce it in the academy:

> In addition, one will find in our mémoires the examination of certain questions that are not ordinarily contained in such works. These are the questions of metaphysics, natural right, and moral philosophy. It is for these that the so-called philosophical class was established.... Metaphysics is without question the mother of other sciences, the theory that provides the most general principles, the source of evidence, and the foundation of the certainty of our knowledge. The truth is that these beautiful characters did not suit the

---

[41] See Lambert's draft text for the 1763 *Preifrage*: *Über die Methode die Metaphysik, Theologie und Moral richtiger zu beweisen*, in *Philosophische Schriften*, hrsg. von Armin Emmel und Axel Spree, (Hildesheim, 2008), X.2, 493–529.

[42] François-Vincent Toussaint, 'Qu'il faut combiner ensemble les lettres et la philosophie', in *HAB*, 1771, 412–426.

metaphysics of scholastics, hostile land, which hardly produced brambles and thorns. And since no others were known when the main Academies were established, it was left out with a sort of contempt.[43]

According to Formey, who expresses here the position of the Academy, philosophical research into the first principles of being, knowledge, and the good must have a place in academic institutions, as is the case in universities, since it constitutes an essential complement to scientific and historical studies. This justification would have appeared obvious to many modern philosophers, who believed that metaphysics is necessary for the sciences, but it is worth recalling that it was put into practice for the first time at the Berlin Academy.

The inclusion of speculative philosophy is surprising for another reason: as one might recall, the conception of speculative philosophy in the eighteenth century was not only opposed to experimental knowledge, a distinction that still existed in the new classification system of the 1740s, but was also contrasted with practical philosophy, and to such an extent that speculation itself was highly depreciated. As previously discussed, Baumgarten and Meier, who belong to the university world, criticized purely theoretical reflections for their lack of utility and practical effect. The expression *speculative knowledge* had for many post-Wolffians quite negative connotations. In contrast, not only did the Berlin Academy create a class for speculative matters, but it also defined it as containing both metaphysical and logical doctrines, on the one hand, and moral and practical subjects, on the other. In other words, speculative philosophy is not only a theoretical domain, but also a practical one pertaining to ethical, political, and juridical matters. In my view, this is probably the most original aspect of the conception of speculative philosophy at the Berlin Academy. It surpasses the traditional distinction between purely theoretical and practical principles, found in various authors such as Malebranche, Locke, and Meier, by associating reflexive and moral disciplines with the general speculative domain. Even Locke's definition, which extends the application of speculative principles to all of natural philosophy, could not have anticipated the conception provided by the Berlin academicians.

Interpreting Speculative Philosophy

Let us examine what the academicians had to say about this new class. Considering the novelty of the situation, it of course provoked a number of reactions within the community. The academicians generally agreed to

⁴³ Samuel Formey, Préface, *Histoire*, 1746, p. iv–v.

include metaphysics and moral philosophy in the Berlin Academy, but there were still other aspects to discuss. Why should we study and analyse metaphysical and moral questions alongside geometry and anatomy, for instance? Why is the Berlin Academy the only academy to include these disciplines as an official field of study, when they were normally discussed in universities? Apart from the official response that Formey gave in the first volume of the *mémoires*, Maupertuis was among the first to provide an explicit answer. In his *Des devoirs de l'académicien*, Maupertuis comes back to the question of the division of classes and explains what the objectives and methods of each class are. He then gives the following definition of speculative philosophy:

> The class of speculative philosophy is the third [class]. Experimental philosophy examined bodies as they are; endowed with all their sensible properties. Mathematics stripped them of most of these properties. Speculative philosophy considers objects that no longer have a single corporeal property. The supreme Being, the human mind, and everything that belongs to the spirit is the object of this science. The nature of bodies themselves, insofar as represented in our perceptions, if indeed they are something different from these perceptions, falls within its scope.[44]

Two points must be emphasized here: on the one hand, speculative philosophy deals with objects and properties that are incorporeal, namely God and spiritual beings. This is in fact a rather common definition of metaphysics that can be found in both Descartes and Leibniz, in virtue of which first philosophy discusses the nature of the soul and the existence and nature of God.[45] And, indeed, in subsequent years, mémoires would be devoted to such questions at the Berlin Academy, for example, to the proofs of the existence of God or of the soul's immortality. On the other hand, Maupertuis's conception coincides with the general reorientation of metaphysics and moral philosophy that took place in the 1740s and 1750s elsewhere in Europe, in particular in France. Philosophers like Condillac and d'Alembert maintained during the same period that metaphysics should be reduced to the study of the capacities of the mind.[46] For them, metaphysics does not deal generally with spiritual entities, including God, but rather exclusively with the mind, which is known through clear and inner perceptions. Yet many papers presented within the class of speculative philosophy concerned the nature of the human mind. This clearly refers to the realm of

---

[44] Pierre Louis Moreau de Maupertuis, 'Des devoirs de l'académicien', in *HAB*, 1753, 516.
[45] René Descartes, *Principes*, preface, in *Oeuvres de Descartes*, éd. par Charles Adam et Paul Tannery, (Paris, 1996) IX–2, 14.
[46] Étienne Bonnot de Condillac, *Essai sur l'origine des connaissances*, (Amsterdam, 1746); Jean Le Rond d'Alembert, *Essai sur les éléments de philosophie*, (Lyon, 1759).

psychology, which will increasingly grow in importance in Berlin. Major contributors, like Formey, Mérian, Sulzer, and Beausobre, would later submit papers on psychological topics. We may even observe how most papers from the 1750s onwards address these problems, in particular, the faculties of the mind and the question of self-knowledge. In other words, metaphysics would increasingly become a domain of psychological investigation, as Condillac and d'Alembert had wished.

Maupertuis raises another sort of question that should be addressed in metaphysics. He claims that the nature of bodies also belongs to speculative philosophy, as long as such bodies constitute objects of perception. This is quite a confused way of expressing a kind of reasoning on which Maupertuis had previously worked. Indeed, the same year he read his lecture, he published his *Essai de cosmologie* in which he examines the principle of least action, which he considered to be of a teleological nature. Accordingly, the search for final causes should thus be part of speculative philosophy since it deals with the intentional representation and causality of the world structure that ultimately originates from a supreme and divine intelligence. In other words, what Wolff called at that time general cosmology should also belong to speculative philosophy. As was the case with psychology, cosmological reflections were the object of numerous mémoires, not only by Maupertuis, but also by people like Euler and Béguelin. In sum, Maupertuis makes two principal claims about speculative philosophy: first, metaphysics deals with spiritual beings in general and thus possesses a distinct object in comparison with experimental philosophy and mathematics. Second, Maupertuis also seems to anticipate what the two main focuses of speculative philosophy will become from the 1750s onward, namely psychology and cosmology.

If the relationship between the class of speculative philosophy, on the one hand, and the classes of experimental philosophy and mathematics, on the other, is discussed by Maupertuis, its relationship to belles-lettres is not explicitly treated. The study of languages, history, and literature would seem to be of a quite different sort of knowledge, one that shares little with physics, mathematics, and philosophy. This was not necessarily a unique position at the time, since many thinkers hoped to separate history and literature from the other disciplines. Let us recall that the French government in the seventeenth century founded distinct institutions for such studies, namely, the Académie française and the Académie des Inscriptions et des Belles-lettres. It is nonetheless surprising to find no link between speculative philosophy and belles-lettres in Maupertuis's paper. This is for the reasons previously mentioned: first, many important mémoires would be devoted to historical matters or take a historiographical approach to philosophical problems. The most well-known example is certainly Mérian's long series on the Molyneux problem.[47] Of course, these contributions belong to a later period, but they show how history, literature, language and philosophy were more intimately connected in Berlin than Maupertuis seems to have thought. Second, many German historians of philosophy of the same period maintained that the study of philosophy requires us to take history into account. For instance, Johann Jakob Brucker asserts such a relationship in his *Historia critica philosophiae*.[48] His syncretic position discusses past and present doctrines with the aim of arriving at a truly eclectic and adequate system of philosophy.[49] Many academicians would agree with this eclectic approach and certainly believed that the history of philosophy was an important part of philosophical methodology. In sum, there seems to have been an important relationship between speculative philosophy and belles-lettres at the Berlin Academy, despite Maupertuis's silence on this matter.

Nevertheless, Maupertuis's general view in the *Devoirs de l'académicien* appears to have been shared by the other academicians. In a public lecture in 1765, Mérian maintains a very similar conception of metaphysics and speculative philosophy. Even though his *Discours de métaphysique* discusses a much wider variety of issues, Mérian agrees with Maupertuis that the main focus of metaphysics should be of a psychological and cosmological nature, since it deals with the foundations of the other sciences.[50] Metaphysics begins where physics ends and penetrates into the very nature of things, whereas physics remains at the level of their sensible properties. Mérian also agrees that this investigation must be done with the help of cognitive tools and must therefore be accompanied by research in psychology as he himself demonstrates in most of his own papers.

This reorientation of speculative philosophy is, of course, interesting for our discussion. It provides us with an original interpretation, and, above all, reaffirms the importance of metaphysics for the purposes of scientific learning. In a period of intense criticism of speculative principles, the Berlin Academy not only defended such knowledge, but also considered it an essential complement to experimental philosophy, mathematics, and belles-lettres. It can also be illuminating to compare this position with another contemporary conception, namely, the one that can be found in the German *Schulphilosophie*. As is well known, Wolff, Baumgarten, and

[47] Jean Bernard Mérian, 'Sur le problème de Molyneux', in *Nouveau mémoires de l'Académie Royale des sciences et belles-lettres*, (Berlin, 1772–1782).

[48] Johann Jacob Brucker, *Historia critica philosophiae*, (Lipsiae, 1766), vol. 4–2, 1–2.

[49] On Brucker's method: Leo Catala, *The Historiographical Concept 'System of Philosophy'. Its Origin, Nature, Influence*, (Leiden/Boston, 2008). On eclecticism at the Berlin Academy, see: Daniel Dumouchel, 'Homme de nulle secte. Éclectisme et refus des systèmes chez Jean Bernard Mérian', in *Dialogue*, 57/4, 2018, 745–765.

[50] Mérian, 'Discours sur la métaphysique', *HAB*, 1767. 455–458.

many other German philosophers during the first half of the eighteenth century provided a general division of metaphysics that would prove to be very influential up until the time of the Kantian and even the post-Kantian philosophies. According to Wolff, who first instigated this division, metaphysics must be divided into four domains: ontology, which is the general science of things and of their possibility, and then three sub-domains, namely, cosmology, psychology, and natural theology.[51] These disciplines are differentiated according to their objects, namely, the world, souls and God, but they have their origin in ontology, which explains the possibility of beings in general. In comparison to Maupertuis's explanations, we can actually draw three major conclusions: first, not only do both Maupertuis and Mérian neglect ontological questions in the Wolffian sense,[52] but in addition very few papers will be devoted to this field in the class of speculative philosophy. Most of the time, contributors discussing general metaphysics either criticized the very idea of Wolffian ontology or addressed ontological questions from a more specific perspective. For instance, Mérian wrote some papers on Leibniz's principle of indiscernibles, in which he rejects the Leibnizian position on the basis of epistemological and empirical arguments.[53] For Mérian, this kind of ontological problem seems to be resolvable with the help of the psychological tool of reasoning. In other words, there seems to be no proper distinct place for ontology or general metaphysics at the Berlin Academy. Second, natural theology was also quite neglected. There are some theological attempts, mainly by Formey, who is philosophically the closest to the Wolffian tradition, but he is an exception. In general, very few papers were devoted to theological and religious topics. The absence of reflection on theology could probably be explained by a passage in Maupertuis's paper: according to him, the Berlin Academy's mission was, notably, to defend the true religion and to attempt to convert unbelievers. Therefore, all four classes should fulfil this task, and this is why there was probably no need to elaborate a distinct rational theology. For example, experimental philosophy helps us to contemplate the wonders of the universe, and thus its divine origin.[54] In a word, speculative philosophy is not the sole and exclusive domain for studying theological matters. Finally, as previously mentioned, the focus is almost entirely placed on psychological and cosmological problems.

---

[51] Christian Wolff, *Discursus praeliminaris*, § 92. On this topic, see: Ernst Vollrath, 'Die Gliederung der Metaphysik in eine Metaphysica generalis und eine Metaphysica specialis', in *Zeitschrift für philosophische Forschung*, 16/2, 1962, 258–284.

[52] Mérian mentions the Wolffian division, but later departs from this conception and raises criticisms of ontology: 'Discours sur la métaphysique', in *HAB*, 1767, 460.

[53] Jean Bernard Mérian, 'Sur le principe des indiscernables', *HAB*, 1756, 383–398.

[54] Pierre Louis Moreau de Maupertuis, 'Des devoirs de l'académicien', in *HAB*, 1753, 521.

Roughly speaking, about three quarters of the *mémoires* concern these two kinds of topics. Yet I think we can draw a general conclusion from these considerations: even if Maupertuis and Mérian were working with a more or less classical definition of metaphysics, according to which it studies the origin and nature of spiritual beings, academicians were in fact mostly interested in two *metaphysicae speciales*, namely, rational and empirical psychology, on one hand, and general cosmology, on the other. And this is I think easily explicable: the Berlin Academy remained a scientific institution in which research focused on topics in physics and mathematics. Academicians were mainly recruited for their contributions in chemistry, geometry, and history. So it appears that when they were interested in speculative philosophy or metaphysics, their approach was often related to scientific problems. This is most probably why metaphysical reflections were either connected to results in physics or mathematics, in what was called cosmology, or conducted on the basis of a scientific method of reasoning in the study of spiritual beings, as was the case in psychology.

The Academic Spirit

The preceding analyses have shown that cosmology and psychology were the main focuses of the class of speculative philosophy during the second half of the eighteenth century. In addition to these points, I would like to emphasize another important element: as I previously mentioned, some mémoires also dealt with the question of how philosophy and science should be conducted within an academy. Contrary to the situation at the London and Paris academies, the existence of such a class enabled scholars to discuss the conditions for undertaking such research in an academic environment and to ask whether a scientific institution should include this class of speculative philosophy in the first place. I will analyse three series of mémoires that go to the heart of the evolution of these questions: first, I will come back to Maupertuis's *Devoirs de l'académicien* and study it alongside Formey's history of the academy, which was published a few years before. These contributions appeared during the academy's renewal period and thus express ideas that were discussed when the class of speculative philosophy was first created. The main idea that both Maupertuis and Formey emphasize is what they call the emergence of an academic spirit that enables one to conduct research in an academy. Second, I will refer to papers produced in the 1760s, in particular Formey's *Considérations sur les académies* in which he provides details about the main advantages of doing research within an academy. Formey believed that the academic spirit helped to eliminate what he calls 'half-scholar' (*demi-savants*); these are people who work in isolation and without a proper scientific method. Other academicians at the time, such as Jakob Wegelin and Dieudonné Thiebault, agreed with him and maintained similar positions. Finally, I will examine a paper from Christian Garve published in 1788-1789, some years before activity in the class of speculative philosophy almost completely ceased. Although he defends, like his predecessors, the fruitfulness of the academic spirit, the most interesting aspect of Garve's contribution is that he holds that such an approach does not concern the study of metaphysics and moral philosophy. In other words, Garve appears to conclude that the class of speculative philosophy no longer has a place within the academy since metaphysics, psychology, and moral philosophy must employ a different kind of methodology.

The notion of an academic spirit can be found in different places, but Maupertuis was one of the first to employ it. Here is a passage from the *Devoirs de l'académicien*:

> All these aids that are found dispersed in the works and discussions of scholars, the academician finds gathered in an academy; he benefits from them easily in the sweetness of the society and has the pleasure of owing them to his colleagues and his friends. Let us add what is still more important; he acquires in our assemblies this academic spirit, this kind of sense of the truth, which enables him to discover it everywhere it is, and prevents him from searching for it where it is not. How many different authors have hazarded systems, of which academic discussion would have made known to them their falsity. How many chimeras they would have not dared to produce in an academy![55]

Maupertuis maintains two views that will be repeated by some of his colleagues during the same period. First, an academy naturally helps gather several scholars within a single institution. This point is, of course, major, but was enunciated by other people before, such as Fontenelle:[56] instead of discovering theories and truths individually, which obliges a single scholar to provide all of the necessary experiments and demonstrations, the academy allows for the development of what could today be called a division of labour. Collectively, rather than individually, it is possible to acquire new ideas and theories. Once again, this conception had an impact on the recruitment procedure: ordinary members were admitted on the basis of their specific scientific capacities, for example in mechanics or algebra. This did not prevent scholars from participating in the activities of more than one class, but they were affiliated first and foremost with one particular area of specialization.[57] Second, Maupertuis maintains that

[55] *Ibid.*, 512.
[56] On this aspect, see: Mitia Rioux-Beaulne, 'Les registres de l'histoire et leurs usages: des parcours singuliers de savants à la trajectoire de l'esprit humain', *Revue Fontenelle*, to appear.
[57] 'Règlement de l'Académie', *Histoire*, 1746, 4–5.

philosophers and scientists conducting research outside the academic world merely tend to build systems, rather than discover genuine theories that draw upon the work of a scientific community. This criticism of systematic thinkers is not new, but Maupertuis adapts it to his own argument: non-academic philosophy will result in a particular and inadequate relationship between scholars, namely, between the instigator of a system and his followers. The target most probably aims at key figures of the German universities. Maupertuis certainly has in mind the Leibnizian and Wolffian schools, which were still a dominant force at the time. For him, Leibniz and Wolff conceived of their doctrines within a system because they proceeded individually and wanted to spread their ideas dogmatically.[58] They believed that they could explain all phenomena on the basis of a single set of truths and structure them architectonically. In contrast, scholarship in the academy is done without any individual systematization. True science and philosophy are based on proper experimentation, which could never be produced through a purely deductive structure of reasoning.

In the *Histoire de l'Académie*, published in 1746, Formey maintains a very similar position. Even if we could consider him to be close to Wolff in many ways, Formey nonetheless makes the following criticisms of the systematic approach, such as the one we find in the Wolffian tradition:

> The philosophers, having shaken the tyrannical yoke of Aristotle, delivered themselves for a spell to the habit of systems. Great geniuses worked towards erecting these chimeric edifices, a time and talent of which they could have made much better use. Fortunately, the vanity of such an occupation was soon detected, and the right path was rapidly taken, by limiting oneself to studying nature, observing phenomena, and recording these observations, while waiting to for them constitute a complete body, from which one can deduce a system based on the unwavering foundations of experience.[59]

A complete body of knowledge seems to be achievable, but not on the basis of a systematic and individual approach. Rather, it must be founded on the work of a community in which each academician specializes, and conducts experiments, and reasons about them. The academic spirit is thus the expression not only of a collective and eclectic approach to research, but also of anti-dogmatism. Therefore, both Maupertuis and Formey agree that an academy is the best environment to share research results and to produce a non-systematic body of learning.

In the 1760s, Formey would provide further details about this approach to science and philosophy. Indeed, he published two mémoires concerning the utility of academies to the advancement of knowledge. Some

---

[58] Pierre Louis Moreau de Maupertuis, 'Lettres', VII, *Œuvres*, (Lyon, 1768), II, 258–261.
[59] Samuel Formey, *Histoire*, 1746, 2.

points mentioned earlier would be repeated, but new arguments were provided. The first publication was more historical and aimed at showing how the academic spirit was developed during the early modern period. Despite his numerous errors, Descartes played a crucial role in the establishment of academies since he taught us how to reason and to do research in an adequate way.[60] Here, Formey seemed to follow the opinion of many French and German thinkers, for example d'Alembert, who believed that Descartes had elaborated a methodology that should still be followed, even if one had to be critical of the Cartesian school.[61] The second mémoire is, however, more interesting for the purposes of our discussion: Formey asserts that academies are not only useful for discovering true theories, but also for detecting inadequate ones. Formey calls *demi-savants* those who maintain that their own approach is self-sufficient. Just like systematic thinkers, half-scholars believe that other disciplines and knowledge must be subordinated to their own. According to him: 'Half scholars are not those who know certain things, but who recognize their ignorance of others. Universal knowledge does not exist'.[62] Of course, Formey did believe that the sciences were related to one another, but not in a dogmatic way. An interesting aspect of this is how he explains what kind of publications should be favoured in the academy. While non-academic scholars mostly publish dictionaries and journals in which errors are numerous and ignorance exploited, academic researchers should work on writing mémoires, which require rigorous and collective work. This claim is surprising, considering that Formey himself produced a dictionary.[63] But I think that his idea here is quite coherent: a non-systematic and truly collaborative way of doing research should produce papers that can be read and discussed among a community of scholars, such as in the case of the mémoires. On the contrary, journals and dictionaries seem to favour dogmatic and systematic approaches.

Formey's colleagues mostly agreed with him on these points. In his *Discours de réception*, read in 1765, Dieudonné Thiebault would later emphasize the link between the academy and this collective way of learning, on the one hand, and the relationship between the sciences themselves, on the other. The entire body of knowledge must be examined by a community of scholars, not by separate individuals lacking any

---

[60] Samuel Formey, 'Considérations sur les académies I', in *HAB*, 1769, 372–373.

[61] Jean Le Rond d'Alembert, *Discours préliminaire*, (Paris, 2000), 127–129.

[62] Samuel Formey, 'Considérations sur les académies II', in *HAB*, 1771, 359.

[63] Samuel Formey, *Dictionnaire instructif où l'on trouve les principaux termes des sciences et des arts*, (Halle, 1767). Actually, Formey explains the reasons why he published this dictionary. Among them was his sense of the imperfection of Diderot's *Encyclopédie*, to which he had previously contributed: iv-vi.

institutional affiliation.[64] Thiebault is thus in agreement with Formey, and before him Maupertuis, when he says that academies offer the institutional conditions necessary for doing research in an adequate way. Since particular sciences are related to each other, scholars should benefit from mutual support. Otherwise, the risk of reverting back to a dogmatic approach is too high. In his own *Discours de réception* of 1766, Jakob Wegelin maintains a very similar idea: an academy is the best institutional organization for fighting dogmatism, or what was called at the time 'l'esprit d'écoles' that was commonplace in universities:

> Academies having much more free range than the schools, they are, as a result, in a better position than the latter to break the chains of authority and example. The narrow spirit of schools often comes from the fact that teaching must be adjusted to the weak and distracted gaze of a worried youth eager to learn.[65]

As was the case in the 1750s, we thus notice similar positions at the end of the 1760s on the advantages of the academic spirit. People generally maintain that the Berlin Academy is the best defence against systematic dogmatism and is the only proper scientific approach to knowledge. They make the distinction between the academic spirit and the spirit of the schools, which would prevail in the universities, and explain the advantage of the former over the latter.

I would like to conclude by analysing one last paper that reveals some important changes with respect to these previous positions. This paper was written by Christian Garve, mostly known for being one of the main partisans of the *Aufklärung* of the end of the eighteenth century. Garve was also a foreign member of the Berlin Academy and wrote a mémoire, published in 1788-1789, entitled *Discours sur l'utilité des académies*. For him, as was the case for his colleagues, the objective was to evaluate the main advantages of academies for the sciences and philosophy. Garve's main point is that academies, and similar institutions, are necessary for the development of scientific ideas and theories. In some aspects, he seems however to depart from Maupertuis and Formey. The most obvious difference concerns the possibility of isolated philosophers and scientists producing rigorous research. As one might recall, Maupertuis seemed to reject the individual approach to science since it would lead, most of the time, to systematicity and dogmatism. Formey and Wegelin appeared to maintain a very similar point of view. Yet Garve holds that great individual thinkers are key players in the development of the sciences, considering that their doctrines could

---

64 Dieudonné Thiebault, 'Discours de réception', in *HAB*, 1767, 518.
65 Jakob Wegelin, 'Discours de réception', in *HAB*, 1768, 527.

gain in rigour owing to the efforts of future generations of scholars inspired by their predecessors. In other words, Descartes, Newton, or Leibniz were important contributors to the history of sciences, but they needed disciples to develop and test their ideas and theories. In the eighteenth century, we can certainly think of Euler, d'Alembert, and Lagrange who helped to complete Newtonian physics. Here is what Garve maintains in his mémoire:

> But they do not think that the great merit of a discovery reveals itself only in the consequences that we draw from it, in the applications that we can make of it, in the usages which result from it. It is thus properly the generation that follows, that can alone fix the price of the works of their predecessors, and the degree of admiration they deserve; from this comes partly the fact that in the sciences and philosophy, the ancients are almost always preferred to the moderns, to those who live and work before our eyes. Even independently of jealousy, it is impossible to pay the same tribute to new ideas – which have not yet entered, so to speak, into the general system of human knowledge, whose depth and richness we have not yet been able to establish – as [is paid] to those that have had the time to mature, which are now linked to our knowledge, and which are therefore generally widespread.[66]

Garve holds that only a collective setting makes scientific progress possible; but he also says that it depends on historical development, and future generations' exploitation of the methods and theories that were discovered by pioneers. We could even find here an explanation for why we tend to favour the ancients over the moderns: the former were obviously instigators. But this makes us forget the work of researchers belonging to subsequent generations who later discover the numerous consequences of the pioneers' theories.[67] And of course an academy is the most appropriate institutional context for developing the theories and arguments of past thinkers, and thus for completing every science in order to attain the general system of human knowledge.

Garve raises another point that is important for the present analysis: what Maupertuis and Formey called the academic spirit is suitable for many scientific fields, owing to their collective and critical nature. For instance, the evolution of experimental physics is closely linked to academies since it requires research groups to discover the numerous consequences of a specific set of laws and phenomena. For example, without the academies, Garve seems to maintain that experimental physics would not have reached the level of rigour and exactness that it possessed in the eighteenth century. The same could obviously be said of other natural sciences such as chemistry and biology. But Garve raises a question that had been addressed

---

[66] Christian Garve, 'Discours sur l'utilité des académie', in *HAB*, 1788–89, 461.
[67] *Ibid.*, 462.

before: what about speculative philosophy? Was Frederic II right to include the class of speculative philosophy when the Berlin Academy was renewed? According to Garve, this was unfortunately a mistake, since speculative philosophy, namely metaphysics, moral philosophy, and logic, are not suitable for collective work. Speculative principles are essentially based on individual and reflexive knowledge.

> Without doubt philosophy is taught and learned, philosophical ideas can be communicated, and philosophers who live together can mutually instruct each other and accelerate their progress in their common career. But it is certain that philosophers take from themselves the materials of their thoughts and draw their ideas from the observations of the inner sense.[68]

Actually, Garve makes a distinction between two ways of discovering ideas, one having its object in nature, and the other in the human mind. The natural sciences obviously find ideas in nature by observing and experimenting with phenomena and elaborating physical laws. Once again, this process of discovery should be undertaken within the scientific community; ideas that are found in nature itself can be easily observed by everyone and are therefore communicable. Philosophical reasoning is, however, different: everyone can discover philosophical ideas in their own minds and does not need the support or work of others. Obviously, exchanges can be made, but the true method of discovering philosophical ideas and arguments is essentially individualistic. Metaphysical and moral theories are not elaborated in association with other thinkers, but through reflection and self-knowledge, and are especially conceived of by individual geniuses.[69]

Let us mention one last point: Garve's position clearly opposes what earlier academicians at the Berlin Academy had believed. In the 1750s and 1760s, most academicians were not only sympathetic to their institutional environment, but also maintained that speculative philosophy should play a central role. Fundamental reflections on cognition and nature, provided respectively by cosmology and psychology, were required in order to complete our knowledge of the universe and the human nature. The class of speculative philosophy would thus have an essential function to fulfil. For his part, Garve expresses a position that seems to be in conformity with the situation at the Berlin Academy at the end of the eighteenth century. Actually, fewer and fewer mémoires were devoted to speculative philosophy in the 1780s and 1790s in comparison with the previous decades. We still find interesting papers by Mérian, Wegelin, and Castillon, but the situation has changed. In the early nineteenth century, the class will be abolished due to lack of interest and new recruitment. In a certain way,

---

[68] *Ibid.*, 467.   [69] *Ibid.*, 462–463.

Garve therefore expressed a more accurate opinion of the presence of philosophy at the academy during this period. Maupertuis, Euler, and others were both philosophers and scientists, believing that these disciplines should be represented in their institution. But this was an exceptional and ultimately temporary situation, which finally resulted in the suppression of speculative philosophy. In the early nineteenth century and afterwards, the Berlin Academy would return to its former structure, one that Leibniz had hoped for, and became quite similar to the other academies in Europe. However, the creation of speculative philosophy provided a fruitful context in which scholars could express their views about the relationship between philosophy and science and discuss the numerous advantages of undertaking research in academic institutions.

Conclusion

In this paper, I have argued two main points: first, the creation of the class of speculative philosophy at the Berlin Academy was not only unique for an academy, but also contributed to the creation of a new conception of speculative philosophy. In comparison with their contemporaries' views on speculative principles, such as those of Boyle, Locke, and Meier, the Berlin academicians elaborated an original interpretation of this concept. For them, speculative philosophy includes a wide variety of questions, but above all seems to be necessary for scientific and historiographical research. At the same time, it offers an interesting orientation for metaphysical questioning, primarily focusing on psychological and cosmological problems. I would even venture to say that this positive reassessment of speculative philosophy must be taken into consideration in order to understand the evolution of speculation in Kant and in post-Kantian philosophers, considering the central role that it plays in this tradition. Second, the class of speculative philosophy enabled some academicians to reflect on the relation between science and philosophy, but more profoundly about the way research is done in comparison with non-academic and university scholarship. We saw that it favours the academic spirit and constitutes a defence against individual dogmatic and systematic approaches in science and philosophy, which would be more common in the universities. However, this conception would change over time. Garve expresses this view accurately: philosophy is perhaps not suitable for academic and collective work since it is mainly based on reflexive and individual thinking. During the same period, the activities of the philosophical class would slow down, to such an extent that they would be entirely suppressed in the nineteenth century.

Université de Montréal
christian.leduc.1@umontreal.ca

The Normalisation of Natural Philosophy: Occasional causality and Coarse-Grained Reality

Andrea Sangiacomo

This violence of landscape, this cruelty of climate, this continual tension in everything, and even these monuments of the past, magnificent yet incomprehensible because not built by us and yet standing round us like lovely mute ghosts; all those rulers who landed by main force from every direction who were at once obeyed, soon detested, and always misunderstood, their only expressions works of art we couldn't understand and taxes which we understood only too well and which they spent elsewhere: all these things have formed our character, which is thus conditioned by events outside our control as well as by a terrifying insularity of mind.

G. Tomasi di Lampedusa, The Leopard

1. Understanding change

In his *Metaphysical Disputations* (1597), Suárez summarizes the key features of efficient causation as follows:

> The efficient cause [...] causes by means of a proper action that flows from it. And in this it is also included that the efficient cause does not give its own proper and formal *esse* to the effect, but instead gives another *esse* that emanates from it by means of an action. In this the efficient cause differs from the formal and material cause, because the latter causes their effect by giving to it their own proper being, and this is why they are called intrinsic causes. The efficient cause, on the other hand, is an extrinsic cause, that is, a cause that does not communicate its own proper and (as I will put it) individual *esse* to the effect but instead communicates to it a different *esse*, which really

Andrea Sangiacomo, *The Normalisation of Natural Philosophy: Occasional causality and Coarse-Grained Reality*
In: *History of Universities*. Edited by: Mordechai Feingold, Oxford University Press (2021). © Oxford University Press.
DOI: 10.1093/oso/9780192893833.003.0008

flows forth and emanates from such a cause by means of an action. (DM 17.1.6/F 10)[1]

Compare Suárez's account with Hume's stance in his *Enquiry Concerning Human Understanding* (1748):

[E]very effect is a distinct event from its cause. It could not, therefore, be discovered in the cause, and the first invention or conception of it, a priori, must be entirely arbitrary. And even after it is suggested, the conjunction of it with the cause must appear equally arbitrary, since there are always many other effects, which, to reason, must seem fully as consistent and natural. In vain, therefore, should we pretend to determine any single event, or infer any cause or effect, without the assistance of observation and experience.[2]

As one might expect, these are two very different accounts of efficient causation. According to Suárez, efficient causation is just one of the four kinds of Aristotelian cause, which all have in common the idea that causes are principles that 'inflow being into something else' (DM 12.2.4). Hume does not consider these distinctions and dismisses the idea that there is any connection between a cause and its effects. In doing so, Hume aims to dismantle *any* conception of causation based on intrinsic metaphysical connections between causes and effects. Moreover, Suárez takes causal relations to hold between *substances*, namely, individual entities, with their own self-standing nature and being, which causally affect one another. Hume, instead, takes causation to hold among *events*.

However, underneath these many differences, Suárez and Hume share a fundamental ontological commitment to the coarse-grained nature of reality. That is, both are committed to the view that reality is composed of entities that can exist independently of one another. For Suárez, this view is embedded in the very idea of *substance*; his way of distinguishing efficient causation from other kinds of causation relies on the specific manner in which an efficient cause relates substances that exist one apart from the other. Hume offers a different framework in which it is possible to rethink the same ontological commitment. For Hume, causes and effects are events, rather than substances. Nonetheless, these events are ontologically discrete and can exist independently of one another. In fact, Hume's argument against necessary causal connections relies on the possibility of

---

[1] Francisco Suárez, *On Efficient Causality. Metaphysical Disputations 17, 18 and 19*, trans. by A. J. Freddoso (New Haven, 1994). In quoting Suárez's *Metaphysical Disputations* (abbreviated 'DM') I mention the relevant number of the disputation, section and paragraph, followed by the page number of the English translation (abbreviated 'F'). When F is not mentioned, the English translation is mine.

[2] David Hume, *Enquiries Concerning Human Understanding and Concerning the Principles of Morals*, ed. by P. H. Nidditch (Oxford, 1975), IV.1, p. 19.

conceiving causes and effects as events that are ultimately independent from each other. Hume would be uneasy with using the notion of substance to characterize these independent events. Nonetheless, he endorses the view that the world is made up of ontologically independent and discrete entities, which he conceptualizes as events rather than substances. This commitment to the coarse-grained nature of reality is neither an obvious nor a natural commitment[3] but is instead a particular philosophical stance on reality, which needs to be supported and consolidated by arguments. To appreciate this point, consider two counter examples. First, in the early modern period, Spinoza rejected the coarse-grained nature of reality by arguing instead for a view in which reality has a *fine-grained* nature. According to Spinoza, reality is an infinitely dense tissue of *modes*, which exist and are constituted by their mutual causal relations. Modes are, by nature, ontologically dependent on one another. No mode can exist independently of or in isolation from all the other modes.[4] Second, in some non-Western traditions, such as the Buddhist Mādhyamaka school, the very notion of substance and coarse-grained reality is the object of sustained criticism. Mādhyamika thinkers maintain that substances exist only at the level of human conventions, which may be helpful for daily practical purposes. A deeper reflection on the nature of things and their dependent co-origination reveals that they have no independent, intrinsic existence.[5] If it is neither obvious nor natural to be committed to the coarse-grained nature of reality, it is worth addressing the question of why this view was so resistant and resilient across the early modern period.

This contribution provides a reconstruction of how a commitment to the coarse-grained nature of reality was defended, preserved and reshaped in natural philosophy. In what follows, I focus on how the view that the nature of reality is course-grained was preserved through a process of 'normalisation' during the early modern period. The general goal is to set

---

[3] By 'obvious' commitment I refer to a commitment shared by all members of a certain broad intellectual environment (i.e., the space commonly shared by many different traditions, which despite their differences do share at least the fact of having evolved in interaction with one another). By 'natural' commitment I refer to a commitment shared by all human beings, independently from the intellectual environments to which they belong.

[4] See Mogens Lærke, 'Immanence et extériorité absolue: sur la théorie de la causalité et l'ontologie de la puissance de Spinoza', *Revue philosophique de la France et de l'Étranger* 199 (2009), 169–190; Francesca Di Poppa, 'Spinoza and Process Ontology', *The Southern Journal of Philosophy* 48 (2010), 272–294; Andrea Sangiacomo and Ohad Nachtomy, 'Spinoza's Rethinking of Activity from the *Short Treatise* to the *Ethics*', *Southern Journal of Philosophy* 56 (2018), 1–26.

[5] See Jan Westerhoff, 'The Madhyamaka Concept of Svabhāva: Ontological and Cognitive Aspects.', *Asian Philosophy*, 17:1 (2007), 17–45; Id. 'On the Nihilist Interpretation of Madhyamaka.' *Journal of Indian Philosophy* 44 (2016), 337–376.

forth a new approach to the *longue durée* history of early modern philosophy and science. My approach aims to study conceptual transformations over time by first identifying those conceptual elements that are progressively assimilated in existent frameworks and thus become 'normal'. Once this process of 'normalisation' has been identified, the approach seeks to explain why certain elements rather than others are normalised. My general working hypothesis to explain this process of normalisation is that historical actors tend to select those elements that are most conducive to defending, preserving and perpetrating certain core commitments that they deem most crucial. I shall call this 'The Leopard Theorem', inspired by the claim from Tomasi Di Lampedusa's novel *The Leopard*: 'if we want things to stay as they are, things will have to change'.[6]

In this contribution, I outline the fundamental methodological underpinnings of my approach and provide preliminary evidence in support of how The Leopard Theorem can be used to interpret and explain some facets of the evolution of early modern debates on causality across seventeenth- and eighteenth-century natural philosophy. I suggest that several authors contribute to the progressive normalisation of an account of 'occasional causality' (i.e., one that understands causes as *sine quibus non* conditions devoid of any intrinsic efficacious causal power to bring their effect about). I contend that the reason why occasional causality is normalised is because it is

---

[6] Giuseppe Tomasi di Lampedusa, *The Leopard*. English translation by Archibald Colquhoun (London, 2007), 19. The original Italian is slightly stronger: 'bisogna che tutto [*everything*] cambi.' I first introduced this theorem in the particular case of Geulincx's occasionalism in Andrea Sangiacomo, 'Geulincx and the *Quod Nescis* Principle: A Conservative Revolution', in *The Oxford Handbook of Descartes and Cartesianism*, eds. Steven Nadler, Tad M. Schmaltz, Delphine Antoine-Mahut (Oxford, 2019), 450–464 . A number of studies noted how the success and circulation of several 'new' ideas has been fostered by the way in which they contributed (in the eyes of historical actors) to defending and propagating certain core features of traditional frameworks. For instance, the circulation of 'new' scientific ideas in the British context offers a good example. Since the beginning of the seventeenth century, the reception of the corpuscularism and the experimental method was determined by the way in which historical actors perceived some of these new ideas as more easily reconciled with religious doctrines than the various types of Aristotelianism in circulation; see e.g. Martin Craig, *Subverting Aristotle. Religion, History, and Philosophy in Early Modern Science* (Baltimore, 2014). The reception of Descartes' natural philosophy in England was deeply determined by the initial enthusiasm (and subsequent delusion) for the way in which Descartes' mechanist physics could have been instrumental in defending the immateriality and immortality of the soul; see e.g. Arrigo Pacchi, *Cartesio in Inghilterra* (Roma-Bari, 1973); Sarah Hutton, *British Philosophy in the Seventeenth Century* (Oxford, 2015). Recent scholarship on the reception and circulation of Newton's natural philosophy shows a similar pattern, insofar as Newton's natural philosophy was soon appropriated and defended by a number of authors as the best means of rejecting deism (and Spinozism) and defending Christian faith; see Jeffrey R. Wigelsworth, *Deism in Enlightenment England: Theology, politics, and Newtonian public science* (Manchester, 2009).

conducive, in an early modern context, to preserving (under a different guise) the fundamental ontological commitment to the coarse-grained nature of reality, which most early modern authors are extremely recalcitrant to abandon.

The transition from late scholasticism to the early modern period has often been seen as the progressive demolishing of the later scholastic framework. Regardless of how abrupt or continuous this process of destruction is seen to have been, it is usually acknowledged that the seventeenth century witnessed the dusk of Aristotelian scholasticism. For instance, Pasnau summarizes one of the key features of this process as follows:

> [The] substance-based ontology lies at the foundation of scholastic metaphysics. To study the decline of scholasticism in the seventeenth century is, in no small part, to witness the collapse of this foundation.[7]

Pasnau stresses the deep theoretical differences between late scholasticism and early modern philosophy. Yet, a study of the normalisation of occasional causality and its impact on the commitment to coarse-grained reality yields a significantly different picture than the one suggested by him. The 'collapse' of late scholastic metaphysics does not concern the commitment to coarse-grained reality as such, but only the way in which this commitment was articulated in the scholastic framework. The metaphysics of substance is the main theoretical framework in which scholastic authors developed and articulated the commitment to coarse-grained reality. However, this fact does *not* entail that the same commitment cannot be preserved, articulated and defended in different (and potentially anti-scholastic) conceptual frameworks. From one perspective (the kind Pasnau expounds), Suárez and Hume's views seem to be polar-opposites to one another. Yet, from another (the kind I am expounding here), they seem to be part of the same conceptual framework: one dominated by a shared commitment to coarse-grained reality. Within this framework, the role of (a certain understanding of) causation shifts from being the 'glue' among substances (e.g. Suárez) to becoming the 'knife' that cuts apart independent entities (e.g. Hume).

A proper articulation of the way in which the normalisation of occasional causality shaped early modern natural philosophy should proceed along two lines of investigation. One line should work backward from the early modern period to scholastic accounts, in order to investigate why occasional causality could even be taken seriously in the seventeenth century, given that Suárez blatantly asserts that it 'is justifiably rejected by all philosophers and theologians' (DM 18.1.5/F 40). Another line should go

---

[7] Robert Pasnau, *Metaphysical Themes 1274–1671* (Oxford, 2011), 6.

forward and reconstruct in detail how the normalisation of occasional causality took place and how it interacted with other conceptual transformations during the early modern period proper. In this contribution, I shall leave aside the first line of research,[8] while I illustrate the second by offering a comparison between four particular cases, which I have previously examined separately in greater detail. The synthesis of these results is not intended to provide any conclusive findings, but rather it aims to build the foundations for a broader historiographical and philosophical narrative about the evolution of early modern philosophy and science.

The four cases I shall examine are Pierre Sylvain Régis (1632–1707), Johan Christoph Sturm (1635–1703), Petrus van Musschenbroek (1692–1761), and Immanuel Kant (1724–1804).[9] Except for Régis, these authors were all university professors, although Régis' work is intended to provide a Cartesian textbook comparable to those used in university courses. Barring Kant, today these authors (unlike Hume, and Suárez in more recent years) do not routinely feature in early modern discussions of causation. However, the Kant I consider is the early Kant of the *Nova Dilucidatio* (1756), which is arguably not Kant's most commonly discussed text. Finally, these are all male philosophers operating between the second half of the seventeenth century and the mid-eighteenth century. To some extent, this fact mirrors the male dominancy of the philosophical scene of the period. Normalisation entails setting standards and prescribing norms. In this sense, it can be seen as a process connected with the establishment and maintenance of power and dominance. However, my goal here is not to *justify* normalisation, but rather to understand its mechanism. While it

---

[8] My hypothesis is that the rise of occasional causality in the early modern period was made possible by an ongoing transformation in the scholastic account of final causation, which in turn created significant conceptual tensions within the scholastic framework itself. For an initial articulation of this hypothesis, see Andrea Sangiacomo, 'Modelling the history of early modern natural philosophy: The fate of the art-nature distinction in the Dutch universities', *British Journal for the History of Philosophy* 27 (2018), 46–74, DOI: 10.1080/09608788.2018.1506313.

[9] See Andrea Sangiacomo, 'From secondary causes to artificial instruments: Pierre-Sylvain Régis's rethinking of scholastic accounts of causation', *Studies in History and Philosophy of Science* Part A, 60 (2016), 7–17, DOI: 10.1016/j.shpsa.2016.08.004; Id. 'Divine action and God's immutability: a historical case study on how to resist occasionalism', *European Journal of Philosophy of Religion*, 7 (2015), 115–135; Id. 'Neither with occasionalism nor with concurrentism: the case of Pierre-Sylvain Régis', in *Occasionalism: From Metaphysics to Science*, eds. Matteo Favaretti Camposampiero, Mariangela Priarolo, Emanuela Scribano (Turnhout, 2018), 85–103; Id. 'Johan Christoph Sturm's natural philosophy: passive forms, occasionalism and scientific explanations', *Journal for the History of Philosophy*, 58 (2020), 493–520; Id. 'Teleology and the evolution of natural philosophy: the case of Johann Christoph Sturm and Petrus van Musschenbroek', *Studia Leibnitiana*, 50 (2018), 41–56; Id. 'Sine qua non causation: the legacy of Malebranche's occasionalism in Kant's *New Elucidation*', *Oxford Studies in Early Modern Philosophy* 9 (2019), 215–248.

is impossible to rewrite the past, understanding how normalisation shaped the course of history can provide conceptual tools to take a more critical stance towards today's use of this past (e.g. in the process of canon-formation and the justificatory practices that unfold from it).[10]

Together, the four cases discussed in this contribution capture the way in which the notion of causality in natural philosophy was reshaped within and across the boundaries of the North European academic milieu, between the end of the seventeenth century and the first half of the eighteenth century. Normalisation concerns how and why existing traditions are altered and transformed and new ideas are selected, adapted and incorporated in existing frameworks. The academic milieu[11] is the ideal scenario to study the phenomenon of normalisation since one of the fundamental purposes of authors working in this environment is to consolidate and transmit to future generations certain accounts of a discipline as 'the' normal account that should be pursued.

My discussion proceeds as follows. In section two, I provide an operational account of normalisation and outline the theoretical underpinnings that I implement in the four case studies. In section three, I outline these cases studies and elaborate on the reasons why the academic milieu is the ideal domain to study normalisation. In section four, I discuss how these cases support my working hypothesis about the normalisation of occasional causality and its impact on the preservation and reshaping of the commitment to coarse-grained reality.

2. An operational account of normalisation

The normalisation of early modern natural philosophy, as I understand it, has yet to be studied thoroughly. As I shall argue, this study is partially prevented by the limits of the current standard methods in the field of history of philosophy and science. My goal in this contribution is not to provide a fully developed theory of normalisation and its implications, which is a task that should be postponed to a later and more advanced stage of research. Rather, I will offer an operational working account of normalisation that, albeit provisional, can orient the research on normalisation in its

---

[10] Concerning the current debate on the Western canon of philosophy and its problems see, e.g. Lisa Shapiro, 'Revisiting the Early Modern Philosophical Canon', *Journal of the American Philosophical Association* 2 (2016), 365–383; Michael Beaney, 'Twenty-five years of the British Journal for the History of Philosophy', *British Journal for the History of Philosophy* 26 (2018), 1–10.

[11] For a methodological explanation of how I understand the notion of the 'academic milieu', see the Introduction to this volume.

initial stages. My account aims to determine specific procedures to investigate qualitative and quantitative aspects that can be associated with normalisation and thus lead to a better understanding of this process. These results will contribute to the development of a more complete and substantive theory of normalisation, understood as a general historical and conceptual phenomenon.

Given the limited goal of this contribution, I shall not dispute whether the account of normalisation that I present is derived or differs from analogous notions discussed by historians and philosophers of science. This kind of historiographical discussion can be developed once normalisation becomes a better known object of study itself. Nonetheless, I will pinpoint (at the end of this section) a few aspects that may help to elucidate how the notion of normalisation I use relates, in particular, to the notion of 'normal science' introduced by Thomas Kuhn (and the problems entailed by the Kuhnian approach) since Kuhn's notion had considerable impact on the scholarship of early modern philosophy and science.

This being said, my operational definition of normalisation is the following:

Normalisation is an ecological process in which exogenous ideas and established traditions mutually adapt to each other.

Before explaining this definition term by term, a disclaimer is in order. This definition appropriates a biological and evolutionary intuition, in which ideas and traditions are understood as quasi-biological entities that work as organisms (ideas) and environments (traditions). This intuition, however, is used for purely heuristic reasons. I do not take this intuition to entail any strict theoretical analogy or conceptual constraint on the way in which normalisation should be understood. Ultimately, the suitability of these heuristics must be assessed against the results obtained by the study of normalisation itself, and its role at this stage is just to metaphorically stimulate a certain way of thinking about the process of normalisation. Nonetheless, this biological metaphor prevents the consideration of ideas and conceptual changes as disembodied ahistorical entities, and instead invites us to consider them as historically embedded phenomena (i.e., phenomena that originate and take place within the domain of human history).

By 'ecological' I refer to the fact that normalisation is a *systematic* process that entails a complex interplay between the actors involved. The key intuition that underpins the use of the adjective 'ecological' is the presence of some recursive feedback mechanism that determines the way in which the changes of the system itself affect the changes of its constitutive components and vice versa.

By referring to normalisation as a 'process' I want to stress that normalisation should *not* be understood as a 'state' or 'condition'. Rather, normalisation concerns how systems of ideas change over time. Something that maintains its diachronic identity over time and does not undergo change may well be defined as a 'state' or as a relatively permanent 'condition'. The transition between different states or conditions might be abrupt or gradual. All these different nuances are captured by the idea that normalisation is a process that happens over time.

By 'idea' I refer to the content of an assertive linguistic statement. I take this as an operational working definition, which should involve investigating ideas by scrutinising linguistic statements.[12] In my account of normalisation, 'idea' works as a synonym for 'concept', 'notion' or 'conceptual content'. I do not take any substantive stance on the theoretical definition of what an 'idea' is. My working definition does not entail that ideas are reducible to linguistic statements (this substantive view about ideas should itself be the object of further debate and investigation). Also, an assertive statement should not be reduced to a single proposition or even to a key-term or slogan, but might be expressed by a network of complex interconnected linguistic structures. Ideas or concepts are not necessarily identical to single key-words, although key-words might signal the occurrence of certain ideas.[13] Finally, ideas can be simple or complex. If an idea cannot be analysed in sub-components that retain in themselves the character of an idea, then the idea is simple. If an idea can be analysed in terms of sub-components that are in themselves ideas, then the idea is complex. Whether an idea is simple or complex should be decided by the actual study of it, while how ideas can be analysed is a matter of methodological investigation (which I shall not develop further here).

By 'tradition' I mean the diachronically continuous and manifold assertion of an idea (or system of ideas) by several authors belonging to different generations. For an idea to become a tradition, three conditions need to be satisfied. The idea must (i) continue to be asserted over time, (ii) be asserted by a network of authors,[14] and (iii) be asserted for longer than the timespan in which one single author is active. Traditions do not necessarily

---

[12] I am aware that normalisation can concern conceptual contents that are *not* expressed in linguistic statements (e.g. images, graphs, schemes). For present purposes, I shall not take these further domains into account and leave for the future the discussion on how to best integrate them within a broader study of normalisation.

[13] On this point see Peter De Bolla, *The Architecture of Concepts. The Historical Formation of Human Rights* (New York, 2013).

[14] By 'network of authors' I mean authors who, rather than simply being a set of disconnected individuals, are directly connected and engaged with the sharing, perpetuation and development of the tradition to which they belong.

need to be supported by the majority of authors embedded in a certain historical context (although they might be), but they need to involve multiple authors who transmit certain ideas from one to the other across generations. Traditions do not need to be uncontested by external or internal opponents. Despite debates that may surround a tradition, the tradition is established if these debates do not undermine the tradition itself, namely, the continuous assertion of its core idea (or system of ideas). Note also that traditions are not identical with historical communities (i.e., socially structured communities of human beings living in a certain historical period in a certain place). Traditions have to do with ideas held within historical communities: one single historical community (like the early modern academic milieu, for instance) can host several traditions, while the same tradition (like scholastic philosophy, for instance) may connect different historical communities.

The transfer of ideas across generations is embedded in the very term 'tradition' (from the Latin *tradere*, to deliver or bequeath). However, for an idea to become a tradition it is also necessary that the *same* idea is continuously asserted over time. It is a matter of controversy how to identify and study whether, and to what extent, the same idea persists over time. In recent scholarship, one approach suggested to distinguish between the *core* and *margins* of an idea or concept.[15] The *core* (which may be in itself a complex network of ideas) is what remains constant and defines the strict identity of the concept. The *margins* are ideas connected to the core but that may be changed, adapted or reshaped without involving a change in the *core*.[16]

I implement this distinction between core and margins not only to the domain of ideas but to the notion of tradition itself. Traditions can be defined by a set of *core commitments*, more or less explicitly spelled out by the authors themselves. In fact, core commitments do not have to be (and in fact are often not) explicitly stated, since they do not represent what is controversial for the authors belonging to a certain tradition. Being

---

[15] Jouni-Matti Kuukkanen, 'Making Sense of Conceptual Change', *History and Theory* 47, (2008): 351–372; Arianna Betti and Hein van den Berg, 'Modelling the History of Ideas', *British Journal for the History of Philosophy*, 22, (2014): 812–835; Id., 'Towards a Computational History of Ideas', in *Proceedings of the Third Conference on Digital Humanities in Luxembourg with a Special Focus on Reading Historical Sources in the Digital Age. CEUR Workshop Proceedings, CEUR-WS.org.*, eds. Lars Wieneke, Catherine Jones, Marten Düring, Florentina Armaselu, René Leboutte, vol. 1681, 2016; Arianna Betti, Hein van den Berg, Yvette Oortwijn, and Caspar Treijtel, 'History of Philosophy in Ones and Zeros', in *Methodological Advances in Experimental Philosophy*, eds. Mark Curtis and Eugen Fischer (London, 2019), 295–332.; Sangiacomo, 'Modelling'.

[16] Note that I adopt this distinction not as a substantive claim about the nature of ideas or concepts, but only as an operational way of studying historical ideas and concepts.

implicit is the privilege that a commitment receives in virtue of its fundamental value for the tradition that surrounds it, and its uncontested position within that tradition. Core commitments are the shared ground on which the tradition itself rests and thrives. The core commitments of the same tradition do not have to be homogeneous among themselves and they can involve a more or less coherent combination of different ideas.

The *marginal* ideas in a tradition are used to spell out, refine, revise, connect, adapt and adjust (the list may go on) the core commitments. To use a metaphor, the core commitments are the *kind of materials* used to build the edifice of the tradition (bricks, wood, stones), while the marginal ideas are the materials used to glue these materials and shape the edifice (cement, malt, sand, plaster). As the edifice, also a tradition as a whole is not reducible to its constitutive (core and marginal) components taken separately, since the *way* in which the components are put together is as constitutive for the tradition as a whole as the separate components themselves. The reshaping of traditions often occurs at the level of these marginal ideas, and brings about macroscopic alterations. However, behind these macroscopic alterations it may still be possible to recognize the older and persistent architectonic structure of the same tradition. What sometimes happened to old medieval buildings that were reinvented and 'modernized' during the Renaissance also happens to philosophical traditions.

This notion of tradition defines boundaries between what is 'internal' and what is 'external' to it. Ideas are internal to a certain tradition if they are part of its system of ideas or derived from it. Ideas are external or exogenous to a certain tradition if they are not part of its system or they are rejected by it. The process of normalisation thus concerns the relationship between a certain 'established tradition', which is taken as the given ecosystem, and 'exogenous ideas', which are ideas that do not belong to this ecosystem but are introduced to it at some point. Exogenous ideas may also remain somehow present within a conceptual ecosystem for some time, without really interacting or becoming part of it, and simply being present in their own relatively isolated and confined niche. Even in this case, such ideas are exogenous because they are not genuinely part of the conceptual process through which the tradition sustains, develops and reproduces itself. The identification of which particular elements count as 'exogenous' and which ones as 'established' is a matter of empirical investigation and depends on the research agenda at stake.

By 'mutual adaptation among each other' I mean that exogenous ideas and traditions do not all interact with one another in the same way. The interaction between a tradition and an exogenous idea can lead to different scenarios. The idea can be simply incorporated or assimilated within the tradition as a helpful addition to it. The tradition itself can have internal tensions and inconsistencies, and the spreading of certain exogenous ideas can interact with these tensions by supporting some strands within the tradition itself or by undermining others. Also, an idea can be shaped in such a way as to enter into dialogue with a tradition, it can be adjusted in order to find recognition and acceptance, or used as a weapon against the tradition itself. These are all just different instances of 'mutual adaptation'. The underlying view is that in the interaction between an exogenous idea and an established tradition elements undergo both some mutual transformation and reshaping. However, this change is neither the simple rejection of the exogenous idea nor the complete collapse of the tradition itself. The notion of 'mutual adaptation' entails a form of equilibrium (reached over time) between change and continuity. Changes in which the introduction of an exogenous idea would destroy an established tradition or changes in which an established tradition simply rejects an idea do *not* count as cases of normalisation.

This point is important because an operational definition of normalisation should be able to distinguish cases of actual normalisation from cases in which some other kind of change occurs. Not all changes can be cases of normalisation, otherwise the notion of normalisation would be operatively and conceptually idle. For instance, the notion of 'progress' assumes that later ideas are 'better' with respect to some preliminary defined criteria. Normalisation is different from progress; not because normalisation excludes the possibility that later ideas may be judged better or worse than former ideas given certain criteria, but because the kind of process of conceptual transformation entailed by normalisation is ruled by an ecological mutual adaptation between exogenous ideas and existing traditions, and it is not oriented to achieve better future states. Unlike progress, mutual adaptation does not necessarily result in a better state, nor is it necessarily captured in terms of better or worse. Whether the end result of a process of normalisation can be judged better or worse is accidental to the process of normalisation itself. Hence, explaining the same process as an instance of progress or as an instance of normalisation yields significantly different understandings of the process itself. Normalisation is also different from strict 'conservativism' because an instance wherein an established tradition managed to simply remain unchanged over time and was systematically successful in rejecting all exogenous ideas would *not* constitute normalisation.

Having clarified my operational definition of normalisation, let me introduce two criteria to determine whether normalisation is occurring in a given domain. These two criteria will be exemplified in the next section, but for present purposes it is worth stating them in more general terms. In my account, *both* criteria are jointly necessary and sufficient to identify a process of change in ideas as a process of normalisation.

The first criterion is that *normalisation requires a multiplicity of different ideas.* The minimal multiplicity is given by some ideas being regarded together as an 'established tradition' and some ideas being regarded as 'exogenous' to that tradition. These two groups of ideas have to be different in some relevant respect (I leave it up to empirical and methodological investigation to define what counts as 'different' and what counts as 'relevant', and how to assess these variables). In a completely homogeneous scenario in which only one idea or tradition is present across time, no normalisation will occur since the idea can only remain unchanged or be dismissed outright. Without multiplicity and difference, the notion of 'mutual adaptation' ceases to be relevant. Most likely, an established tradition has to deal with many exogenous ideas at the same time, many exogenous ideas are in competition among themselves and, in fact, different rival traditions are in competition among each other.

The second criterion is that *normalisation requires a selection among ideas.* By 'selection' I mean here the fact that only some ideas succeed in maintaining diachronic continuity over time. This can apply both to ideas that belong to the established tradition itself (when despite some changes, several authors from several generations keep asserting some ideas of that tradition), and to exogenous ideas (when some of these ideas are established themselves as new traditions). Selection entails two consequences. First, not all ideas have the same adaptive success during the same period and some of them, at some point in time, are no longer asserted. Second, every idea tends to become (at least part of) a tradition, although not all ideas are equally successful in this effort.[17] The criterion of selection is necessary to identify normalisation because without selection there would be either the diachronically continuous co-existence of mutually different ideas, or the constant appearance and disappearance of different ideas that do not mutually adapt to each other. Neither of these scenarios allows for a 'mutual adaptation between exogenous ideas and established traditions', and thus neither of them counts as a process of normalisation.

Multiplicity of different ideas and selection are jointly sufficient to identify normalisation because when they both occur, it is possible to identify the relationship between different ideas in terms of 'established

---

[17] The underlying working assumption here is that ideas strive to be propagated, and becoming (part of) a tradition is the most effective way to achieve this goal. For present purposes, again, I do not take this assumption to entail any substantive consequence about the nature of ideas (e.g. whether ideas *qua* ideas strive to propagate themselves, as memes, or whether this is a by-product of the attachment of the human individuals defending the ideas themselves).

tradition' and 'exogenous ideas', and the selection occurring among them. Since this selection process does not entail either an identical perpetuation of the same ideas across time, nor a constant emergence and rejection of new ideas all the time, it can be understood as a 'mutual adaptation' of some exogenous ideas to the established tradition.

The account of normalisation I have presented so far is designed to determine whether a specific phenomenon is a case of normalisation. However, this account leaves it open for actual fieldwork to identify the causes and mechanisms that explain why a specific case of normalisation unfolds in the way in which it does. In this sense, normalisation can work both as an *explanans* (that which is used to explain and understand the meaning of a certain process) and as an *explanandum* (the process that needs to be explained and understood), although at different levels. Let me elaborate on this point.

Given a domain in which some change in ideas occurs, this change can be explained in several ways. For instance, as already mentioned, the notion of progress may be one of the explanations (i.e., by showing that the ongoing change is an instance of progress). Normalisation offers another kind of explanation. If the change constitutes *progress*, then the explanation is mostly axiological; that is, based on values such as 'better' or 'worse', as in the case of judging a certain historical change to be 'progress towards a better condition'. If the change is a *normalisation*, then the explanation is (for lack of more specific terminology) 'ecological' and 'evolutionary'; in the sense that, as I stated above, it does not necessarily involve any axiological judgment or consideration about the fact that the change leads towards a *better* state. This entails that by understanding a change as progress or as an instance of normalisation, the phenomenon of change itself is understood, conceptualized and explained in two significantly different ways.

Nonetheless, identifying a change as an instance of normalisation is just the beginning of a more specific kind of explanation, which concerns the causes and conditions that determined this specific kind of normalisation to occur in this specific way. Epistemological complexities aside,[18] my point here is only that normalisation, as an *explanans*, concerns the identification and description of a certain conceptual change *as* an instance of normalisation, while normalisation as an *explanandum* asks the researcher to provide an account of the causes and conditions that rule the particular

---

[18] It is contested amongst philosophers of science whether explanations are best understood as answers to why-questions, or whether there are explanations that answer different kinds of questions, such as how-possibly questions. See e.g. Wesley C. Salmon, *Four Decades of Scientific Explanations* (Pittsburgh, 1989), 137.

process of normalisation at stake. Once a phenomenon of change is identified as a case of normalisation, the actual process of normalisation itself
demands further explanation. The key question, at this junction, is: *why
has this* exogenous idea, rather than its many other rivals, been normalized
in *this* tradition? The assumption behind this question is that conceptual
change does not have to be linear or straightforward but that several alternative and divergent routes are possible at any crossroad. Methodologically,
it is thus important to assume a *principle of sufficient historical reason*,
which requires an explanation why, given the possible alternative scenarios,
ideas changed in the way in which they did. In this way, normalisation
goes from being an *explanans* to being the *explanandum*.

Moreover, the *principle of sufficient historical reason* offers an initial
working criterion (which may well be further refined and integrated by
other criteria as the research advances or requires so) to assess what counts
as a good explanation of normalisation. Taking normalisation as an
explanandum, its sufficient reason concerns why certain historical actors
select certain ideas, over others, and deal with them in a certain way, rather
than another, by then instantiating a certain process of normalisation,
rather than another. For instance, one may observe a process of mutual
adaptation between certain exogenous ideas and a given tradition, and this
fact would be sufficient for this process to count as an instance of normalisation (taken as *explanans*). However, this identification does not explain
why it is this particular kind of mutual adaptation between these particular
ideas that takes place. Asking why *this* exogenous idea (rather than others)
mutually adapts with this tradition in this way (rather than in any other
way) pushes the explanatory work one step further back, by taking the fact
of normalisation as an *explanandum*. The sufficient reason for normalisation can be any set of causes and conditions that determines certain historical actors to foster the mutual adaptation between certain ideas and
certain traditional elements (rather than others), by thus producing this
specific process of normalisation instead of others.

In the next two sections, I shall illustrate this point more concretely.
I first identify the *fact* of the normalisation of occasional causality (taken
as an *explanans*) in four cases across the seventeenth and eighteenth centuries. I shall then suggest that the explanation of this process of normalisation (taken now as the *explanandum*) lies in the effort of historical actors
to safeguard their commitment to the coarse-grained nature of reality. This
kind of explanation can be generalized in the form of The Leopard
Theorem, the claim that normalisation is aimed at preserving some core
commitment of a certain tradition, which may be regarded as capturing
one kind of sufficient historical reason for the normalisation of occasional
causality (i.e., the effort of safeguarding core commitments of the tradition

in which this normalisation occurs). Whether The Leopard Theorem may be further generalized and validated, or perhaps even considered as some sort of 'law of normalisation' (without mentioning further and even more ambitious questions about whether there are such laws or what they may be), remains open for future investigation.

In the following discussion it will become increasingly clear that the study of normalisation (especially when taken as an *explanandum*) runs against and makes apparent the methodological limitations of the standard and most common approaches used in the history of philosophy and science (which I have employed myself in the four cases I shall discuss here). This is why The Leopard Theorem can only be taken, for the moment, as a preliminary working hypothesis. The problem is not theoretical and the consequence is *not* that The Leopard Theorem does not successfully capture the reasons for normalisation that are instantiated in the cases that I discuss. The problem is rather methodological, since the methods I have been using (and which are the methods most commonly used in the field) to analyse these cases are *not* capable of legitimately licensing the generalizations that would be required to consider The Leopard Theorem as a proper 'law of normalisation'. Appreciating these methodological limitations is crucial because they show how the study of normalisation can push the current methods in history of philosophy and science to their edge. By revealing these limitations, my discussion aims to justify the introduction of new methods to support and enhance the current research practice.

Before concluding this section, let me make a few remarks about how the notion of normalisation that I have explained so far relates to Kuhn's account of 'normal science'. As mentioned in the introduction, it is beyond the scope of this paper to offer a proper discussion of this point. I shall thus focus on just two notable differences between Kuhn's account of normal science and the account of normalisation I have presented, leaving room for further reflection on the issue of whether the two can be reconciled.

The first difference is that Kuhn's account of normal science relies on the notion of *paradigms*, while my account of normalisation relies on a notion of tradition that is much broader and more flexible. According to Kuhn, one way of understanding what a paradigm is amounts to thinking about paradigms as 'universally recognized scientific achievements that, for a time, provide model problems and solutions for a community of researchers'.[19]

---

[19] Thomas Kuhn, *The Structure of Scientific Revolutions* (London, 2012⁴ [50th anniversary edition, first edition 1962]), xlvii.

Normal science progressively deepens and expands the heuristic potential of a given paradigm. When a paradigm is discarded in favour of a new paradigm, a 'revolution' occurs (in Kuhn's sense). My definition of normalisation does not concern 'paradigms', but ideas and traditions, as I operationally defined them above. Moreover, my account does not focus on what happens within a given tradition, but on the interaction between this tradition and exogenous ideas. This process of mutual adaptation can consist in a number of changes and transformations that are not necessarily captured by the Kuhnian conception of the deepening and systematization of a paradigm associated with normal science. In this respect, my notion of normalisation is broader than Khun's notion of normal science.[20]

The second difference is that my account of normalisation relies on a continuist understanding of conceptual change, while Kuhn's account is discontinuist. According to Kuhn, conceptual change occurs when there is a change in paradigm. This led to the vexed issue of the change of worldview associated with scientific revolutions and the problem of incommensurability of different paradigms. My account aims to avoid these problems. Since my definition of normalisation entails that change occurs as a process of mutual adaptation between different ideas, the possibility of an abrupt emergence of some new idea and simultaneous disappearance of some other idea is ruled out by the very definition of normalisation. Mutual adaptation is a continuous process spread over time that actually rules out radical or abrupt discontinuity. However, this continuist approach does *not* entail that there must be some continuous consensus over time either, nor that revolutions (in Kuhn's sense) are impossible. Mutual adaptation entails that both established traditions and exogenous ideas change over time. In this respect, a diachronically consistent and unchanging tradition cannot be said to have undergone normalisation and normalisation can only be said to have occurred when traditions are transformed. Radical change may be observed by considering sufficiently distant points in the continuum of the process of mutual adaptation. While on shorter segments of the continuum, different ideas share a common ground (i.e. some ideas that are *not* changing at the same time), this common ground may itself change and be different in different periods. When there is no common

---

[20] Nonetheless, the later Kuhn introduced a more flexible and malleable way of conceiving of normal science, by stressing that normal science can be understood as a process of progressive adaptation of scientific ideas to specific core normative commitments endorsed by a scientific community. See Thomas Kuhn, *The Essential Tension. Selected Studies in Scientific Tradition and Change* (Chicago and London, 1977); Id., *The Road Since Structure. Philosophical Essays, 1970–1993, with an Autobiographical Interview.* Ed. by J. Contant and J. Haugeland (Chicago and London, 2000); James Marcum, *Thomas Kuhn's Revolution: An Historical Philosophy of Science* (London-New York, 2015), 139.

ground between two traditions that are diachronically ordered and causally connected, it is legitimate to say that they are as different as two
'worldviews' before and after what Kuhn would call a 'revolution'.[21]

3. The normalisation of occasional causality

This section presents some preliminary evidence for the normalisation
of occasional causality in early modern natural philosophy. The evidence
I provide is based on four cases that I have examined in recent years. The
goal of this section is not to argue about the details of each of these cases,
which I discussed in the separate publications. Rather, the goal is to outline the most relevant points which allow us to see these four cases as
symptomatic of an underlying process of normalisation. Before presenting
the cases, let me add a few words about the common domain of investigation from which they are derived, namely the academic milieu to which all
the four authors belong.

In principle, normalisation can be studied either by focusing on exogenous ideas and then by studying how they spread within a certain established tradition, or by focusing on an established tradition and then
studying how it changes due to exposure to, and the dissemination of,
exogenous ideas. Based on her particular domain of investigation and
research agenda, the researcher has to decide which of these two approaches
is more suitable and whether they can be combined. Existing scholarship
tends to privilege the focus on exogenous ideas, by mostly investigating
the introduction and development of 'original' ideas against the background of established traditions. For present purposes, however, I maintain that it is methodologically preferable and operationally easier to focus
on established traditions.

I shall not offer *a priori* criteria for empirically identifying and recogniz-
ing traditions as such. Heuristically, it is more fruitful to leave this issue
open for actual empirical research and adopt a flexible enough understanding of 'tradition' to include different kinds of traditions. However,
as a general working assumption, I presuppose that traditions construct
themselves in such a way that they become recognizable *as* traditions
(leaving it open to empirical investigation to determine *how* one can best
identify them). Traditions self-construct their identity and strive to acquire
resources to propagate it, both intellectually (by reproducing their ideas)
and materially (by disseminating these ideas via various means, such as

[21] I am grateful to Laura Georgescu for very insightful discussions we had about the
topics covered in this section.

through books, teaching structures, advocacy and so forth). Since exogenous ideas are exogenous with respect to some established tradition, it is methodologically plausible to first identify the established tradition with respect to which certain ideas are considered exogenous. Moreover, since established traditions are such because they have managed to make themselves visible as traditions, they are operationally easier to identify.

A tradition may establish, identify and support itself by many different means. Nonetheless, teaching (in any way or context in which this practice may be framed) is always essential to the constitution of a certain tradition. Traditions exist because authors transmit certain ideas from one generation to the other. While this transmission may occur in different ways, teaching is crucial since it entails the normative injunction that the object of teaching is worth learning. That is, teaching is the vehicle by means of which the core commitments of a tradition find their way in new generations and reproduce themselves at the foundations of the future worldviews. Teaching is essentially concerned with finding the best way to transmit, above all, the core commitments of a tradition. This injunction is explicitly or implicitly supported by the fact that it flows from two poles with unequal power and social status, namely, from authors in a position of (intellectual and social) prominence (i.e., 'teachers') towards individuals who are in a neutral or subordinated position (i.e., 'students') who are often 'young' and not yet established members of society. Teaching is a practice of intellectual co-optation, and is always deeply entrenched within the core commitments of the broader socio-historical landscape in which it takes place. Teaching is thus a necessary component of a tradition. Without teaching, the ideas and material means that convey these ideas may long survive without making any impact on the development of the intellectual landscape. The indeterminate mass of 'unread' material stored in the libraries around the world is a good example of this point. If nobody teaches certain ideas any longer, these ideas cease to be part of a tradition at that time, even if their material instantiations can still be existent.

Teaching practices are not only the way in which traditions are established, but they are one of the most plausible domains in which normalisation becomes more apparent. If normalisation occurs, this affects the content of teaching as well. Hence, teaching practices over time will not have the same content. If a particular change is an instance of normalisation, then the change in the content of what is taught offers one of the best domains to investigate the process of normalisation itself. This is the reason why the four cases I shall now introduce have in common the fact that they instantiate different kinds of teaching practices. All the four authors whom I shall present were prominently engaged in teaching and propagating a specific brand of natural philosophy and, within it, a specific understanding of causality. Three of these authors (Sturm, van Musschenbroek and Kant) were working at universities, while one (Régis) was working as a competitor who was trying to establish an alternative tradition (Cartesian philosophy). In this respect, all four authors can be regarded as belonging to the academic milieu of early modern Northern Europe.

In order to make the comparison easier, I offer a synoptic presentation of the four cases in the following table. The table presents the four cases side-by-side and assesses them against eleven different criteria. These criteria are intended to draw attention to the aspects that I consider most relevant to the study the normalisation of occasional causality. Criteria 1–2 are purely historical (dates and genre). Criteria 3–5 concern the broad positioning of the four authors within early modern natural philosophy and in connection with the debate on occasionalism, in particular. Criteria 6–10 concern the details of the theory of causality admitted by the authors, since my focus is on the normalisation of occasional causality as a doctrine of causality. Criterion 11 frames the four authors against the commitment to the coarse-grained nature of reality, which my working hypothesis assumes to be relevant to explaining why the normalisation of occasional causality occurs.

Comparison criteria	Case 1: Régis	Case 2: Sturm	Case 3: Van Musschenbroek	Case 4: Kant
1. Date	1691	1698	1726–1762[22]	1756
2. Genre	University textbook	University textbook	University textbook	Academic essay
3. Key canonical authority in natural philosophy	Descartes	Descartes	Newton	Newton
4. Explicit engagement with occasionalism	Yes	Yes	No	Yes

[22] Van Musschenbroek kept working and expanding his textbook throughout his career. In my study, I focus on the last and posthumous edition that appeared in 1762 under the title *Introdutio ad philosophiam naturalem*. For an overview of van Musschenbroek's work and a reconstruction of the evolution of his thought, see Steffen Ducheyne, 'Petrus van Musschenbroek and Newton's 'vera stabilisque Philosophandi methodus'', *Berichte zur Wissenschaftsgeschichte* 38 (2015), 279–304; Id., 'Petrus van Musschenbroek on the scope of physica and its place in philosophy.' *Asclepio* 68 (2016), doi: http://dx.doi.org/10.3989/asclepio.2016.02; and the contribution by Pieter Present in this volume.

5. Attitude towards occasionalism	Explicit rejection	Explicit acceptance	No explicit stance	Explicit qualified rejection
6. Kind of causal relation	*Sine qua non* relation between powerless relata	*Sine qua non* relation between powerless relata	*Sine qua non* relation between powerless relata	*Sine qua non* relation between powerless relata
7. Modal status of causal relations	Conceptually necessary	Hypothetically necessary	Contingent	Contingent
8. Role of laws of nature	General constraints	General constraints	Establish connections between relata	Establish connections between relata
9. Role of God	Source of causal activity	Source of causal activity	Source of the laws of nature	Source of the laws of nature
10. Kind of causal relata	Modes	Modes	Phenomena	Substances
11. Commitment to coarse-grained reality	Yes	Yes	Yes	Yes

Criteria 1–2 show that the four cases are similar in regard to time and genre. Although Régis' textbook was not adopted in universities, it was intended to present a systematic and comprehensive Cartesian textbook. The *Nova Dilucidatio* is Kant's doctoral thesis, which is thus aimed at earning Kant status recognition within the academic milieu. Sturm and van Musschenbroek's textbooks are designed by established university professors for university practice.

Criterion 3 reflects a sharp change in the canonical authorities to which the four authors refer in the domain of natural philosophy. This change is expected, given the standard picture of eighteenth century natural philosophy witnessing the victory of Newton over Descartes. Criterion 4 shows that, except for van Musschenbroek, all these authors refer at some point to the debate surrounding occasionalism. Criterion 5 testifies that, except for Sturm, none of these authors self-identify as a supporter of occasionalism, and that both Régis and Kant argue against some version of it. Again, this remark is in line with the standard picture of occasionalism as a somewhat idiosyncratic mid-seventeenth century philosophical position that ultimately had little long-term impact on the evolution of eighteenth century philosophy and science. While this standard picture may be accurate on some level, it is largely an over-simplification. The remaining criteria offer more specific points of comparison to assess how the four authors deal with crucial key issues connected with occasionalism, and how their attitude toward these issues shows, in fact, a process of normalisation of occasional causality.

To better appreciate this comparison, let me make a few remarks on how the debate on occasionalism should be understood. Occasionalism can be taken to refer to two fundamentally distinct (although connected) questions: (1) what is the kind of causality that belongs to certain entities? and (2) what is the source of causal efficacy in phenomena?[23] Concerning (1), occasionalism entails that, in a given domain, entities are only *occasional* causes of their effects; in other words, they are only *sine quibus non* conditions for their effects to obtain.[24] Concerning (2), occasionalism entails that finite beings (at least some kinds) are occasional causes, while God is the active efficacious cause that brings about the effects associated with occasional causes. Depending on how inclusive the domain is to which *sine qua non* causality applies, God may remain the only active

---

[23] Steven Nadler, *Occasionalism: Causation among Cartesians* (Oxford, 2010) distinguishes 'occasional causation' (i.e., the theory according to which a cause A occasions—without direct efficient causal influx—the cause B to bring about the effect *e*), and 'occasionalism' (i.e., the doctrine according to which finite creatures do not have efficacious powers and God is the only true efficacious agent). According to Nadler (*Occasionalism*, 35), 'the relationship between occasional causation and occasionalism is that between genus and species. Occasionalism represents one species or variety of occasional causation, namely, that species in which the proximate and efficient cause whose operation (through efficient causation) is elicited by the occasional cause is God.' In this contribution I do not follow Nadler's distinction. I find Nadler's characterization of occasional causation too broad and his characterization of occasionalism too narrow. By 'occasional causality', I shall refer to the doctrine of *sine qua non* causality, which is compatible with Nadler's account of occasional causation. By 'occasionalism', I mean the way in which the causal labour is divided among different entities. This may well entail (e.g. in the case of Malebranche) what Nadler characterizes as full-blown occasionalism, but several other options are also possible. On this point see Andrea Sangiacomo, 'Louis de La Forge and the non-transfer argument for Occasionalism', *British Journal for the History of Philosophy* 22 (2014), 60–80; Id. 'Samuel Clarke on Agent Causation, Voluntarism and Occasionalism', *Science in Context* 31 (2018), 421–456. I shall use the term 'causation' more loosely to refer to doctrines of causality in general or to the phenomenon of causation. For an outline of the main themes and authors usually associated with early modern occasionalism, see Jean-Christophe Bardout, 'Le modèle occasionaliste. Émergence et développement au tournant des XVIIe et XVIIIe siècle', *Quaestio*, 2 (2002), 461–492; Nadler, *Occasionalism*. I first introduce this twofold approach to the study of occasionalism in Sangiacomo, 'Samuel Clarke', in order to clarify the sense in which Samuel Clarke appropriated occasional causality.

[24] For the interpretation of occasional causes as *sine quibus non* conditions, see Sangiacomo, '*Sine qua non*'. In the following discussion I use the expression *sine qua non* causality to refer to the understanding of causal relata as *sine quibus non* conditions.

efficacious cause (as is the case, for instance, in Geulincx or Malebranche's versions of occasionalism).

Early modern occasionalism is usually presented as the claim that finite creatures (2) are not endowed with intrinsically efficacious causal powers (1); but are instead only occasional causes (1) for God's (2) constant causal activity in the world. This standard formulation may capture some crucial features of early modern occasionalism. However, it does not capture the distinction between the two different issues with which occasionalism deals. For instance, in scholastic debates occasional causes (1) were used in specific domains as *ad hoc* solutions to particular problems connected with sacramental causation or the theory of cognition.[25] This use of occasional or *sine qua non* causality did not have the same domain of validity (2) that early modern occasionalists aimed to establish, and it was definitely *not* the kind of causality that scholastic authors deemed most relevant in natural philosophy. However, this does not entail either that occasionalism—understood as a theory of *sine qua non* causality (1)—was not put to work in crucial, albeit more specific, medieval debates.[26] For the rest of this discussion, I shall focus on occasional causality (1) as the idea that undergoes a process of normalisation in these four cases.

Seen from this perspective, criterion 6 shows that the four authors considered in the table accepted an occasionalist solution to problem (1). This claim is perhaps the most controversial, but also the most important for the comparison. For present purposes, I will limit myself to briefly describing how each author adopts a version of *sine qua non* causality.

Régis discards Malebranche's occasionalism insofar as occasional causes would require some form of operation of finite things on God in order to

---

[25] See, e.g. Marilyn McCord Adams, 'Powerless Causes: The Case of Sacramental Causality' in *Thinking about Causes: From Greek Philosophy to Modern Physics*, eds. Peter Machamer and Gereon Wolters (Pittsburgh, 2007), 47–76; Jean-Luc Solère, '*Sine Qua Non* Causality and the Context of Durand's Early Theory of Cognition', in *Durand of Saint-Pourçain and His Sentences Commentary. Historical, Philosophical, and Theological Issues*, eds. Andreas Speer, Fiorella Retucci, Thomas Jeschke, and Guy Guldentops (Leuven, 2014), 185–227.

[26] The standard historiography on the connection between early modern and medieval occasionalism aims to find in medieval debates those authors who anticipated the early modern stance on *both* the questions I introduced. See e.g. Dominik Perler and Ulrich Rudolph, *Occasionalismus. Theorien der Kausalität im arabisch-islamischen und im europäischen Denken* (Göttingen, 2000); Nadler, *Occasionalism*. This is why the standard picture points to Arabic philosophers and a few later authors, such as Pierre d'Ailly and Gabriel Biel, as the medieval predecessors of early modern occasionalism. While this picture is largely accurate, it overlooks the way in which occasional causality received a much broader discussion and implementation even by authors who would *not* adopt an occasionalist position similar to that of early modern authors, in other domains such as natural philosophy.

determine God to produce certain effects.[27] Later, Régis reinforces his rejection of occasional causes by arguing that Malebranche's account breaks the conceptual necessary connection that links causes with their effects.[28] Régis' contention is that this necessary connection, in Malebranche's account, depends entirely on God's free establishment of the laws of nature and thus bears no intrinsic relation to the nature of the causal relata themselves. According to Régis, causal relations have to be grounded instead in specific features that the causal relata have and that determine why certain causal processes require particular causal relata instead of others.[29] Régis' alternative to occasional causes is thus to conceive of causal relations as connections between modes (as opposed to substances), which have specific natures and definite features.[30] These modes do not have any intrinsic causal powers, but they channel God's own power, which somehow flows through them and produces different effects in virtue of the distinct features and dispositions of the modal entities that it traverses. Despite Régis' rejection of Malebranche's occasionalism, Régis' account of causal relations does maintain that causal relata operate as *sine quibus non* conditions for certain effects to obtain, even if Régis denies that these causal relations are extrinsically established by God and roots them within the very nature of the relata themselves.[31]

---

[27] Pierre-Sylvain Régis, *Cours entier de philosophie, ou Systeme general selon les principes de M. Descartes* (Amsterdam, 1691), 110: 'les causes occasionelles paroissent répugnantes à l'idée de Dieu ; car si par causes occasionelles, j'entends des causes qui déterminent Dieu à produire quelque effet qu'il ne produiroit pas, ces causes ne luy en donnoient occasion d'elle-memes, et sans qu'il les ait prevenues, cela suppose en Dieu une indetermination qui est incompatible avec son immutabilité; et si j'entends des causes qui determinent la volonté de Dieu qui est d'elle-meme generale, cela suppose encore le meme défaut. Je ne diray donc point que les causes secondes sont des causes occasionelles'.

[28] See Pierre-Sylvain Régis, *L'Usage de la Raison et de la Foy ou l'Accord de la Foy et de la Raison* (Paris, 1704), livre I, partie II, ch. 36, 208: 'Qu'on ne dise donc pas qu'on ne voit point de liaison necessaire entre les causes secondes et les effets qu'on leur attribuë, comme l'on en voit entre la cause premiere et ses effets; car à moins de renoncer aux sense et à la raison, on y voit une manifeste.'

[29] See Régis *Usage*, livre I, partie II, ch. 36, 205: 'C'est une verité incontestable qu'ils ne peuvent agir s'ils n'ont de certaines dispositions. Si le feu, par exemple, ne s'insinuë dans le bois, s'il n'en écarte les parties, s'il ne leur imprime un mouvement pareil au sien, jamais il ne convertira ce bois en flame. Il en est de même de tous les autres agens naturels: Si vous leur ôtez leur forme, leur figure, leur situation, leur pesanteur, leur legereté, leur liquidité, etc. vous renversez tout, ils ne produiront plus aucun effet.'

[30] Régis, *Cours*, 109–110: 'Quand je fais reflexion sur la maniere particuliere dont les estres modaux agissent, je conçois qu'ils n'ont rien d'eux-mêmes qui soit efficace; c'est pourquoy, pour marquer cette difference par rapport aux effets que Dieu et les estres modaux produisent ensemble, je veux appeler Dieu, *Cause efficiente premiere*, et nommer les Estres modaux, *Causes efficients secondes*, entendant par cause efficient premiere, celle qui agit d'elle-même et par elle-même, et par cause efficient seconde, celle qui agit par la vertu d'une autre.'

[31] Régis struggled to maintain a balance between distinguishing his position from that of Malebranche and avoiding the claim that finite entities are endowed with intrinsically

Sturm's case is more straightforward since he explicitly accepts an occasionalist metaphysics of causation (questions 1 and 2 mentioned above).[32] Sturm offers an interesting way of taking into account Régis' arguments against Malebranche. He stresses that causal relations among relata are grounded in some form of conceptual necessity, according to which certain relata, in virtue of their specific nature, are suitably connected with particular effects rather than others. However, Sturm explicitly emphasises that this conceptual necessity is nothing but the result of God's free establishment of these causal connections, and thus, metaphysically speaking, it is a hypothetical necessity.[33]

Van Musschenbroek does not explicitly discuss whether bodies have intrinsic and efficacious causal powers. In fact, van Musschenbroek denies that natural philosophy is concerned with causal powers and that causes are even accessible to human cognition.[34] According to van Musschenbroek, natural philosophy deals with *phenomena*, which are a product of the way that bodies appear to human senses and are perceived to undergo changes.[35]

efficacious powers. Régis' main conceptual device to accomplish this task consists in rethinking the scholastic (and Scotist) notion of (artificial) instrumental causality by radicalizing the scholastic claims that secondary causes are *instrumental* causes of God's own action. While this view was widely held, especially mong Thomists, the major difference between Régis and his scholastic predecessors is that they mostly maintained (while Régis resolutely denied) that natural beings, even when understood as instruments, have intrinsic causal powers.

[32] See Johann Christoph Sturm, *Physica Electiva sive Hypothetica*. 4 volls. Hildesheim-Zürich-New York: G. Olms, 2006 (Christian Wolff Gesammelte Werke, Band 97.1.1/97.2.2) [First edition: first part 1697; second part 1722], I, 178: 'Deum hoc loco statui agere et operari in natura omnia, non secundum absolutam suam potentiam, qua, quicquid vult, sine omni mora et errore perfectissime expedit, sed secundum potentiam respecivam et hypotheticam, cujus exercitium ipsemet a certis materiae vel humane mentis conditionibus liberrime suspendit.' See also *Physica Electiva*, I, 117: 'causae sine qua non, ut Scholae loquuntur, vel occasionalis nomen mereri.'

[33] See Sturm, *Physica Electiva*, I, 178–179: 'Nam, postquam *voluntatis Divina infinitam efficaciam* et potentiam vera puraque actione, facere fecisseque omnia, generaliter innotuit; cum interim constet, non absolutam illam ubique, sed conditionatam aut materiae rerumque materiatarum variis habitudinibus ac circumstantiis accommodatam fuisse, nec immediate illam immediatione suppositi, sed per diversa media passive se habentia peragere omnia; in singulis porro effectuum generibus et casibus specialibus operae pretium est inquirere [...] quibus materiae conditionibus usus sit motor potentissimus, h.e. quaenam et qualis sint illae causae mediae sive secundae, per quas ipsi placuit hunc aut illum effectum producere, quos alias absoluta sua potentia absolute quoque, praeteritis intermediis omnibus, conficere potuisset.'

[34] On this point see Ducheyne, 'Petrus van Musschenbroek and Newton' and Id. 'Petrus van Musschenbroek on the scope'.

[35] See Petrus van Musschenbroek, *Introductio ad philosophiam naturalem*, ed. by Johannes Lulofs, (Lugduni Batavorum, 1762), 5: 'omnes situs, motus, mutationes, et actiones corporum, quae sensibus observantur, sive uno, sive pluribus, appellantur *Phaenomena*, vel *Apparitiones*.'

All phenomena, he argues, depend on motion.[36] However, human beings do not experience the causes of phenomena directly, they experience regularities in how phenomena occur and change. These regularities are expressed as the 'laws of nature', and they consist in the fact that, given certain occasions or states of affairs, certain other phenomena will follow.[37] The laws of nature are not the cause of the phenomena, but rather the effects of the operation of genuine causes. The laws of nature ultimately depend on God's free will, which established that certain effects will obtain in particular occasions.[38]

Van Musschenbroek does not rule out the possibility that there might be some entities (aside from God) endowed with genuine causal powers. However, he does rule out the very idea that natural philosophy can be concerned with investigating this issue. In the domain of natural philosophy, causation is nothing but a regular relationship between different phenomena, in which certain phenomena are observed to always occur at the occasion of other phenomena. Phenomena are thus *sine quibus non* conditions for the unfolding of natural effects, in the sense that they are not in themselves the active principle that causes the change, but rather the condition or state of affairs that is required for the effect to occur (in virtue of its unknown cause). If one considers occasionalism with respect to the question of what is the source of causal efficacy in phenomena (question 2 above), then van Musschenbroek is methodologically agnostic and dismisses occasionalism, since he dismisses the very legitimacy of such a question in the domain of natural philosophy. Nonetheless, from the point of view of the question about the kind of causality that belongs to certain entities (question 1 above), van Musschenbroek's position entails that *sine qua non* causality is the kind of causality that connects phenomena.

In the *Nova Dilucidatio*, Kant maintains that the bare existence of substances is not sufficient to establish causal relations, unless God further establishes how these substances should relate to one another.[39] Kant stresses that these causal relations (which amount to the laws of nature) are

---

[36] See van Musschenbroek, *Introductio*, 5: 'omne enim incrementum vel decrementum, generaio, corruptio, vel qualiscunque alteratio, quae in corporibus contingit, a motu pendet.'

[37] See van Musschenbroek, *Introductio*, 5: 'Omnia corpora secundum certas moveri regulas observantur, quaecunque causa movens exstiterit. Hae regulae etiam vocantur *Leges Naturae*, et sunt constantes apparitiones vel effetus, qui, quotiescunque corpora in similibus sunt occasionibus, semper eodem eveniunt modo.'

[38] See van Musschenbroek, *Introductio*, 6: 'Pendent autem omnes a liberrima Creatoris voluntate, qua statuit, ut nonnulli motus in similibus occasionibus semper essent iidem.'

[39] See Immanuel Kant, *Kants Gesammelte Schriften, herausgegeben von der Deutschen Akademie der Wissenschaften*, 29 vols. (Berlin, 1902–), I, 415; English translation Immanuel Kant, *Theoretical Philosophy, 1755–1770*. Ed. and trans. by D. Walford (New York, 1992), 44: '[N]o substance of any kind has the power of determining other substances, distinct from itself, by means of that which belongs to it internally (as we have proved). It follows

freely established by God and do not depend on the intrinsic features of the substances themselves. Kant explicitly rejects a qualified version of occasionalism (which, following Leibniz, he attributed to Malebranche), in which God is understood to constantly intervene in nature.[40] However, insofar as causal relata are considered in themselves and independently of God's establishment of the laws of nature, Kant does accept the occasionalist account of causation in terms of *sine quibus non* conditions.

Despite differences in the way in which each author spells out their views in regard to criterion 6, it is safe to conclude that all four authors accept (some qualified version of) occasional causality. This point has important consequences. Criterion 7 shows that, over time, the modal status of causal connections drifts towards contingency. Only Régis insists on the conceptual necessity that intrinsically connects causes and effects, and exploits this claim as a device to counter Malebranche's own occasionalism. However, from Sturm to Kant, causal connections are understood to be intrinsically contingent when considered with respect to the nature of the causal relata themselves. The nature of causal relata is simply unable to ground their causal relations. This point becomes the consequence of a metaphysical principle in Kant (the principle of co-existence[41]) and, in both van Musschenbroek and Kant, is connected with their discussion of the laws of nature.

Consider now criterion 8: neither Régis nor Sturm think that the laws of nature establish the particular causal connections between the causal relata. Rather, for both authors the laws of nature (in the physical domain) only put general constraints on physical processes, such as the fact that the quantity of motion in the universe cannot decrease or increase.[42] According

from this that it only has this power in virtue of the connection, by means of which they are linked together in the idea entertained by the Infinite Being. It follows that, whatever determinations and changes are to be found in any of them, they always refer, indeed, to what is external. Physical influence, in the true sense of the term, however, is excluded.'

[40] See *Kants Gesammelte Schriften*, I, 415; Kant, *Theoretical Philosophy*, 44: 'there exists a universal *harmony* of things. Nonetheless, this does not give rise to the well-known *Leibnizian pre-established harmony*, which is properly speaking *agreement* between substances, not their reciprocal *dependency* on each other. For God does not make use of the craftsman's cunning devices, carefully fitted into a sequence of suitably arranged means designed to bring about a concord between substances.'

[41] See *Kants Gesammelte Schriften*, I, 412–413; Kant *Theoretical Philosophy*, 40–41.

[42] Régis' account of the laws of mind-body union (see *Course*, 126–127) is more complex and entails substantive claims about how physical and mental states are connected. This is due to the fact that bodies and minds are heterogeneous in nature, from an ontological point of view, and thus establishing causal relations among them cannot rely on any conceptual necessity intrinsic to their own nature. Bodies and minds are simply not related *by nature* or in virtue of their own nature, but only by God's own laws of mind-body union. Remarkably, Régis does not use the term 'laws' to describe God's ruling of the mind-body relation, but 'conditions' (French *conditions*).

to both van Musschenbroek and Kant, instead, causal connections cannot be understood as arising from or being grounded in the nature of things themselves considered independently of the laws of nature. The laws of nature do more robust causal work in van Musschenbroek and Kant's accounts, since the laws establish not only general constraints on causal processes but the actual kind of causal processes that can take place among certain causal relata. The explicitly asserted contingency of the causal relations is directly correlated with the explicitly asserted extrinsic nature of these same relations (which depends on God's establishing the laws, rather than on the nature of things themselves). This is not a coincidence: since God's will is free, if causal relations (codified in the laws of nature) depend on God's will, then they are contingent with respect to the nature of causal relata themselves, because God could have established completely different relations holding among the same relata. Moreover, God's will was not necessitated by the relata themselves to establish certain relations.

Consider now criterion 9. As the contingency of causal relations becomes more explicit, God's role shifts from being the provider of causal efficacy in nature to being the free establisher of the laws of nature. Surely, Régis and Sturm agree that there are laws of nature and that these depend on God. Sturm also explicitly maintains that God is free in his decision to establish certain laws rather than others. However, Régis and Sturm both emphasize God's involvement in nature as the source of causal efficacy in the unfolding of natural effects. Van Musschenbroek and Kant shift the emphasis towards God's free establishment of the laws of nature themselves, which come to play a more robust role in their account of causation. Van Musschenbroek does not suggest, and Kant explicitly rejects, the idea that God directly intervenes in the actual production of natural effects. In this sense, they both conceive of God's role as that of a metaphysical ruling principle that provides the foundation of the laws of nature, which also makes these laws both contingent in themselves and accidental with respect to the nature of natural entities themselves. It is worth stressing that such a conception of the laws and their grounding in God's free will is conceptually and systematically connected with the understanding of the causality of finite beings in terms of *sine qua non* causality.

To conclude this synoptic presentation, consider criteria 10 and 11 together. All four authors are convinced that reality is coarse-grained; however, the way in which they spell out this commitment is rather different. Régis and Sturm accept that natural beings are modes rather than substances. Van Musschenbroek speaks of phenomena, which are epistemological constructions based on the human perception of bodies and physical events. The notion of a phenomenon potentially encompasses both modes and substances and is reducible to neither. Kant, in the *Nova*

Dilucidatio, explicitly defends the view that the world is made up of substances. From the point of view of criterion 11, the cases of Régis and Sturm are problematic, since modes are not self-standing beings and an ontology of modes may easily lead to a fine-grained ontology (as Spinoza's case shows). However, both Régis and Sturm strenuously resist this potential outcome and insist on the fact that modes do have specific natures. Arguably, this provides a further explanation of why they both have to preserve some form of conceptual necessity in causal relations. While conceptual necessity arises from the nature of causal relata, it also has a reverberating effect on these relata by reinforcing the idea that, despite their being modes rather than substances, they have an ontologically discrete consistency and they can be conceived as having their own individual, discrete nature.[43] Van Musschenbroek and Kant somehow overcome this problem. My suggestion is that this is possible because the contingency of causal relations (entailed by their accounts of *sine qua non* causality) offers a different criterion to preserve the coarse-grained nature of reality.

4. The Leopard Theorem and the study of normalisation

I would like to draw both a philosophical and a methodological conclusion from the synoptic presentation of the four cases I discussed. My philosophical conclusion is that The Leopard Theorem explains the normalisation of occasional causality. My methodological conclusion is that new methods are necessary in order to duly validate and explore the implications of this theorem. In the rest of this section I spell out these two claims in turn.

The Leopard Theorem, introduced in section one, states that exogenous ideas are normalized insofar as they allow historical actors to preserve core commitments of the tradition in which they operate. In the four cases presented, the exogenous idea is that the kind of causality at work in natural philosophy is *sine qua non* causality. This idea is exogenous with respect to the established late scholastic and Aristotelian tradition. Moreover, a number of seventeenth century *novatores* were also reluctant to give up the scholastic notion of power and were looking for mechanistic surrogates of them.[44] In the eyes of these authors, *sine qua non* causality would also have appeared rather exogenous and far from what they were looking for.

---

[43] This account of modes in which modes are dependent on substances but nonetheless genuine real beings endowed with their own essence can be traced back to Suárez's realist account of modes (DM 7.1.16–17). See Pasnau, *Metaphysical Themes*, 253–58.

[44] See e.g. John Henry, 'Occult Qualities and the Experimental Philosophy', *History of Science* 24 (1986), 335–381.

Nonetheless, the normalisation of *sine qua non* causality in natural philosophy entails a progressive emphasis on the contingent nature of causal relations and their extrinsic origin with respect to the nature of causal relata themselves. Causal relations do not arise from the nature of the relata themselves, but from God's free establishment of them. Causal relations are thus contingent in themselves (since God could have established completely different relations) and accidental to the nature of things (since causal relations do not follow from the nature of things).

My working hypothesis is that the normalisation of occasional causality resulted from its potential to safeguard the coarse-grained nature of reality in a period in which its previously established traditional support (i.e., the scholastic metaphysics of substance) was declining in popularity. As is well known, the first half of the seventeenth century witnessed a virulent assault on scholastic ontology. The notion of substantial form, and forms in general, was under violent pressure. According to the traditional scholastic worldview, the notion of substantial form is ultimately responsible for establishing the coarse-grained nature of reality. Rejecting substantial forms thus threatens the core commitment to coarse-grained reality. At least two strategies are available to preserve this commitment. On the one hand, authors might defend the traditional scholastic account against the assaults of the *novatores*. On the other hand, authors might *normalize* particular exogenous ideas that could turn out to offer new resources to defend the coarse-grained commitment in a new way. Although these two options might be contrasted as 'conservative' and 'progressive' respectively at a superficial level, they actually represent two different attitudes to safeguard the same core commitment. For present purposes, I shall not discuss the first option; the four cases illustrate the second option.

Consider again the connection between criteria 6 and 7, on the one hand, and criteria 10 and 11 on the other. From the point of view of criterion 10, the earlier cases of Régis and Sturm can be interpreted as inheriting a wider process of rethinking of the notion of substance that traverses the seventeenth century. Although these authors were not the instigators of this process of rethinking, they had to respond to it since this process is in tension with their commitment to coarse-grained reality. The later cases of van Musschenbroek and Kant show a progressive resolution of the tension and a reaffirmation of the notion of substance. This does not entail that one has to expect a restoration of a substance-based ontology in the second half of the eighteenth century. My suggestion, rather, is that the progressive normalisation of *sine qua non* causality and the consequent contingency of causal relations (criteria 6 and 7) offer a new way of defending the core commitment to coarse-grained reality (criterion 11). This removes much of the pressure on the notion of substance as the main device for embodying and defending the commitment to coarse-grained reality, and thus allows for the reintroduction of a substance-based ontology (criterion 10). Occasional causality is the new device that allows authors to parcel out reality in virtue of the contingency of causal relata. Since causal relata do not bear any conceptual necessary connection to each other, they can be conceived of independently from one another, even without having to assume that they are substantial entities. Coarse-grained reality can be established independently from the ontological debate on the nature of substances, modes or events.

I stated in section two that normalisation is a process of mutual adaptation and this feature is particularly crucial if we are to appreciate the meaning of the transformation captured by the four cases presented. The fact that Kant can accept both the contingency of causal relations and that causal relata are conceptualized as substances may suggest that the effect of the normalisation of occasional causality is a sort of restoration of the very idea of substance that was under scrutiny during the mid-seventeenth century. Superficially, the mutual adaptation between occasional causality and coarse-grained reality creates the conditions for a revival of the notion of substance itself. In this revival, however, it is no longer the notion of substance as such that supports the commitment to the coarse-grained nature of reality, but rather it is the normalized account of occasional causality that makes room for the understanding of entities in terms of substances again. With respect to scholastic traditions, this process of normalisation entails a radical transformation of the notion of substance itself, since substances are no longer endowed with intrinsically efficacious causal powers. In this sense, the normalisation of occasional causality does not lead to a *restoration* of metaphysics of substance but to a complete reshaping of it.[45] My conclusion is that the genuine and deep continuity between the periods before and after the normalisation of *sine qua non* causality does not lie in the metaphysics of substance, but rather in the preservation of the core commitment to the coarse-grained nature of reality. To paraphrase *The Leopard*, all the marginal ideas changed in order to allow the core commitment to stay the same.

From a methodological point of view, my working hypothesis is just that: a working hypothesis. It has some prima facie plausibility and the cases I discussed provide some initial evidence in support of it. However, normalisation concerns quantitative trends of change across time. These

---

[45] One may speculate that Kant's critical philosophy offers a further clue in this direction. Even if in the *Nova Dilucidatio* Kant partially restores a metaphysics of substance, this metaphysics is no longer the pivotal support for the commitment to coarse-grained reality and thus the critical Kant can let it go again.

trends represent a statistical tendency among several authors to operate along analogous lines, but they do not presuppose that all authors operating in a certain context will reach some form of consensus. Trends are manifold and diverse; thus, it would be crucial at this point to assess these trends quantitatively.

The analysis I provided is a purely qualitative analysis based on close reading of particular cases, but close reading is simply not suitable to produce quantitative insights. The common move to generalize claims based on particular cases is to assume that the cases examined are representative and stereotypical of general trends. This assumption is deeply entrenched with the justifications used to consider certain authors as 'canonical'. Scholars license inferences based on the close reading of say Descartes, Leibniz, Hume and Kant because these authors are seen to be milestones in the evolution of ideas, and somehow the embodiment of different philosophical alternatives.

However, canons are deeply problematic constructions.[46] Among their many problems, it is important to stress that being assigned the role of representing a tradition, idea, or line of thought is a qualitative feature attributed to canonical figures, which is used as a surrogate for genuine quantitative investigations of trends in the evolution of ideas. Qualitative surrogates may be handy, for lack of better resources, but are hardly ideal when it comes to reliability. To study normalisation, qualitative surrogates are deeply problematic because they are constructed by the standpoint of what has already become normal, and thus do not allow for a more objective study of the process of normalisation itself. Canons are built from the standpoint of an already established tradition and in virtue of how that tradition understands itself. For these reasons, canons exist always and only in the present, even if they concern the past. Since traditions are constantly in the process of justifying themselves, they tend to constantly overwrite the process of their own origination. There is a discrepancy between how the history of a tradition presents the ideas that are taken to be formative of that tradition, and the way those ideas were understood at the original time of their introduction. Now-normal ideas were exogenous, and the now-established tradition looked different. Studying normalisation from the standpoint of what is understood to be normal at any given moment of time is like studying the evolution of species based only on the

---

[46] Arguably, the most significant flaw in the early modern canon is the complete absence or recognition of the contribution of women philosophers. On this point see Eileen O'Neill, 'History of Philosophy: Disappearing Ink: Early Modern Women Philosophers and Their Fate in History', in *Philosophy in a Feminist Voice: Critiques and Reconstructions*, ed. Janet A. Kourany (Princeton, 1997), 17–62; Jonathan Rée, 'Women philosophers and the canon', *British Journal for the History of Philosophy* 10 (2002), 641–652; Shapiro, 'Revisiting'.

way in which certain individuals of a species look in the present. What is missing is precisely the broader diachronic perspective on the evolution of that species.

The integration of quantitative methods in the study of the history of early modern philosophy and science is necessary not only to verify my hypothesis about the normalisation of occasional causation, but to study normalisation as such and to determine whether The Leopard Theorem may be generalized as a law of normalisation. The aim of this paper is not to spell out these quantitative methods, nor is it to investigate how they should be articulated or integrated with traditional close reading. My goal, rather, has been to stretch to its extreme limits the standard method of close reading and show how, faced with the phenomenon of normalisation, this method reveals its own insufficiency.

Before concluding, let me address two rather immediate objections that may be raised against my approach. First, one may object that my whole reconstruction is fundamentally biased as a result of my own interpretation of these four authors. Perhaps, since my interpretation is contestable, the working hypothesis and all the conclusions I derive from it are too. In turn, one might argue, this means that they do not capture the actual forces that drove the conceptual change in early modern natural philosophy.

What is interesting about this objection is that it relies on the assumption that it may be possible to reach some sort of objective understanding of historical ideas. By 'objective' I mean an understanding that is not in itself a form of interpretation and thus can claim to represent matters of facts as they genuinely exist. If pushed further on how one may have access to these matters of fact, an objector would perhaps state that a close reading of the texts themselves is what objectively establishes what the authors thought and defended. Although this sounds plausible, this assumption is blatantly false. Close reading is nothing but the careful examination and analysis of, for the most part, limited portions of texts. Close reading is always interpretation-laden, and rightfully so. In order to analyse any text, it is essential to distinguish between different conceptual layers, to establish the goals that the text aims to achieve, to assess whether different conceptual elements play as premises, as intermediary steps or as conclusions in an overall argument. The reconstruction of the context of the text introduces even greater complications (how to identify and select sources, how to assess their role, and the list may well include many others). None of these activities are possible without relying on some (at least) preliminary interpretation that is not directly derived by the text itself. Without these activities, there is no analysis of texts, and thus no close reading.

In response to the objection, then, I grant that my interpretation is an interpretation and that all interpretations are contestable. As mentioned,

I provided more extensive arguments for my particular interpretation elsewhere, and I shall not present an extensive defence of the details of my interpretation here. For present purposes, it suffices to say that (i) it is false in general to pretend that the understanding of historical texts can rely on any form of direct, and thereby hermeneutically un-mediated, access to the content of a text; and (ii) it is wrong to suggest that close reading is the method to achieve this alleged objectivity.

Second, one may object that normalisation leads to the construction of grand narratives, which are by definition unable to capture the fine-grained evolution of ideas and remain faithful to the nuances introduced by the different historical actors themselves. One should simply abstain from grand narratives and focus the research on close reading of particular authors.

In response to this objection, one might suggest that it is impossible to completely dispense with narratives of some sort in order to meaningfully frame the way in which particular authors engage with the ongoing historical development of ideas.[47] However, for present purposes, I would simply like to stress that this objection is a self-defeating one. Close reading and canonization go hand in hand. Canonical authors are the main objects of close reading, and close reading is mostly concerned with canonical authors and works. In turn, this implies that sustained close reading of authors who are not yet canonical may help to establish them as part of the canon. The canon itself is the best exemplification of a grand narrative and is itself an attempt to establish and secure 'The Grand Narrative' or a certain tradition. The objection against grand narratives in general can be seen as the effort of a *particular* grand narrative—one embedded in the currently established canon and supported by the currently established tradition—to preserve and defend itself. This reaction is more extreme than might be expected, but it also sheds light on a further layer of normalisation: in order to study the normalisation of ideas, it is necessary to normalise quantitative methods in the study of the history of these ideas.

The academic milieu in which natural philosophy evolved during the early modern period is the vast scenario in which the process of normalisation took place. To understand this process, it is not enough to cherry-pick a few authors. Ideally, all authors who inhabited that environment should be studied and taken into account. This is not because they all played the same role, shared the same views or had the same impact. On the contrary, they should all be studied because the process of normalisation can be

---

[47] On this point see John Henry, 'Essay Review. The Scientific Revolution: Five Books about It', *Isis*, 107 (2016), 809–817 (with respect to narratives in the history of science). For a broader case for the necessity of developing new kinds of *long durée* history, see Jo Guldi and David Armitage, *The History Manifesto* (Cambridge, 2014).

understood only by comparing how different authors achieved different results and how different ideas had different fates within the evolution of natural philosophy. This study cannot proceed case-by-case because the object of the study itself is not any particular author. The study of normalisation is rather a study of how the whole environment in which these authors existed evolved and how the ideas defended in this process mutually co-evolved and co-affected each other over time. Pursuing this line of research requires a deep integration of qualitative and quantitative methods that has not yet properly begun. The history of the academic milieu of early modern Europe awaits this new course of research to take off in order to become the laboratory for the study of normalisation.

Faculty of Philosophy
University of Groningen
a.sangiacomo@rug.nl